HIGH PRAISE FOR

The Brownsville Incident of 1906

"Both Colonel Baker's imaginative recreation of the Brownsville Affair and his account of his fight to redress the wrong done to the disciplined black soldiers add considerable depth to this important story. Although several books have been written about this unfortunate piece of America's racial history, Baker demonstrates that there is more to be learned. His is a remarkable tale of courage, persistence, and conviction. Get the book: it is a great read."

~ Tweed Roosevelt, University Professor, Long Island University; Chairman, Theodore Roosevelt Institute

* * *

"Colonel Baker skillfully interweaves two distinct stories. First he offers an imaginative reconstruction of a shameful and widely-reported 1906 incident: the events that led President Theodore Roosevelt to discharge without honor 167 African-American soldiers for allegedly participating in—or refusing to identify the participants in—a shooting rampage in Brownsville, Texas. (Doris Kearns Goodwin's The Bully Pulpit calls Roosevelt's action 'a permanent scar on his legacy.') Second, he gives a first-person account of his own ultimately successful efforts—sixty-six years later—to exonerate those same soldiers. Racism, sectional tensions, political machinations, careerism, and sheer human malevolence all rear their ugly heads in Colonel Baker's fascinating narrative."

~ Professor Baird Tipson, Adjunct Professor, Gettysburg

* * *

"An inspiring story of one honorable man's commitment to correct a 'gross injustice' and to remind Americans that these lessons transcend race and time: 'Innocence before guilt. Due process of law. These basics of constitutional protection cannot, should not, be superseded by anyone, including the president of the United States.'"

~ Sam Roberts, *New York Times.*

* * *

D1522562

"With a keen eye for truth and justice, Lieutenant Colonel William Baker provides a road map for those with the courage to successfully fight the most powerful political institution in America."

– Judge Greg Mathis (Ret.), First cousin, Lieutenant Colonel William Baker

* * *

"LTC Baker has written a book that should be required reading in all military schools. As an analyst, historian, critical thinker, and philosopher, LTC Baker has fashioned the most comprehensive story of the Brownsville Affair to date. His efforts led to the redemption of 167 African American soldiers whose lives were forever altered and ruined by racism. The Brownsville Affair had implications that ultimately fleeted up to the White House. Included in this group of innocent soldiers was Master Sergeant Mingo Sanders, who was considered to be one of the best leaders in the Army. LTC Baker's magisterial efforts led to a modicum of vindication and justice for these soldiers' unjust treatment. His remarkable scholastic ability and moral courage set a high standard for all future investigations into this matter, and may provide a moral compass for similar investigations going forward."

– Dr. Benjamin Swinson, LTC (Ret) Infantry, U.S. Army

* * *

"Two sad things emerge from Lieutenant Colonel William Baker's phenomenal research in *The Brownsville Texas Incident of 1906: The True and Tragic Story of a Black U.S. Army Battalion's Wrongful Disgrace and Ultimate Redemption*: first, that only two of the 167 Black soldiers dishonorably discharged lived to know of Baker's determination to exonerate them; and, secondly, Baker did not live to see his book to publication. Still, there is one great thing readers can derive from Baker's relentless drive and a discipline annealed in the military is the satisfaction that he corrected a terrible wrong. Lieutenant Col. Baker, Presente! And let the 21-gun salute begin."

– Herb Boyd, *Black Detroit: A People's History of Self-Determination* adjunct professor at City College in New York and author of numerous books.

* * *

The

BROWNSVILLE TEXAS INCIDENT OF 1906:

The True and Tragic Story of a
Black Battalion's Wrongful Disgrace
and Ultimate Redemption

Lieutenant Colonel (Ret)
WILLIAM BAKER

Library of Congress Control Number: 2019953114

978-1-943267-71-2 paperback

978-1-943267-92-7 hardback

Cover Image belongs to Bettye F. Baker

Edited by David Lott

Designed by Joyce Faulkner

Printed in the United States.

*

Red Engine Press

Fort Smith, AR & Pittsburgh, PA

To the men of the First Battalion,
Twenty-fifth Infantry, U.S. Army, for whom
justice was denied for more than 66 years.
"Truth crushed to earth did rise again."

May my grandchildren,
Andrew Bryant Walker, Wesley Baker Walker
and Julianne Frances Walker
come to know why standing-up for justice
is their true freedom.

Contents

Book III: Aftermath

ACKNOWLEDGMENTS

Books and great works evolve because of the largess of people. I have many to thank.

I would first like to state my deep appreciation and indebtedness to the late Major General Harry W. Brooks, Jr., who gave me the Brownsville Project while I was stationed at the Pentagon in 1972, and set me on the path to writing this book.

I would also like to thank the late Lieutenant General DeWitt C. Smith, Jr., Army Deputy Chief of Staff, Personnel and the longest serving Commandant of the U.S. Army War College, who believed in, and supported, my research and civil rights at the Pentagon, 1972; Dr. Bruce Aiken, historian, author, and member of the Texas Historical Commission; the staff at the National Archives Division and Pentagon Law Library; Louise A. Arnold-Friend, Chief, Reference & User Services Divisions, Library Collections Manager, United Starts Army Military History Institute, U.S. Army War College, Carlisle Barracks, Carlisle, Pennsylvania.

I would also like to thank my lifelong friend, Lieutenant Colonel (Ret.) Benjamin L. Swinson who was a sounding-board for my efforts to move the exoneration process through the Pentagon; my editor, David C. Lott of Vineyard Haven, Martha's Vineyard, MA, who surely made the story better, Carl Holt, Director of Martha's Vineyard Television, who filmed my initial efforts in recording the Brownsville story and assisted in archival photo research on the men of the First Battalion Twenty-fifth Infantry; our publishing team to include my daughter Janet L. Baker, Esq,; and Joyce

K. Faulkner, publisher principal who had enormous faith in the book.

I also want to thank the supporters of my literary efforts, Richard Purdy of Gettysburg, Pennsylvania; Sam Feldman of Martha's Vineyard, MA; my son William Rhett Baker, and finally, my wife Bettye Foster Baker, who inspired me daily.

FOREWORD

Connection to the Story and the Author

IT WAS 1993 WHEN this book began to find its voice after incubating for more than 18 years in the mind of my husband, retired Lieutenant Colonel William Baker. You would think that important stories such as the Brownsville Redemption are immediately recognized the moment they reach a publisher's desk, or more significantly, the eyes of an agent. That was not the case in *The Brownsville Texas Incident of 1906: The True and Tragic Story of a Black Battalion's Wrongful Disgrace and Ultimate Redemption*. The manuscript was viewed by several well-known publishing houses, but they had no interest. Who would buy it? How would they make money?

Publishing history, particularly Black history, is rife with stories that never see print, and those that do, barely squeak by. We have come to understand that these are not stories that white America welcomes or digests easily, whether on the battlefield or the cotton field. However, these stories lay bare a stark reality that demands telling.

Brownsville, in particular, is a classic example of how truth is ignored—by the president of the United States no less—to advance a political agenda or deny Black justice. Colonel Baker pushed ahead against institutional opposition and threats to his career to uncover the hard facts of the incident and reveal a truth hidden and disbelieved for nearly 70 years. It is also a story of the deep and abiding pain that was levied on the men and families of the First Battalion, Twenty-fifth Infantry, (Colored) most all of whom went to their graves disgraced and unknowing that their innocence would one day be proclaimed.

A Story Determined to be Told

Brownsville was a story determined to be told. And because of that imperative, I was successful in securing posthumous publication of his manuscript. From start to finish, my husband carefully researched and documented this work, which consumed nearly 40 years of his life. Lt. Colonel Bill Baker died on September 24, 2018, just weeks after the ink on the final page of the manuscript had dried. Bill's painstakingly accurate research led to both the Pentagon's and President Nixon's correction of President Theodore Roosevelt's unjustified leveling of dishonorable discharges against the soldiers.

The Brownsville tragedy transcends racial boundaries and time. The universality of its themes: due process, fair play, and the presumption of innocence are enduring precepts. For that reason, it should have wide appeal to all who value justice, especially among African Americans, soldiers, and former soldiers of all stripes. Because of its similarities to the Dreyfus Affair and the Japanese internments, this book provides a poignant chronicle of our past that demands that those who ignore our history and the stunning impact of racial discrimination and injustice shall have the task of establishing why race and social justice matters.

The foundation and tentacles of what moved my husband to correct the Brownsville injustice reach back to the inception of this country, long before the nation had set its precepts and ideals on paper. Yet, it is clear that his motivation stems from his life experience growing up in the Jim Crow South in Attapulgus, Georgia, where he was the grandson of a freed slave named Ned Keaton. It was Keaton who would first tell him the story of the Brownsville debacle.

The notion that black men are dispensable, undeserving of the same justice, opportunity or consideration as their white brethren defined Bill's circumstances, but not his upbringing or belief system. For this reason, and this reason alone, did Bill make the decision, once Brownsville officially came to his attention, that he would dedicate his life to the rectification and vindication of these innocent men.

This work begs the question: What makes a man stand up in spite of threats to his livelihood, to his career, and yes, even to his life?

Bill Baker will tell you: "Knowing that 'Might Makes Right' had won in Brownsville and Washington for 66 years has caused me to distrust certain judicial expressions that often give the illusion of justice, the sort of stereotyped bromides that politicians and judges are given to, such as: 'All men are equal before the law,' and the inscription over the U.S. Supreme Court building, 'Equal justice under law.' President Roosevelt made similar statements as he rationalized his action against the Brownsville soldiers. His statements were barren then, and such lofty pronouncements are barren now, and will always be barren, for they assume the law is just.

"I am convinced that justice is not always inspired or achieved by the law, and certainly not by well-meaning platitudes, and not even by just having constitutional rights. Those rights must be activated. It was goodness, the God within, and struggle that achieved a measure of justice for the soldiers. What they got was delayed, imperfect, but redemptive. Truth prevailed. And in this case, 'truth crushed to the earth' did rise again."

Relevance Today

The story of Brownsville is strongly relevant today. Back in 1907, claims of the black soldiers' innocence would have been labeled 'fake news.' There was compelling evidence that would have supported those claims, but there was no imperative to find and interpret it. In fact, it was just the opposite. Roosevelt couldn't come up with a reason to not find the men guilty. It wasn't until Bill Baker made the effort to dig up the evidence and analyze it decades later that a true and accurate account of the incident was told. In today's parlance, the 167 men of the Twenty-fifth were guilty of acting as soldiers 'while being black.'

On July 17, 2014, Eric Garner, a black man, died in the New York City borough of Staten Island after a New York City Police Department officer put him in a chokehold while arresting him. Before he died, Garner is heard on video as saying, "I can't breathe" 11 times while lying face down on the sidewalk. Despite his role in the incident, Daniel Pantaleo, a New York City Police Department Officer, remained on desk duty, collecting a salary and pension benefits, and avoided any legal punishment for his role in Garner's death. Pantaleo was ultimately fired—five years later in August 2019. Garner's crime? He was suspected of allegedly selling loose, unlicensed cigarettes.

The list of such lethal incidents continues to grow. But so do the efforts to counter them and to get to the truth of what really happened. That's why Bill Baker's effort must be recognized, applauded and cited as an example of the ongoing need to continue to fight for black justice. Justice is not easy. It must be fought for. It must be believed in. And it requires men and women of good conscience to step forward and do the hard work, just like Bill Baker did.

Refer to: https://www.nytimes.com/2018/10/08/obituaries/william-baker-dead.html.)

Dr. Bettye Foster Baker

PROLOGUE

A Night of Terror

Midnight, August 13, 1906. Unidentified bandits viciously raid the town of Brownsville, Texas, where the First Battalion, 25th Infantry of the United States Army, a unit of 167 black men, is stationed. The raiders unleash a 10-minute barrage of bullets that kills a young bartender, wounds a police lieutenant, breaks windows, studs the sides of houses, fells a horse out from under its rider and causes wide-spread panic among the white townspeople.

The next day, the August 14 edition of the *Brownsville Daily Herald* newspaper proclaimed, "DASTARDLY OUTRAGE BY NEGRO SOLDIERS," setting the tone for subsequent media coverage as well as the arc of events that would lead to what could be called 'President Theodore Roosevelt's biggest blunder.'

Those deadly few minutes have lived long in history. Sometimes called the Brownsville Texas Affray or The Brownsville Texas Riot, I call it the Brownsville Texas Incident. Whatever one calls it, the harrowing event resulted in a rush to judgment that tragically changed the lives of those soldiers forever.

Roosevelt charged that all 167 black soldiers of the First Battalion, Twenty-fifth Infantry who were stationed in Brownsville that day were responsible for the carnage. The men were subsequently discharged without honor and without trial. Their pain and suffering, however, did not end with that humiliation. They also lost their pensions and were barred from any future government service. Worst of all, they were forever stigmatized with the dishonor of a crime they never committed—a tragic mistake that set me on a decades-long quest for justice.

My grandfather first told me the Brownsville story when I was a child and that he didn't believe that the black soldiers did the shooting. Further, he accused Roosevelt of deceiving them, and disgracing the "Colored race." I recall the deep sadness in his voice when he recounted what he called the president's betrayal of his brothers-in-arms. Some of these same black soldiers fought with then-Colonel Roosevelt during the Spanish American War in 1898. They helped him capture Kettle Hill by first capturing the village of El Caney near San Juan Hill. And they faithfully served him during the Philippines insurrection. They deserved better.

A Reconstruction

This book is divided into three parts. Book I is a reconstruction of the events surrounding the Brownsville Incident, using newspaper reports, court documents and depositions from the National Archives, Library of Congress and the Pentagon Law Library. I created conversations between the players in Book I with the help of these sources, plus my own knowledge and experience in military protocols. Book II is a memoir of my quest for justice and my search for the real story of what happened on that fateful day in Texas. Book III details the aftermath of my successful discovery of the innocence of the black troops and the long delayed compensation for the affair's lone survivor—a payment 67 years in the making.

I believe this investigation satisfies a role worthy of national record and of much needed closure to an important event. To a limited extent it is also autobiographical, in that it portrays a glimpse of a particular slice of my life.

Government reports constituting the official records of the 'Brownsville Affray,' the incident's name, included:

- Three presidential messages

- War Department reports

- Hearings of the Senate Military Affairs Committee

- Courts-martial records of the white officers—Battalion Commander Major Charles W. Penrose, and Company Commanders Captain Samuel P. Lyon and Captain Edgar A. Macklin

- Military court of inquiry proceedings published by the U.S. Government Printing Office in Washington, D.C.

These published reports included many volumes, some of which constituted thousands of pages. They purported to tell the story of what really happened at Brownsville and, in fact, offered valuable information.

However, as I reviewed and analyzed them, I grew to distrust much of what they presented and eventually rejected many of their conclusions. Other sources included telegrams, cablegrams, memoirs, contemporary newspaper accounts, letters and autobiographical materials of some of the major characters.

Official reports I studied were from the Law Library in the Pentagon. I also used U.S. National Archives original source documents located in boxes numbered 4499 through 4504, adjutant general document file number 1135832 and newspaper accounts. Sworn affidavits, depositions, testimony of the black soldiers, white townspeople and officials, court-martial records from the white military officers who commanded the black troops and technical reports by ballistic experts and others were of special legal significance.

Book II, My Quest for Justice, is based largely on the strength of the evidence I relied upon to tell my story. They include the same government records and the same original source documents in the National Archives, official government letters and memoranda from 1971-1974, my private papers, my own memory and some of the official documents purporting to tell the story of what happened at Brownsville.

Notwithstanding my distrust and rejection of some of my source information, I am satisfied that I have been fair and true to all of my sources. However, I have not been able to keep myself out of the story. It was impossible. My quest to exonerate the innocent has become itself an integral part of the whole story.

Politics of the Early 1900s

It is helpful to review the politics of that time. When President Theodore Roosevelt assumed the presidency in 1901 after the assassination of President William McKinley, he did something no other president had done—he invited a black man, Booker T. Washington, to the White House for dinner. Roosevelt further signaled his intention to promote civil rights for black Americans by appointing blacks to Federal positions. Roosevelt's appointments and his public statements against the lynching of blacks created hope in the black community. They also solidified the political alliance between Washington and Roosevelt. As a result, the black electorate, encouraged by Washington, flocked to Roosevelt and the Republican Party. The Brownsville incident, however, brought that progress and the hopes of the black community to a sudden end.

To me, the historical importance of the Brownsville Incident lies in the universality of its themes. They transcend racial boundaries and time. When Americans are charged with the commission of a crime, they are entitled to a trial and all of the rights associated therewith. Innocence before guilt. Due process of law. These basics of constitutional protection cannot, should not, be superseded by anyone, including the President of the United States. In addition, the underlying theme of redemptive justice—craving it, pursuing it and finally getting it—flows throughout this book. It is never too late to correct injustice. This story, chronicled here in three sections, illustrates that powerful truth. Together, they form the chronicle of my fight to exonerate the innocent, and the ultimate triumph of justice denied.

ONE

STRANGER AT THE DOOR

***

The Beginning

Southwest Georgia, 1936

DECADES AFTER THE BROWNSVILLE incident of 1906, the stigma of dishonor still haunted the soldiers of the 25th Infantry. It followed almost all of them into old age. It drove some into insanity. And cruelly, it followed most of them to their deaths. Along the way, as they wandered across the country, they told stories of their innocence to anyone who would listen. My grandfather, Ned Keaton, a storyteller himself, had heard the Brownsville story and passed it along to me, when I was a boy of five or six years of age. It was the heart of the Great Depression.

One day, late in the evening, I sat on the front steps and watched a stranger walking down the dirt road toward my grandpa's house. The old man walked with an air of dignity. His steps suggested he had been a soldier, coming with a deliberate, rhythmic, and precise cadence. As he walked, his shoes kicked up little clouds of red dust, which rose to the top of his boots. His clothes were clean, but old and tattered and dotted with holes that had been patched many times. He wore a quaint, funny-looking wide brimmed hat, one that I had never seen before.

I scampered up the steps, ran into the house and told Grandma Angeline that a beggar was coming. She took a hoecake of bread from the cupboard, wrapped it in newspaper and went to the door. As she was coming through the door with the bread, the man was mounting the steps. I was hanging onto Grandma's apron. When the stranger saw grandma's face, he retreated down the steps. He apologized, saying something to the effect that he was sorry and calling her 'Miss.' He said that he didn't mean anything, begging her not to holler for the sheriff. She assured the man that she was a "Colored woman," and that she had some bread for him.

Looking at the black boy (me) huddled so close to the woman's skirt, a faint smile of recognition came over the stranger's face. Reaching into his pocket, he pulled out some pennies and offered to pay. Angeline walked to the edge of the porch with the bread and told him she wouldn't take anything for it. The stranger insisted, telling Angeline that he was not a beggar. She told him to take the bread and, 'May the good Lord be with you.' He accepted the bread gracefully, turned and left.

The next day I was standing beside Grandma Angeline at the corner of the Country General Store. We were waiting for Grandpa to return from the Gulf of Mexico with oysters. It was not yet dark, but evening shadows were beginning to fall. We expected to see him coming over the hill at any time now. Suddenly, I heard the screeching sound of a car skidding on the road, brakes squealing as it tried to stop. The smell of burning rubber permeated the air. A cloud of red dust trailed the skidding car. I saw an old man trying to cross the road. Someone shouted at him, 'Watch out! Car! Car!' Too late. There was a dull thud, a cry of pain. The car dragged the man several feet, then sped away.

I turned away from the noise and buried my face in Grandma's apron. A cloud of red dust mixed with leaves swept by, caught in the wind from the speeding car. The dust covered my shoes and clung to my pants. People were running across the street, forming a crowd around the still figure lying in the street.

Grandma held on to me tightly, but I broke free, ran across the street and picked up the old man's hat. Then I rushed into the crowd, working my way through the people to the interior of the circle. I looked at the old man lying motionless on the ground face up, eyes wide open. People stood around talking, shaking their heads, certain that the man was dead. Their voices were low, hushed and respectful. No one tried to help. I recognized the man as the stranger who had come to Grandpa's door.

All the commotion drew the attention of Mr. Kauffman, the white storekeeper at the meat market. He left his store and pushed into the crowd, elbowing people out of his way. When he got through the crowd, I ran to him. I grabbed the corner of his apron and pulled him toward the man on the ground. I looked up into his face, wanting so much for him to help the stranger. Kauffman stared down at the man quizzically, looked up at the crowd, and asked, "Who's the dead nigger?"

My grandfather knew. He came up through the crowd and knelt down beside the man. He lifted up the stranger's hand, felt his wrist, then looked off into the distance. I approached Grandpa slowly and handed him the hat. Grandpa placed the hat over the dead man's face. Then, he told me that he knew the old man from a long, long time ago. The man was one of the soldiers from Brownsville.

Two

THIRTY YEARS LATER

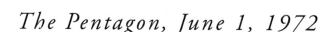

The Pentagon, June 1, 1972

The Brownsville Papers

MOVE FORWARD MORE THAN three and a half decades later to June 1, 1972. I am in the U.S. Army. I'm a staff officer at the Pentagon while also holding an unpleasant job with the White House which I didn't like. On this day I am sitting at my desk in the Pentagon, engrossed in a letter addressed to me from the White House staff. The letter was full of petty complaints and projects the Special Adviser to President Nixon wanted me to do. My desk was stacked high with paperwork. I had been away in Europe on a White House project for the Nixon administration. When I returned, the papers on my desk had mounted to an impressive height.

The phone rang. I answered it, not knowing that it would change my life forever. My boss, Colonel Harry W. Brooks, Jr. the Army Director of Equal Opportunity Programs, was calling. I detected a sense of crisis in his voice. He told me to come to his office right away, and to bring the Brownsville papers.

What was he talking about, I thought? I told Colonel Brooks that I didn't know anything about any Brownsville papers. Brooks grew irritated. "Helen said she put the file on your desk weeks ago. Find it. Bring it over to my office immediately."

When I did not find the Brownsville file among the pile of papers, I started to tear my office apart searching for it. As I ransacked the place, I thought my office looked uglier than ever. It wasn't really an office at all, but a cubicle painted sub-ugly government green. It had one desk, an old typewriter, an old-style black telephone, a chair and several metal, six-drawer file cabinets in assorted shades of dull gray and drab beige.

My office was a part of the newly established Army Department of Equal Opportunity Programs. It was a lowly stepchild in the Pentagon—understaffed, generally ignored and poorly housed. It reminded me of those endless cubicles set in large government mail rooms and the U.S. Post Office where I had worked during the Christmas recess in 1954. There I saw low-level clerks (many with college educations) who had grown old working long hours in the mail room. They stood hunched over long tables, leaning with one shoulder lower than the other, sorting huge piles of mail. These men hobbled down the marble steps at the end of the work day. But once they hit the streets, they straightened up and strutted with exaggerated pride, casting off the drudgery of the day. They walked the be-bop walk, heads held high with one shoulder higher than other, one arm swinging stiffly.

These men belonged to an army of inopportunity, of broken hopes and lost dreams. I was beginning to think that I was becoming one of them. How was I going to get anything accomplished in this department? I escaped up the ladder of equal opportunity, but it was not up a self-made ladder. It was an opportunity made available by others.

When I opened the last of the old metal file cabinets, I caught sight of a document with a red tab attached to the top with a paper clip. It was lying flat on top of other papers in an overstuffed file drawer. I took it out, leaned against the file cabinet and read a document with big, bold letters emblazoned on the top, "H.R. 6866, 92ND CONGRESS, 1ST SESSION." It was a proposed bill introduced by Congressman Augustus F. Hawkins of California (Hawkins was the first black politician west of the Mississippi River elected to the House of Representatives.) Hawkins' bill had been referred to the Committee on Armed Services. The bill, if approved by the Congress and signed into law by President Richard M. Nixon, would direct Secretary of Defense Melvin Laird to rectify certain official actions taken as a result of the Brownsville Raid of 1906.

Brownsville! The name awakened memories that I had never been able to forget. The stories my grandfather told me about a violent shooting spree in Brownsville, Texas. Those memories took me out of the Pentagon back to Southwest Georgia in 1938 when I was a boy. While sitting on the banks of a creek fishing, my grandfather told me how President Theodore Roosevelt misjudged and mistreated a regiment of black soldiers in Texas. Roosevelt accused the black soldiers of getting drunk, of breaking out of their army camp and of shooting wildly into people's houses. My grandfather did not believe the black soldiers participated in the shooting. He said Roosevelt deceived them and disgraced the colored race. I recalled the sadness in his voice when he recounted the president's betrayal of his brothers-in-arms.

Leaning against the side of the hard metal file cabinet became uncomfortable. I pulled the folder out of the drawer, went back to my desk and continued reading. I knew that

Colonel Brooks wanted the file right away, but I couldn't stop reading. Attached to the bill were three intriguing letters. The first was from Congressman F. Edward Hebert of Louisiana addressed to Defense Secretary Melvin Laird, requesting his views on the proposed legislation, H.R. 6866. The bill proposed to overturn the Discharge Without Honor meted out to the 167 members of the 25ᵗʰ Infantry who were charged in the Brownsville Incident. The resolution was the culmination of nearly 66 years of effort by the country's black leadership to reverse what many had thought was a miscarriage of justice.

The second letter was written by Army lawyers in the Judge Advocate General's office (JAG) on behalf of Secretary Laird. It was addressed to Congressman Hebert in response to his letter and stated Laird's opposition to the bill.

As I probed deeper into the Army's opposition, I found the Army's official version of what happened:

The Brownsville Affray occurred on the night of August 13-14, in 1906, in Brownsville, Texas. Some 16 to 20 unidentified soldiers of Companies B, C, and D furtively left the Army garrison, and ran amuck through town, firing into homes and stores. One man was killed, two men were wounded, and the horse belonging to the lieutenant of police was killed.

The letter went on to explain that because none of the soldiers came forward to identify themselves as participants or to offer any evidence to incriminate any other members of the unit, President Roosevelt accused all of them of participating in a successful 'conspiracy of silence.' Therefore, he punished all of them, discharging them without honor. It appeared to me that the alleged 'conspiracy of silence' was the legal basis for Roosevelt's mass punishment of 167 soldiers. It was also the basis for JAG's current opposition to Hawkins' bill. JAG's opposition to enactment of the bill disappointed me.

Fortunately, I felt, Director of the Office of Management and Budget George P. Shultz had returned the Army's letter. He requested additional reasons for the Army's opposition. His office, commonly known as OMB, was the clearing house for proposed legislation in the Nixon Administration.

The third letter was addressed to Shultz. It had yet to be sent to OMB, but was on its way out the door. It too had been written by JAG. The Army dug in its heels, refusing to offer any additional reasons for its opposition except to assert that the discharges were supported by ample historical precedents. I was certain that if that letter got out, it would kill the bill.

After having been approved by a maze of high level departments, the proposed opposition letters had reached the end of the line for agreement. They were on my desk.

I looked at the date of the bill. It was dated March 29, 1971. The Congressman's letter was dated April 9, 1971, and JAG's response was dated April 23, 1971. These papers had been kicked around for a year now—first over at OMB, then the White House, then at the Justice Department and back to the Pentagon. It was now June 1, 1972. The deadline for response was upon us. We had only three days to concur or non-concur.

While studying the legal arguments in the letters, I felt the presence of someone standing over me. I looked up and saw Colonel Harry Brooks. The quizzical look on his face made me blurt out, "What's the matter with those lawyers over there in JAG? I know you couldn't agree with them, Colonel Brooks. I don't agree with them. We must non-concur."

Brooks wanted to know where I found the Brownsville papers. He and Bob Dews had been looking all over for them for some time now. I told him that I found them stuffed in the file cabinet. Apparently, the secretary got them mixed up with my papers.

"But here, you take 'em." I handed the papers to him.

Brooks didn't take the papers. He smiled slightly, and his face settled into a relaxed expression. The anxiety and irritation were gone. "Let's get Bob Dews and go to my office and talk about this," he replied.

On the way to Brooks' office, I stuck my head into Dew's open office door. I told him that I had found the Brownsville papers and motioned for him to come with us. Lieutenant Colonel Robert Dews, the senior staff officer in our department, was a brilliant, savvy and experienced man. Brooks relied heavily on his judgment in critical matters.

We went into Brooks' office and sat down around a small conference table. Dews glared at me and said. "You want this project?"

"What's the matter, Bob?" I said, still holding onto the Brownsville file. "Don't be sensitive. I just want to help."

"Do you know something about it?"

"You can have the whole damn thing."

I spared Dews an excursion into the past by simply telling him that I had just read the file and I'd like to work with him on the project.

Brooks intervened. He wanted to know whether we were going to agree with JAG's opposition to Hawkins' bill on Brownsville.

"Bob, can we concur with JAG?"

"We can't do it!" I said before Dews could answer. "We just can't do that!"

"Wait a minute, Bill," Brooks said softly. "I was talking to Bob." Then he asked Dews again, "Can we go along with JAG?"

"I'm not sure. I haven't had time to do much on it," Bob said.

Turning his attention to me, Brooks asked me what I knew about Brownsville. I still clutched the folder in my hand.

"I've read most of the papers in this file, sir," I said. "We have an issue with JAG."

"Well, I'm not so sure at this point," Brooks said.

Now more excited than ever, I felt confident. I wanted to take on this fight with JAG. I wanted to persuade the Army to drop its opposition to Hawkins' bill, so I volunteered to take the case. Shuffling the papers in the Brownsville folder, I showed Colonel Brooks that, without getting our agreement, JAG had already sent the first opposition letter to Shultz, and JAG stated that their opposition was not controversial in the Department of the Army.

"Look here." I pointed. "Nowhere on this piece of paper can you find our signature agreeing to that statement. They bypassed our office. They must be hiding something."

Brooks picked up the telephone and called Colonel Wade Williamson over at JAG and told him he was sending Bob Dews over to resolve some issues on the Brownsville case. After the phone call ended, Brooks said to me, "Sorry, Bill, I want Bob to handle this."

The next day, early in the morning, about six o'clock, I stopped by Dews' office. He was sitting at his desk, having a cup of coffee. I could tell from his facial expression that he was in a sour mood. He was angry and he wasn't trying to hide it.

"Those bastards' skirts aren't clean," he said. "You were right, they are hiding something." He, too, believed that the lawyers in JAG deliberately bypassed our office and intentionally sent that first letter out to OMB without our concurrence.

Dews was convinced that Colonel Wade Williamson wouldn't support Hawkins' bill because of his distaste for the Congressional Black Caucus. He said that Williamson was adamant, dogmatic, and unyielding in his position, and that he believed JAG had joined forces with the Army adjutant general to oppose the bill. He asked me whether I still wanted the case, and I told him, "Yes, by all means."

Later that morning, Colonel Brooks called me into his office, where he and Dews had been in a meeting for some time. Brooks didn't even ask me to sit down.

He looked up from his desk and said, "We'll non-concur. Bill, you have the Brownsville project."

That phone call from Brooks, followed by the assignment of the Brownsville project to me in 1972, led me to do a quick study of the history of the Brownsville affair and set me on the path for a deep incursion into history. What I found was a strange story of a town seized by fear and anger, a web of lies, deep-rooted racial passions and prejudices and murder.

A Violent Beginning

The town of Brownsville had a violent beginning. It was fathered, birthed and nurtured by the guns of the United States Army in 1846 during the Mexican American War. General Zachary Taylor was leading his troops against the Mexican Army and constructed an earthen bastion on private property. That property was later named Fort Brown and the name they gave to the tiny civilian settlement nearby was Brownsville. Congressman Abraham Lincoln of Illinois characterized the genesis of Brownsville in a letter to Rev. J.M. Peck in 1848. In the letter he stated the facts of the action and sought to determine whether the United States had, in fact, not committed an aggression against Mexico in prosecuting the Mexican War. This account was taken from Carl Sandburg, *Abraham Lincoln-The Prairie Years, Volume One*. p. 372.

Brownsville sat in the lower Rio Grande Valley in a flat river delta. It was the very bottom of southeastern Texas, just north across the Rio Grande River from Matamoros, Mexico. Fort Brown was located next door to Brownsville just across Garrison Road at the end of town. Here the fort nestled against the big bend curve formed by the Rio Grande River where it flowed southeast to the Gulf of Mexico.

Brownsville was a rough and tumble Southern town in 1906. The population of 6,000 people was about two-thirds Mexican. The rest were white with a handful of blacks. It was a poor town of dirt farmers just eking out a living. Ranchers, shopkeepers and saloon owners operated establishments that were heavily dependent upon the patronage of white soldiers from nearby Fort Brown. Brownsville was also a haven for smugglers.

The railroad came to Brownsville in July 1904, bringing unanticipated problems. Incoming cheap Anglo labor added to a town already surfeited with cheap Mexican labor and inhabitants imbued with deeply-rooted racial prejudices arising from the old cotton field, tobacco road and unreconstructed South. Since there were just a few black families in Brownsville, lawlessness, violence, and most all other ills were blamed on the Mexican population along with the occasional cowboy gunslinger, rough-neck white newcomers and smugglers. All that changed on July 25, 1906, when the all-black 25th Infantry came to town.

Author's Note: As the blame for lawlessness and violence changed, so did the deepening crisis of fear. That did not surprise me. What intrigued me most as I researched and wrote this book is how a shooting incident in Texas could have such an impact in American history? Well it did, and even has currency today. Between 1906 and 1910, the Brownsville Affray was a cause célèbre and a national crisis. President Theodore Roosevelt's punitive action against the black soldiers created a huge public outcry and a Senate investigation which challenged the legality of the president's action. Roosevelt accepted the challenge with dramatic effects.

Another amazing result of the incident was an irrevocable split in the black community. Long before the Brownsville Incident, the black community had been drifting into two political camps—those following Professor Booker T. Washington's philosophy of self-help and accommodation to segregation, and those adhering to the W.E.B. Du Bois School of Civil Liberty Advocates, demanding full equality.

THREE

BROWNSVILLE, TEXAS, 1906

Anger and Fear Take Over

The Announcement

WEEKS HAD PASSED SINCE last May when Dr. Fredrick J. Combe, the white mayor of Brownsville and also a medical doctor, announced the news at a special town meeting that the War Department was planning to send black soldiers to Fort Brown. They would replace the current battalion of white soldiers. Not long after the announcement, Mayor Combe began hearing rumors that his citizens would not accept the "nigger soldiers." Some white citizens were making violent threats, boasting that all they would have to do was kill a few niggers, and that would drive the other niggers out of town in a week or two. William Howard Taft, Secretary of War under President Theodore Roosevelt, received many complaints, all of them saying, "Don't send the colored soldiers to Texas. Change the orders."

While assuring his citizens that they had no reasons to fear the new arrivals, Mayor Combe neglected to tell the townspeople that he had served with some of these soldiers. He had been their surgeon (medical doctor). *Perhaps*, he thought, *it would be unnecessary, since it was taking so long to make a final decision.*

Figure 1: Mayor Frederick J. Combe, Circa 1903, in his military uniform
Courtesy of the Brownsville, Texas Historical Association

Fearing that Taft would not heed the complaints, Combe set up several meetings with his police chief, George Connors, to plan a strategy. He wanted to do anything he could to avoid trouble. But trouble was now only a few weeks away.

Sentiment ran high against stationing black troops at Fort Brown. Families and friends congregated around their kitchen tables and discussed the situation to no end. A frightful expectancy of bad things to come gripped Brownsville. They conjured up all kinds of irrational calamities. *Black heathens will rape, rob, and murder us in our beds*, they thought. They had nothing but contempt for them. It was widespread. People were nervous, and they felt the coming of a reign of terror.

One would have thought that the black soldiers were foreign conquerors, storming in to occupy their town. The unsettling fantasy was fueled by rumor, anger and fear. Brownsville was about to have a general panic on its hands.

Captain Benjamin J. Edger, Jr., the doctor for the white unit that was leaving Fort Brown, told Mayor Combe that all the white people he had spoken to, even his friends, didn't want "colored soldiers" in Brownsville. And they were loud and insistent when they voiced their denunciations.

The Mexicans residents worried, too. Police Chief Connors told the mayor that some Mexicans, especially those who thought they were white, felt the same way about the coming blacks. Mayor Combe believed their fears were groundless. Nevertheless, he knew that he had to find a way to quiet them.

"They'll get used to the colored soldiers, for sure, with time." He tried to sound reassuring.

Chief Connors said he didn't know about that, his voice hesitating. He shook his head, indicating mild disagreement. Talk was getting violent. Threats were being made.

"My policemen tell me that they heard a group of roughnecks talking about joining a posse to meet the train and stop the soldiers from getting off," he said.

The mayor wanted to know who was behind it, and what their names were. The police chief wasn't quite sure, but believed the saloon keepers were in it down to the last pissing details.

"They are an unhappy lot, worried they're going to lose beer drinkers when the white soldiers leave," Connors said. "The last thing they wanted to lose was that business. And you know, they're saying that they're not going to serve the Negro soldiers. Joe Crixell said all he wanted in his saloon was white officers' business."

According to the chief, one of the policemen heard H.H. Wellers say to a crowd of rabble-rousers at his saloon, "The people will get rid of the niggers some way."

"Then, there's John Tillman. He just opened the Ruby Saloon, and it's just beginning to take off. His business is going to be hit pretty hard unless he serves the Negroes. He's gotta do something to make up his losses, else he's going out of business. I heard him said he may have his bartender set up something in the back of the Ruby Saloon for the colored soldiers. If he can't make money that way, I heard he threatened he would have the 'Negro soldiers run out of town in three weeks.'"

"That's nonsense," the mayor said. "Who's he going to find to do that? Who's going to shoot first? And they damn sure better aim straight. They won't get a second shot. I know these soldiers from Cuba."

Chief Connors continued his report, "And oh, yes, there's something else I heard. The preachers are calling for a mass meeting next week."

"They can be trouble," Mayor Combe said. "I want you to keep your eye on them. They can stir up trouble and wrap it in the sanctity of God."

This conversation took place while Brownsville was still waiting on the final decision from the War Department.

The chief leaned forward. "You better get some kind of answer soon. You saw the crowd gathered near City Hall the other day. It was getting pretty angry till Captain Kelly stepped in and cooled them off a bit."

The mayor thought for a moment, and then said, "When I saw Captain Kelly out there addressing the crowd, I knew the situation was in good hands. Now there's a man I can count on."

"Kelly is a good man," Connors agreed. "We don't have to worry about him. But you better watch out for your political enemies, especially Sam Wreford. Don't take your eyes off him. He'll use this thing to embarrass you or break the law in some fashion. You know he breaks the law at every opportunity he can." The chief had finished his report and stood up. "The streets are quiet today," he said as he turned to leave. "I'm going fishing."

After walking with the chief to the door, Combe returned to his desk pondering the political aspect of Connors' warning. *Was that letter complaining about the soldiers that Wreford wrote to U.S. Senator Culberson intended to embarrass him? After all, it was Wreford who made the letter public.* Combe had read the letter in the *Brownsville Daily Herald*. He disagreed with Wreford's position that "black troops always cause trouble." *Not these soldiers*, Combe thought. They weren't strangers to him.

They were soldiers of Companies B, C, and D, units of the 25th United States Infantry Regiment (Colored), an all-black battalion except for its white officers. The soldiers were stationed out West on the plains of Nebraska at Fort Niobrara near the small town of Valentine. On the plains and in other places in the West, Native American Indians feared and respected black soldiers as warriors. They held them in such high regard that they honored them with the name of their sacred buffalo and called them "Buffalo Soldiers."

Combe kept reminding himself that he knew these soldiers. Wreford didn't. His citizens didn't. However, his sympathies were clearly with the citizens of his town.

He began to brood. He would rather not have black soldiers stationed in his town if his citizens didn't want them, but he knew these black soldiers. He knew First Sergeant Mingo Sanders. He was friends with some of the white officers. He had served with them as a combat medical officer in Cuba and the Philippines during the Spanish American War of 1898. He knew their reputation as honorable, well-disciplined, fighting men. In addition, he was aware that they were equipped with the new M1903 Springfield, an American-made, five-round, magazine fed, bolt-action service repeating rifle. Combe believed that it would be disastrous for his citizens if they attacked these well-armed soldiers. Clearly, there could be no armed clash between his citizens and the soldiers, should they come to Brownsville. Even though the chief's report was disappointing, even saddening, and certainly not reassuring, Combe was not convinced that his citizens would fight to keep the soldiers out.

An Anxious Wait

The weather was hot and humid on this day in mid-July. The air barely stirred at all in the sweltering heat. Many of the townspeople scurried to the beach near Point Isabel on the Gulf of Mexico to cool off. Mayor Fred Combe was performing his doctor duties. He glanced into the waiting room. There had been few patients this morning. He drew a sigh of relief. Maybe there wouldn't be many heat stroke patients for him to see this summer.

Still troubled by the chief's report from a week ago, Combe decided to close his medical office early and go to his other office in City Hall. It was worrisome that he still hadn't received anything final from Washington. Senator Culberson had promised that the Secretary of War would give his reply any day now. That was weeks ago, and still no answer. The suspense was stressful.

As Combe walked toward City Hall, he saw Captain Benjamin J. Edger, Jr., a white officer and the post surgeon for the departing white soldiers at Fort Brown. The captain was allowed to conduct his own medical practice in his spare time. Edger waved him down from across the street and approached him. "Fred, got a minute? I've something for you."

Combe sensed some urgency in the captain's voice. He greeted his old friend, then paused. "Yeah, Ed, what do you have?"

They walked up Ninth Street toward City Hall on Adams Street.

"I have the Army contract for you to sign to act as post surgeon until they can get a new doctor here to replace me," said the captain. "You know, there is no colored doctor coming with the 25th Infantry."

Combe looked over his shoulder. "Let's wait until we get to my office, lest we contaminate Mexican people's minds with the fears of white folks." His voice was barely above a whisper. "If there's going to be a problem, and I don't believe there will be, it will be with the white people, not with the Mexicans. In fact, the black soldiers will probably just melt in with them. You know, some Mexicans do look like Negroes."

Chuckling sardonically, the captain shook his head. "Don't tell that to the Mexicans."

Edger followed the mayor and waited for him to unlock his office. The two men walked in, closed the door and sat down. Edger reached into his black bag, pulled out the contract and handed it to Combe who made no move to take it. His hesitation lasted so long that Captain Edger let his hand, and the contract, fall to his side. "What's wrong, Fred? Did you change your mind?"

Combe felt uneasy but he managed to say, "Oh, it's nothing, Ed. Give it to me, I'll sign it." He took the contract, signed two copies, and handed the Army copy to the captain.

Edger stood up. "We're leaving the day before the 25th Infantry gets here, Fred. Word is that they'll arrive on the 27th of July. Between now and then, there's a lot of packing to do. I better get going."

Combe dropped his copy of the contract on top of a pile of papers stacked on his desk. All were waiting for his signature. He sat down and signed paper after paper, resigned that there would always be something to sign. The paperwork took longer than he thought it would. When he finished, he put it in a basket on a small table near the large grandfather clock in the corner. He used to love the sound of its ticking. He often marveled at the enormous golden pendulum as it moved with precision. But now it irritated him. Each tick seemed to extend time. He sat down in his brown leather armchair and propped his feet up on a long marble table. He drew in a long-awaited breath of relaxation and reflected on his two years in office.

It seemed that all of his progress was about to go up in smoke. Just as he began to feel good about the strides he made in cleaning up and securing the town, trouble was heading straight at him. He feared riots would rip the community apart. Why hadn't he told the people at that special town meeting that he knew some of the soldiers? Maybe that would have eased their fears. Who was he kidding? He knew why he neglected to tell them, and now he regretted it.

FOUR

BROWNSVILLE AWAITS

The Final Decision

The Telegram

ON THE 23ʳᵈ OF July, Mayor Combe was alone in his office with the door closed. He was reclining comfortably in his great leather armchair, reading the *Brownsville Daily Herald*, when he heard a light tap on the door. It startled him. He had grown more and more edgy every day, waiting on the word from Washington. He didn't respond immediately, but took a deep breath. *Was the final decision waiting at the door?* Finally, he said, "Come in."

His clerk opened the door and smiled warmly. "Doctor Combe, I think this is what you've been waiting for." He handed him a telegram.

Combe took it and the clerk left the room. Getting up from his chair, he walked to his desk, stared at the envelope for a few seconds and ripped it open. As Mayor of Brownsville, Combe saw many telegrams, but this one was different. Typed on dull, rough, yellow paper with big bold capital letters jammed together, the words seemed more official, more powerful and final than he had ever seen before. He read the first line, and then slumped down in his chair, sagging beneath the news. "They've made the decision. The colored soldiers are coming."

Taft had simply refused to change the orders, but his response was intended to allay the townspeople's fears.

The fact is that a certain amount of race prejudice between white and black seems to be universal throughout the country, and no matter where colored troops are sent there are always some who object to their coming. It is a fact, however, as shown by our records, that colored troops are quite well disciplined and behaved as the average troops of other troops, and it does not seem logical to anticipate any greater trouble from them than from the rest. Army records also showed that white soldiers averaged a greater degree of intemperance than colored ones. Sometimes communities that objected to the coming of colored soldiers have entirely changed their view and commended their good behavior to the War Department.

Although Combe didn't agree with Taft's decision to send the soldiers, he readily agreed with Taft that black troops were well disciplined. He thought that the townspeople's fears were overblown, and had to admit that even he, a man of science, a combat veteran and a medical doctor, had allowed himself to fall into the fear trap. Suddenly, he had a startling revelation about his fears which surprised and enlightened him. He was not afraid of the black soldiers, but of the fears of his own citizens—and the likely consequences of their fears. It was his citizens he must convince. He felt foolish that he allowed himself to be overcome by fear the last few weeks. He no longer felt depressed. He resolved not to let fear enslave him again and that gave him new strength.

The News Gets Out

Even before Mayor Combe could inform his policemen and his staff, the word hit the streets of Brownsville that Taft refused to change the order—and indeed, black soldiers were coming to town. *How could the word have leaked out?* Then Combe remembered. It must have been through Sam Wreford, who probably got the word through Senator Culberson.

Combe needed time to organize a citizens committee to calm the fears of the people and set up a welcoming party that would work to keep the peace.

He rang the police chief to discuss his plan to organize a welcoming party.

"The preachers are one step ahead of you," Chief Conner said. "They're holding a protest meeting tomorrow in front of the Federal Courthouse."

"Do you think they'll draw a crowd?"

"Yeah they've been whipping them up for weeks now."

Combe felt he must act quickly. "Get hold of Captain Kelly," he said. "Tell him to round up some stalwarts and meet me in my office tonight at eight o'clock. Tell 'em it's urgent."

At ten minutes after eight o'clock, Mayor Combe was sitting alone at the head of a small mahogany conference table in the downstairs conference room at City Hall when he heard Captain Kelly's voice. "Damn fools! They'll incite a riot."

The mayor raised his head and called out to Kelly and the group of men entering the lobby. "Captain, in here! I'm in the conference room."

Since he heard of the threats, Captain Kelly managed to gather some of the town's most prominent officials for the meeting—John Bartlett, the county judge; Frank W. Kibbe, the city attorney; Jesse O. Wheeler, the editor of the *Daily Herald*; and Celedonio Garza, the sheriff. George Connor, the Chief of Police, was also in attendance.

Mayor Combe got down to business. "You all know why you're here. We've got to get control of this situation before those rabble-rousing preachers spin it out of control. Thank God they are meeting in front of the Federal Court House, and not here on the steps of City Hall. But how can we stop them?"

Chief Connor said, "I don't have anything on them. I think the preachers are pretty much straight. Anyhow, I believe Sam Wreford is really the one behind this meeting."

"Get me some charges, and I'll throw his ass in jail, cool him off a bit," Judge Bartlett said.

Combe spoke up. "And he wrote that letter to Washington, giving the impression that the whole town is against the colored soldiers."

"Well, what else have you got on Sam Wreford?" The judge looked around the table. "Anybody got anything more on Wreford? I can smell shit a mile away. Got to be some more shit somewhere."

"He's dirty all over," City Attorney Kibbe said.

"Give me some specifics," the judge said.

"He's been fornicating with a Mexican woman."

"So what!" Bartlett raised his eyebrows. As a county judge, he knew that, under the laws of Texas, having sex with a woman other than one's wife was a crime—and was encoded as fornication. "There are a lot of white men in this town fornicating with Mexican women."

Wheeler would not be dismissed. "I have proof that he's not a resident, and hasn't paid his taxes in several years."

Judge Bartlett peered up over his glasses. "Now you're getting somewhere."

"Just listen to this," Wheeler said. "A few years back, Sam Wreford tried to smear Jim Powers, Superintendent of the National Cemetery at Brownsville, accusing him of stealing money from the cemetery funds he managed for the quartermaster general. Jim came to me for help in clearing his name. While looking into the matter, we found some stuff on Sam, including a record in the Court of Cameron County showing him to have been guilty of living in fornication with a Mexican woman at Brownsville. No penalty was imposed on him on the condition that he take the woman back to Mexico. And the record showed further that Sam Wreford paid no taxes in Brownsville for several years, and that he was, in fact, a resident of Mexico."

When the drift of the meeting turned to specifics on possible criminal behavior, Jesse Wheeler excused himself and left.

"Jesse seemed uncomfortable with our discussion," the city attorney said.

"Go to Sam," the judge said to the city attorney. "Get him to call off the meeting tomorrow."

Mayor Combe had listened intently, forming a new strategy as the discussion went along. Finally he said, "I raised the question about stopping the meeting, so now I will resolve it. The momentum for the meeting is probably too great to stop it now. Besides, somebody responsible needs to address the citizens, and that man is me."

He turned to the city attorney. "Kibbe, present your stuff to Sam. If you need the leverage, use it. Tell him we appreciate the preachers' leadership in calling the meeting, but the mayor needs to talk first—after an opening prayer by one of the preachers, of course. After I finish, one of preacher can give the benediction, and then I'll leave."

Combe knew that this strategy would marginalize the preacher by confining him to the invocation and the benediction. The mayor assumed that by that time, his words should have cooled down the crowd some. As an afterthought, Combe said that perhaps Sam Wreford should be allowed to make a few remarks.

The mayor instructed Kibbe to go to Wreford, strike a deal and tell him the mayor would support his business interests, if he would simply agree to a joint meeting under the auspices of the mayor's office. He also instructed the city attorney to tell Wreford that the mayor's office would handle the set-up, the podium, the flags and all the patriotic details.

"Tell Wreford that he must get the preachers to tone down their rhetoric in the town. Persuade him to go along, and, do not use the word 'dirt' unless you have to," Combe concluded.

After the mayor finished giving his instructions to the city attorney, he motioned to Kelly. "Captain Kelly, after I leave the stage, you stay up there, take the questions, and keep that crowd pacified, okay?"

Shortly after the meeting broke up, the city attorney met with Sam Wreford. Combe was relieved when Kibbe called back and reported that he had struck a deal with Wreford that allowed the mayor to handle the substance of the protest meeting. Combe was especially pleased that there was no need to confront Wreford with the derogatory information.

A Unique Distinction

The next day at five o'clock the streets were lined with throngs of people going to the Federal Courthouse. The square in front of the court was already packed—and people were still coming. Mayor Combe sat on the platform, which had been hastily erected for this special town meeting. He was conspicuously apart from the rest of the dignitaries. It was his practice to have his massive, over-stuffed, brown leather chair transported from his office to wherever he was speaking. It dwarfed the rickety, cane bottom, wooden straight-back chairs upon which the other dignitaries sat. *I get a lot of strength and power from sitting in this chair*, he thought, *and I'll need it today.*

The rest of the dignitaries, Captain Kelly, the banker, Jesse Wheeler, the editor of the *Daily Herald*, Judge Bartlett and Sam Wreford, were sitting in chairs behind a table draped with red-white-and blue bunting. A pitcher of water stood in the center of the table. Several glasses had been put on the table in front of the places where each person was supposed to sit and marked by artistically-penned nameplates. The mayor's fruit jar, filled with water, sat on the floor beside his great chair, as it always did during all his speeches. Whenever he was lost for words or needed to get his thoughts together, he took a small sip or two from the jar, using it as a distraction. There was a joke around town that one could tell whether the mayor made a good speech or a bad one by measuring the amount of water left in the jar. A good speech left the jar nearly full, a bad speech—empty.

One of the preachers, stood at the podium, poised to offer up a prayer to Almighty God. The place had all the trappings of a political rally rather than a protest meeting. Colorful red-white-and blue bunting was tacked up just about everywhere. Old Glory and the Texas state flag rippled in the breeze from the Gulf of Mexico. With the exception of a band, all the elements were there. The air was heavy with expectation, as if some political heavyweight was about to announce his candidacy for office.

After a few more late arrivals elbowed their way in, the preacher said, "Let's bow our heads in prayer." Then he offered up a short prayer, so short, in fact, that it probably set a record for brevity for preachers in that part of Texas.

Then, Mayor Combe rose to address the crowd. "My good citizens, my friends, you know me. I am Fred Combe, your mayor, and for some of you, your doctor. Our relationship is long, close and deep. Like most of you, I was born here in Brownsville. I grew up here. This is home. I like living here, like living in my house where I can look out of my windows and see our beloved Rio Grande River which flows by my garden, flows by our town—bringing water for our crops—and flows down yonder to our beautiful Gulf of Mexico.

"My roots are deeply embedded in the soil of our ancestors who were born and died here—strong men who built this town from nothing, nothing but a virtual cotton patch. Our ancestors loved this town. You love this town. And like you, I love this town—its traditions, the way we talk, our food, the soil from which it comes, the pungent smell of barbecue rising from the smoking pit, the salty air we breathe. I love this part of Texas."

The crowd broke out chanting. "Yes! Yes! Yes! Texas! Texas! Texas!"

A man up front yelled. "Tell it! Tell it! Tell it, Fred." The mayor was encouraged.

After several more interruptions of loud chants, Combe drum-rolled the crowd by reminding them how much he had accomplished since he became mayor just two years ago, and how well off they were under his administration.

"Since becoming your mayor, I have reformed our great city. I have reformed the city administration, cleaned up the streets and brought order to our town by cleaning up the police force. I put the police in new uniforms similar to the military and gave them the dignity they deserved. In winter, I dressed them in double-breasted blue coats with brass military buttons, and with Cavalry blue felt hats trimmed in gold cord. And in summer, with the familiar wide-brimmed campaign hats and the military khaki pants.

"So now, as you know, they look like soldiers. And that's good, for like the soldier, they are here to protect our mothers, our wives, our children, all of our citizens. I have seen the transforming magic of the uniform while I was a soldier. I know the uniform of a well-dressed soldier brings discipline, honor and respect to the soldier, to his community, to his country. And I knew the uniform could do the same for our policemen.

"Now with a more professional police force, you, the citizens, feel more secure, and I feel more secure. There is less open display of weapons, less shooting and gunplay in our streets, fewer dead people. I know you love your guns. I love my guns. But the gun isn't the quickest way to settle a dispute, and I know you own many guns. I see you toting Winchester rifles, Remington rifles, shotguns, six-shooter pistols and even a few old Krag-Jorgesen rifles you managed to buy from soldiers at Fort Brown willing to sell a rifle for a buck or two."

Then the mayor dropped his voice and eased into the crux of the matter:

Now we are being consumed by a crisis of fear, a contagion, spreading hate among us. Irrational fear that has invaded our minds, our bodies, our spirit, and is about to invade our very souls. It is a fear that threatens our Christian way of life and is propelling us toward the gun, toward destruction of our town, urging us to believe in salvation through the gun, instead of salvation through our God.

Sam Wreford sat stoned faced on the platform with the other dignitaries. He was becoming uneasy with the tone of the mayor's speech.

A heckler near the front shouted, "Git to the point, Mayor! The colored soldiers are coming. What are we gonna do about it? Thought this was a protest meeting. We're not here to talk about our souls!"

Looking directly at the man, the mayor said, "I know what we are here for. I'll get to it in a minute."

"Deal with it now, Combe," the heckler called out. "We're tired of waiting! Why are you making a campaign speech?"

Mayor Combe recognized the heckler as the man who had supported his opponent in the last mayoral election. Turning his head away, Combe looked straight ahead at the sea of citizens before him. Then, as if speaking confidentially and privately to each group, the Mayor spoke to the middle, to the left and then to the right.

"You have nothing to fear from these soldiers," he said firmly. "They wear the uniform of our United States Army. They are coming to protect our border from thieves, smugglers and bandits. And remember, it was the ancestors of these soldiers, who, as soldiers themselves, drove many Mexican bandits from our land, from our Texas."

"Rubbish!" the man shouted. "Liar! White men drove the bandits out of Texas. White men!"

Again, Mayor Combe ignored the man. "And, my dear citizens, I want you to know it was these very soldiers, these valiant men, who are coming to our town who fought the Spaniards in Cuba, who captured El Caney, tore down the Spanish flag, and raised old glory, your flag, my flag, over the hill of El Caney. They shared their rations with Colonel Roosevelt, and with him captured Kettle Hill."

The crowd gasped at this revelation of history, and the mayor thought he was beginning to win the people over. Now was the time to call on Jesse. Turning to the table where Jesse Wheeler, Editor of the *Daily Herald*, was seated, the mayor waved him up to the podium. "Come on over here, Jesse. You tell'em."

The editor walked over to the flag-draped podium and stood at the mayor's side.

"The mayor is right, he tells the truth. These are the brave soldiers who captured El Caney." He held up a copy of the *Daily Herald*, and waved it at the crowd. "It's in the paper today. You can read it for yourselves."

A woman in the crowd, stretching, and standing on tiptoe, asked politely, "Mr. Wheeler, would you read it for us?"

Jesse Wheeler nodded. "It's a long article, but I'll read a few lines. You can get the paper and read the rest for yourselves." Then he began to read from the paper:

The 25th United States Infantry, which lay over in San Antonio yesterday on its way from Nebraska to a different post on the Texas border, enjoys a unique distinction in the military Annals of America.

It was that body of troops, composed entirely of Negro Soldiers, that charged El Caney hill in the face of continuous fire, pulled down the Spanish ensign, and with the assistance of the Fourth and Twelfth regiments, made prisoners of the Spaniards that survived the attack.

After reading these short passages, the editor said, "It goes on to say the Negro soldiers then went over and joined Colonel Roosevelt, now our President, and his Rough Riders, and assisted them in capturing Kettle Hill."

Still skeptical, the man turned his back on Mayor Combe and, facing the crowd, he hooted. "It's a fake, folks. They say anything in the newspapers." Then he turned, and, pointing at the mayor, challenged him again. "You don't know, Combe. How could you know? You weren't there!"

An old man standing on the ground, near the corner of the stage and who obviously knew the heckler, looked over at him and said. "You ain't been there, neither. Shet your mouth."

Sensing that the mayor was winning the argument and turning the crowd in his favor, Sam Wreford decided to speak out. He was sure he had an ace in the hole to turn the crowd around. Best use it at once, Wreford thought, or Combe would surely win. Besides, the mayor had tricked him and the preacher by taking over their meeting. What was supposed to be a protest meeting now appeared to be turning into a political meeting supporting the soldiers, President Roosevelt and the Republicans.

"As I was trying to point out, my good citizens," Combe continued, "the records of these soldiers demonstrate that we have absolutely nothing to fear."

Wreford stood up, interrupted the mayor's words, and pointing at him, said, "Their records be damned! Fred, sounds like you have gone over to the enemy. Sounds like you're supporting the soldiers coming. I've got a question for you. Are you going to act as medical surgeon at that post when the colored soldiers get here?"

Mayor Combe reached down, took a sip of water from the fruit jar wondering how Wreford found out he'd agreed to act as post surgeon? It was supposed to be a confidential deal. Nobody was to know about that contract. He was to go on an emergency basis only. He didn't believe his old friend Captain Edger would have told anybody about it, and Edger had assured him that nobody in the departing white battalion knew about it, not even the commander. Who else knew? He would deal with the snitch later. For now he had to deal with Sam Wreford's question.

But before the mayor could answer, Wreford went on, "Didn't you sign a contract the other day, knowing in all likelihood you'd be serving the colored soldiers, that they'd be coming? You signed that contract, didn't you?"

The mayor turned away from Wreford, faced the crowd squarely and spoke. "Now folks, Sam knows, and you all know, that I go to the post on an emergency basis when I am called. I've been going for years. They never asked me to sign a contract before. This time they did. Yes, I signed it, but it don't say nothing about the color of the patients I'm supposed to operate on in an emergency. It says nothing about colored soldiers coming to the post. It just says 'soldiers' and anybody can come by my office and read the contract for themselves. I have nothing to hide."

The mayor was relieved to see the crowd nodding in approval. He felt the sentiment in the crowd flowing toward his argument again.

By this time the mayor knew he had defused the contract issue Wreford had raised. He decided he'd better disclose his past connection to the 25th Infantry, the regiment of the black soldiers. Getting back to the hecklers' question, he said. "Sir, would you please repeat your question?"

The man gladly obliged. "I asked you how you know that Cuba stuff in the paper is true. How could you know? You weren't there."

Standing erect, Mayor Combe squared his shoulders and looked directly at the crowd, and said, "I served with them. I was their combat medical officer. And some of the white officers are my friends. I do not fear these men, and you should not fear them. They are honorable men, good United States Army soldiers. I returned from Cuba with them on the same boat. The boat stopped in Tampa, Florida. There was no ...."

Seeing Sam start to get up from his chair again, the mayor stopped in mid-sentence. He looked directly at Wreford and said sarcastically, "Okay, Sam, I guess it's your time to speak. Come on over before you pee in your little britches."

Then the mayor raised his voice, "Don't tell too many lies, and keep the poison out!" The crowd broke out laughing.

Wreford walked to the podium, glaring at Combe. He reached in his pocket for his prepared speech, and, not finding it, he fumbled around in his other pockets. He began sweating profusely when he realized he had indeed lost it. He faced the crowd, and said, "Folks, I lost my speech, but ...."

Before Wreford could finish his sentence, the mayor curled his right hand, making a bull horn, and yelled toward Wreford's right ear.

"But what? Yeah, we know, Sam—a little bird stole it." The crowd broke out laughing again.

The mayor was making a fool out of Sam Wreford. Perhaps, he should have let one of the preachers give the speech. If Wreford didn't get it together quickly, he was going to be a laughingstock all over town.

Someone shouted, "Let him talk! Quiet! Quiet!"

When the crowd quieted down, Wreford began again.

"As I started to say, I don't need a piece of paper to tell you that the mayor is selling out to the enemy. He's selling out to Roosevelt and that Republican crowd up yonder in Washington, D.C. who's trying to foist these colored soldiers off on us."

"For your information," Wreford continued, "my pastor and I called this meeting today. The mayor jumped aboard our bandwagon, and sent his man, begging us, sweet-talking us, asking us to let the mayor speak first. Out of respect for his position, we agreed, thinking we had a common purpose, to keep the nigger soldiers out of our town. Now, the mayor used to be my friend. But no more. He's done switched sides. He's done gone over to the enemy."

Leaning over the podium, Wreford looked intently at the crowd, and, slowly moving his head up and down, said, "You know, he really gave us a political speech, telling us how much he loves our town, how much he loves Texas."

He turned his head briefly toward the mayor. "Well, Fred, we all love our town, we love Texas, and we even love that old muddy Rio Grande River. But as good Christians, we didn't come here today to talk about love, to congratulate ourselves, to lick our own boots. We're here to talk about how to stop those colored soldiers from coming to our town. We want to send a message to Washington. We're not going to allow them niggers in here. I say, if he loves this town so much," he raised his voice to a shrill crescendo, "why in the hell is he letting the niggers in? Don't believe him. If he loved us that much, he would join us in stopping them from getting off that train. But by God, we're going with or without him. We're gonna stop 'em!"

The crowd stood in dead silence. They were so quiet that Wreford dropped his voice almost to a whisper. He leaned over on the podium as if he were about to let the crowd in on a very big secret, and said quietly, "I'm a good Christian. I know there's a lot of good Christian men out there among you. God said love your neighbor, but he never said nothing 'bout loving niggers. Them nigger soldiers are just like rats. You let 'em in your home and they will infest the whole place. You don't hafta hate rats to kill 'em. You just kill 'em."

He raised his voice to an emotional pitch, and shouted, "They don't want our land. They don't want our money. Gentlemen, they want our white women! I say, let's go meet that train and clean 'em out!"

The people in the crowd were stirring around and murmuring to themselves.

Wreford paused and waited for the reaction to what he thought were the most powerful words of his speech. He then repeated them, "Gentlemen, they want our white women!" But there was only silence.

Finally, a man near the back, called out, "Shet up, Sam. You ain't nothing but a barnburner."

Wreford held his hand to his ear. "Speak louder, I didn't hear you."

The man called out again. "I said you're a barnburner. You talking about gitting rid of rats. You're jest like the Dutchman who burned down his barn jest to git rid of the rats. You risk all these people's lives, if you attack them soldiers. Don't listen to him, folks. Don't go down to that train. You'll all git killed."

"Coward!" Wreford yelled. "You're a coward, old man."

"Yeah," shouted another man supporting Wreford. "I could take fifty men and go clean out the whole Negro outfit. Let's march on the train!"

Captain Kelley was boiling. Itching to say something, he couldn't sit any longer and listen to such foolishness about stopping the train. And it pained him to hear United States Army soldiers being compared to rats. He stood up from his seat on the stage and said derisively, "Stop the train? With what? That old rifle you got there that you keep around the house to shoot doves and deer? Those old shotguns I see some of you carrying that you use to shoot rabbits? The soldiers got the new Springfield rifles. They're trained to fight. None of you've ever been a soldier."

Sensing that he was about to lose control of the situation, Wreford figured that he had better get in a few last words. He needed to slam the mayor for good, and perhaps this was the moment. "Folks, we got a rat among us, and we all know who he is. He just finished talking to us and there he sits!" He pointed to the mayor.

"It's plain as the hair on his head," Wreford said emphatically. "He's a double-crossing, double-dealing rat! He's a traitor to the purity of our white women. He's a traitor to the chastity of our girls."

The crowd became very quiet and ill at ease with this vitriolic attack upon their mayor whom most of them believed in, honored, and even loved. They were stone-faced, grim, in total disbelief.

Wreford fired off another volley of attacks. "And why won't he go to that train station with us? I'll tell you why. 'Cause he's made his bed with them, and I want to tell you, he's in that bed with 'em. By his own admission, he's lived with 'em."

The mayor was steaming, seething with anger, he leaped from his seat. "Why, you son-of-a-bitch! That's enough. You son-of-a-bitch! You just crossed the line. You've gone too far.

You've assaulted my honor. You impugned my character, my integrity. You called me ugly names.

"Now you're trying to incite my citizens to riot, to take the law into your own hands. You will not destroy our town." He walked over to Wreford, stood chest to chest with him, looked directly in his face and made a promise. "You'll regret this day, you rascal." Mayor Combe brushed past Wreford's shoulder, and started to turn away.

He stopped cold when he heard Sam Wreford say. "You double dealer! You asked for it."

Mayor Combe jumped in Wreford's face again, started jabbing his index finger into Wreford's chest, and backed him against the table and chairs, "You! You! You!"

Wreford stepped backward until he sat down. He tried to get up, but the mayor stood over him. "Sit down. You shut up. You fornicator!"

Shocked, the crowd let out a loud gasp.

"Oh, my God," one woman yelled standing near the front row.

Aghast that the word 'fornicator' had slipped out, the mayor knew that now he had to offer some proof of this crime. *I can't stop now*, he thought. *I must destroy him completely.*

Wreford flinched, astounded that the mayor would make such an accusation in public. Visibly shaken, he waited to find out what else the mayor knew about that old incident with Jim Powers. He tried to get off the stage quickly, but the mayor blocked him and shoved him back down in his chair.

Leaning close to his face, the mayor looked him dead in the eye. He had more for him. "Oh no, you're going nowhere, you tax cheat! You dirty the chair you're sitting in. You defile this stage."

Figure 2. Map of Brownsville and Fort Brown
Drawn by Craftsmen
in the Office of Quartermaster General December 1909
Modified by Lt. Col. (Ret) William Baker
NOTE: Garrison Road Separates Brownsville from Fort Brown

Mayor Combe walked back to the podium and addressed the crowd, "My good citizens. My friends. I apologize for my language, but there's more you should know about this man, and I regret it has to come out this way. I was hoping he would go back to Mexico where he belongs. He's been pretending to be one of us. But I've got to tell you, he is not a resident of Brownsville, not a resident of Texas, not a resident of these United States. He's a resident of Mexico. The Cameron County Court found him guilty of fornication with a Mexican woman. I want you to know the woman wasn't his wife. The judge ordered him to get out of this country and take the woman with him, or be thrown in jail. He didn't obey the law. Instead he remains here, stirring up trouble, poisoning your minds. The records show he hasn't paid his taxes in several years. If you don't believe me, go down to the courthouse and see for yourselves."

Mayor Combe paused, took a couple of deep breaths and pointed to Wreford. Then, buoyed by his success, he took a rhetorical flight of fantasy as pure nonsense fell from his lips.

"There he sits, still in this country. He's a bad man. He's a liar. He's a notorious introvert. He was a dangerous celibate before he met that Mexican woman," he said with righteous conviction. "And my friends, I tell you something else, he even practices nepotism with his sister."

One of the preachers was totally devastated, hearing his favorite deacon being accused of what he misunderstood to be horrific offenses. He could take everything he had heard, but to think that this man, a deacon in his church, was a fornicator, was too much for him. He could excuse a tax cheat, a liar and all those other shameful things the mayor had said. There was redemption for them. They could be forgiven, but not fornication, not in concept of morality and debauchery.

God would never forgive a fornicating deacon, and neither would he. There could be no redemption for such a sinner.

He got up from his seat, walked over to the mayor at the podium and tapped him on the shoulder. The mayor turned, and the preacher whispered something in his ear.

The mayor shook his head in disagreement. Then he said, "Please give the benediction, Reverend. This meeting is over."

But one of the distraught preachers wouldn't hear it. His faith required that he disavow Sam Wreford the fornicator, then and there.

The mayor decided he had better let the distraught preacher speak. Certain that he had already won the crowd and that Wreford, his biggest political adversary, was disgraced, the mayor turned to the audience.

"My good citizens, my friends," he said. "I thank you for coming, and for your understanding. The Reverend has a few remarks to make."

Then he sat down. The crowd roared its approval.

The preacher steadied himself. Holding both sides of the podium, his face stern, he faced the crowd.

"Good Christians, you should know, I don't tolerate my deacons fornicating with Mexican women who are not their wives." He walked over to Wreford and pointed directly at him.

"You're no longer a deacon in my church," the preacher declared. "You git off this stage. You ain't fit to sit here."

Wreford flinched but didn't get up. The preacher moved closer and closer to Wreford, moving his outstretched arm, up and down with his finger pointed in Wreford's face.

"Git! Git! You ought to be horsewhipped."

Wreford swayed so far back in his chair to avoid the jabbing finger that he tumbled over backward, hitting the floor.

The preacher dropped his arm down, stepped back and looked at the fornicator struggling to get to his feet. Standing over him, he moved both hands up and down as if summoning his church members to stand until Wreford moved.

"Git up! Git up!" the preacher shouted.

When Wreford was on his feet, the preacher clenched his fists. It appeared that a fight was about to erupt. The sheriff quickly intervened by standing between the two. The preacher backed off, and the sheriff escorted Wreford from the stage.

"My good Christians," the preacher said, "there goes my worst 'sinner.'"

During this commotion the mayor slipped from the stage and moved through the crowd, shaking hands as he went. The audience dispersed, following the mayor down the street until hardly anybody remained except for a few members of the preacher's church.

Captain Kelly and the other dignitaries got up and left.

Seeing most of the people walking away, the preacher shouted, "Let the slackers go! All the God-fearing people will stay. God's on our side! We'll stop that train!"

FIVE

BUFFALO SOLDIERS ARE

Coming To Brownsville

July 23, 1906, Valentine, Nebraska

DESPITE WARNINGS FROM MILITARY officials in Texas and Senator Culberson of Texas that colored troops should not be sent to Brownsville, despite the well-known, strong anti-Negro sentiment in Brownsville—and despite the bad blood between the Texas Militia and the colored 25th Infantry, the War Department issued its final directive on May 26, 1906. The black soldiers must depart from Nebraska for Brownsville, Texas.

A throng of well-wishers, mostly whites along with a few Indians and blacks, gathered at the train station near Valentine, Nebraska, to say their good-byes to the black soldiers of Companies B, C, and D of the 25th Infantry who had been stationed at Fort Niobrara, Nebraska, for the past four years. (Company A was out in Montana protecting settlers as they seized land from the Indians.) The citizens of Valentine hated to see these men leave, for they had found them to be good neighbors and some had become good friends. Owners of saloons, cafés, and restaurants in Valentine had never refused them service, nor had the townspeople ever made racial distinctions against the soldiers. When the soldiers boarded the train for Brownsville, the townspeople stood on the sidelines waving good-bye and calling out, "We are going to miss you!"

Just as the train was pulling off, an elderly white woman shouted a warning, "The people in Texas are gonna give you hell! Don't go down there!"

Leaning his head out of the window of the train, Private John Amos Holomon shouted back, "If the Texans bring hell, they gonna get hell!"

The men of the 25th Infantry were on their way to Fort Brown without any trepidation. Many of them were seasoned veterans of the Spanish-American War in Cuba, the Philippine Insurrection, and the Indian wars on the Great Plains. They had also seen action in the hills of Montana and Wyoming. Their character, military skills, and acts of heroism were acknowledged in their military records. They were the sons of Northerners and Southerners. They were sharecroppers, farmers, musicians, carpenters, bricklayers, mechanics, cooks, maids, and laborers—and all shared the common bond of honor, duty, and country as black soldiers of the United States Army.

Unlike the black soldiers who had no fears about going to Fort Brown, the five white officers dreaded taking their troops to Texas. Being white, they were in the dubious position of hearing all the ugly racial talk emanating from Brownsville that was being communicated through the white military grapevine from the white soldiers of the 26th Infantry stationed at Fort Brown.

The officers of the 25th Infantry were highly qualified professionals. Two of them were graduates of the United States Military Academy at West Point. The white Battalion commander, Major Penrose, was not a West Point graduate.

(The Senate Military Affairs Committee later made a mistake in stating Penrose was a graduate of the Point. During my research, officials at West Point denied this error.) The other two officers came up through the ranks, and the fifth officer received his commission by direct appointment.

The officers dreaded taking their black troops to Texas. They knew their leadership skills would be tested and their burden heavy. Penrose was ambitious. He had aspired to becoming a general ever since being commissioned an officer 22 years before. He had always been thoroughly committed to his military career. Penrose saw the military as a stepping stone into Michigan politics, a move which he hoped would lead to the governorship.

I reviewed his medical records at Walter Reed Army Hospital. From the standpoint of health and physique, Penrose seemed to be scorned by the gods at birth. He was a slender man, 5 feet, 7 ¼ inches tall, with a puny build and little strength. He weighed about 130 pounds stripped, and never seemed to be able to gain much weight, no matter how much he ate. He had a pallid, dusty complexion and suffered from frequent bouts of sickness. These interludes included recurring attacks of typhoid fever, diarrhea, amoebic dysentery, and marked constipation—all of which frequently caused him to be irritable. Penrose had been wearing glasses for several years. He was a heavy smoker and moderate drinker. Notwithstanding all these infirmities, he fancied himself destined for leadership as a great general.

July 25, 1906, Austin, Texas

As the train moved across several states and farther south, the weather grew hotter and more uncomfortable. But discipline was maintained, and there were no incidents. Major

Penrose and his soldiers had been traveling three days when the train neared Austin, Texas, and something began to bother him. It was something his father had said that kept nagging him, worrying him, paining him like a migraine. It was always there, casting doubt on his future. Now the words came to him. He suddenly remembered vividly that evening last summer when his father returned to Lancaster, Pennsylvania, from a Republican political meeting at the Union League in Philadelphia. Recalling that conversation was unsettling, even chilling. Penrose's father, the old general, said, "Charlie, you've got to change regiments."

The sense of immediacy in his father's tone seemed curious. "What do you mean, change regiments?"

"Why, your career's in jeopardy. It's as simple as that."

"How so? I'm in the finest regiment in the army. We proved that in Cuba."

"Undoubtedly, that's true. But it's a Negro regiment," the old general said.

"I know that, sir." Trying to be as respectful as he could to his father, but showing his impatience, Penrose said, "Dad, cut to the chase."

"It's the uniform, son. There's resentment, and it's growing—resentment against the colored man wearing the U.S. Army uniform."

"That's petty prejudice. That's what it is. What's the uniform got to do with it?"

"The uniform is a symbol, a powerful symbol of honor. It represents acceptance of the black man, deference to him. It dignifies him, praises him, and ascribes nobility to him. It's the acknowledgment by official policy that the black man is equal and entitled to wear the same uniform as the white man."

The younger Penrose stiffened. "You mean the black soldiers have the same rights and privileges under the constitution–the right to fight and die in war? And yet, not the right to reap our respect or gratitude?" He hoped he hadn't sounded sarcastic.

But his father had no interest in debating the rights of Negro soldiers. His only concern was for his son's career and future. "Command of black troops by white officers is considered inferior duty," he said. "It's a drag on your career. Many senators are unlikely to confirm you for promotion above major, if your principal duty has been commanding Negro troops. To get right down to it, Charlie, it's a matter of social equality."

Last summer's conversation now was stuck in his brain, and he knew it would be there for a long time.

With knowledge that the protests had reached all the way to Washington, Penrose was troubled that his battalion was coming to the attention of the officials in Washington in a negative way. Stern-faced and serious, he got out of his seat, stood unsteadily with the rocking of the train, smoothed the front of his uniform, and went to check on his men. He was aware that he and his black troops would be arriving in Brownsville, Texas, under protest of the citizens of the border town his command was supposed to protect. He wondered what form the protests would take when they arrived. *How unfair*, he thought, *that his command was being rejected for doing nothing more than being born black.*

The Texans' prejudice flew in the face of the contributions his men had made and could still make. It shattered his belief that they would be measured by the professional quality of their military performance—and not by their color. It destroyed his sense of fairness, and yet, his father had undoubtedly spoken the truth. So, as the train neared Austin, he felt a new sense of foreboding. An uneasiness settled deep in the pit of his stomach. Fortunately, he had one friend in Brownsville—Fred Combe.

The troop train stopped in Austin and was one hour late departing Austin for Brownsville. Penrose decided it was not wise to allow his men or officers to get off the train to stretch their legs or get a breath of fresh air. Previous threats of violence by the Texas Militia in Austin, and warnings by the military authorities made the idea seem unwise.

July 25, 1906, Brownsville, Texas

In Brownsville, crowds of people stood along Levee Street on the southeast side of town all the way east to where it intersected Garrison Road. Masses of people lined Garrison Road up to Elizabeth Street which led to the main gate to Fort Brown. To maintain crowd control, split-rail fence barriers were set up along the route the soldiers would take to Fort Brown.

Mayor Combe and his police force waited at the depot for the train to arrive. The mayor was tense, anxious and still worried about threats to stop the train. Standing near the train station in the background on the west side of 12th Street near Levee Street, behind a split-rail fence barrier, Fred Combe watched everything. He looked for any sign of a posse—Wreford and the preacher might still show up to carry out their threats. Although he didn't see them or any signs of a posse, he was still apprehensive. Searching for shade from the hot July sun, he moved to a cooler spot near an orange tree in back of the split-rail barrier in a vacant lot. Things were quiet thus far and he relaxed.

His mind drifted back to the days he spent in Cuba during the war with his friend, Charlie, Major Charles W. Penrose. He remembered their friendship as more than soldierly camaraderie. Professional, yes, but it was more than that. It was respectful and warm, a genuine friendship when they first met in 1898, a long time ago. Now he wondered what his old friend would look like, how much he had changed and if he would still be the same old Charlie. It will be a good reunion. He was sure that the two of them could work out any difficulties that might arise between his citizens and the soldiers.

Figure 3. Elizabeth Street looking toward Fort Brown
U.S. Archives, AG File 1135832

Combe had heard that First Sergeant Mingo Sanders, a black noncommissioned officer who also fought in Cuba in '98, was still in the 25th Infantry Regiment. Combe recalled Sanders' reputation as a combat soldier—in battle, he was heroic under fire, and as a professional soldier, a strict disciplinarian who brooked no foolishness from his men. He was fair, reasonable, and one of the best soldiers in the Army, black or white. Although Sanders had to be getting old and near retirement, Combe knew he and Major Penrose could count on Sanders to keep any trouble-making soldiers in line.

Mayor Combe had thought about planning a public welcome, a warm greeting for the troops, but changed his mind for political reasons. Now he began to think that an outward show of friendship, even for his old friend, might be misunderstood. But how could he stand in the background and watch his friends get off the train and say nothing?

Two years ago, when the white soldiers from the 26th Infantry Regiment arrived, greeting the troops hadn't been a problem. Combe was right up front shaking hands, smiling, welcoming them to Brownsville along with other citizens. Now he was uncertain. Should he go up and greet them or not? He decided he would go to the post later and welcome them in private. The decision pained him, and he was a little ashamed for having to do that. It reminded him of his childhood, when he had to play in the backyard with his colored playmates or in the kitchen. He was always required to hide his friendship. These rules were forced on him by his parents. He now forced the same rules on himself.

The 25th Infantry Arrives

When Combe felt the ground shaking under his feet, he knew it was the heavy vibrations of the train radiating down the railroad tracks. He heard the train's whistle signaling everyone to stand back, get out of the way and let the train rumble in. The rust-colored iron engine pulling the troop train rolled into Brownsville, puffing clouds of black smoke high into the air. Blowing off billows of steam, it came to a jerky stop. The black troops had arrived.

When the doors rolled back, the conductors swung off the train to the ground and placed steps beneath the doors. The first soldier to get off the train was Sergeant Mingo Sanders who was in charge of the security detail.

Sergeant Sanders was a tall, wiry black man, with chiseled features, high cheek bones, long arms and large hands. He had the look of an ancient African warrior king. His posture was stern and formal—regal and yet a king from the people and still of the people, and fiercely dedicated to protecting them when needed. His eyes were black, deeply set, and somehow remained friendly even when he was angry. He had entered the Army in 1891 and fought in Cuba and the Philippines, a brave soldier and an honorable man. He loved the United States Army. Having spent 26 years in devoted service, he was just two years from retirement.

After disembarking from the train, Sanders looked around, scanning the streets and observing the crowd of people near the train station. He took notice of the policemen standing at the intersections of Levee Street and 11th and 12th Streets—and imagined how to best use the wooden split-rail fence barriers for security. He looked for any sign of people carrying guns, stepped back aboard the train, and said, "Security guards, disembark! Take up your pre-planned positions."

At Sanders' command, twelve armed soldiers jumped off the train, took up positions on both sides of Levee Street, facing outward, and stood at parade rest.

As Combe observed all of these precise military moves, he was reassured. The leadership of the old 25th Infantry was still in charge. *Nothing untoward was going to happen in his town between these soldiers and his citizens,* he thought.

Penrose saw no smiles. He heard no clapping, no bands playing. He saw just hostile, suspicious faces glaring at his soldiers as they marched along the streets of Brownsville, through the large black iron gate guarding the main entrance to Fort Brown.

What a cold reception. It's not going to be easy for us here, he thought.

Figure 4. Main Gate, Fort Brown, Texas, Circa 1906
Courtesy Professor René Torres, University of Texas at Brownsville

The wives and children of the officers and the noncommissioned officers were the last to get off the train. They followed the troops, carrying suitcases, hat boxes and an assortment of belongings. Some of the children had their pets with them—dogs, cats and even some birds in cages. They were being assisted by their personal military orderlies and their military cooks. Under the regimental organization, the unit regiment was a closely-knit collections of soldiers, wives, children, and sometimes other close relatives, all of whom lived together as a big family. While the lower-rank soldiers lived in barracks, the married noncommissioned officers and their families lived in separate quarters. The commissioned officers and their families also lived in separate quarters. It was a military tradition to allow the families of the married men to accompany them except in extremely dangerous outposts.

A lone soldier with a big black dog, Company B's mascot, followed the troops through the gate.

Each company unloaded personal belongings, supplies, boxes of ammunition, boxes of spent cartridges, empty shell casings which had been fired, and ammo clips used on the rifle range at Fort Niobrara, Nebraska. Then teamsters came, loaded everything on horse-drawn wagons and hauled it off to Fort Brown for storage. When space ran out, the overflow of boxes filled with empty cartridges shells and clips were placed on the back porches of the companies.

As the men began to unpack, a delegation from the black community, about four families, came to welcome them. But they also wanted to warn them that the white people weren't happy with their arrival and had made it clear that they did not want "these damn niggers trading down here," or even coming downtown.

That warning turned out to be prophetic.

Six

THE TROOPS GO

―――❧―――

To Town

A Breeding Ground for Mosquitoes

THE NEXT DAY BEGAN with heavy rain—and it continued until late that afternoon. The falling rain did nothing to cool off the sweltering town. In fact, it made things worse. Sheets of water fell onto the sidewalks and rose back up into the air as steam, raising the humidity to insufferable levels. The old soldiers hadn't experienced such hot, humid, miserable weather since their sweaty days in the Philippines. The young ones had probably never seen such weather.

Brownsville, with its low-lying topography, lagoons, ditches and semi-tropical climate, was a fertile breeding ground for mosquitoes. They attacked at any time of the day—morning, noon, or night. Typhoid fever was rampant.

That afternoon, Private William E. Jones was in the kitchen, preparing dinner for Captain Lyon and his wife. It would be their second meal at their new post. Willie, as Mrs. Lyon called him, was busy trussing a chicken. As he pinned its wings back and tied the legs together to hold in the savory stuffing, he stopped frequently to scratch his arm which was peppered with red welts from mosquito bites. After wiping his hands on his apron, he began to scratch, but scratching brought only temporary relief. He picked up a box of bicarbonate of soda, made a white soda paste, and smeared it all over his arm, trying to get some relief. Mrs. Lyon gave him an occasional stare as she observed him plastering his arm with white paste.

Finally she said, "Willie, that looks awful. Why don't you go to the drug store in town and get some salve after dinner?"

"It'll be all right, Miss Lyon. My mother used to put soda powder on her arms all the time to stop the itching."

"You should go get the salve, anyway," she said. "Besides, I need some."

After dinner, Mrs. Lyon handed Private Jones some money and cautioned him, "Don't linger. Be careful. Don't forget, you're in Texas."

Private Jones walked out the iron gate, crossed Garrison Road and hurried down Elizabeth Street looking for a drug store. This was the first time he'd been to town. As he walked and searched for a drug store, he studied the store signs on both sides of the street. In the middle of the block he saw a short white man with a heavy mustache standing outside on the sidewalk, just a few feet ahead of him. He was well dressed in a dark suit, white starched shirt, black vest, and a white bow tie.

As Private Jones neared the store, he called out, "Evening sir." The man said nothing, but his face turned hostile. He walked toward the doorway and blocked the entrance. Jones looked up at the sign which read, "Dotgrain Drug Store." Then he looked at the man—and realized he was not wanted there. He knew that black soldiers weren't welcome in the beer joints, but this was a drug store.

The man folded his arms across his chest. His eyes squinted with loathing. His mouth twisted and he cursed in a low tone, just above a whisper, "Damn you, we don't sell beer here."

"I don't want no beer," the private answered. "I want some of that salve I hear you got to stop this mosquito itching." Jones stretched out one arm, still white-washed with soda paste.

Barely parting his lips, which were hidden beneath his thick black mustache, the druggist shifted to his right side. "I don't want your business. Leave!"

"Mister, I got money, I can pay." Jones held out a quarter.

"Boy, are you some kinda idiot? Don't you get it? I'm not selling you a damn thing."

Jones put his money back into his pocket and turned away, crestfallen and puzzled. "It seems kinda funny I can't buy salve in a drugstore," he mumbled to himself.

Resigned to a night of discomfort, Private Jones was headed back down Elizabeth Street to the fort, when he saw Private August Williams and Private McGuire coming toward him. Seeing them gave him some comfort. They were approaching a white man who was walking just ahead of him. Private Jones walked faster. He wanted to tell McGuire and Williams how he had been treated at the drug store, because he thought they might be looking for something to stop the itching too.

McGuire, who was ahead of Williams, passed the white man on the narrow sidewalk, and their shoulders lightly brushed.

The man got angry, stopped and whirled around, pointing at McGuire. "Why, you black son-of-a bitch, don't you know this is a white man's town?"

McGuire, who liked to avoid trouble, quickly moved on. Williams moved on, too.

Figure 5. Artist's rendition: Nelson Potter
Private August Williams and Private McGuire are insulted as a white
man tries to pass between them. As McGuire moves to the left, nearer to
Williams, the man yells, "You black son of a bitch. Don't you know this
is a white man's town?"
SOURCE: Private Collection William Baker

Jones, who had seen and heard the whole thing, ran up
to meet them. "What's wrong with these people? The man
at the drug store wouldn't let me in the store. He wouldn't
sell me salve. We ain't done nothing to them. What with the
mosquitoes and all, I'm about tired of this place already."

McGuire looked back over his shoulder. "Our shoulders
barely touched. Hell, it don't look like they want us to even
walk on the sidewalk here."

When Jones went back to Captain Lyon's quarters and
told Mrs. Lyon what had happened, she shook her head, but
said nothing. A confused feeling of guilt mixed with denial
came over her, one that she had never experienced before.

She was a white woman and the daughter of a general officer, accustomed to privilege, and had been with the 25th Infantry for many years. She knew first-hand that the men were good, disciplined soldiers and wouldn't cause Brownsville trouble. Why wouldn't the druggist sell Willie some salve? She had a strange feeling that she had been denied the salve, not Willie.

She sat at the dining room table and looked down. "It's not right, not right, not right for a drug store." When she looked up, she saw Jones' outstretched hand giving her the money back. She put the coins in her dress pocket. "I'll go tomorrow, myself, and get the salve."

Not knowing what had happened to Jones, Williams, and McGuire, John Holomon led a group of soldiers into town that evening to quench their thirst for beer. Among them were Dorsie Willis and James Newton. Holomon wished he could have also brought along an old buddy, an ex-soldier named Bugs. The way the soldiers talked about him, it is easy for me to imagine what he looked like. The soldiers called him Bugs, which actually was his real last name, but they called him Bugs for another reason. His eyes were big and wide apart like those of an insect. He was a giant of a man, and his neck was short and stubby like a tree trunk cut too close to the ground. His head appeared to be bolted directly to his shoulders. His shoulders were broad with long arms that fell almost to his knees when he was standing. He had big hands, like baseball gloves. In fact, he had once been a baseball pitcher who throw the ball at dangerous speeds.

Legend had it that Bugs joined the Army because he liked fighting. It was said that he would rush into hell looking for the devil, find him, fight him, split his head open, piss on his brain and roast him for supper. There was a rumor that back in 1904 Bugs led a secret society of thugs, desperadoes and shakedown men in B Company. He demanded money from soldiers for guarantees of immunity from discipline. They said that he was a bad man, feared nothing and no man. But Bugs wasn't with them. He wasn't in the army any more.

They walked up Elizabeth Street and stopped in the first saloon they came to—the Ruby Saloon, owned by John Tillman. They walked in, stepped up to the bar and ordered beer. Frank Natus, the bartender looked over at Tillman, who shook his head.

Tillman leaned back against the whiskey racks. "Sorry, boys, I can't serve you here in the front. I'll set up something in back of the saloon. You boys go around in the back through the alley. I'll have Frank put some beer back there for you."

Turning to the bartender, Tillman said, "Get some crate boxes and set them up in the back. That'll do for now. We'll fix it up better tomorrow."

The men left. They refused to go to the back of the saloon. They crossed Elizabeth Street to Crixell's Saloon. Joe Crixell was standing in the door as if he had been waiting for them.

"Boys, we have the officers' trade," he said. "Some of 'em are in the back drinking. We like it that way. My guess is you boys would rather drink by yourselves and not mix with the officers."

Private Holomon caught his drift. "Never mind, fellows," he said. "There's another joint across the street. Let's go there."

They had started out the door when Lieutenant Lawrason stepped out from behind the curtains of a back room, holding a bottle of beer.

"Aw shucks, Joe," he called to the owner, "Get 'em the beer. We just got in town and all of us are thirsty. They got money. These are my men. I don't mind."

"Yeah, lieutenant, but some folks in this town do mind," Crixell replied. "I can't serve 'em. They'll kill my business."

Private Newton leaned his head in the doorway. "That's all right, lieutenant," he said. "We'll leave."

The five men went next door to H.H. Wellers' Saloon, the rowdiest, toughest tavern in town. Half drunk, H.H. stood at the bar. The place was filled with locals. It was standing room only.

"Well, well, well. Look what we got here, folks!" H.H. announced in a slurry voice. "A bunch of nigger soldiers looking for Mexican whores. I tell you, boys, we don't serve no Mexicans, no whores here. And I damn sho' ain't serving no niggers. Just keep walking 'till you think you can't walk no more—that's the tenderloin section. You'll find the Mexican bars and all the whores you want out there."

Then H.H. staggered over toward them.

Private Holomon stepped forward. "Stand back, fellows, he's mine," he commanded. "Y'awl just go on down to that Mexican bar and git your beer like this here man says. As soon as I take care of this here business, I'll catch up with you."

Boyd Conyers, James Newton and Dorsie Willis were reluctant to leave.

"To hell with that," Conyers said "We'll wait for you."

Conyers walked over and gathered the men in his arms, shuffling them outside. They grudgingly accepted and left.

Several toughs wearing faded black 10-gallon hats got up from their table and stood behind H. H. to back him up. The bartender reached under the counter for a pistol and slid it down the bar to a man waiting at the other end. Holomon saw the gun. Instinctively, he grabbed a beer bottle off one of the tables and threw it, striking the pistol a split second before it reached the man's outstretched hand. The firearm fell behind the bar while the bottle shattered, sending glass flying everywhere.

"I'll be damned!" H.H. stood in awe. However, he was not impressed by the crashing beer bottle. Smashing bottles was a common occurrence in Weller's Saloon. What got Weller's attention was Holomon's glaring eyes inviting a fight, his quickness and most of all, the power of his arm.

H.H. muttered to himself, "Where the hell did he learn to throw like that?"

Holomon gave the room a menacing look.

"We may not git beer here, but we sho' gonna git respect," he declared. "We are men of the United States Army, soldiers, and don't you forget it." His voice trailed off in an easy whisper. He opened the door and calmly walked out.

Holomon and the soldiers walked slowly up the street. Holomon slapped young Willis on the back and with a loud belly laugh roared, "We scared the hell out of 'em, I can tell you that. You should have seen us fight those Texans back at Fort Riley. Ever heard about it, Dorsie? Bugs was with us, then. All I know about Bugs was what they say, he was a big, bad, mean man."

The soldiers kept walking up Elizabeth Street toward the tenderloin district. Holomon glanced at the other soldiers, but said nothing to them. He hoped to God that they hadn't done too much damage. They hadn't come to town to cause trouble. They had come for beer and they weren't giving up. It was damn hot, and they were determined to find a bar that would take their money and serve them.

As they continued walking, Willis saw a sign that read White Elephant Saloon. "Look, there's another saloon. Let's go in there." The proprietor of the White Elephant saloon was V. L. Crixell, Joe Crixell's brother, who ran a combination beer joint and pawn shop. It was also a place where white men could meet women. Euphemistically, he advertised that part of his business as "Polite Attention."

Behind the bar next to the whiskey bottles was a big notice, WE BUY AND SELL GUNS. Accordingly, along the walls were racks with a variety of guns and rifles—Winchesters, Krag-jorgensons, Maulins, Springfied 03, Shot Guns, pistols—you name the gun, and it was there.

"I don't know, it looks more like a pawn shop to me," Conyers said.

With an overly friendly gesture, Crixell waved them in. "Come on in, boys. You got them new Springfield rifles, I hear. I know you come to sell me some guns."

"No, sir. We're thirsty. You sell beer here too, don't you?" Holomon asked.

"Yeah, but...

"But what?"

Crixell's friendly disposition changed abruptly. He looked Holomon up and down with a quizzical, scornful air and motioned to the bartender. "Looks like we got John Henry here. He's a big black steel-driving man. Wants a beer. He just scares me to death," he said. "Bartender! Get the big man a beer!"

The bartender handed Holomon a glass of beer. Holomon looked in the glass, inspected it carefully and then swallowed it down in one gulp.

Crixell looked up at Holomon in amazement and said, "Give me the glass. You need a refill, BOY."

"No, I don't," said Holomon.

He paid 15 cents for the drink and headed for the door, but Crixell demanded more money.

"For what?" Holomon asked.

Crixell snatched the glass from Holomon's hand and threw it to the floor, smashing it to pieces. "For the glass, you idiot! White people don't drink after colored!"

Holomon was ready to fight again. "You called me 'boy!' You call me 'idiot!' I'll rip your heart out, you cracker!"

He advanced while Crixell retreated, backing up against the gun racks. The other soldiers jumped between the two men, but it took all of their strength to restrain Holomon.

That bout of excitement increased their thirst for anything cold—beer or water, anything. It didn't make much difference at that point.

"Let's push on," Holomon said. "Couldn't be much farther. I haven't felt this kind of heat and humidity since I left Luzon Island."

After walking many blocks, thirsty and drained by the heat and humidity, they heard Spanish music drifting across the railroad tracks. Relief was in sight. They had finally reached the tenderloin district which was lined with mostly Mexican bars. It was like stepping into an oasis. Their search for something wet and cold was over.

Hot and sweaty, the men piled into the first saloon that they saw. A Mexican bartender welcomed them, offering a shot of something stronger than beer. But they ordered beer and drank up. After several glasses had been emptied, the soldiers paid up and walked back to Fort Brown. All went but John Holomon. He stopped at the Ruby Saloon to speak to the owner.

A Talent for Making Money

Private John Amos Holomon, a tall lanky, athletic man with curly brown hair and a heavy mustache, had a talent for making money. He was the hard-nosed, no nonsense money lender in the outfit. He was also the company's fastest runner, the lightning-fast outfielder and captain of the baseball team. He'd been a sergeant but had been "busted," as soldiers would say. He had been demoted back in March 1905 to the grade of private for fighting with another soldier named Arvin over money—a debt of a dollar and a half.

Holomon's story was that Private Arvin owed him the money but refused to pay. When Arvin wouldn't pay, Holomon attempted to collect it and Arvin ran off. Holomon ran him down, threw him to the ground and punched him several times. Then he took a five dollar bill out of Arvin's pocket and gave back the change from what Arvin owed him.

Holomon operated an intricate financial business at every post he had been stationed. Fort Brown would be no different. Coming up with a unique scheme to make money from the soldiers and local merchants was his specialty. No one in the battalion came close to his financial prowess. An enterprising soldier, Holomon had set up a "pay for ride into town and back" stage line to carry his fellow soldiers from Fort Niobrara, Nebraska, to the small town of Valentine. There the men paid for wine, whiskey, beer, and women on credit, charging almost anything to Holomon's account for a fee.

Holomon's account was a line of credit he had set up with the local Valentine merchants. All a soldier had to do was sign a hand-written note and present it to receive whatever he wanted on credit until payday. Holomon also lent the soldiers hard cash, charging 25 percent interest for any fractional part of the month until payday. He also ran gambling games and took a cut of the winnings.

Holomon saw a ripe opportunity before him in the saloon business. *With the four white bars in town refusing service to the black soldiers, there was quick easy money to be made,* he thought. He knew that the soldiers would be too tired after their grueling duty to make the long trip to the Mexican bars. Significantly, he also knew the men had too much pride to buy beer from Tillman's newly-opened bar in the back of the Ruby Saloon. Now, if he had his own bar, Holomon's Saloon, the bar problem could be solved—and he'd make a killing. All he needed was a local white saloon to supply him with beer, soda pop, cigars, and tobacco. This proposal was what he had in mind when he dropped in to speak with John Tillman, owner of the Ruby Saloon.

He told the bartender that he wanted to speak to Mr. Tillman.

The bartender stopped wiping off the bar and looked up suspiciously at Holomon. "Did I hear you say you wanted to speak to Mr. Tillman?"

"You got that right."

"You don't have to see Tillman, I can take ...."

"Yes, I do," Holomon interrupted.

Natus pointed to the back room. "I got the place set up in the back. Just go around back, and ..."

Holomon interrupted him again. "I'm not here to drink beer. I want to see Mister Tillman, the owner."

"What do you want to see me about?" Tillman suddenly appeared from the back room.

Holomon put his hands in his front pockets and rocked backwards. "I'm John Holomon. Can I talk to you in the back room? It's kinda private."

Tillman studied Holomon's face for a second. "Come around to the back door."

Holomon walked outside and entered the back door of the Ruby Saloon. Crate tables and chairs where placed haphazardly around the dingy, windowless storage room. Unopened crates of beer and liquor were stacked along one wall, held securely with ropes. There, Holomon laid out his plan to Tillman.

"I've figured over half of the soldiers won't buy beer back here from you, Mister Tillman. Both Weller and the Crixell brothers have refused them, and the Mexican saloons are too far away."

Tillman looked at Holomon quizzically, surprised he had remembered his name. He was unaccustomed to this kind of conversation from a black man.

Holomon continued. "Both of us can make money. You help me get a license, supply me with beer, soda pop, cigars, and tobacco at five percent over your wholesale price and we got ourselves a new business." Holomon gestured with both hands toward the boxes and crates. "Looks like you got a plenty of everything I need."

Tillman listened intently, his face relaxing some. "Go on."

"I see you have a little dry goods business going on, too, in your other store. I want to set up a line of credit with you. Some of the boys run out of money before payday. I want you to give them credit, charge it to my account. You don't have to worry about being paid by them. I'll pay you, and we'll settle up at the end of the month."

Tillman reared back, a smirk forming around his mouth. "Where'd a colored boy like you get an idea like that?"

Holomon said nothing, but studied Tillman's tightening eyelids.

Tillman began taking him more seriously. "And how are you going to get your money? What's your take?"

Holomon leaned back on a crate, looked Tillman directly in the eyes and shoved his right hand in his pants' pocket. He rattled the five gold coins he always carried, drawing strength from their sound and feeling their power. Still rattling them, he exaggerated his answer.

"You don't worry about me, I'll get my money." He gathered the coins, still in his pocket and jangled them once again.

Tillman looked at Holomon with both interest and skepticism. Uncomfortable and intimidated by the boldness of his proposal, Tillman thought, this is a smart nigger, talking about percents and things. It was a full minute before he spoke.

"You got some nerve, trying to horn in on my saloon business," he said. "I can't believe your nerve. Colored boys have had their asses kicked for less. Nigger, what did you say your name was? Yeah, I remember, you said, 'Holomon.' Why, you must be a half-Jew. Holomon, that's a Jew name, ain't it? Yeah. You look like a Shylock."

Holomon bristled at Tillman's insults. 'Half-Jew' was a fighting word. *I'm going to bust 'im upside his head*, he thought. Holomon saw a wooden water bucket on the floor. Reaching down, he gripped its handle. He gripped it so tightly that his hand shook and water sloshed and spilled out over the over the top. Then he thought better of it. This was not something he should do, but something he wanted to do. He wanted to hit this man, but he needed to avoid trouble in this new town and focus on starting his business. He suddenly recalled an incident with an old man and a banjo that he regretted. *It's not worth a riot*, he thought. And he left.

A Deal Is Made

It was a blessing that he kept his temper. He always felt bad after a fight, even when he won. Holomon's anger took him back to 1904, when his outfit was on maneuvers with the Texas National Guard at Fort Riley, Kansas. The Texans brought their own entertainment for the floor show at the Junction City Saloon—a "colored man" with a banjo. He remembered that night all too well. When the "colored man" began singing offensive coon songs, Holomon went after him with a vengeance. He took the old man's banjo and smashed it over his head. That's when the fight with the Texans began. Three burly Texan militiamen beat up Holomon until Bugs joined the fight. Then it was all over. Bugs picked up two of the Texans and hurled them through the air like toys. They crashed against the whiskey bottles and glasses lining the shelf behind the bar and rolled like logs to the floor.

What felt momentarily like triumph later dissolved into a sense of shame for himself and pity for the old man. Holomon regretted having hit him and destroying his banjo, his only means of livelihood. He knew the old man was singing those old songs only for money.

Although quick to anger and to fight, Holomon was nonetheless a patient man. He was not easily discouraged. He was determined when seeking something he wanted—especially a business deal. After his failure at the Ruby Saloon, he walked across the street to Joe Crixell's place. The same man who was standing in the doorway earlier was still standing there. Holomon asked him if he could speak to the owner.

"That's me."

"You're Joe Crixell?"

"Last I heard, I was Joe Crixell. What do you want now? Told you earlier we had the officers' trade."

Holomon stood near the doorway. "Might you step outside for a minute?"

Joe Crixell looked at him suspiciously. "I told you we serve the officers."

"Now, I don't wanna talk to you about drinking beer in this here saloon. I want to buy it by the crate and take it to my place."

Joe Crixell stepped out side. He was immediately intrigued by Holomon's proposal to buy whole crates of beer, thinking maybe he could make up some of the business he'd lost when the white soldiers left. "Come on in the back," he said. "Let's talk about it."

Holomon was heartened by Crixell's interest and laid out the same deal he'd just offered to Tillman.

Crixell could see a way of making himself some good money and competing with the new back room bar at the Ruby Saloon. He was impressed with Holomon's plan. *Yeah, I can make up some of my losses,* he thought. *If I don't do it, the Ruby saloon will take all the soldier business through the back door.*

Crixell made up his mind right on the spot. "I'll do it. You pay me a nickel on the bottle above my cost for beer, two cents on the bottle above my cost for soda pop and two cents above my cost per cigar. I'll work out something later on the cost of cigarette tobacco."

Holomon reflected and made some quick calculations in his head. "No." he said, "I'm buying by the crate. Give me crate prices for the beer and soda pop, big box prices for the cigars and tobacco."

Suspecting Holomon wanted to dicker with him, Crixell hesitated. He was not in the mood to negotiate—he was still tempted by the high probability of this new source of income. "Boy, are you trying to Jew me down?"

Holomon disliked that familiar insult. Growing up in Macon, Georgia, he'd heard it all his life. Southern white gentiles used that expression all the time to denigrate Jewish merchants. It was a term he was sensitive to, but he also knew he had to keep his wits about him and ignore it, lest he scuttle this deal. So he ignored Crixell's question. "You know I can't make any money at the prices you want me to pay," he said. "If I can't make any money on this proposition, you can't make money on it either. If I make money, so much the better for me, and so much the better for you. If I don't make any money, so much the worse for me, and so much the worse for you."

Crixell was impressed by Holomon's reasoning and decided to show him some respect. "Very well, you can have it by the crate and boxes. I'll work out the prices, so that you'll make a profit. By the way, where do you plan to set this up?"

Holomon did not answer the question and stretched out his hand and Crixell shook on it. A gentleman's agreement. "I'll find a place and let you know." He shoved his right hand deep into his pocket, started rattling the five gold coins and walked out the door.

"Get Off the Sidewalk!"

Sunday evening, August 5th, was hot and humid. Fred Tate, a U.S. federal customs inspector, and his wife were standing on the sidewalk on Elizabeth Street, talking to a party of six white women. They were all hoping to catch an evening breeze from the Gulf of Mexico. Two black soldiers, Private James W. Newton and Private Frank J. Lipscomb, were walking down the sidewalk, approaching the group. Newton, walking slightly ahead of Lipscomb, passed between Fred Tate and the women.

"Hey, Boy, don't you know how to get off the sidewalk when you see white people?" Tate called out to him.

Figure 6. Artist Rendition: Nelson Potter
Private James W. Newton is pistol-whipped as he and Private Frank
K. Lipscomb walk down Elizabeth Street on Sunday night, August 5,
when passing Custom's Inspector Frank Tate and other white women in
the community.
SOURCE: Private Collection of William Baker

When Newton said nothing, Tate took it as an insult. He pulled his pistol from his jacket, rushed up behind Newton and struck him on the head with the butt of the gun, knocking him to the ground. Then he began pistol-whipping him about the head and shoulders. Newton curled up into the fetal position, holding his head trying to protect himself.

Private Lipscomb ran up to intervene. When he saw blood streaming down the side of his friend's face, he pleaded, "Don't hit 'im any more, mister. You gonna kill 'im."

Rising slowly to his feet, Tate pointed the gun up at Lipscomb's face. "Get back, boy," he warned, "before I blow your head off."

Lipscomb looked down the barrel of Tate's .45 caliber Colt pistol. He stepped back.

Tate turned back to Newton who was lying on the sidewalk, still holding the side of his head. Tate held the pistol over Newton. "Get up, you black bastard. Get away from here. Go! I've got a good mind to blow your brains out."

Dazed, Newton said nothing. He struggled to his feet, holding his hand over his right eye. Not understanding why he had been beaten up, he staggered on down the sidewalk. Seeing Newton still on the sidewalk, Tate ran up behind him and shoved him into the street. "That'll teach you to get off the sidewalk, when you see white ladies standing there." Where Newton grew up, he had not experienced this type of bullying.

On Monday morning, Private Newton stood in formation, waiting for the routine morning inspection with a grossly swollen face and a bruised, half-closed black eye.

Sergeant McCurdy stopped in front of him and, looking closely at him, said, "What in the hell happened to you, Newton? Been drinking and fighting again, Huh?"

Newton was known to be a heavy drinker and frequently got into the losing end of a fight. But before he could answer, McCurdy brushed him off.

"Go over to the hospital and get that face fixed up," the sergeant said, and moved on down the line to the next soldier.

Just two days later on the Wednesday after the pistol whipping, Private Clifford J. Adair returned from Matamoros, Mexico, after spending a day shopping and sight-seeing. He was stopped by a federal custom official on the U.S. side of the border as he was getting off the ferry on the Brownsville side.

"What are you bringing back from Mexico, boy?" the custom officer asked.

"I have a pen I paid fifty cents for," Adair said.

"Let me see it," the customs officer said. Adair took a little blue pen from his pocket and started to hand it to the customs officer. But before he could, the officer snatched the pen out of his hand and glared at it. His face was contorted with displeasure.

Adair, sensing that something was wrong, said, "I'll pay the duty on it. I got money. It's for my mother back in New York."

"You're not in New York," the custom agent said. "You're in Texas. I don't care how much money you've got, and I don't give a good goddamn about your mama."

With that he flung the pen into the Rio Grande River. "Swim for it. You damned niggers are too smart around here, anyway." Then the agent turned and walked away.

Adair told his commanding officer, Captain Macklin, what had happened when he got back to the fort, but Macklin brushed him off, telling him to be a good soldier and not make waves.

The abuse the soldiers were taking in Brownsville didn't sit well with Holomon. It made him more determined than ever to find a place he could turn into a saloon. He wanted to give the soldiers a space they could call their own, drink freely, tell war stories, and raise hell among themselves as soldiers were accustomed to doing.

Holomon was an enterprising man, and after days of intense searching, he found a place at Sixteenth and Monroe Streets in Brownsville at the edge of the northwest corner of Fort Brown. He rented an old wooden clapboard house that looked like a small barn. There, he set up his saloon.

Some folks called it ugly, but it had character. Looking as if it had been resurrected from an architectural cemetery of dead and broken buildings of bygone years, it stood like a primitive, splendid, friendly ghost of the past. Its adobe foundation rested on 4x4 wooden pilings which held up the long, cracker box of a building. A steep, sloping wood-shingled roof slanted within a few feet of the ground on one side—a roof simply adorned by a few small brackets. It had rough-hewn, clap-board vertical siding with wood-shuttered windows and doors affixed with metal box locks. Three plain wooden steps led up to each of the three entrances. All its simple, unadorned features combined to give it an innocent, unpretentious, and defiant eloquence in sharp contrast to the garish saloons on Elizabeth Street.

Holomon named his bar "Allison's Saloon" after Private Ernest Allison. Allison was a recently discharged soldier who decided to stay in Brownsville. Holomon hired him to operate the saloon.

Holomon and Allison worked feverishly to get the old building ready for business. They scrubbed it down with homemade liquid potash soap made from Red Devil lye and hog lard. If the saloon were a success, Holomon would have the money to send for his son, Robert, who lived in

Macon, Georgia, with his mother who was barely able to support herself.

"How old is he?" Allison asked.

"He's nine—fine boy," Holomon said, smiling.

Holomon's wife declared a long time ago that she was through following him from post to post while he chased Indians. Holomon had given up trying to persuade her. But if he had enough money to offer her, he thought he could talk her into letting the boy go with him. And once she did, he swore he would never give up his son again. He had already made plans to bring Steller Harris, his housekeeper in Valentine, Nebraska, to Brownsville to care for the boy.

"Think your wife will let the boy go?" Allison asked.

"I'm sure she will when I offer her money," Holomon responded, "She'll take the money, I know that."

The two finished scrubbing down the building. Next, they set up the bar and counter in the front room which served as the main part of the saloon. They set up tables for drinking and gambling in a back room—and converted a small room into a storeroom to keep its stock of beer, soda pop, cigars, and tobacco. Holomon planned to add whiskey later when he got a chance to go up to San Antonio to fetch it.

Opening Day

Friday, August 11, 1906, was John Holomon's big day—the day he was to open his saloon. He went behind the bar and checked the icebox to make sure the beer was cold. Then he pulled out his record book to see who owed him money. Tonight, like never before, the soldiers would drink at Holomon's bar. They could get what they wanted from Holomon—loans for gambling, money or credit to buy beer, soft drinks, and anything else they might need. They had received credit from Holomon at other forts and towns, but always to spend at somebody else's saloon.

The difference tonight was that the men would buy directly from him. A swell of pride ran through Holomon as he looked at his watch. It was time for him to head back to the fort to stand inspection and prepare for the "Retreat" ceremony. "Retreat" was an army custom in which the soldiers honored the U.S. flag as it was lowered down the flagpole at five o'clock to officially end the day.

Anticipation, expectation, and excitement filled the air. The word had gone out that the saloon would open that day after evening "Retreat." Men polished their boots to a high spit shine and wore their best and cleanest uniforms for the ceremony. They were filled with anxiety, since no soldier wanted to be kept on post for failing inspection at "Retreat." That evening they lined up and stood at rest on the parade field, facing the flag with B, C and D companies standing in that order. The flag was flying in red, white and blue ripples with furls softly undulating in the light breezes coming from the Gulf of Mexico.

Finally, it was almost time to sound "Retreat." The bugler, Private Hoyt Robinson, strutted out onto the field like a proud peacock, took his position and waited for the command.

The officers took their positions. Major Penrose gave the order, "Sound 'Retreat!'"

A moment later the haunting music of "Retreat," signaling the end of day and inviting refuge, flowed over Fort Brown. The music enveloped the newly arrived companies, evoking powerful emotions—a deep sense of patriotism, duty, honor, and country. Sergeant Mingo Sanders and his men of the 25th Infantry especially felt it. It stirred feelings of honor and pride in wearing the uniform of the United States Army.

On the last note of "Retreat," the evening cannon fired. The gun barrel lurched forward, then recoiled. The blast created the sound of war without war, shook the ground and filled the air with the smell of gunpowder. It sent black smoke floating upward into the air. Over and away from Fort Brown it moved, drifting with the breeze until finally disappearing into the sky.

Major Penrose brought his battalion to attention and saluted the flag. The soldiers snapped to attention in unison—so precisely that 167 pairs of boot heels clicked as one. When Private Robinson blew the first note of the National Anthem, the soldiers all saluted. The color guard started slowly lowering the flag.

Sanders, who was nearing retirement, stood ramrod straight. He felt a rush of emotion. His throat swelled, his lips quivered—and he choked up. He tried to fight back tears. Feeling an urgent need to cover his face with his hands, he struggled not to lower his salute. He looked straight ahead, motionless, except for the tears flowing down his face. He realized that there wouldn't be many more "Retreats" for him. The sun was lowering in the evening sky, not yet setting, but going down, and he knew it was going down for him, too, and would soon be gone, as he would be in just two years. He regretted that he would soon have to retire from his beloved army, the army he idolized. He wished he could stay forever.

The music was coming to an end. The flag reached the bottom of the pole, flowing into the outstretched hands of two soldiers who completed the ritual. Robinson lowered the bugle and tucked it under his arm. With the flag folded into a neat triangle, "Retreat" was over. The troops were dismissed.

Allison's Saloon opened after "Retreat." All were free to go into town—and town that evening meant going to Allison's. Soldiers poured into the saloon, filling the place to capacity in a few minutes. Private Newton, who had been pistol-whipped by Tate just a few days earlier, was one of the first soldiers through the door. When he saw an empty spot at the bar, he grabbed a bottle of beer, yanked out the cork, and climbed up on it—his head almost reaching the rafters. Raising his beer in a toast, Newton looked around, and called out, "Here's to the soldier! We're all soldiers and let's drink like soldiers!"

Figure 7. Allison's Saloon
Saloon of Private Holomon, Company B, 25th Infantry

Holomon was late getting to his saloon on opening day. He had gone to the Western Union office just across the street on Garrison Road to send a telegram to his wife. He wanted to tell her about his good fortune and to ask her to let young Robert Holomon visit him before school opened in the latter part of August.

By the time he got to the saloon, the place was packed. Soldiers stood elbow to elbow at the bar. There were so many people that they spilled outside into the yard. Holomon made his way through the revelers, slapping them on the back, greeting them like a politician running for office. Once inside he put on his apron, went behind the bar, and checked the cash register. Then he helped Allison and the three other bartenders he'd hired fill orders.

Everybody was drinking, laughing, and having fun. Some told war stories—recounting their military exploits in Cuba, the Philippines, and duty on the western plains. Some went outside and sang the old cavalry songs they sang when riding with the 9th and 10th Cavalry.

There was friendly banter about the last time C Company won a baseball game. Company B's team had won the championship and the players let everybody know it—rubbing it in and making the other teams relive their losses. Private Boyd Conyers proudly passed around a photo of the champion baseball team. Mingo Sanders was especially proud of the team and he had worn his dress blue uniform for the team picture.

Somebody shouted, "Hey, Holomon, when you gonna get some whiskey and women in here?"

"Damn the whiskey, just git the women," another soldier yelled.

"You know where the whores are," Holomon called back as he walked to the back room to deliver drinks. "Catch the ferry, go to Matamoros. The girls are just waiting to take your money."

Private Newton hadn't stopped drinking since Allison opened the place that night.

"Newton, stop drinking," Conyers yelled. "You're as full as a pig that's been drinking slop all day. You gonna be big as a barrel. Ain't you drunk enough?"

Newton, looking sleepy, his eyelids almost fully closed, turned on his stool and nearly fell off. "Yeah, I'm drunk, and I like it."

A soldier sitting at the other end of the bar laughed. "Tell the truth, Newton. We're all drunk, and you won't lie." The crowd roared with laughter.

Watching everything, the designated bouncer sat on a stool in a corner, looking like a giant Buddha. His huge frame overlapped the stool. He watched everything. He wasn't drinking beer that night. For some strange reason, he was moody.

Holomon came out of the gambling room. He saw Newton, looked at the Bouncer and nodded toward Newton. The bouncer got up, walked over to Newton, picked him up and threw him over his shoulder like a sack of rice. The bouncer walked out, carried the drunken soldier back to the barracks and dumped him on his bunk.

"Stay here, don't you come back here tonight," he growled. "You drunken coward. You let that cracker beat your head. If you come back, I gonna whip your ass!"

Newton mumbled something and fell asleep.

Every kind of gambling was going on in the back room— poker, blackjack, craps, you name it. Holomon went in and out of the gambling room, carrying drinks, picking up the house share of the pot and lending money. As he moved around, he heard fragments of gambling talk which he described in his deposition:

"Put my money down."

"I put five down there."

"And I put ten."

"Put your bones in the pot."

"Shoot the dice or snake eyes."

It was getting late and most of the soldiers had already gone back to their barracks. Many had gone to bed, but were still talking about the good time they had. When the bugler sounded taps at eleven o'clock, the lights were put out. All was quiet when the sergeant in charge of quarters conducted bed check.

As John Holomon lay awake in his bunk, thinking about the day's events, his mind slipped into deep reflection. He was struck by the changes he had observed among the men—a new spirit, new vitality, a new *esprit de corps*, an upbeat morale he had not seen in them since their arrival in Brownsville. It began at "Retreat." He sensed that the tensions of Brownsville had disappeared. There were no signs of bitterness over their treatment or rejection by the citizens.

However, the soldiers' attitude was more than just the absence of ill will. A cohesive spirit was rising, a brotherhood that went beyond the common bonds of the soldier, some kind of burgeoning racial pride. The men seemed to have more respect for each other, honor for each other, honor among themselves. Was it the beer? No, he didn't think so. It was something else. It was something about his saloon itself, he was sure. They knew they had a place to relax and mingle, a place owned by one of them.

The saloon was alive—and it had become one of them, a soldier, a buddy, a welcoming friend. *Yes, that's it!* he thought. It had worked magic on the men that night. It was their saloon, a place of their own. Each soldier must have felt he owned a piece of the saloon, even though he owned none of it.

A powerful sense of ownership, possession, and control seeped into Holomon's psyche. "What is it in men that evokes that deep emotional drive for control?" he asked himself. "What ignites it, drives it, perpetuates it?"

As he pondered this, the only thing he could think of was the men's craving for respect, honor, and recognition. That answer came to him just as he drifted off into a deep sleep.

No soldier went through the back door of the Ruby Saloon that Friday night. And no soldier went through it Saturday night or Sunday night, August 12th. It was late on that Sunday, when John Tillman became angry as he looked in the back of his empty saloon and saw no black soldiers there. He'd lost business, and he knew why. He blamed Joe Crixell for distributing beer and other goods to the new saloon. Crixell double-crossed him, betrayed the other white saloon keepers and the other merchants. After they got the final decision that the soldiers were coming, they all pledged not to do business with the black soldiers. They had agreed to work together to bring the white soldiers back. Tillman walked out of the front door of the Ruby Saloon and looked down Elizabeth Street toward the fort. He spat in the street. His voice filled with angry disappointment as he grumbled aloud to himself, "I'm going to see Joe Crixell about this!"

SEVEN

THE YELLOW ROSE

Of Texas

The Assault

IT WAS TEN O'CLOCK Sunday night, August 12, when Private Oscar W. Reid and Private Jimmy Brown returned to Brownsville from Matamoros, Mexico. They had taken the advice given the previous night at Allison's Saloon to go there and get women. And they did just that. Having had a bit too much to drink and feeling good, Reid and Brown sang some old ribald cavalry songs as they sat on the ferry crossing the Rio Grande to 14th and Levee Streets in Brownsville. They didn't know that they were about to encounter one of the most dangerous men in Brownsville. A. Y. Baker, a U.S. custom inspector and former Texas Ranger, sat on his horse on the Texas side of the river, watching and listening to the two frolickers aboard the approaching ferry.

Baker was a lawman with a hazy past who had been involved in a highly-charged case of murder by mutilation and dragging. The crime landed him in jail. However, he could have been given a long prison sentence or even the gallows, had he not been defended by one of the best and politically well-connected lawyers in the state of Texas. James B. Wells of Brownsville, his defense lawyer, kept Baker out of prison and perhaps saved him from the gallows.

On this particular night, Baker appeared to enjoy the ribald cavalry songs sung by the two black soldiers. As the ferry came closer to the landing, he chuckled and made no move to stop them (although he could have, for Baker was a dead shot). He didn't even shout at them as they came off the boat. He just savored the erotic songs. But that all changed when the black soldiers started singing, most likely, the Yellow Rose of Texas. It was written by a black man, according to the University of Texas.

> *There's a yellow rose in Texas*
> *That I am going to see*
> *No other darky knows her*
> *No one only me*
> *She cried so when I left her*
> *It like to broke my heart*
> *And if I ever more find her*
> *.We nevermore will part.*
> *She's the sweetest rose of color*
> *This darky ever knew*
> *Her eyes are bright as diamonds*
> *They sparkle like the dew*
> *You may talk about dearest May*
> *And sing of Rosa Lee*
> *But the yellow rose of Texas*
> *Beats the belles of Tennessee*
> *Where the Rio Grande is flowing*
> *And the starry skies are bright*

She walks along the river
In the quiet summer night

As Baker listened more intently, his mood changed from amusement to indignation. He raised himself up in the saddle and canted his ear more toward the men, then looked over toward Fred Starck, another custom agent mounted on his horse nearby.

"Them niggers done gone too far," Baker called out. "Now they're singing about a white woman, I knew it, I knew it. They're lusting for our women."

He pulled his gun, then hesitated, thought about his earlier troubles with the law and his narrow escape from the gallows. He re-holstered his gun, shook his head from side to side, gritted his teeth and rode off in a full gallop toward the merrymakers. As the soldiers stepped off the gangplank, he almost rode into them. He pulled up on the reins until his horse reared up high on his hind legs.

"Cut out that racket!" Baker yelled. "You got no business carousing about a white woman. That's our song! Stop singing it! Stop it!" He shoved Private Reid into the shallow part of the Rio Grande River and rode off.

Private Reid landed in the water up to his waist. "Don't know what that crazy man talking 'bout." Reid staggered out of the water onto the riverbank. "That's a colored soldier's song. We been singing that song all our lives."

The ferry captain laughed heartily as the soldiers headed back to the fort. That same Sunday night, a white woman named Mrs. Evans alleged that she had been accosted by a big black soldier as she entered her home about nine o'clock. She claimed the soldier fled when she cried out.

On Monday afternoon, Lon Evans, the alleged victims' husband, burst into the mayor's office, and said, "Doctor, as mayor of the city, we want you to go with us to the post to interview Major Penrose and report this outrage on my wife."

Visibly upset, Mayor Combe stood up at once. "How many citizens did you say?"

"At least fifty," Evans said.

"No, I will not go with fifty citizens," Mayor Combe said, "I see no necessity for that. You and I can go down and do just as much by ourselves. I know Major Penrose, and if this is true, he will do all he can to find the guilty man. Let's go now."

Grudgingly, Lon Evans climbed aboard the mayor's carriage. They went to Fort Brown where they found Major Penrose walking along the parade ground. Penrose was a troubled man. The gossip mills and rumor dens had already spread the word all over town that a black soldier raped Mrs. Evans.

Penrose, seeing the mayor's carriage pull up, walked over and greeted them. "I can guess why you're here."

"And you'd be right," the mayor said as he and Evans dismounted without shaking the major's outstretched hand. Evans launched into his complaint as he was stepping down from the carriage.

"Major, last night about nine o'clock, my wife was assaulted by a colored man whom she positively identified as a Negro soldier. My wife and I were returning from the train and were met by a friend riding my wife's pony. My friend

Figure 8. Artist's Rendition: Nelson Potter
A.Y. Baker, Customs' Inspector shoves Private Osker W. Reid into the Rio Grande on Sunday night, August 12
SOURCE: Private Collection Lt. Col. (Ret) William Baker

insisted that my wife get on her own pony and ride home. So he assisted her to mount and she went on ahead. My friend and I walked on slowly behind. My wife went on home, dismounted and entered the back gate. When she was near the steps and near the ashcan, she was seized by a man from behind by her hair and was thrown violently to the ground. She screamed and the man fled."

Penrose crossed his arms and asked, "What did he look like, Mr. Evans?"

"Oh, he was a large, dark Negro wearing a slough hat, blue shirt, and khaki trousers."

"Can your wife provide me a more detailed description? I have a lot of large dark men under my command."

"No! She was too frightened." Evans was clearly annoyed by the question.

"Why did you wait so long to report the attack to me?"

"She was so upset, I was afraid to leave her."

"Well, somebody was well enough to report it to the newspaper," Penrose said. "A reporter called me last night and gave me a detailed account of what will appear in the *Daily Herald* today, and it is precisely the same as you've told me. Why didn't you bring Mrs. Evans with you today so she could point out the man?" Before Evans could answer, Penrose spoke again. "I want you to know I have already ordered an investigation into the matter, Mr. Evans."

It was obvious that Mayor Combe didn't like the way Major Penrose questioned the veracity of Evans' wife. Becoming increasingly irritated, the mayor decided he'd better say something to support his constituent. His eyes narrowed to a slit, his jaws tightened, his lips pursed and he turned his head from side to side to indicate his disagreement with the drift of the conversation.

Finally, he said, "Penrose, you know you're my friend. We go way back to the days in Cuba." He leaned forward over toward the major, and looking him straight in the eye continued. "But I've got to tell you—get to the bottom of this thing quickly."

He glanced at Evans as if to measure his reaction, then turned back to Penrose. "I don't want a lynching in my town. You find the man."

While the three men were talking, Wilbert Voshelle, the corral master, passed by them on the way home to Brownsville. The three lowered their voices, but Voshelle was able to catch a little of the conversation. He heard Evans say, "Major, if there is not an arrest between now and 11 o'clock tonight, every black enlisted man seen on the streets in Brownsville will be shot."

Hearing the threat, Penrose became angry. His head snapped back; his eyelids batted rapidly. "Mr. Evans, did your wife say she was raped?"

"No, I didn't say that."

"Then what are you saying?"

"I'm saying she was attacked."

"Then you are not accusing my men of rape."

"Rape or no rape, she was assaulted."

Penrose drew in a deep breath, showing some sympathy for Evans. "I'm sorry this thing happened to your wife. I will give every assistance in helping locate this man, but I can tell you that the man is not to be found among my soldiers."

Evans' tone was aggressive, insistent. "I expect more than that. I want the soldier."

"None of my men have ever been accused of such a thing. We just left Valentine, Nebraska. They never assaulted white women there, and they freely associated with white people around town."

Rocking forward on his toes, and putting his face within inches of Evans' face, he emphasized, "And in bars!" Then, lowering his voice, he added, "And they were on friendly terms with them." Then, the major raised his voice. "Why in God's name would they come down here in Texas, in this hostile place, and do such a thing? Besides," he added rather dryly, "with the number of Mexican prostitutes in this town, I hardly think rape would be necessary."

"Major, could I speak to you privately for a minute?" Combe said.

Penrose nodded. "Sure."

"Excuse us for a minute, Mr. Evans." The mayor took Penrose's arm and led him aside and then spoke quietly. "Major, don't you think it best for you to keep your men in the post tonight? Right or wrong, I fear this may cause a great deal of trouble."

"Yes, I already made up my mind as to that. I would rather anything in the world have happened than this very thing. And while I don't think it was one of my soldiers, they will undoubtedly get the blame. I'll keep them out of town and send out to get them all in before dark."

Mayor Combe and Evans climbed into the carriage and drove off while Major Penrose rushed back to the administration building, bounced up the steps and stuck his head into the sergeant major's office. "Sergeant, find Captain Macklin. Tell him to report to me immediately," he said. Then he went into his office and closed the door behind him.

Sergeant Major Taliaferro was straight as an arrow. Stern, unflappable, no-nonsense, he had worked for Penrose several years. Penrose chose him to be the Battalion Sergeant Major for just those qualities. As Penrose put it, "He's just like me, only black—cool under fire."

The sergeant didn't get up immediately, but sat in a thoughtful mood, holding the *Daily Herald* while tapping it lightly on the edge of his desk. Then he got up, walked to the commander's office and tapped three times, signaling to Penrose that it was he at the door.

"Come in."

The sergeant stepped inside, closing the door behind him. He found his commander standing with his back to him, staring out the window onto the parade ground. Turning around, Penrose said, "It's bad, Scottie."

Scottie was the nickname Penrose gave the sergeant-major, but only used it in private.

In all the years they'd worked together, Taliaferro never saw his commander's face so troubled.

"It's the rape gossip, isn't it? But I don't see anything in the paper about rape. Here, you read it." The sergeant handed the newspaper to Penrose.

Without a word, Penrose took the newspaper, and with his hands and heart beating rapidly, he began reading the *Daily Herald* datelined Brownsville, Texas, August 13, 1906:

Infamous Outrage
Negro Soldier Invaded Private Premises Last Night
Attempted to Seize A White Lady

After reading the complete article, Penrose sighed, feeling almost relieved. "Well, I don't see anything about rape either. The newspaper says nothing about it. And Evans didn't say anything either."

But when he thought about it some more, he became agitated and slammed the paper down on his desk. "That may not be the end of it though."

"What's the matter? There was no rape. You didn't see it in the paper. The paper said, 'Attempted to seize a white lady.'" The sergeant major tried to comfort his commander.

"Yes, I know, but the gossip mills say she was raped, and that's what the mob will act on. It's what comes after the charge of rape, or rumor of rape, that's worrying me. Rape or rumor of rape of a white woman by a black man is the rallying cry for mob violence. You know that, Scottie."

Penrose paced back and forth. Then his eyes lit up as if he had a revelation. "It's the garrison! It's the fort! These Texans may attack my command. So help me God, I'll defend this post. Go get Captain Macklin."

Just as Taliaferro turned to go find Macklin, Penrose looked out the window. "Wait, Scottie, I see 'im. He's coming this way."

Captain Macklin was walking from the guardhouse toward the administration building. Penrose stuck his head out the window and yelled, "Captain Macklin, I want to see you right away. Come now."

Macklin was on duty as the officer of the day. In this role, he was in charge of the guards, responsible for the protection of the garrison and took care of any routine matters that might arise during non-duty hours. Macklin stepped into Penrose's office, closed the door and saluted.

Still standing, Penrose walked from behind his desk and partially returned the salute. "There may be trouble in town tonight," he said. "Mayor Combe and a Mr. Evans just left. The mayor is afraid this rape talk may cause trouble."

Realizing that the captain was still standing at attention, he said, "At ease," and motioned for Macklin to sit down.

"What do you want us to do, sir?"

"See to it that all the officers are informed that all passes are canceled as of eight o'clock tonight. See to it that all the men are notified of this order at "Retreat." No one, not anyone for any reason whatsoever, Macklin, is to leave the post after eight p.m. As officer of the day, send out three patrols to round up any stragglers. Check all of the white bars personally. Don't forget the Mexican bars. Have the patrols check them. Now you better get going. It's getting late."

Macklin looked at his watch and left.

"Excuse me, sir," the sergeant interjected, "...but you didn't mention defending the fort in case a mob does attack."

"I didn't want to excite him. I've got to run this thing through my mind."

"So do we all." Having said that, the sergeant left and returned to his office.

A Hobson's Choice

Penrose stood at the window, looking into the distance across the parade ground—and analyzed the situation, running military tactics through his mind. His mission came first, he decided, and then the welfare of his men. What were his courses of action? And what were the advantages and disadvantages of those courses of action? But what was he to do if a mob attacked the fort? What then were his choices? What would be the appropriate course of action if that happened? The questions frightened him. He was trapped on the horns of a dilemma—to defend the fort or not to defend the fort. Those were his options, but they were nothing more than Hobson's choice, Penrose told himself.

Penrose began to pace. Not to defend would allow some of his men to be taken at random by a mob. The only thing that would matter to that mob would be the color of the men. Not to defend was the path to ignominy. It would dishonor the uniform, the soldier, the fort, the U.S. Army itself. It would be a shameful capitulation, a disgrace, he lamented. And he would be disgraced now and forever, a discredit to himself, his family and the U.S. Army. It would undoubtedly lead to trial by general court martial, the end of his career. His ruination.

Penrose paused at his desk for a moment, then went back to the window. *To defend means to fire on civilians, but are they citizens? They remain citizens until they breach his gate or jump over the garrison wall. If they did that, they would become the enemy, just like a foreign enemy.* He turned and walked back to look at the Springfield 03 rifle mounted on the wall. He grabbed it and examined it, patting the stock. He estimated there might be 150 to 300 townspeople, good rabbit shooters maybe, he thought, but no match for his men with the new Springfield 03 rifles.

If they crashed the gate, they would be bunched up, massed, a perfect target to be gunned down, a funnel to shoot into, maximizing the deadly cone of fire. If they jumped the wall, their backs would be to the wall—a perfect shooting gallery just like in a carnival. There would be no escape for them. May God have mercy on their souls if they took such a foolish action. Many would die, and so would his career, but not his honor. *I will defend this fort, so help me God!*

Penrose dug deeper into his analysis. Then another outcome, another option, a peaceful way out, came to his mind. What if Mayor Combe reasoned with his people, maybe talked them out of it? But that was his option, not Penrose's. He walked back to the window facing toward the town. It didn't look peaceful to him. Several white men milled around, openly carrying guns. Seeing that, the mayor felt internal pressure to do something else—but he didn't know what else he could do except get out of his office and inspect the fort.

At the main gate, two guards were alert. Such a small thing as that made Penrose feel better. It was clearer than ever in his mind that his first priority was to defend Fort Brown.

In town, the crowds grew larger. Exaggerated, bizarre, embellished stories about the alleged attack on Mrs. Evans circulated on Elizabeth Street. People jeered, hooted and heckled any and all black soldiers on the streets, calling them "niggers," "coons," and "darkies."

When the battalion mail clerk entered the U.S. Post Office to pick up the soldiers' mail, angry white men stopped him several times, trying to engage him in conversation about the attack on Mrs. Evans. He tried to get rid of them as best he could, but they obviously wanted trouble. As he was about to leave the post office carrying two bags marked U.S. Mail over his shoulder, one of the hecklers called out, "It's a damn good thing your commanding officer ordered all you niggers in, because some of you are going to get killed tonight!"

Before the mail clerk delivered the mail to each company, he went to see Captain Macklin. "Sir, the people in town are talking about killing us tonight."

Macklin felt the pressure. Later that day he carried out Major Penrose's orders, announcing the eight o'clock curfew at "Retreat." Patrols went into town to warn those who might not have gotten word that all passes were canceled.

After "Retreat," some soldiers hurried to Allison's Saloon to have some fun and still get back to the fort before the eight o'clock curfew. Business was brisk and the place was packed, just as it had been on the last two nights. But there was no heavy drinking. Even Newton moderated his intake of beer. The frivolity that characterized the first two nights was gone.

Some of the sergeants huddled in a corner, sipping beer. Mingo Sanders shook his head. "I don't believe it. Nothing like that ever happened before. What black fool would assault a white woman down here in Texas?"

Holomon walked over to where the sergeants sat. "Time to go. We're closing early tonight, fellows. You got the word."

The men grudgingly left the saloon and went back to the post. Some went fishing in the lagoon, some started a baseball game, others played cards, went to the library or started shooting pool.

Stragglers and slowpokes squeezed out the last minute of fun before the curfew began. Captain Macklin stationed a guard at the ferry dock to intercept any soldier going to Mexico. He went into Brownsville and combed the town. In the end, he was satisfied that all but two soldiers were accounted for. Sergeant George Thomas and Private Edward Lee, who were given 24-hour passes, had apparently not gotten word about the curfew.

Unlike earlier in the evening, at nine o'clock the streets in town were quiet and peaceful. Across the street from the garrison, a children's birthday party was in progress at Louis and Anna Cowen's house. Several children were invited to the party, including the children of the white officers from Fort Brown. The Cowens lived in a plain bungalow on 14th Street between Elizabeth and Washington Streets on the south side of the alley that ran between Elizabeth and Washington Streets. It was called Cowen's Alley.

Louis Cowen worked as a New York Life Insurance agent. He also ran a small, but successful, dry goods business on the side. Citizens around town concerned with social status questioned his ethnicity. Some said Louis Cowen was three-fourth Mexican, not quite white in the eyes of the purebreds who lived in white-columned mansions in the better parts of town. Others whispered that he really was a renegade Russian Jew, who had shortened his name from Cowajiian to Cowen. His complexion was considered too olive for a white man. He had such tight, curly brown hair that his friends called him "Curly Top." No matter what they thought about him, or what they called him, Louis Cowen was handsome—a lady's man and a fastidious dresser. He slicked his hair back and may have even used a hot straightening comb on it. Certainly his drinking buddies didn't seem to care about his ethnicity. They liked Louis Cowen, his jokes and his self-deprecating humor.

Figure 9. Louis and Anna Cowen's House
U.S. Archives AG file 1135832

Anna Cowen was a Mexican-American woman and a devout Catholic. She was quite nervous and easily upset. She was tired and worn out even before the party began. The hustle and bustle from the birthday party fatigued her even more, and she left the party to seclude herself in a back bedroom. Seeing her husband leaving, she called out to him. "Louis, bring me back a couple of sandwiches and a bottle of Schlitz beer."[1]

But behind the mask of this fast-talking, wise-cracking man was an impatient striver who was in a hurry to make money and win complete acceptance. Cowen was unusually jumpy that night. He'd been thinking of how to escape to the Ruby Saloon since the party began. Finally, he couldn't take it anymore. About 10:30, he left his house which was full of guests attending his daughter's 13th birthday party. Before he walked out, he told his wife who was in the back bedroom trying to sleep, "I've had enough. I gotta git outta here." As he left, he told Amada Martinez, the maid, to take over.

Figure 10. Louis R. Cowen, Circa 1906
Courtesy of Ralph Cowen, Nephew of Louis R. Cowen
Lt. Col. (Ret) William Baker Private Papers

---

1   Schlitz Beer - 1898.

Cowen nodded, and headed for the Ruby Saloon where he felt more at home than in any other of the four white saloons in town.

Although Anna Cowen went to bed early, long before the party ended, she was unable to sleep. But now that the party was ending and the guests leaving, and with Louis still out at the Ruby Saloon, she got up and got dressed as if she were going out. She opened the dresser drawer, took out her rosary beads, held them tightly in her hand and went into the dining room. She sat at the head of the table and told Amada Martinez to bring her some hot water.

Before Cowen reached the Ruby Saloon, one of those unexpected light Brownsville summer rains began to fall. To get out of the rain, he stopped at the house of his next door neighbor, Katie Leahy. He found the rain a convenient excuse to exchange gossip with Katie about the attack on Mrs. Evans. He boasted to Leahy that if any one of those niggers ever touched or insulted his wife or his children, or one of his lady friends, that he would take out his Winchester and kill them.

He stopped frequently on the way to the saloon, engaging in conversation with small groups of white men who came together in some kind of brotherhood stemming from the Evans' affair. They offered whiskey to anyone on the streets who would stop and discuss what to do about the soldiers at the fort. However, nobody offered Cowen a drink. Nobody wanted to talk to him or hear his jokes.

When Louis entered the saloon, he looked around and saw that it was almost empty. He thought it strange that none of his old drinking buddies were there. They usually beat him to the bar, and he was late getting there tonight. *Where is everybody?* He crawled up on the bar stool and slouched over the bar, feeling disappointed. He looked like he was already drunk.

What he thought would be a relief from the birthday party turned out to be less than a warm welcome from his youthful friend, Frank Natus, the bartender. Frank stood at the other end of the bar and appeared to be ignoring him.

"Where in the hell is my beer?" Cowen grumbled.

"I'm looking for the tin cup," the bartender shot back.[2]

"The tin cup! What're you talking about? I ain't drinking out of no tin cup," Cowen cried. "That cup was used for slaves and niggers, so you wouldn't have to give them a real glass. Git me a real glass, a glass of Schlitz. And don't you insult me again, you pucker-faced bastard!"

Hearing himself called a bastard hurt. Natus was an orphan who had lived an uneven life. He never knew his mother or father. After hearing the insult, he decided he would not force the tin cup on Cowen, nor would he trade insults with him. "I know what you want," he said.

Instead of sliding the glass of beer down the bar as was his customary practice, Natus took his time. He leaned over while handing him the beer. "I hear talk 'bout 'cha. They say you are doing business with the colored soldiers and your girls are getting awfully nice with them. Better watch your back."

Cowen was unnerved by Frank Natus's warning. He knew Natus had picked up some bar room talk about him, and that probably Natus meant well in trying to warn him. But his family had been friendly with the soldiers, and he himself sold a few insurance policies to some of the black non-commissioned officers. And, of course, some of the white officers'

---

2   The tin cup was a way of dishonoring any patron who acted up in the saloon.

children were at his daughter's birthday party. He thought he should go over to Weller's saloon and see if he could pick up some more information. He quickly downed his beer, paid the tab and left.

Once outside, he stood erect and broadened his shoulders, trying to summon some courage. Then he marched across the street into Weller's saloon. He was about to go to the bar, but he changed his mind when H.H. frowned at him, turned his back and walked away. Cowen decided he didn't want another beer after all. What he really wanted was something to eat. So he went to the restaurant in the rear of the saloon and ordered a ham sandwich.

At about 10 minutes to midnight, Anna Cowen still sat at the dining room table, sweating profusely. She called to her oldest daughter, "Gertrude, do not go to bed. I don't feel well. Stay by me. I am nervous."

"Don't worry. I won't go to sleep, Mamma." Gertrude came up to her mother and stood next to her at the table.

"Feel my heart, Gertrude," she said. Anna took Gertrude's hand and placed it over her heart, "Hear it? It's just going a' thump, thump, thump."

EIGHT

MIDNIGHT ATTACK

On Brownsville

August 13, 1906

THE DRIZZLING RAIN HAD just about petered out, but a heavily overcast sky made it more difficult for the sentinels at Fort Brown to see on an already dark night. They walked their posts expecting trouble. When Captain Macklin made his final inspection, he came within five feet of the sentinel on guard post No.2 before Private Joseph H. Howard challenged him. "Halt! Who goes there?"

"Captain Macklin, officer of the day."

"Advance, captain, and be recognized."

Captain Macklin took two steps forward before Private Howard recognized him. "Captain Macklin recognized."

"Why did you let me get this close to you, soldier, before you challenged me?"

"Sir, it's dark out here. I didn't see you."

"Anything unusual happening around here?"

"No, sir. All's quiet and peaceful."

Just then, at 11 o'clock, the bugler blew taps. At the sound of taps the lights went out in all the barracks. In the darkness, each company's charge of quarters (CQs) conducted the check roll call. Shortly thereafter, Samuel Wheeler,

Corporal of the Guard, received the check roll call reports, and reported to Captain Macklin that all the soldiers in the companies were present or accounted for. Since Wheeler knew that Sergeant George Thomas and Private Edward Lee were on 24-hour pass, they were reported accounted for. While making his reports, Wheeler reassured Captain Macklin. "Everything is very peaceful. None of the men have been drinking or in anyway acting ugly."

Figure 11. Garrison Wall and Barracks, Fort Brown, Texas, Circa 1906

Certain that all was in order, quiet and serene, Captain Macklin retired to his quarters to get some sleep. It was about 11:30. On the way, he heard a dog growling near the gate to the officers' quarters. Then he heard muttering, then children crying. He unhooked his saber and ran up to where a big black dog had cornered several children who were huddled in a group and backed up to the gate. Some of the little girls were sobbing.

Recognizing the dog as Company B's mascot, he waved his saber, shouting, "Get away, Trooper, leave 'em alone. What in the hell's wrong with you?" Immediately, Trooper ran off toward B Company barracks.

"What are you doing out here this time of night?" Macklin asked Wesley Bailey, who at 13 was the oldest of the children.

"We were over at the birthday party at Mr. Cowen's house."

Macklin escorted the children across the parade ground and pointed to the officers' family housing. "Y'all go straight home," he admonished them mildly.

Macklin went to his quarters, got a bottle of beer from the icebox, sat down on the side of his white iron cot, and drank his second beer of the night. *Maybe Penrose overreacted imposing that curfew*, he thought. Nothing had happened. Then he lay back on the cot and fell dead asleep with his clothes on.

About 10 minutes before midnight, Private Joseph Howard, sentinel at post Number 2, heard a dog whining and running up and down along the inside of the garrison wall.

Howard recognized the dog as B Company's mascot, Trooper. "Trooper, come here. What's wrong, boy?"

Trooper ran at once to the sentinel, but turned and raced back to the wall, this time with a low, deep growl as he sniffed along the wall, following a sound. Private Howard didn't think too much about Trooper's behavior. He hadn't heard or seen anything of concern. And, it was not unusual for some kind of activity to occur outside the fort on the town side of the wall. But then Trooper began racing up and down along the wall, barking loudly. Howard heard running, and a few seconds later two pistol shots rang out down the road behind him near the vacant set of barracks reserved for A Company. Howard looked over in that direction but saw nothing.

The Shooting Begins

A band of some 16 to 20 men emerged from the darkness near the garrison wall. They moved cautiously like a military patrol probing enemy lines. Their heads were lowered, chins buried in their chests, bodies hunched over in low, military crouches. They crossed Garrison Road into the town of Brownsville.

Garrison Road separated Fort Brown from Brownsville and was better known by locals as "the firing line." It was along that line that drunken cowhands, gunslingers, and soldiers traditionally engaged in fist fights, gun play and various forms of lawlessness.

Figure 12. Cowen Alley
U.S. Archives file 1135832, box 4053
Modified: Lt. Col. (Ret) William Baker

The raiders ducked into Cowen Alley, a narrow passageway between Elizabeth and Washington streets. There a single-frame house with a covered porch stood alone. Its lights still burned as the birthday party had broken up only a short time before.

Anna Cowen's heart beat frantically. She still wasn't feeling well. Amada Martinez came into the dining room with a pitcher of hot water. As she sat down at the table to console her mother, loud shots rang out from the alley.

One of the marauders, apparently the leader, fired several shots into the back of Cowen's House with his pistol, shattering windows and piercing walls. Then he directed the men crouched behind him to send more fire at the structure. Two or three of the men raised their rifles and took dead aim at the lights. One by one they went out. A student lamp sitting on the dining room table was shot out. So was a light shining directly at the raiders through an open window. A single shot shattered the lantern in the kitchen that threw light into the backyard. Another bullet hit a large Rochester lamp hanging in the center hallway illuminating the three back bedrooms. All shots were made with military precision. The house was in total darkness.

Amada fell to her knees and became hysterical. "Madame, Madame! 'Tis the day of judgment," she cried out as she crawled about the floor in total darkness. "The soldiers are going to kill us."

It was the custom in Brownsville to discharge shots with a gun to signal a fire. The children, thinking there was a fire in town, ran into the dining room yelling, "Fire! Fire! Fire, Mamma!"

Anna Cowen yelled back to her children, "It's not a fire. It's the soldiers. Go to the bedroom. Get under the bed." But the children stayed with her, hanging onto her dress.

She crawled along the floor with the children and Amada. When they reached the dining room wall, they turned around and pressed their backs into the corner. Terrified, she held her rosary beads close her heart and began praying. "Mary, Mother of God, save us from the soldiers." She urged the children, "Pray to God, children, to save our lives. If we are alive tomorrow, we will go to church and thank God."

While Louis Cowen's house was being shot up and his family terrorized, he wasn't there. He was wandering around town, in and out of saloons, trying to find out why he had become persona non grata.

As he was about to eat his ham sandwich, he heard several shots. Dropping the sandwich, he ran out of the restaurant and down Elizabeth Street toward his house, stopping again at the Ruby Saloon.

Flinging the screen door open, Cowen saw Natus at the bar. "Hey, Frank, did you hear those shots? You gotta lend me a pistol."

"I heard 'em, all right. What's all that shooting about, Louis? I don't got but one gun—and I'm keeping it for myself."

Failing to get a gun from Natus, Cowen remembered Teofilo Crixell, Joe Crixell's brother. Teofilo was known for accepting guns for unpaid debts at his saloon, the White Elephant. Surely, Cowen could get one from him.

As Cowen left the Ruby Saloon, he stumbled off the saloon porch into the street, complaining, "Damn! It's dark as hell out here." As the sound of gunfire drew nearer, Cowen became afraid that he might be shot before he made it all the way to Teofilo's saloon on Market Square. So, he changed his mind, scurried across the street and rushed to Joe Crixell's saloon, stumbling through the door. "There's shooting going on out here!"

Joe Crixell was enjoying a winning poker hand, playing for drinks in the back of his saloon, when he saw Cowen. In that instant, Crixell heard four or five shots. He threw his cards down and waited. When another shot rang out, he said, "There's some shooting, boys."

"That's what I said when I came in." Cowen panted, as if he were totally out of breath. "Joe, gimme a half pint of whiskey." Holding onto the bar with one hand, Cowen tried to tell the others what he had seen, but he was interrupted by Martin Hanson, one of the poker players.

More preoccupied with the poker game than the shots, Hanson glanced up and immediately dismissed Cowen's concern. "That's nothing but firecrackers, Louis," he said. "Come on, Joe, give Cowen the damn liquor and play your hand."

Crixell grabbed a half-pint of whiskey from the shelf and tossed it to Cowen, who caught the bottle with one hand and clutched it to his chest. He fumbled with the cork until he got it out. After taking a drink, he stretched out his hand and pleaded, "I need a gun, too. Got to get home to protect my wife and children."

Crixell shook his head. "Don't have no more pistols here. Plenty at the White Elephant." His voice trailed off as he listened a few seconds more. Then he sat down and picked up his cards. Ten or more shots rang out, and all of the players jumped up. Cards flew everywhere. "I'll be damned if those were firecrackers, Martin. Those shots came from United States Army rifles," Crixell said.

Cowen shuddered at the sound of more gunfire. "That's what I was trying to tell you when I came in here," he gasped over gulps of liquor. "I seen ...I saw gun flashes down toward the fort near my house when I crossed the street."

"It's trouble, all right." Crixell pushed the chairs out of his way and hurried from the back of the saloon to the front door. Looking across the street toward the Ruby Saloon, he saw Frank Natus and several other men standing on the sidewalk. "Close up your doors, boys. Here come the niggers."

He stepped back inside and was about to bolt the door when Hal Shannon spoke up. "Wait! I got to git my bicycle." His bicycle was leaning against a post in front of the saloon. When he reached for the handlebars, a bullet whizzed past his head and hit the post, barely missing him.

"Get back in here, you damn fool!" Crixell yelled. "You'll get yourself killed out there!"

As Shannon stepped back inside, they heard several more shots.

Cowen paced nervously, still bemoaning the fact that he was trapped in town unable to protect his family. He kept saying over and over again, "I've got to get home to protect my wife and children."

Crixell looked at Cowen as if he thought he were crazy. "You haven't any business out in the street now. No telling what those black bastards will do. Let's go upstairs. We'll be safer. In case those soldiers get here, the first place they will break into will be the bar." Crixell locked the front door.

At first, Cowen was reluctant to go upstairs and asked Crixell to unlock the door and let him out, because he was going home no matter what. But then he realized that without a gun he wouldn't be able to do much anyway. He stayed where he was.

Cowen went upstairs with Crixell and the other patrons, took another swig of whiskey and blew out the flames of the

Route of Attack

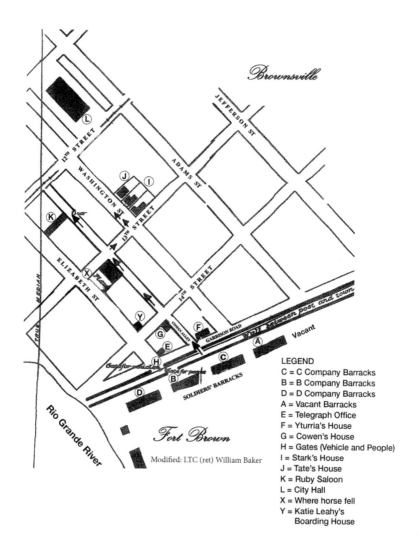

Brownsville

LEGEND
C = C Company Barracks
B = B Company Barracks
D = D Company Barracks
A = Vacant Barracks
E = Telegraph Office
F = Yturria's House
G = Cowen's House
H = Gates (Vehicle and People)
I = Stark's House
J = Tate's House
K = Ruby Saloon
L = City Hall
X = Where horse fell
Y = Katie Leahy's
      Boarding House

Modified: LTC (ret) William Baker

Figure 13. Modified: Lt. Col. (Ret) William Baker

oil lamps. *I'll go home when this fray has died out*, he thought. *My family didn't do anything to the soldiers. All in all, they have been friendly to us. I don't guess they will hurt my family*, he rationalized as he sat in the darkened room.

No lights were lit in Cowen's house. It was dark and silent. The raiders saw to that with such ferocity that it appeared that they specifically targeted the lights. From their position in Cowen's Alley, the raiders fired sporadically with high-powered rifles. They took aim at the Western Union Telegraph building, the Yturria's house and the Martinez's Cottage.

"Fire High"

"Fire high and over the fort," the leader ordered. Twisting around and elevating their rifles, the raiders fired several shots in the direction of the fort.

Across the street from Cowen's house on the corner of Elizabeth and 14th Streets, near the raiders' path, stood a rambling, two-story building owned by Katie Leahy. She called it the Leahy Hotel, although it was nothing more than an old-fashioned rooming house.

Katie Leahy, a tall, wiry, 36-year-old, ruddy-faced woman, was as opinionated as she was loquacious and sharp-tongued. Strong-willed and resolute, she was quick to command her guests and others not only what to do, but how to do it. She had spent most of her life in and around army posts and had been married to a former soldier from the Eighth Calvary. Together they ran a saloon in Brownsville. Since her husband's death, she managed the boarding house. However, she planned to get back into the saloon business some day.

Leahy sat on the edge of her bed in her first-floor bedroom, her nightgown pulled up over her knees. Holding a bottle of liniment, she shook small drops onto her aching legs. She had had a hard day running up and down the stairs, cleaning up after her boarders and gossiping with Anna Cowen. "That's that," she said with a sigh as she set down the bottle.

Suddenly, she heard the shots. At first she thought it was a fire alarm. But when she heard several more, she ran outside into the middle of Elizabeth Street, trying to see where the shooting was coming from. She saw gun flashes near the Cowen's house and heard bullets whistling over her head. Horrified, she ran back inside and went upstairs. She looked out the window. Two policemen sauntered down Elizabeth Street. They called up to her, "Where is the fire?"

She didn't answer. Instead she ran back downstairs. Standing in the door, she waved her hands, urging the policemen inside. "Come in! Come in! The Negroes are shooting up the town."

When the policemen heard more shots, they scrambled through the door, almost knocking Leahy down. "Get in the bathroom! You'll be safe in there. Get in the bathroom." She pointed and shoved them inside. Before she closed the door, she gave them specific instructions. "Under no circumstances do you leave till I tell you. It doesn't matter who comes. You stay here until I give you the all clear and let you out. Don't leave for any reason whatsoever." Then she went back to the second-floor bedroom window.

Once upstairs, she observed about 16 men whom she believed to be Negro soldiers wearing khaki uniforms. From her vantage point she guessed that they were about 30 feet away, near the corner of 14th Street and Cowen Alley. To her they seemed to be firing into the air, not aiming at anything. She could tell by the upward flashes from their guns, she later said. One of the men was having trouble with his gun. Another came over to help him. She saw one of the men look up at her, and heard him say to the other, "That's Mrs. Leahy. Keep straight to the front and shoot ahead."

"They got Frank!"

Judge Parks was an out-of-town guest at Katie Leahy's hotel. He was a tall, thin, sickly man, but discreet and well respected. He didn't gamble or socialize with any of the judges, lawyers or ranchers in his judicial district. When he wanted to have a little diversion, he got away to Brownsville. Then he slipped across the border to Matamoros, had a little fun there and thus kept his reputation intact. Tonight, as on all nights when he was away, even on his escapades, he penned his wife a letter. He was sitting in his bedroom on the second floor writing, when he heard shooting. He went to the window and saw the "whole thing." But he was unable to discern who the shooters were.

When the raiders approached 14th Street, they fired off a volley of shots in the air and divided into two groups. One group dashed across 14th Street at full speed, entering the mouth of the alley on the other side. The other group ran up 14th Street and turned left onto Washington Street, firing in the air as they ran. Flashes of light from gunfire pierced the darkness. The sound traveled far through the night, awakening townspeople from an uneasy sleep. At the same time, the gunfire startled and awakened the soldiers and officers at Fort Brown.

When the shooters had passed 14th Street, continuing up the alley, Katie Leahy heard someone pounding on her front door. She got her pistol, went to the door and listened before opening it. It was a terrified Anna Cowen, her six children and the maid seeking refuge.

"Get your asses in here quickly!" Katie commanded.

Several blocks away at the time the shooting began, Police Lieutenant Joe Dominguez was sitting on the steps of the police station at 12th and Washington streets. Thinking he heard gunfire, he turned his head toward the sound. When he heard more shots, he mounted his horse and set off at a full gallop down Washington.

Another policeman, Genaro Padron, heard the shooting around the same time as Lieutenant Dominguez. Running to the corner of 14th Street and Washington, Padron was just in time to see silhouettes of the raiders, whom he decided were Negro soldiers shooting up Cowen's house. Frightened, he ran around the corner and fled north on foot up Washington Street toward 13th Street. There he met Dominguez in the middle of the block.

Dominguez jumped off his horse, tightened his saddle girth and shouted to Padron, "Where's all this shooting coming from?" He pointed in the general direction of Cowen's house.

"The soldiers are shooting up Cowen's," Padron said.

Dominguez remounted his horse and trotted back up Washington, then south on 13th, toward the Miller Hotel on Elizabeth Street near the alley.

Meanwhile, the raiders moved up the alley toward 13th Street. They paused in the back of the Miller Hotel where a light shown through a window. "Git the light," the leader whispered. A single shot missed it. As they headed farther up the alley, the leader held up his hand, "Wait, I hear something."

A pounding of hooves came down 13th Street. "Git down! Git down!"

The men crouched low.

When Dominguez passed the mouth of the alley on 13th near the Miller Hotel, he looked down the alley but didn't see anything.

The leader hissed through his teeth, "There goes the son of a bitch! Let's git 'im!"

Dominguez pulled up on the reins as he got closer to the Miller Hotel. Standing up in the saddle, he hollered to the people in the hotel:

Wake up! Put out the lights! The colored soldiers are firing into houses and killing people! Wake up! Defend yourselves!

While Dominguez's back was turned, the raiders rushed out of the alley and stood up. They fired a volley in the direction of the policeman, hitting him in the arm and wounding his horse. Just as they rounded the corner, the horse stumbled and fell at 13th and Elizabeth Streets.

"We scorched his ass. That will teach him. We learned him a lesson," the leader said as the raiders continued on up the alley toward 12th Street.

When John Tillman, the owner of the Ruby Saloon, heard the shots, he was drinking beer with two friends, Paulino Preciado and Nicholas Alanis. Tillman rushed to the door just in time to hear Joe Crixell's warning from across the street. Immediately, Tillman stepped back into the doorway and yelled to his bartender, Frank Natus, "Get back in here, Frank! Bar the doors!"

Preciado rushed to the bar, but Alanis ran to the bathroom in the back of the saloon.

Natus came right in, slammed the doors shut and locked the door by dropping the crossbars in the metal U-slots riveted to the doors. Then Natus realized the door to the alley was open. He grabbed the lantern and a pistol from under the bar and ran toward the open back door.

Preciado, a bookbinder by trade, pulled a small pistol from his boot and followed the bartender to the door.

Alanis, who was sitting on the toilet in the bathroom that backed up to the alley, ran out—pants still down. "Don't go out! I heard noises in the alley."

Natus stood at the back door of the saloon, holding up a lantern, trying to see what was going on. He stepped into the courtyard. A single shot fired. Natus fell dead.

Preciado darted back inside, calmly closed the door, and walked to the middle of the saloon where Tillman and the rest waited. "They got Frank."

"What? That can't be!" Stunned, Tillman struggled to process the awful news.

"A group of five or six armed men appeared in the alley and fired. Frank cried, 'Ay Dios,' and fell dead," Preciado explained.

Tillman turned on his heels, visibly shaken. He lifted the bar on his saloon door and walked out. It was the height of the shooting. He walked down Elizabeth Street, turned left and went up 13th. Turning on Adams, he headed toward his house which was across the street from the garrison. His wife, badly shaken by all the shooting, met him at the door. When he told her about the tragic death of the young bartender, she flopped down in a chair and held her head in her hands. "Poor Frank," she said in almost a whisper to herself. "He didn't have an enemy in the world. Why did he have to die? Who in the world would want to hurt him?"

Tillman shook his head, "I don't know," he said, but he looked aside as if something else had gone terribly wrong.

After consoling his wife, Tillman went next door to see his neighbor, J.P. McDonnel, and they walked back up town together.

The other group of raiders was running northwest on Washington Street when they spotted a light coming out of one of the three houses near the corner of 13th and Washington. A lantern was burning in Fred Starck's house. A hail of bullets hit the two-story residence, knocking out the lantern in his little girls' bedroom and ripping the mosquito net covering them. The bullets came within 18 to 20 inches of killing them. Had Fred Starck or his wife been standing in the children's bedroom, they may well have met their death as well.

Gunshots rang out all over Brownsville. Some people heard them at the same time. The noise awakened others at different times. Mayor Combe was no different from most of the citizenry. Suddenly shaken from his sleep by the first shots as he lay on a cot on his back porch, he jumped up, put on his trousers, and grabbed his pistol. He called to his brother, also a medical doctor, who was sleeping upstairs. "Joe, I hear pistol shots down the street."

A sinking feeling flooded over Mayor Combe, reawakening his fears that despite his best efforts, his town was about to explode in racial violence. *It's here! It's here! Trouble is here*, he thought. He grabbed a handful of cartridges, pointed the revolver up, rolled the chamber and saw that it was already fully loaded. Sticking the pistol in his front belt, he went to the window and looked down the street. "Joe," he called, "I don't see anything, but I am going down the street to find out what that firing was about."

"Wait for me, Fred," his brother said, "I'm coming with you." Fully dressed by now, Joe Combe checked their father, also a doctor, who still slept undisturbed in his room. Then he picked up his pistol and hurried downstairs to join his brother.

The two men walked to the corner of Ninth and Elizabeth Streets, turned the corner and headed down Elizabeth toward the garrison. It seemed to Fred Combe that gunfire punctuated each step they took. He walked on one side of the street and his brother Joe took the other, both with their pistols drawn.

When they passed the post office on Elizabeth Street, Joe Combe yelled, "Fred, hug the wall. They are shooting down the street."

The mayor crept along the wall with his pistol drawn until the shooting stopped.

Then both brothers ran. Just as they reached Twelfth Street, a figure scurried around the corner onto Elizabeth and almost ran into the mayor.

Mayor Combe shouted, "Stop!"

The man skidded to an immediate halt. With the barrel of the mayor's revolver pointing directly at his face, he cried, "Mayor, it's me, Genaro, please don't shoot!" It was a city policeman Genaro Padron.

The mayor lowered his revolver. "My God! I almost shot you." He stuck the gun back in his front belt.

The policeman put his hand on the mayor's shoulder. "Don't go any farther, mayor," Genaro pleaded. "You will be shot."

Convinced that the policeman was in full panic, the mayor ignored him and continued down Elizabeth to the middle of the next block. In front of Crixell's saloon, Combe saw

Jose Garza, who sometimes worked as a special policeman. Tonight the police chief hired him in case the rumors about Mrs. Evans' rape stirred up potential trouble.

The mayor walked up to him and, smelling whiskey on his breath, realized that Garza had been drinking. He also saw that Garza held a Winchester rifle. *That's strange. Brownsville policemen only carried pistols.*

"What are you doing with that rifle, Garza?" The mayor grabbed the rifle away from the hired policeman. "Give me that thing!" He stepped inside Crixell's saloon, followed by Garza whose pant legs, the mayor noted, were splashed with fresh mud.

Combe pulled the rifle bolt back, looked down into the breech and saw that there was an empty cartridge inside the magazine which the ejector had failed to eject. *It sure looks like this gun has been fired recently*, the mayor thought.

The owner of the saloon stood near the bar, watching the mayor's inspection of the gun and its malfunctioning ejector with great interest. Garza said nothing, but Crixell spoke up. "The damn rifle doesn't work. It probably was like this for a month. I took it in on a bad loan some six months ago." Crixell went on to explain that Garza had borrowed the gun from his brother over at the White Elephant saloon, when he heard the shooting.

Mayor Combe seemed satisfied with the explanation.

Just then George Connor, the chief of police, and two other policemen walked up.

The mayor addressed him at once. "George, where have you been? And for Christ's sake, where are the rest of your men? Have you accounted for all of your officers?"

"All but three."

"Who are they?"

"Dominguez, Brisneo, and ..."

In the excitement, the chief couldn't remember the other officer's name. That memory lapse by his chief of police caused the mayor to drop his head in concern. While looking down, he saw a dark spot on the ground barely visible in the dim light of the lamp post. He reached down. It felt wet. He held his fingers up to the lamppost light and looked at them.

"Joe!" Fred Combe called to his brother. "Come here. Look at this. It's blood."

Joe Combe stepped closer and the mayor showed him the blood on his fingers and pointed to the ground. "There's blood. Somebody's hurt. Follow the bloodstains. We need to see if we can find out who it is."

The chief and his policemen examined the spot and went off into the night, looking for the raiders and the other policemen.

The Call to Battle

Meanwhile, down the road at the garrison, the soldiers and officers heard the same gunfire as the townspeople. A minute or so after hearing Trooper barking and running on the inside of the garrison wall, Private Howard, the sentinel at Guard Post Number 2, heard the first shots. Then came a fusillade near Cowen Alley, directly across Garrison Road to the right of where he stood.

Hearing the sound of creaking wheels, Howard looked around. Tamayo, the scavenger (the fort's garbage collector), was emptying ash cans and trash into his mule cart when the shooting began. The frightened mule bucked, reared and shook herself violently. Her shaking rattled the chains and traces connected to the cart. Tamayo gripped the reins tightly as the animal struggled to escape the loud bangs. She was nearing the administration building with Tamayo pulling back on the reins and shouting, "Whoa! Whoa! Whoa!"

Poised for action with his rifle at the ready, Howard ran to the edge of the parade ground near a clump of trees and fired three times straight up in the air. "They're shooting us up!" He shouted to the guard on post Number 3.

The rest of the guards picked up the warning and repeated it. "They're shooting us up!"

Lying in bed, disturbed and anxious—and unable to fall asleep, Major Penrose sat straight up and said to his wife, "Those are pistol shots."

Knowing that his sentinels were not authorized to carry pistols on guard, he became even more concerned. Then he heard a high-powered rifle volley.

Mrs. Penrose raised up on her elbow. "A fire alarm?"

"I am afraid it's something worse than that." Penrose listened intently. More shots rang out—then repeated banging on his door—and shouts.

"Major Penrose! Major Penrose, they are shooting us up."

"Okay, I'm coming." Penrose threw the bed sheet back and jumped out of bed. He put his uniform on over his pajamas, latched his pistol belt around his waist with his pistol still in its holster and pushed his bare feet into his boots. Within seconds he was dressed. As he reached for his hat, he heard more shooting. The pounding on the door persisted until he opened it.

It was Private Charley Hairston, the sentinel stationed near Major Penrose's quarters. "We're under fire, sir," he shouted.

"How do you know?"

"I heard bullets whistling in the air over my head."

"Go to the guardhouse and tell the sergeant of the guard to sound the call to arms."

"Yes, sir." Hairston saluted and raced off to the guardhouse.

Penrose was running across the parade grounds toward the enlisted men's barracks when he heard the clattering sound of the scavenger's mule cart and Tamayo's voice shouting, "Whoa! Whoa. Whoa!"

Within minutes, the call to arms sounded across Fort Brown and every company responded, believing they were being attacked.

Sergeant Mingo Sanders was in bed with his wife when they were awakened by their next door neighbor, Hattie, knocking on the door, shouting, "Fire!"

At that moment Sanders heard the trumpet play the call to arms. He'd heard that sound many times over his long military career, calling him and all soldiers to battle. Never uncertain, never doubtful, never iffy. It's always clear and forceful. Every soldier knows its meaning.

"That's no fire. It's a call to battle," Sanders told his wife. He dressed, ran out the door and sprinted across the parade ground to the barracks while still buttoning his shirt. He heard gunfire, which he determined was from mixed weapons—pistols and high-powered rifles of many kinds. He heard bullets whistling high overhead, coming from the town and going in the direction of the hospital.

When he got to the Company B barracks, Sanders picked up his rifle, strapped it diagonally over his shoulder and across his back. He grabbed a lantern and the company roster—and rushed to the parade ground where he gave the command, "Company B, fall in!"

Although most of the soldiers lined up in their usual positions, a few men assumed the prone position, lying on their stomachs. Some dropped to their knees, trying to avoid being in the line of fire.

"Stand up!" Sanders ordered. "Stand up! If you get killed, you will die like a soldier."

"Dim your lantern! You'll get all of us killed. I hear bullets whistling over our heads," Holomon complained.

"Don't you think I hear 'em? Those shots are high and wild. They wouldn't even hit Maggie's drawers,"[3] Sanders responded.

"Why don't you put out that light, sergeant?" Holomon pleaded. "It'll draw fire. You're gonna get us all killed,"

By this time, Sergeant Sanders was getting annoyed with Holomon. "Damn the light and you, too, Holomon. Stand up before I kick your God damned guts out!"

That was enough to convince the ground huggers to get up. All the men fell in line—and while Mingo Sanders called the muster roll, bullets from Winchesters, Mausers and Remingtons whizzed high over their heads.

Lt. Lawrason, the company commander, heard the shots, got dressed and rushed out of the officers' quarters. He reached his company just as Sanders began calling the roll. Each man in line repeated his name and yelled, "Present!"

"All present or accounted for, sir," Sanders reported to Lawrason.

Lieutenant Lawrason took two steps forward, facing B Company. "Prepare to defend the fort. Issue ammunition. Take up your defensive positions. Hold your fire. Wait for orders to shoot from me."

---

3 'Maggie's drawers' was the soldier's slang for missing the whole target during rifle practice, when the red flag is waved at the shooter.

When First Sergeant Jacob Frazier, Company D, heard the first two shots, he wasted no time getting dressed. A six-foot, four-inch giant of a man who towered over most of the men in his company, Frazier won the allegiance and loyalty of his men through patient instruction, gentleness and persuasion—and showing toughness by his own example. Frazier had served 14 years in the army. He and his wife Hattie lived in army quarters next door to Mingo Sanders and his wife.

Frazier, partially dressed in his trousers and shoes, raced to Company D's barracks, but Captain Samuel P. Lyon, his company commander, beat him there.

The noncommissioned officer in charge of quarters, commonly known as the CQ, heard the call to arms and quickly unlocked the gun racks. Since the men already had their rifles in hand, Captain Lyon issued a quick order. His voice was urgent. "Sergeant! Get the men downstairs. Get them lined up as quickly as possible, call the roll, deploy in a skirmish line facing the town, fire on my order and shoot to kill!"

Lyon had been in the army more than 14 years. He was a no-nonsense officer, hardened in combat in Cuba, a strict disciplinarian and a man of few words who would rather shoot than talk. He came up through the ranks from an enlisted man and gained instant social status by marrying a general's daughter.

Lyon stood a half step behind Sergeant Frazier, looking over Frazier's shoulder as he called the roll. When the roll call was completed, Lyon wasn't satisfied. He had a tough time seeing in the darkness, and because he wanted to be doubly sure of the roll call count, he ordered, "Do it again, sergeant! Move quickly, go down the line, look into each man's face, get nose to nose!"

Sergeant Frazier did as he was ordered. He called the roll a second time, and reported, "All present or accounted for, sir!"

"Who are you accounting for? Who's absent, sergeant?"

"Corporal Charles Hawkins and Private Walter Johnson, sir!" Sergeant Frazier reminded Lyon that he had signed a three-day pass for the two absent men, and apparently, they were unaware of the cancellation of all passes. Their whereabouts settled, D Company was ready to move to its defensive position.

All the companies were assembling simultaneously as the raiders continued shooting in Brownsville, firing high over Fort Brown. All had completed their roll call and accounted for their men except C Company which was in a state of chaos.

Sergeant Brawner, the C Company charge of quarters, was making routine inspection checks of C Company when he heard shots and the call to arms. Stopping his routine inspection checks, Brawner immediately went looking for Sergeant Harley. Harley was acting as first sergeant for the official first sergeant who was away at rifle competition at Fort Riley, Kansas. Brawner knew the first sergeant's duty was to assemble his men, when the call to arms was sounded. Brawner turned the corner from the upstairs hall and was about to go down the staircase when he saw Sergeant Harley coming up the stairs.

"Sergeant Harley, I am going to open the gun racks."

Harley looked shocked. "What for? Are you crazy?"

"We're being attacked!"

Harley was skeptical. "You must be joking. Who's attacking us?"

Brawner became impatient with Harley. Determined to open the gun racks, he yelled, "How do I know? The shots are coming from town. I have the keys. I'm going to open the racks."

Sergeant Harley pulled rank on Brawner. "No, you're not. I am the acting first sergeant. Wait for orders! I didn't hear any call to arms. You wait for orders!"

In disgust, Brawner brushed past Harley on his way down the staircase, turned around, looked up the stairs at Harley's back, and muttered, "You bonehead! You're gonna be shot dead some day waiting for orders." Then he took off running toward the guardhouse, looking for Captain Macklin, his company commander.

By this time, Major Penrose had made his way to C Company's barracks to find out for himself what was holding them up. The other two companies had already been deployed for defense of the fort. He was downstairs on the bottom porch when he heard men upstairs scrambling and shouting.

"Sergeant Harley," one of them said, "why don't you open these gun racks?"

Penrose yelled up the stairs, "Why don't you men hurry up and get down here?"

"We are not going to fall out without our guns to get killed," Private Rudy, the company gun repairman, shouted back.

"Why don't you get your guns?" Penrose shouted.

Looking down from the second-floor porch, a soldier tried to explain. "Sergeant Harley won't open the gun racks."

"What?" Penrose couldn't believe it.

"Says he is waiting on orders," the soldier yelled back.

Penrose went to the head of the staircase and issued Harley a direct order, "Sergeant Harley, this is your battalion commander. You get those gun racks open."

Harley was distraught. He had been given a direct order to open the gun racks, but he couldn't comply. "I can't, sir. I don't have the keys."

Penrose became highly agitated. "What are you talking about? What do you mean, sergeant? Who has the keys?"

"Sergeant Brawner, sir. He just left, looking for Captain Macklin."

"Get the ax! Break the locks! Get them open some way. Get the ax! Get the ax!"

A soldier standing outside heard Major Penrose screaming. He ran to the woodshed, found the ax, ran up the stairs and broke open the gun racks. One by one, the men picked up their rifles, hurried down the stairs and finally fell in line.

Sergeant Harley realized his mistake in refusing to authorize Sergeant Brawner to open the gun racks. He knew Major Penrose was going chew him out when he saw him coming toward him, hollering. "Sergeant Harley, get these men organized. Call the roll. Where in the hell is your company commander?"

Harley attempted to offer an explanation. "I didn't hear the call to ..."

"Forget that. Where's Captain Macklin?"

"I don't know. Maybe he's in his quarters."

Major Penrose walked over to the first soldier in line and put his finger on Private Clifford I. Adair's chest. "Soldier, you go to Captain Macklin's quarters. Tell him to meet me at his company's defensive position, immediately!"

Penrose sent for Captain Lyon and ordered him to take a patrol into town to search for Macklin. Major Penrose put

Lieutenant Grier in charge of Company C until Captain Macklin could be found.

Penrose issued his final orders to the company commanders. "Defend your sectors of the fort. Do not allow anyone to enter the garrison. You are not to fire under any circumstance unless it is for the preservation of life. Your men are not to fire unless you order them. And you are not to fire unless I order you to do so. I will be stationed at the Central Gate. Return to your companies on the defense line."

When the shooting had died down and Macklin still had not shown up, Penrose really began to worry. Macklin was officer of the day. Had he heard the shooting? Had he jumped over the wall on the town side? Had some harm come to him? Penrose sent for Captain Lyon and ordered him to take a patrol into town to search for Macklin.

Lyon took his whole company, formed a patrol, and before heading out of the fort into the darkness, he issued the patrol order. "We are going into Brownsville to find Captain Macklin. This is a search patrol, not a combat patrol, but we will be in combat formation. The situation dictates that I am the point man. Keep your interval, and if fired upon, return the fire immediately. Do not wait for an order. Follow me!"

They searched the lower part of Garrison Road first. They continued to the upper part, then along Madison Street until they reached 12th Street near the county jail. There the patrol encountered 40 or 50 men armed with rifles, shotguns and pistols standing in front of the jail.

At first sight of the crowd, Dorsie Willis warned Lyon, "Captain! Those men have guns."

With that warning, the soldiers took a defensive posture. They knelt down with their guns drawn and pointing at the armed men.

Standing at the head of the patrol, and with his right hand on his pistol, Lyon called out, "Who are you?"

"Officers of the law! Officers of the law!" a man shouted.

Lyon wanted clarification. "Stand back! I want to speak to the sheriff!"

A man standing amongst the men spoke up quickly. "I'm the sheriff." He stepped out in front of the crowd. "It's me, Captain Lyon. I'm Celedonio Garza."

"I'm looking for Captain Macklin. Have you seen him?"

"I don't know any man by that name. Wouldn't know him if I saw him."

Captain Lyon didn't like the sheriff's answer. "Tell me, sheriff, do you have a white man in your jail?"

"No, I have one man in jail, and he's black."

Captain Lyon was curious. "Is he a soldier? What's his name?"

The sheriff was eager to deny that he had any soldiers in jail. "Why no. It's old Mack Hamilton. I just put him in for safe keeping. Captain, who's doing this shooting?"

"I don't know," he answered. And with that, the patrol moved out, turned left on 12th Street and continued the search for Macklin.

NINE

DID THE SOLDIERS

———— ⚬⚬⚬ ————

Shoot Up the Town?

"He's gone."

As suddenly as it began, the shooting stopped. The raiders vanished into the night, creating a mystery as to their identity in the mind of the mayor. He was baffled. *Who were they?* A chorus of clamoring voices filled his ears with answers.

"I saw colored soldiers."

"I heard coarse voices."

"I saw big bulky men jumping the wall."

"It was the nigger soldiers, all right. It couldn't have been anybody else. Everybody knows it was the niggers."

"I know it was the soldiers because I saw their khaki uniforms."

"Mayor, we told you to keep them out of our town. Now look what they gone and done."

Some of their reasoning didn't make sense, but some of the townspeople were certain they saw "colored" soldiers. Fred Combe wanted to believe them, but he was doubtful. There was no question in his mind that some of the people saw the raiders. But did they see black soldiers? And how the black soldiers could have done it was a mystery to him. He was not yet ready to join the citizen chorus blaming the soldiers. The question looming in his mind was, who had the raiders really been? And, just as important, why?

But for now the mayor was concerned with the safety and status of his policemen. He stood in front of Crixels' Saloon, receiving a disturbing piecemeal report on the status of his officers from Connors, the chief of police.

"I heard Dominguez got shot out of the saddle," said Connors. "Don't know his condition or where he is. It's rumored that he was killed, but somebody said they saw him crawling on the ground away from his horse. Three other men are missing, Macedonio Ramirez, Florencio Briseno and Jose Coronado."

Hearing such bad news gave the mayor reason to think that the raiders were trying to wipe out his police force. He had better wait for the facts, he chastised himself. Saying nothing to his police chief, he lowered his head and continued walking down Elizabeth Street with a policeman.

Not too far away, he saw something that appeared to be a pile of bodies stacked up on the sidewalk. As he drew closer to the corner of 13th and Elizabeth Streets in front of Sam Wreford's office, he realized it was a horse. The animal contorted its body, writhed about, twitched its hind legs.

"That's Lieutenant Dominguez's horse." The policeman pointed his pistol at the horse's head. "Want me to put him out of his suffering?"

He shook his head. "No, no need. The horse is in the throes of death. He'll be dead in a second. A pity. We don't need to hear any more shooting."

As the mayor crossed the street going toward the Miller Hotel, a man called out to him, "Mayor, they can see you from the garrison. Don't go out in the street."

Believing that he would not be harmed by any soldier from Fort Brown, and still doubtful that the soldiers had caused the trouble, the mayor crossed the street anyway.

A bright light burned in the hotel, but no one was in the lobby. Convinced that the frightened hotel guests were hiding, he stood in the courtyard and called out, "Does anyone know anything about this shooting?"

He didn't get an answer.

Suddenly, a man in his pajamas bolted through the front door and ran past him without saying a word.

Only seeing the disappearing back of the man, the mayor couldn't tell who he was. From his limp, he guessed that it was the hotel clerk. Seeing the limping man's fright gave the mayor pause—and he rethought his intention to go to the post and consult with Major Penrose. While he still harbored doubts about the culpability of the soldiers, he remembered the old cliché that caution is the better part of valor. He turned around and walked back up Elizabeth Street, warning citizens as he went along, "Don't go near the garrison."

What disturbed the mayor most was the sight of an old man running toward him, gasping for air. "Mayor Combe, Mayor Combe," wheezed the man. "You are wanted at the Ruby Saloon. The Justice of the Peace wants you to examine a dead body."

When Combe reached the Ruby Saloon, a huge crowd of people, even larger than what he had seen earlier when he passed on the other side of the street, had congregated at the front of the saloon. They were silent, as if they were attending their own wake, heads hung low. They barely moved. But when the mayor approached, they respectfully opened a path to let him through. When he got to the door, it was locked.

Tillman had the good sense not to let any more onlookers in before the place got packed.

Tillman let the mayor in and directed him to the courtyard of the Ruby Saloon, where the coroner was waiting on him to examine the body of Frank Natus. Frank was lying in the pool of blood where he had fallen. The mayor knelt down, lifted up Frank's left wrist, felt his pulse, looked at the wound and noticed that he had been hit with a single shot at close range, apparently with a large caliber gun. He shook his head, "Poor fellow, he's gone. His body is cold." He closed Natus' eyes and removed the nickel-plated Smith and Wesson pistol from the corpse's right hand. Natus clutched the gun fiercely as if he were still expecting it to save him.

When the mayor came out of the Ruby Saloon, some of the people wanted to know if the young bartender was going to make it. Others wanted to know if the doctor could save him, while others, who had heard that Natus was already dead, wanted to know if he was really dead.

Passing through the crowd, Mayor Combe said simply, "He's gone."

"Justice comes at the end of a rope."

Katie Leahy and Judge Parks had been looking for Louis Cowen. They stood on the outskirts of the crowd with Anna Cowen and her children in tow, trying to console her. When Anna Cowen heard the mayor confirm the bartender's death, she began sobbing. "The soldiers tried to kill us, too! They tried to kill us! Where is Louis? Where is Louis?"

Katie Leahy grabbed her by the shoulders and shook her. "Anna! Get a grip on yourself, woman. This is no time for hysterics."

Judge Parks, who was known for his compassion, spoke up. "Go easy on her, Katie. She's scared—like the rest of us."

Leahy sneered at the judge, "Fearful? I don't know what you're talking about. I don't know what the word 'fear' means."

By now Anna Cowen had calmed down, but her plaintive cries that the black soldiers tried to kill her and her children stung the mayor. Leaning her head on Katie Leahy's shoulder, she was a pitiful sight. Combe began changing his mind about the culpability of the soldiers. Maybe they did do it. The mayor stepped closer to Anna Cowen, "Mrs. Cowen, did you see the soldiers?"

"No, sir, I didn't have to see them. Amada, here," pointing to the maid, "saw them."

Before the mayor could ask Amada, Katie Leahy interrupted. "I saw 'em. One of them was a freckled-faced, yellow nigger. He stepped in a mud puddle, when his gun jammed."

During his search for Louis Cowen, Judge Parks learned that Policeman Dominguez escaped serious injury. He'd crawled away from his dying horse and someone helped him into the nearby drug store. Judge Parks said, "Dominguez is okay, shot in the arm. Two other policemen are missing. I fear they're dead."

"Oh, Lord! How could I have forgotten?" Katie Leahy covered her mouth and looked embarrassed.

"Forgot what?" The mayor asked, bewildered.

"They're safe in my bathroom."

"In your bathroom? The policemen are in your bathroom? Is the door locked?"

"No, sir. Just closed."

"And they can come out anytime?"

"Yes, sir, but I told them not to come out until I told them to do so."

The mayor shook his head, wondering if Katie Leahy would ever learn to mind her own business.

As he moved away from the group, their mood turned ugly. The respectful silence and deference the mayor usually enjoyed vanished. The already huge crowd swelled as more angry people ran in from all parts of town. They were armed with a variety of weapons—Winchester rifles, old-style military Krag rifles, pistols, and shotguns. People ran about, shouting, "The soldiers shot up the town! They killed Frank!"

The crowd quickly grew into an angry mob. Raising their arms over their heads and waving their guns, they yelled, "Let's go down to the post. Let's go down to the post and do those fellows up."

Tempers boiled over. Arguments began breaking out between those who wanted to charge the fort immediately and those urging calm.

"Get the hell outta my way! Let me through! I'm going now," one man demanded. He was not alone.

The mayor looked at Judge Parks who stood a short distance from him. "Get me a box or something to stand on."

Judge Parks saw a large wooden barrel full of water, sitting at the edge of the street. It was used to dampen the dirt on the street. "Wouldn't it be useful to dunk some of these hotheads in this water barrel?" he said. He tilted it over to empty it, rolled it to a clear spot, stood it up—and helped the mayor climb on top.

Fred Combe raised his hands and tried to speak. "Please calm down, I have something to…." But the noise drowned him out. He waved his arms up and down, trying to quiet the crowd, as if he were about to begin one of his campaign speeches. Nobody paid any attention. Judge Parks handed him a shotgun and the mayor fired a single blast into the air. The crowd startled. Having gun blast so near to their ears got their attention. Nobody ran toward the fort. The mayor started speaking.

"I appeal to you, first as your mayor, and next as an ex-Army officer, not to rush that fort. As I told you a week or so ago, I served with those troops. I know them to be as efficient as any in the world. They are splendidly armed. If you go down there, many valuable lives will be lost. Besides that, you are within the law now. Remain so, and we will get justice."

Even though they'd quieted down, the frightened citizens were still restless.

"Justice comes at the end of a rope for murderers," one man yelled.

"That's right," the mayor shot back. "But after a trial, not a lynching."

Seeming to give a bit, the man spoke of Texas' honor and shifted the burden squarely on the mayor's courage. "Our honor is at stake. We're Texans! You go tell Penrose to give up the guilty sons of bitches now, or we'll go and take 'em."

The mayor got the message. Either he went to see Penrose or the mob would go. The decision to the dilemma was easy. "All right, I'll go," the mayor replied.

"Now, how are you gonna do that without getting shot?" Kate Leahy spoke up again. "Don't risk your life, mayor. You're not a stupid man. Don't you go acting like one now."

"I'll crawl down the sidewalk within hailing distance of the guards," Combe said. "When they hear my voice, they'll let me in. Go to your homes. I'll call Major Penrose on the phone. We'll get this ironed out and punish the guilty parties."

The crowd began to disperse. The mayor went inside the Ruby Saloon, but even after numerous tries, he was unable to get Penrose on the telephone.

It was about 1:30 in the morning. Not having found Captain Macklin anywhere in town, the patrol was headed back down Elizabeth Street to the fort, when they came upon the mayor surrounded by the last few stragglers from the crowd.

When he saw the soldiers take defensive postures, the mayor stepped forward and called out, "Captain Lyon, order your men not to shoot." To reassure Captain Lyon that the small group of men with him were not hostile, the mayor turned and pointed to the men in back of him. "All these men with me are officers of the law! I need to talk to Major Penrose. Take me to him."

The soldiers lowered their weapons at the order of their captain.

"I'll provide armed escort for you only and your uniformed policemen," Captain Lyon said. "Tell the other men to get back!"

"It's okay." The mayor pointed to the other men. "You can go home. We won't need you anymore tonight."

They all started to move away except Joe Combe, who said, "Captain, I'm Doctor Joe Combe, the mayor's brother."

"Okay, you can join us."

The two Combe brothers joined the captain at the head of the column and together they marched down Elizabeth Street toward the fort.

"Have you seen anything of Captain Macklin?" Lyon asked the mayor.

"No." The mayor was concerned. He and Macklin were close friends.

"We cannot find him anywhere on post, and we're afraid he's been done away with in town," Lyon said.

"That's nonsense." The mayor dismissed that notion.

Stationed just back of the Central Gate, Major Penrose saw Captain Lyon and the patrol returning. At the head of the column with Captain Lyon were the two Combe brothers, but there was no sign of Macklin. He wanted to rush out to meet them, but he was frozen in place. Finally, he managed to shout out, "Lyon! Did you find Macklin?"

"No, sir," Lyon called, as they marched toward the gate. "I'm going over to the officers' quarters and look around for him myself." He sent the patrol back to the company's defensive position and headed across the parade field.

By now, three soldiers had been dispatched to Macklin's quarters. The first soldier knocked on Macklin's door. "Captain Macklin! Captain Macklin! Major Penrose wants to see you."

"All right," Macklin answered. Not fully awake, he turned over and went back to sleep.

Because Macklin never showed up, the second soldier arrived and knocked on Macklin's door. "Captain Macklin! Captain Macklin! Major Penrose wants you to come now."

"All right," the soldier heard him say. But Macklin went back to sleep again.

The third soldier pounded on a door he thought was the right door. "Captain Macklin! Major Penrose is looking for you." When there was no answer, the soldier left, too.

The first two soldiers had not reported back to Major Penrose that they had spoken to Macklin, because they assumed he'd gotten up. The third soldier reported that Macklin didn't answer, but it turned out that he'd knocked on the wrong door.

Major Penrose then sent Corporal Burdette to Macklin's quarters.

Corporal Burdett met Private Hairston, the sentinel on duty near Macklin's quarters. The sentinel said to Burdett, "I know he's in there. He answers, but he won't get up."

Corporal Burdett slung his rifle off his shoulder. "Come with me, I'll get him up." Both men went to Macklin's door. Burdette banged the butt of his rifle against the door three times.

"Captain Macklin, they're shooting on the officers' quarters!"

Macklin leapt straight up fully clothed. He'd fallen asleep in his uniform. Stumbling over the empty beer bottle on the floor, he flung the door open. "What's the trouble? What's the trouble?" Not waiting for an answer, he bounded down the stairs and ran full speed across the parade ground.

Back at the central gate, Major Penrose greeted the mayor politely, and acknowledged the presence of the two uniformed policemen with a lackluster wave of his hand. However, he was curious about the other person. "Mayor Combe, who is this other man with you?"

"This is my brother, Dr. Joe Combe. I don't believe you've met him."

Deliberately not reaching to shake his hand, Major Penrose was all business. "No, I have not. I hope he can help you explain what all this shooting is about. Come inside the gate."

The mayor sensed that Penrose was trying to shift the burden of blame directly upon his constituents and by proxy upon his shoulders. The chilly reception indicated that he was attempting to do just that. The mayor realized that politically it was no time to straddle the fence. He made up his mind in that instant to join his citizens in blaming the soldiers.

"To the contrary, sir, you and your officers have some explaining to do. Your men have gone into town and killed one man, seriously wounded the lieutenant of police, killed his horse, and shot into several houses."

To say Penrose was shocked to hear those accusations would be an understatement. Furthermore, they presented grave implications for his command—and for him personally. "Doctor, I can hardly believe that. I am told that the citizens fired on the post."

"No! Your men fired on my citizens. They were seen by several people."

"By whom? How can they be sure they saw soldiers in this black, moonless, cloudy night?"

"By several people, I tell you, Major."

"I can't believe it, doctor. I have had a roll call. The men are all present or accounted for. Some of your people fired at my command."

Mayor Combe was getting exasperated. "Major, who is the officer of the day? He ought to be able to shed some light on this."

Major Penrose told Mayor Combe that Macklin was the officer of the day, and reminded him that Captain Lyon was still looking for him.

"Inspect your barracks for bullet holes."

Captain Lyon walked across the parade field toward the officers' quarters. In the distance, he saw someone who looked like Captain Macklin running toward him. When he got closer, he recognized that it *was* Captain Macklin. Lyon was glad to see him.

"Where have you been, Ed? We've been searching all over for you."

"Asleep in my quarters," Macklin answered, surprised at seeing all the activity around him.

"You better go and report to Major Penrose. He's at the central gate."

Mayor Combe and Major Penrose were still wrangling about who shot up the town when Captain Macklin rushed up to the two men, interrupted the conversation, and saluted Penrose. "Sir, I report!"

"My God, Captain Macklin! Where have you been?"

"I have been asleep in my quarters."

"I sent three men looking for you. When you never reported in, I assumed the worst for you. You mean to tell me that you were sleeping in your quarters all that time, and you never heard any of that shooting?" Then he softened his voice, relieved to find that his best friend, Ed Macklin, was still alive.

"My God, Ed, I am glad to see you. Take command of your company."

"Yes, sir," Macklin said in a whisper, clearly embarrassed.

Mayor Combe expressed his relief at Macklin's safety. "Thank heavens you're safe, Ed, and not involved in this mess." Then he related his assessment of the meeting to Major Penrose. "Major, we've not accomplished anything here tonight except to butt heads. Don't allow any of your officers or men come into town under any circumstances, as the people are very much wrought up."

Major Penrose agreed. "I'll issue an order at once that no man is to leave the fort."

Hoping to keep peace, the mayor readily made a promise that he knew would be difficult to keep. "I'll keep the citizens in town."

"No one will be allowed on post except you," Penrose added.

Relieved that he had reached an agreement with Penrose, and believing that all of the soldiers were back at the fort, the mayor was satisfied that he had prevented a deadly confrontation between the townspeople and the soldiers. He and his group left.

Penrose walked over to C Company's defensive position and gave Captain Macklin a new order. "Ed, redeploy your company to maintain defense of the fort. I'm sending B and D Companies back to the barracks. Make sure no man cleans his weapon. Conduct a full shakedown inspection at daylight, after reveille. Conduct a rifle inspection, verify ammunition and check your barracks for bullet holes."

He then made his way to B and D Companies and relieved them. At about 3:15 a.m., he issued an order. "Make sure all guns are locked up. Conduct a shake down inspection at daylight. I want a rifle inspection after reveille. Verify ammunition. Oh yes, I almost forgot. Inspect your barracks for bullet holes."

After milling around from bar to bar, restaurant to restaurant and crowd to crowd, Louis Cowen went home about two o'clock in the morning. His wife, his children, and the maid had gone home with Katie Leahy and were staying with her. Not knowing this fact, Cowen didn't go to Katie's hotel.

Katie Leahy sat on Cowen's porch, waiting for him.

Cowen staggered up to the gate with a brown paper bag in his hand. In it, he had sandwiches and a bottle of Schlitz beer. In his back pocket, he had what was left of a half pint of whiskey.

Katie Leahy met him at the gate of his house. She gave him a piece of her mind. "Where have you been, you lousy cuss?"

"Get outta my way, Katie. I gotta protect my family."

"You been drinking."

"Gotta protect my family," he pulled on a section of the white picket fence, thinking it was the gate, not recognizing that the gate was already standing wide open.

"They're not in there, Louis. Anna and the children are at my hotel."

"I'm gonna sue the government for fifty thousand dollars," Cowen threatened, his voice slurring.

Katie Leahy started to walk away. "I'm sick of listening to you. I'm going home."

"I'll stand guard," Cowen said.

"Guard what? Don't be ridiculous. You guard me?" Katie Leahy went to her hotel.

Louis Cowen followed her there. He lit a lantern and sat in the Leahy Hotel yard the rest of the night, without a gun, believing he was guarding his family.

"This is a shakedown."

There was no more hostile activity against the fort for the rest of the night, and no one heard any more shooting. At dawn, Major Penrose withdrew Company C from its defensive position, and Captain Macklin marched his company back to their barracks for the shakedown inspection. The shakedown was kept secret from all the enlisted men and even from the battalion sergeant major. All soldiers were ordered to their barracks and instructed not to leave.

The commanders of all three companies walked into their respective company barracks and announced:

This is a shakedown, a full shakedown. Non-commissioned officers block the doors. Everybody strip down to your underwear. Dump your footlockers on your beds. Dump all bags on the floor.

A most thorough inspection was conducted, but no unauthorized ammunition, pistols, knives or other contraband was found.

Just at the conclusion of the shakedown, the bugler sounded assembly. The men hustled into their uniforms and stood reveille at precisely 5:30 a.m. At that time an inspection of all rifles was made. No residue of gunpowder was found in any rifles or any evidence that any of the guns had been fired.

After the inspection, Macklin decided he would go outside the garrison gate into Brownsville and look around. At the mouth of Cowen's Alley, he spotted something that shook him to his knees. He couldn't believe his eyes. *It can't be*, he thought. He picked up several empty cartridge shells, rolled them around in his hand, looked at them in disbelief and then put them in his pocket. He picked up six empty clips. "Oh, no!" he cried. It was no mirage. The empty cartridge shells and empty clips had been made for the Army's new Springfield rifle, 1903 Model.

Putting the other damaging evidence in his pockets, Macklin stood up, looked around guardedly and went directly to the administration building where he found a despondent Penrose sitting at his desk. Taking the empty shells and empty clips from his pockets, he walked over to Penrose and, holding the curious evidence in both hands, he showed it to him. "Look what I found in Cowen's Alley."

Penrose examined the empty shells and empty clips. He took off his glasses, looked at the evidence again and put his glasses back on. Then he took his glasses off again and dropped his arm by his side, the glasses dangling in his hand. "Well, Macklin," he said sadly. "It looks as if our men are responsible for this shooting."

Penrose was in a state of shock. He still couldn't believe it. On the one hand, all men were present or accounted for, and there was no evidence that any weapons were fired. On the other hand, here was this bizarre evidence of shells and clips. What was he to make of it? Did his men shoot up the town? Were they murderers? He was desperate and needed advice. He knew he had to conduct a preliminary investigation before he reported anything to his regimental commander. Since Macklin had found those spent shells, there must be more in the streets that other people would surely find and turn over to Mayor Combe. Combe would probably come to confront him anytime now. He would have to admit what he now was sure was the truth, and he dreaded meeting with the mayor again.

He debated with himself. "I'll talk with Creager, that's what I'll do. No, I won't talk to Creager. He's too narrow minded. He's too prejudiced against Negroes. He's a bigot, but he's all I got. I'll call Creager."

Renfro B. Creager was an attorney. He was also the United States Commissioner and the deputy clerk of the United States District Court for the Southern District of Texas. When Penrose called, Creager responded promptly.

They met in Penrose's office and after a brief exchange, Penrose was convinced that Creager could not be of any help at all. Talking with him would be of no value.

But before the meeting broke up, Penrose heard the knock on his door that he had been dreading. It was Mayor Combe. He joined the meeting and promptly confronted Penrose with one clip with one cartridge in it and about seven empty shells. "Major Penrose," he demanded. "What do you think of this evidence? Your men did this."

"Where did you get that?"

"About two o'clock this morning I stepped on these shells at the corner of the Miller Hotel alley, and..."

"Are there more?" Penrose asked, examining them.

Mayor Combe's attitude turned haughty. "Yeah. About daybreak I picked up some empty shells in front of Mr. Stark's house. He also found some, and turned them over to me. Mr. Houghton turned over some ball cartridges this morning."

"Live, ball ammunition?" Penrose raised an eyebrow.

"Yeah."

The mayor's arrogance in presenting the physical evidence showed. His tone cut Penrose deeply. Penrose felt that the mayor knew he had him on the run, forcing him to nearly concede his men's culpability for raiding the town.

"Combe," he said, "this is almost conclusive evidence, but who did it and how they did it, I don't know. It's a mystery to me."

Creager and Fred Combe left together, leaving Penrose confused.

TEN

PANIC

❧

In Brownsville

"The soldiers have to go."

ON THEIR WAY BACK to City Hall after they left the meeting with Penrose, Mayor Combe and Commissioner Creagar discussed what to do next.

Creager was blunt. "Fred, you got to get these soldiers out of town. You have no other choice."

From past meetings and discussions with Creager, Combe knew Creager was no friend of the "Negro." In fact, he hadn't wanted the black soldiers in Brownsville in the first place. Yet, he believed Creager was right in his conclusion that the soldiers must go. "You're right. But don't you think we need a group of citizens to investigate?"

"All that matters now is to get all of them out of town," Creager insisted.

Shoulders slumped and head hung low, Combe mounted the steps of City Hall in deep thought. "Creager is right. All of the soldiers have to go. My town is in a state of panic."

Fred Combe assessed the situation correctly on that Tuesday morning, August 14, the day after the attack. It was a day that began with fear and uncertainty. The air was thick with rumors. People were on the edge. Imaginations ran wild.

The townspeople believed all kinds of preposterous things—that drunken soldiers were roaming the streets, plundering homes, raping women, snatching babies from their mother's arms, and shooting and killing at will.

White men locked their women and children behind closed doors and ordered them not to venture out for any reason. Some people fled to Matamoros, others to outlying ranches. Anna Cowen was one of them. But she remembered her prayer and her promise to God to give thanks if He allowed her to live through the shooting. She went to church before she fled to the country.

Armed angry white men roamed the streets expecting to find that their town had suffered major damage. But they didn't find the pillaging they had imagined. They looked for bullet holes and picked up empty shell casings and clips. They entered the bloodstained courtyard of the Ruby Saloon and compared stories on how many shots they heard, how many raiders they saw. Horrified, they stared at the dead horse still lying in the street. By now, a long line had formed in front of Cowen's house and curiosity seekers were going through it. Overnight, it became like a museum or tourist attraction.

After leaving Creager, Fred Combe cloistered himself in his office and listened to his own inner counsel. He accepted Creager's advice to get rid of the black soldiers, but not until after an investigation. He called a meeting in his office to consult with two of the most prominent Republicans in town, Major Armstrong, a former army officer who still used his army title, and E. H. Goodrich, a former Grand Union soldier. The three concluded that the mayor should hold a "mass meeting of the thinking people in town" in the courtroom of the Federal courthouse at eleven o'clock.

A ranting crowd congregated in the center of town near City Hall, demanding to see Mayor Combe. "Get out here, Fred! Do something! We got to get these nigger soldiers out of town! Come out now! Stop hiding behind your desk!"

"Behind his desk? He's hiding under his desk," Sam Wreford interjected.

"We've waited long enough!" Al Billingsley shouted.

The mayor recognized Sam Wreford's high-pitched voice and was immediately agitated. *That Wreford just won't go away. I better get outside and lay down the law.* The mayor's face was tense, his jaws tight, his eyes puffy and surrounded by dark circles. He hadn't gotten much sleep and was near exhaustion. But he braced himself, went outside, and confronted the crowd.

"I'll arrest anybody who keeps this up," Mayor Combe called out, "especially you, Al Billingsley. And as for you, Sam, I'll have you deported. As for the rest of you, my good, law-abiding citizens, meet me at the Federal courthouse, in the courtroom, at eleven o'clock. I need your help to resolve this problem."

When the sheriff and two policemen came out and stood near Mayor Combe, the threat of imminent arrest worked. The crowd quieted down and Combe went back to his office to prepare for the mass meeting. He didn't want to make a fool of himself, for he knew his credibility was on the line this time—more so than ever before.

At eleven o'clock the court room was packed with people with an overflow that spilled outside onto the steps and into the street. Captain Kelly, the old banker, said to the mayor, "I think all the respectable citizens are here."

"How many do you think?"

"I guess about five hundred, including the folks outside."

The mayor stood at the podium and called on the chief of police to give an assessment of the casualties and damages, and then he sat down.

The chief had been busily going up and down the streets all morning, in and out of houses and buildings, talking to people, looking for damage and injured people. He had just about completed writing his report and was making a few last minutes changes when he was called on. He went to the podium, looked over the crowd, and announced, without preamble, "Pray for Frank Natus. Last night we lost him." He paused for a few seconds before continuing, "Police Lieutenant Dominguez was shot in the arm, but he's okay."

Then the chief began to read from his report. "As it turned out, God almighty was with us. Only a few houses and buildings were hit. Cowen's house took the worst of it. The soldiers shot it up pretty bad. Anna Cowen and her children barely escaped death. Fred Stark's house took some terrible hits. They almost killed his three little girls."

The chief stopped reading his report for a few seconds, looked to the back of the crowded room where Fred Starck stood. He spoke directly to Starck. "Fred, I don't have to tell you that you're a lucky man. You and your wife, yourselves, barely escaped death."

Fred Starck nodded in agreement, but there was something else on his mind, *Did Avila have something to do with this?*

Starck was a U. S. custom officer, who enjoyed quite a reputation for chasing and catching smugglers inside Texas along the Mexican border. His arrest record had been high— more than 600 smugglers captured and jailed. However, of late, the smugglers seemed to be evading Starck's traps. His capture rate had plummeted.

One night recently Starck was chasing a smuggler on foot along the border. When he finally caught up with the man, he hit him in the back of the head with his revolver and knocked him to the ground. Starck prided himself in having never killed a smuggler, but now his reputation was at stake. It was time for him to make an example, to send a message. He put the barrel of his pistol to the back of the man's head. As he was about to fire, a familiar voice cried, "Mr. Starck, don't kill me. It's me, Avila."

Starck stepped back, the barrel of his revolver shaking in his trembling hand, "No! No! No! Not you, Avila. How could you go back to smuggling after I trusted you—and gave you a second chance?"

"I needed the money. Please, please let me go!"

That voice was convincing. It was also pleasant. Starck had liked it at once, when he first arrested Avila years ago for smuggling. It was that voice that convinced Starck to get Avila out of jail, to trust him and to give him a job in his house. In time, Avila became almost one of the family.

But it was obvious that Avila had betrayed Stark by tipping off smugglers about the techniques and the plans he used to apprehend them. Starck's anger dissipated into disappointment, and he said, "I hate to do this, but I must take you in. Get on your feet."

Later, Avila jumped bail and went into hiding. Starck wondered if smugglers shot up the town. *Where is Avila?*

The Way of the Heathen

The chief continued reading, "They fired into Yturria's house at Washington and 15th Street, the Telegraph house and Tillman's Saloon. Some of you call it the Ruby Saloon. That's where poor Frank got it. The Miller's Hotel had a bullet hole in the jamb of one of the windows on the alley side and was hit twice in the brickwork on 13th Street. There was a bullet hole in the door of Mr. Wells' office on 13th Street, and one bullet hole in Wreford's office. A few lamp posts here and there and a building column or two got hit. Preciado claims he was grazed. That was about the extent of the damages and the casualties. Oh, yes, Old Gray. He suffered an agonizing death." The chief folded his papers and stepped down.

Mayor Combe took the podium and addressed the crowd. "My people, my good citizens, we had a terrible night. We had a night of terror! But as the chief said, our God stood watch over us. All those bullets flying around in the air, and only one soul was taken from us. Our God was here protecting us. The murderers took a young life, a young boy, just twenty-three years old. He was a good boy, an orphan. God took care of him when he was a baby. He found a home for him when he was abandoned. Last night, He, our God must have had a good reason for calling him home 'cause Frank had no enemies. And I want you to know, Frank is with our Lord! And our Lord is with us." The mayor paused and looked over the crowd before he resumed.

"And what I want you to understand is that we don't have to go out and avenge his death. I understand the fires that burn in your hearts because they also burn in mine. They urge you and me to action. Revenge urges us to take up arms, to take the law into our own hands, to move against the fort. But citizens, I have to tell you, that's not the way. It's not the American way. It's not the Christian way. It's the way of the heathen. It follows the path of the uncivilized. And if we go that way, it'll be the ruination of Brownsville, your town, my town, God's town!"

Fred Combe paused and asked for water. Captain Kelly handed him his fruit jar. After taking several sips, Combe dropped his voice into a pleading tone. "Now I agree with you that this hideous crime, this crime against God, was committed by some ruffians at Fort Brown. But we should not condemn all the men. So far most of them have comported themselves like good citizens, just like you and me. However..." The mayor saved the words the crowd wanted to hear for last. "All black soldiers and all the white officers must leave Brownsville. I demand this."

Abruptly, the mayor moved from behind the podium, stood in front of the crowd, balled up his fist, raised it above his head and shouted at the top of his voice. "I will go to the highest authority in Washington, to our president, my friend, the great Theodore Roosevelt. He will take these soldiers out of Brownsville, out of Texas. I guarantee you. I promise you. I promise my God! They will go. They will go. They will go—and never come back!

"I vow to you the guilty ones will be caught and brought to trial. They will be hanged at Fort Leavenworth." Then Combe raised his voice to a shout. "They will never walk upon this land again."

He lifted his chin up, tilted his head back and looking to the ceiling, stood on his tip toes and began leaping into the air, jumping up and down so fast that some in the crowd thought he was levitating.

He continued to yell, invoking God. "Oh, God, if I lie, if I lie, strike me dead now! Strike me dead, now!"

"Ah. Ah. Ah," the people uttered in agreement. Then they went wild, cheering as Combe's passion overflowed onto them. The people were captivated, mesmerized by the mayor's theatrics. It was politics mixed with old-time religion. It also brought hope to the minds of those who secretly wished to escape this new danger to their town—the new, deadly Springfield 03 rifle in the hands of rampaging soldiers. Combe's argument was compelling and soothing to them. They were convinced that their mayor would keep his promise.

By now, Combe was sweating profusely. Beads of perspiration rolled down his face. His shirt was dark with sweat. Although emotionally exhausted, he had still more to say. He pushed his hair back, took out a white handkerchief, wiped the perspiration from his face and looked over at Captain Kelly to his left. "Captain Kelly, I want you to select a committee of citizens to investigate the night of horrors. I am appointing you chairman. Select the best people. I will sit on the committee. I also appoint the sheriff and the chief of police. You select the rest. I will not accept NO from any man you select. Start now. Let's go and talk with Major Penrose now, today. We can't afford to wait."

ELEVEN

INVESTIGATION BY

The Citizens' Committee

"It's a mystery to me."

CAPTAIN KELLY LIKED TO boast that there was less racial prejudice in Brownsville than any other place in Texas. Nonetheless, he chose mostly Northern men who he considered had no special animus against Negroes—the county judge, Frank W. Kibbe; the city attorney, James A. Brown; an alderman, E. H. Goodrich, a Republican as well as a former Union soldier; Jesse O. Wheeler, the editor of the *Daily Herald*, and John G. Fernandez, a banker.

As soon as the committee was chosen, someone said, "Let's go to lunch."

Captain Kelly disagreed. "No, there's no time like the present. We'll go at once to see Major Penrose."

Major Penrose sat in his office with his elbows on his desk and his chin resting in the palms of his hands. He was a disturbed man, hopelessly perplexed, even dumbfounded by the contradictory evidence before him. He'd just finished reviewing the military records of the three noncommissioned officers in charge of quarters and had scrutinized their sworn statements. They swore that they had given the keys to no one. These men had been entrusted with the keys to the rifle racks and were accountable for keeping them locked. They were authorized to open them only upon orders or upon hearing the call to arms.

In his quandary, Penrose had absentmindedly placed the empty cartridge shells and two empty clips on top of the military records and sworn statements. Perhaps this was just a reflexive act, to hold the papers down and keep the breezes coming through the window from blowing them away. However, a gust of wind, seemingly from nowhere, blew through the window, whipped across his desk, and scattered not only the papers, but also the empty cartridges shells and empty ammunition clips. Penrose quickly picked up the papers, clips, and empty cartridge shells. While holding one of the shells, he noted something he had not observed before. The date on the base of the empty shell was missing.

Back at his desk, he sat down, laid the empty shells and clips back on top of the papers. He then reached in his desk, took out the Articles of War book, and placed it on top of the items on his desk. It was in this book that he would check the offenses he would have to charge the men with under military law.

He started talking to himself. "I know these are good men. They have impeccable records. They are right here in front of my eyes. I've never had any reason not to believe them in the past, yet now I must challenge their sworn statements and the validity of these records."

Penrose looked again at the empty shell casings and the empty clips lying on top of the men's records. This physical evidence did more than just act as a paper weight. It was a psychological barrier, keeping him from believing in his men, a conundrum befuddling his brain.

Penrose went over the information in his head again, reviewing fact after fact. All of the men in charge of the rifle racks swore that they kept them locked at all times, except when issuing rifles to the sentries for guard duty—and that they never left the rifle racks unattended at any time.

"If my men shot up the town," he asked himself, "where did they get the rifles? How did they get the rifles? What soldiers did it?" He continued to ponder. "I was out there when the rolls were called. All were present or accounted for. How then did this thing happen?"

Recognizing that he was not getting anywhere trying to reconcile the sworn statements with the physical evidence, he turned to the affidavit of Tamayo, the post scavenger. Tamayo swore that the shooting began on the town side of the garrison wall, and that he didn't see any soldiers shooting.

Three taps on his door startled Penrose, even though he knew it was the sergeant major. "Come in, Spottie."

"Sir, Captain Kelly, Mayor Combe, and several other people are here to see you."

"Take them to the staff room, I'll be right in. Tell Captain Lyon and Lieutenant Grier to meet me there"

They wasted no time with introductions. Kelly went directly to the point, "Major Penrose, your men did this shooting." He threw some empty cartridge shells across the table at Penrose. "There's the evidence. No one else has those arms or ammunition."

"It cannot be. I have the best battalion in my regiment. I know my men," Penrose said. "They could not be guilty of this outrage."

Kelly raised his eyebrow. "Well, who did the firing?"

Not all convinced himself, Penrose said, "I think it was an attack on the barracks from town."

Kelly raised his voice, "What? Have you examined your barracks and buildings? Nothing could be shot from the town without hitting them."

Penrose was forced to admit that none of the buildings at the fort showed signs of having been hit.

Mayor Combe was itching to lay out more physical evidence. Finally, he interjected, "Penrose, here are some more empty shells. They were given to me this morning after I met with you."

The room fell silent for a moment as Penrose held the empty shells, evidence he couldn't reconcile either in his mind or in his heart. "Gentlemen, I do not understand this at all. I do not know how my men could have done it. It's a mystery to me."

"They did it!" Captain Kelly said roughly, while the other committee members sat stone-faced.

Backed into a corner with what seemed to be overwhelming evidence, Penrose conceded, "I am afraid that's true." Then, with tears in his eyes, he added, "I would give my right arm to find out the guilty parties."

With that admission, Captain Kelly, Fred Combe and the rest of the members of the Citizen's Committee got up from the conference table and left without shaking hands or showing any other courtesies.

A despondent Penrose went back to his office and slumped in his chair. Then he picked up his pen and wrote the following telegram to the military secretary, Department of Texas, San Antonio:

Regret to report serious shooting in Brownsville last evening, in which one civilian was killed and the chief of police so seriously wounded that his right arm had to be amputated. Brownsville officials claim shooting was done by enlisted men of this command, and borne out in their opinion by empty shells and clips picked up in the streets.

He handed the message to Lieutenant Grier, the acting adjutant. "Take this to the telegraph office. Send it immediately."

"Send a telegram to the president."

When Kelly and his committee got back to town, he turned to the police chief. "Get somebody in here for us to talk to." Then they went to lunch.

After lunch, they went to Wells' law office, closed the drapes, and set up shop. A long mahogany conference table surrounded by heavy, dark brown leather chairs stood prominently in the middle of the room. The committee members took their seats. Kelly sat at the head of the table. The decorous and orderly setting of the law office with scores of law books aligned neatly on the shelves stood in sharp contrast to the mob scene outside. Armed vigilante groups patrolled the streets, ready for an old-fashioned lynching.

The police had no trouble finding people willing to talk to the committee. They pulled people in off the streets, all men, lined them up at the door, and ushered them in one by one. The committee immediately started taking testimony.

Captain Kelly, the chairman, greeted them by asking each one to state what they knew about "this attack of the Negroes on the town." He did not put any of them under oath or have them swear on the Bible. "You know the object of this meeting. We know that this outrage was committed by Negro soldiers. We want any and all information that will lead to the discovery of those who did it."

Charles S. Canada.

Questioner: We are inquiring into the matter of last night with a view to ascertaining who the guilty parties are. We know they were Negro soldiers. If there is anything that throws any light on the subject, we would like to have it.

Witness: I was raised among them. I know their voices pretty well. I heard one of them Negroes say, 'We got him.'

Questioner: Did you see them?

Witness: No. I know that coarse voice.

Miller Hotel Proprietor.

Witness: I heard someone shout, 'There goes the son of a bitch! Get him!'

Questioner: Did you see them?

Witness: No. I heard the coarse voice.

He finished his testimony by saying the voice came from the alley in back of the hotel.

C.C. Madison.

Witness: I heard someone say, 'Halt.'

Questioner: Did you see any soldiers?

Witness: No.

Dr. Thorn, dentist who lived near the Miller Hotel.

Witness: I heard the voices of two men. One said, 'There he goes, give him hell.' The other man said, 'God damn him!' It was a Negro's voice.

James P. McDonnel.

Witness: I knew there was bitter feelings in town and thought that if they caught any Negro soldiers uptown, they might do them up. So I laid awake, never pulled off my shoes. When I heard the shooting, I ran down Elizabeth Street to the alley between Washington Street and Elizabeth Streets. I heard more shots, just inside the garrison wall. I saw about twenty men assembled on the town side of the wall near the telegraph office. I have no idea where they came from.

Questioner: Did you see any soldiers jump the wall?

A: No.

Questioner: Were they Negro soldiers or white men?

A: I don't know if they were Negroes or white men, but they were United States soldiers.

Questioner: How do you know that?

McDonnel assured the city attorney that they were soldiers "because they wore uniforms," and left the stand.

George W. Rendall, one-eyed and hard of hearing

A retired mechanical engineer, Rendall had the habit of counting and measuring everything. He was a religious man. He lived almost on top of the fort near the main gate. Rendall ambled up to the head of the table, took his glasses off and laid them on the table.

Witness: Kelly, where is the Bible?

Questioner: Anybody got a Bible?

Committee: Indicates no.

Questioner: George, you don't need a Bible. Just tell the truth.

Witness: I want a Bible!

Questioner: George, you know the soldiers shot up the town, I know it, and our Lord Jesus Christ knows it. Now tell us what you saw and heard.

Witness: All right. Pistol shots woke me up at 10:00 p.m., fired close to my house, 60 feet from inside the garrison wall. When my wife and I went to the window, I could see soldiers moving back and forth inside the fort, and they were shooting. One man in particular. I watched the shots, seeing the fire leave the pistol. It was elevated in the air. I heard someone say, 'There he goes.' Then the men moved toward the wall. They were 150 feet from me."

Policeman Genaro Padron

Witness: I knew they were soldiers because they "were in their uniforms.

Questioner: Were they white or black men?
Witness: I couldn't tell because they were firing at me.

Kelly and his committee rushed through 15 more witnesses for a total of 22. Eight said the raiders were black. Five out of these eight testified that they actually saw the raiders and recognized them as black soldiers. Three said they heard voices, and from those voices knew the raiders were black. The others gave confused and contradictory statements.

Some committee members fidgeted, blinked their eyes, and moved around in their chairs. Others cupped their mouths with their hands forcing back persistent yawns after a trying morning and a late lunch. It grew increasingly obvious that committee members had grown weary of the meeting. Kelly called a brief recess. He went to a window, pulled back a corner of the draperies and looked outside. A long line of restless, impatient men waited to get in to tell their stories.

But Kelly decided they had heard enough. After recess he congratulated himself and the committee. "Gentlemen, we have conducted a most diligent inquiry. I'll go outside and give the people our verdict. We must get a telegram off to President Roosevelt."

There were no dissenting opinions.

Kelly stepped outside the door. "We have concluded our investigation. We find that the black soldiers at the fort perpetrated this heinous crime. We are sending a telegram to the president to remove them and punish them."

Katie Leahy pushed her way to the head of the line, and tried to come in the door. "You didn't talk to me."

"Now, Katie, you know this is a men's thing."

Having pacified the crowd, Kelly stepped back inside and said, "Let's go home. We'll meet again tomorrow and write the president."

Physical Evidence, Testimony and a Telegram

Once the citizens' committee left the fort, Penrose began his own inquiry. He agonized over the physical evidence, going over it again and again. Something peculiar about the base of two empty cartridge casings caught his eye. He picked one up and rolled the empty cartridge case around between his fingers with the base side up, looking at the bottom. It was marked U.M.C.30 S. He picked up the other empty shell case and examined it. It was marked the same. Then he compared them with other empty shell casings and said, "Aha, they are different." They were marked 'U.M.C. Co.,' followed by the date. He knew these markings identified the manufacture of the ammunition as Union Metallic Cartridge Company of Bridgeport, Connecticut. He was baffled. *Why the difference?*

Penrose decided to have some of the enlisted men brought to his office for questioning. Corporal John H. Hill, who had been stationed in the rear of post, was the first soldier questioned.

"Corporal, Captain Lyon tells me you saw some civilians near the wall last night. Tell me more about it."

"Sir, I saw some civilians running from a dark place near the stone wall toward town in front of Company D's quarters. I think they'd been hiding there," Corporal Hill said.

Penrose perked up with that answer and leaned over closer to Hill. "Yes. How many do you think?"

"About five. Maybe a few more."

"That's all you can tell me?" Penrose seemed disappointed that Hill had nothing else to say.

"Yes, sir."

Next, Private William Mapp of Company C told Penrose his story, "I heard voices on the outside of the company barracks saying, 'Come out, you black sons of bitches.'"

Finally, Private Charles E Rudy, Artificer of Company C, "I was sleeping on the back porch when I was awakened by a shot. Then I heard a number of shots. I saw the flashes of guns being fired along the wall. It looked as if they were being fired from outside the wall toward B company headquarters, but the fire was aimed high. I heard cursing and calls. 'Come out, you black son of bitches, and we will kill all of you.'"

Penrose wanted to believe his soldiers, but the physical evidence of the empty cartridge shell casings was overpowering for him. Besides, who at the Military Department of Texas was going to believe the words of Negro soldiers over the words of white men? *I need some hard, physical evidence.*

He decided that he had to inform his superiors of the conclusion. He sent this telegram to the military secretary, Department of Texas.

> *After further investigation, I am convinced the killing of a citizen and wounding the chief of police at Brownsville last night was done by from seven to ten men of this command, abetted by others in post.*

If any citizens or anybody else harbored any doubts as to who shot the town up, all they had to do that afternoon was scan the front page of the Brownsville *Daily Herald*, and it would disabuse them of such doubts:

Tuesday, August 14, 1906

DASTARDLY OUTRAGE

BY NEGRO SOLDIERS

*Fired On Private Residences and Other Places —
Houses of L. R. Cowen And F. E. Stark Riddled
with Bullets.*

*MIDNIGHT ATTACK ON CITIZENS —
VOLLEY UPON VOLLEY OF KRAG-JOR-
GENSEN BULLETS*

*Frank Natus, Bartender at Ruby Saloon, Killed In-
stantly by Murderous Fiends. Wounded Policeman Joe
Domingues and His Horse Killed under Him.*

The next day the Citizens' Committee dispatched a telegram to President Roosevelt, telling him, among other things, that about 20 to 30 black soldiers armed with rifles and plenty of ammunition broke out of Fort Brown just before midnight on August 13, and fired into the homes of citizens and buildings. They concluded the telegram with the following:

*...we ask you to have the troops at once removed from
Fort Brown and replaced by white soldiers.*

TWELVE

THE BLOCKSOM

Investigation

What Katie Leahy Saw

SINCE WILLIAM HOWARD TAFT, the Secretary of War, was on vacation, the telegram was sent directly to President Roosevelt at his home in Oyster Bay, New York. He responded immediately and ordered an investigation. However, he refused to call for the immediate removal of the soldiers, stating they would remain in Brownsville pending the conclusion of the investigation.

Major Augustus P. Blocksom, an Assistant Inspector General (IG) of the Southwestern Division, was assigned the task of conducting an investigation. His selection happened this way. The commanding general in Texas, William S. MacCaskey, expressed this view of the townspeople in Brownsville, "Citizens of Brownsville entertain race hatred to an extreme degree." Blocksom was a northern native, born and reared in Zanesville, Ohio. Perhaps MacCaskey wanted an investigator who was not a native of the South, so there would be no questions about his taking sides with a populace known to harbor severe racial prejudice.

Also, MacCaskey knew Blocksom to be a careful, methodical man, though somewhat plodding. He also knew him to be malleable and willing to accommodate any decision or outcome suggested by his superiors.

But there was something else about Blocksom not commonly known in military circles. It was known and expressed in Zanesville, however. He was the son of a radical Democratic politician, an aggressive Copperhead. His father was a northern sympathizer with the breakaway Confederate States, who attended and took his son to political rallies where Copperhead white women carried signs expressing their fears of miscegenation, "SAVE US FROM NIGGER HUSBANDS."

Blocksom took a train immediately to Brownsville, the first of several trips he would make, arriving there on August 18, 1906.

The next day, August 19, Blocksom plunged headlong into the investigation, interviewing a string of willing witnesses. *He had to get something out quickly to headquarters*, he thought. He brushed aside all formalities. He took unsworn statements, spoke to people in bars, hotel lobbies and on the streets—anywhere he could find them.

He interviewed Judge Parks. The judge told him he saw the whole thing, but didn't tell him he recognized the raiders as Negroes. That disturbed Blocksom because he knew Parks would be a credible witness.

Several people asked him if he had talked to Katie Leahy. They told him that Katie Leahy had been trying to contact him and that he could not leave town without speaking with her.

When he finally met with Mrs. Leahy, he felt that he already knew her and that she had a lot to say. He wanted to hear all of it. "Now, Mrs. Leahy," he instructed. "Just tell me all you know."

She admonished him right away. "I have been trying to catch up with you. Where have you been? You can just call me, Katie."

"Fine, Katie."

"They were shooting indiscriminately from the galleries," Leahy said.

"Who are you talking about? Who was doing the shooting, Katie?"

"The Negroes. I went outside in the middle of Elizabeth Street. Bullets were flying all around me. I ran back inside and stood in my second-floor window. I counted sixteen men at the corner of 14th Street and Cowen alley. It had been raining, and they stopped at a mud hole and then went around it. One of the men had trouble with his gun, and another man stopped to help him. The man that was helping him looked up, and saw me in the window, and said, 'That's Mrs. Leahy. Keep straight to the front and shoot ahead.' They were just shooting in the air."

"You say they were Negroes?"

"Yeah, I know they were Negroes. The one who looked up in my window was quite dark. The other one who had trouble with his gun was light. I could see spots on his face."

"How far do you think they were from you?"

"About thirty-five feet."

"Was anybody else standing in the window with you."

"Yes, Judge Parks."

Blocksom seemed aware of this. "Did Judge Parks see the Negroes?

"Yes, I think he did, but he didn't have on his glasses."

Blocksom considered Katie Leahy's account the most convincing. It was the most compelling to him, and he believed it was the most damning to the soldiers. He had heard enough for now—and he could see that the situation was deteriorating.

Blocksom could see that Brownsville was an armed camp and he feared the worst. Special deputies patrolled on the town side of Garrison Road opposite 65 armed soldiers standing guard on the garrison side. He felt that one wild shot by a citizen who had been hastily deputized would certainly create a rapid return of fire by well-trained soldiers taught to immediately return fire. In a "fire fight," these deputies would surely lose. *It'll be a massacre, and it might be the end of my career for letting it happen*, he thought. The possibility of this gory consequence horrified him while the potential damage to his career dismayed him.

He wired a preliminary report to headquarters on August 19, "The cause of the disturbance was racial. People did not desire colored troops here. Showed they thought them inferior by slights, denial of privileges. Soldiers resented this."

He concluded that the soldiers shot up the town. He also acknowledged that there was a rumor circulating in the lower part of town that the citizens fired first, but he believed that rumor was without foundation. He recommended the removal of the black soldiers and their replacement by white soldiers.

Blocksom's preliminary report went through the chain of command to Taft, who was still on vacation in Canada. Major General F. C. Ainsworth, Military Secretary, kept the President informed by telegram—and by bundling up his mail and sending it to Canada.

By the time Roosevelt received Blocksom's report, he had already received demands from the two Texas senators to "transfer the disorderly troops." Senator Culberson had warned Roosevelt not to station Negro soldiers in Brownsville. Now he chided the President, "I told you so."

The pressure was building up on Roosevelt. The Citizens' Committee sent another telegram to Roosevelt:

> *Our position is misunderstood. We cannot convince our women and children that another outbreak may not occur at any time...Many of our citizens have moved and are removing their families elsewhere. A Texas town should not be left unaided in this condition.*

Roosevelt approved Blossom's recommendation, and ordered the removal of all black soldiers and the closing of Fort Brown. A contingent of white soldiers from the 26th Infantry hurried to Fort Brown to secure it.

THIRTEEN

A TEXAS RANGER

Comes to Town

"You will never come out alive."

CAPTAIN BILL MCDONALD, A Texas Ranger, was in Dallas, Texas, when he first heard about the trouble in Brownsville. Since then he had followed the situation closely. He called the governor's office almost daily, called Mayor Combe, and read every scrap of news he could find on it. When there were no immediate arrests, and none seemed forthcoming, he became impatient. "I tell you boys," he said to the two Texas Rangers under his supervision, "It's gonna take me to go down there and straighten this here thing out."

When McDonald got word that Roosevelt ordered the black soldiers out of Texas and there were no arrests, he became alarmed. He decided to go to Austin, Texas, to speak to the adjutant general of Texas (AG). He wanted approval for a contingent of Texas militia troops to follow him to Brownsville and settle what he called "that Brownsville business."

The adjutant general, a big beefy man distinguished by a shock of red hair, sat at his desk, reading through a stack of papers, when his *aide-de-camp* announced, "Sir, Captain Bill McDonald is here to speak to you."

"Let him in."

"McDonald, I've been expecting you," the AG said without looking up.

"Then you know what I want."

"I can't authorize any Texas Militia troops for use at Brownsville. You don't have the authority to enter the fort and investigate Federal troops."

"Why, them hellions have violated the laws of the state of Texas, shooting into the people's houses and committing murder," McDonald said.

"You can't enter that fort!"

"I'll show ya."

"Stay out of Brownsville, McDonald!"

Figure 14. Captain W. J. (Bill) McDonald
SOURCE: The Texas Rangers, by Walter Prescott Webb
University of Texas Press, May 1965

McDonald started to go out, but stopped at the door, and turned around. "George, why don't you get off your big fat ass and do something for Texas?"

Even without the Texas Militia, McDonald knew that he must go to Brownsville. After all, he was a Texas Ranger with a big reputation as a lawman. He was known throughout Texas for always getting his man, though usually dead.

McDonald was a small man, but with a big presence—a legendary fighter for law and order in Texas. A dead shot with a six-shooter, he packed two pistols, but his favorite weapon was his automatic, double-barreled shotgun. Most of the time he wore it strapped across his chest. However, he frequently carried it in one hand and waved it around for maximum intimidation over anyone who disagreed with him.

McDonald's reputation always preceded him. The legendary accounts of his bravery, often told by himself and embellished by his friends, was passed along to the newspapers. The press buildup made his coming to Brownsville something of an event within itself. Legend had it that McDonald was so brave that he would rush into hell with one bucket of water.

His friends loved to tell the story of the time McDonald faced down Bat Masterson, the dapper, but notorious, gunslinger. As the story goes, while waiting to be served in a restaurant, Masterson became angry with the Chinese cook because he was slow bringing his food. Masterson picked up an iron table-castor and was about to strike the cook on the head. But before he could, McDonald jumped up, grabbed Masterson's arm, and said, "Don't hit the Chinaman."

"Maybe you'd like to take it up," Masterson said.

"I done took it up," McDonald said.

Masterson put the castor down and waited quietly for his food.

McDonald left the adjutant general's office, wondering who would give him the authority to enter the fort.

Eventually, he turned to the one man he knew would not defer to the niceties of Federalism, a Texas judge who wouldn't be afraid to give him the go-ahead to investigate the shootings in Brownsville.

That man was District Judge Stanley Welch, an unrestrained man and unabashed street fighter. With little provocation, he would rather fight than adjudicate. Every bit the patriotic one-armed cowboy, he brokered no nonsense in his court and certainly did not suffer fools gladly. When McDonald called him, Judge Welch joined McDonald in Corpus Christi, Texas. The two men caught the train for Brownsville and arrived Tuesday evening, August 21, at about six o'clock. McDonald hopped off the train first, looked around and was surprised that no one was there. "Stan, I don't see a damn soul here to meet us—no policeman, nobody. Them bastards knew we were coming."

"I don't care. I need to rest up a bit," the judge said, and headed for the Miller Hotel.

Instead of going to the hotel with the judge, McDonald went directly to the mayor's office, where he found Mayor Combe and Captain Kelly going over the Citizens' Committee report. McDonald swaggered in unannounced, huffing and puffing, threatening to turn Fort Brown upside down. "Combe, just who in the hell is in charge down there at that damn fort?" Before Mayor Combe could answer, McDonald said, "I'll shake 'em till them murderers come tumbling ass-first into my lap."

"You're not going to do that single-handedly. We don't want any more trouble, McDonald. We can handle it."

"You can do what? You sod-busters been down here dilly-dallying for over a week now, wasting time, letting a bunch of niggers outsmart you."

Captain Kelly and Mayor Combe were taken aback by such rudeness. Trying to placate McDonald, Combe held up a copy of the message they'd sent Roosevelt, "Here, look, we sent the president a telegram."

"I don't wanna see that shit." McDonald raised his hand, and brushed the telegram away. "You keep it to wipe your ass with. That's about all it's worth." Then he left, kicking the door shut behind him with the heel of his boot. He was going to meet up with the two Texas Rangers who had reached Brownsville before him.

McDonald met the Rangers in the lobby of the Miller Hotel, and said, "Let's get some privacy."

Blaze Dalling offered his room. No sooner had they entered the room than McDonald chewed them out for not meeting him at the train station. "Where were you? I didn't see you at the station."

Intimidated, the two Rangers said nothing.

"You half-steppers better show some respect from now on. You're working for me now. What in the hell have you found out?"

McDonald sat and listened to Dalling.

"We discovered some important information, sir."

"Let me hear it," McDonald said.

"There's this soda water man who works for this Negra soldier who opened a saloon on the edge of town. The soda water man told me that some shooting had been done last night, and that Company C could have taken the whole town if they had wanted to, and that they could take the whole damn state."

"Hardly," McDonald hit the wall with his fist. "Not my Texas!"

"The night of the shooting, this here Negra saloon closed early," one of the Rangers said.

McDonald rubbed his chin and thought about it. "Downright suspicious."

"The sheriff caught a Negra man out on the street that night and..."

McDonald adjusted his gun belt. "Did they kill'm yet?"

"No, he's in jail," the ranger said.

"Good. What are we waiting for?" McDonald asked. "Let's go and see what this nigger has to say."

The sheriff let McDonald in and led him to the one black prisoner in the county jail, whom McDonald began to interrogate. "Who are you, and what do you know about this shooting?"

"Sir, I am Mack Hamilton."

"Are you a soldier?"

"No, sir. I am a citizen. I used to be in the cavalry. I got out."

"Do you know any of them soldiers at Fort Brown?"

"Yes, Sir."

"You know a damn lot more than you're telling. You better get on with it, boy!" McDonald grabbed him by the scruff of his neck and pushed him against the bars. "You better tell me every god-damned thing you know. Stop stalling."

"Corporal Willie Miller, he's my cousin, he's the only soldier down there I know. I been talking to him 'fore I went to bed. Shooting woke me up. I gone outside to see what's going on. Sheriff seen me, says to me, 'Mack, you gonna git killed.' He puts me in jail. I've been here ever since. I want to see my wife. I ain't done nothing."

McDonald became impatient and, figuring he had gotten all the information he was going to get, instructed the sheriff, "Keep his black ass in jail. He's lying to shield himself."

"He aint' going nowhere!" the sheriff reassured him, and added, "Oh, yeah, Captain, I forgot to tell you that a company of soldiers came to the jail immediately after the shooting and wanted to know who had been put in jail. They claimed that the citizens had fired on the post."

Seemingly unimpressed with this bit of information, McDonald stood up and moved toward the door. "Got anything else?"

"Yes. Here's a soldier's cap. It was picked up in the street the morning after the shooting. Look, it has the initials "C.W.A." I checked it out. There is a Private Charles W. Askew at the fort." The sheriff was obviously proud to have that piece of evidence to show McDonald. "I'm saving it for the grand jury."

"Grand jury, hell! Gimme that." McDonald wasn't waiting for any grand jury. Snatching the cap, he looked around the room. "Where is your telephone?"

Concluding that he had made tremendous headway, McDonald called the governor and left a message for him reporting his progress. "I got good evidence. Some of it gonna be pretty hard for you to believe. I believe the white officers were in on it up to their assholes. They sent the nigger soldiers to attack. My impression is that Captain Lyon and his company was to go and finish up the job."

"I'm going to the fort tomorrow morning," McDonald said to the sheriff after the call. "If you got any guts, you all will come with me."

"You will never come out alive," the sheriff said.

"What do you yellow-bellies use around here for balls?" McDonald muttered and left, slamming the door behind him.

"I have a warrant for the arrest of your men."

The next morning McDonald marched on Fort Brown accompanied by two Texas Rangers armed with Winchester rifles. He strutted down Elizabeth Street toward the fort, his automatic shotgun at the ready, the heel of the gun resting on the hump of his potbelly. The barrel was slightly elevated, pointing straight ahead. The way he walked, one would think he had a cannon mounted on his gut, ready to blast down the gate with one shot. When he got within 10 feet of the gate, he heard a loud voice.

"Halt!" It was Mingo Sanders, standing at the gate with 20 soldiers with brand new Springfield rifles trained on the two Texas Rangers.

"I'm Captain McDonald of the Texas Rangers. I'm down here to investigate a foul murder you scoundrels have committed. I'll show you niggers something you've never been used to. Put up them guns!"

"This is Federal property, mister. Advance, show your papers, and be recognized."

McDonald looked at the guns aimed at him, and for a moment he seemed slightly intimidated. He strapped his shotgun across his chest, walked up to Sanders and reached in his pocket to take out the order from Judge Welch. Then he became extremely agitated and changed his mind. "I don't need any god-damned paper to get in here."

He started to move past Sanders, but found himself blocked by the rifles of two soldiers. Turning back toward Sanders, McDonald reached up, grabbed the rifle of Sanders, and tried to wrestle it away, but he couldn't move it. He pulled and jerked at it again. The rifle didn't budge. It was as if it were embedded in stone. Recognizing that he was out gunned, and unable to wrest away the rifle, McDonald had second thoughts about not presenting his authority paper. He reached into his pockets and waved Judge Welch's order in Sanders' face. "See this, boy?" he barked. "I got an order from a judge."

Sanders snapped his heels together and said politely, "Yes, sir. Where are you going? Who do you want to see? Can I help you?"

Emboldened again, McDonald snubbed the offer. "Yeah, you can get the hell outta my way!"

"Holomon! Escort these men to the administration building," Sanders said.

McDonald bounced up the steps, strolled into the administration building, and looked around. Sergeant Major Taliaferro was sitting at his desk. Immediately McDonald shouted, "Sergeant! Where is your commander?"

"He's in his office. I'll see if he can speak to you."

Then, McDonald saw the sign 'Battalion Commander' on a closed door. "Never mind." He brushed past the sergeant major and barged into Penrose's office where he was holding a meeting with Captain Macklin.

"Where is Corporal Miller?" McDonald asked.

"Captain McDonald," Penrose said, and reached out to shake McDonald's hand. "Sergeant Sanders called from the gate and ..."

"Major, I asked you a question. Where is that Miller nigger?"

Penrose withdrew his hand, turned to Macklin and said, "Have Miller brought in."

"Get Private Askew too," McDonald said.

Macklin stuck his head out of the door, and told the sergeant major to bring the two men to headquarters.

McDonald sat down and started questioning Penrose.

"Major, what have you found out?"

"We have the empty cartridge shells, nothing else," Penrose said.

"Tell me something new. I know your darkies did it. I just want to know which ones."

Penrose stared at McDonald, but said nothing. McDonald turned to Macklin. "Captain, where were you during this here shooting?"

"Sleeping."

"Sleeping? Cracker! Don't you trifle with me. What the hell do you mean, sleeping?"

Macklin bristled. He looked at Penrose, and asked, "Do I have to answer this man?"

Penrose leaned over and put his hand on Macklin's shoulder, "Ed, you don't, but go ahead. We have nothing to hide."

Macklin tightened his lips and said slowly, "Sleeping means sleeping, McDonald. I was in my quarters."

The sergeant major ushered Corporal Miller in for questioning. "Miller, where were you on the night of this here shooting?"

"I went to Matamoros on a twenty-four hour pass. When I got back, I stopped by Mack Hamilton's house. You see, he's my first cousin. I left him and went to a Mexican saloon. When I heard the shooting, I showed the bartender my pass. He'll tell ya."

"Damn right, you did. You're the only son-of-a-bitch telling the truth around here." McDonald got up from his chair, took out his pistol, walked over to where Miller was sitting, got in his face and began sweet-talking him. "Now, boy, you are doing good so far. You showed that bartender your pass, 'cause you knew your buddies was planning to get even with them crackers. Didn't ya? You're a good boy. You are not a murderer. You didn't want any part in this here killing." Raising his voice, McDonald said, "All right, now tell me who did it!"

"Sir, I don't know."

"Come, come, come, boy. Tell me, tell me. Now!"

"Sir, if I knowed, I would tell ya."

McDonald was getting angrier and angrier. He sensed his most promising lead slipping away. He raised his pistol and slammed it down on the arm of the chair, barely missing Miller's hand. The pine arm rest broke into pieces, throwing splinters into Miller's lap and on the floor.

Miller flinched and scooted his chair backward. McDonald raised his pistol again and shouted, "Tell me. Tell me! You better give me names. Now, boy! Now, boy!"

"I don't know."

McDonald started to bring the pistol down on Miller's head. Macklin moved quickly, jumped to his feet and blocked McDonald's arm. "That's enough, McDonald! Miller, go back to your barracks. I believe you."

"You take your goddamned hand off me." McDonald lowered his voice to a whisper. "Take your damned hands off me. You'll pay. You'll pay. By God, you'll pay."

Macklin let go of McDonald's arm, took a step backward and balled up his fists.

Penrose stepped between the two men and spread his arms like a referee. "Don't do this. We got enough troubles. It's hot in here. Miller, on your way out, tell the sergeant major to bring a pitcher of lemonade in here."

Private C. W. Askew was the next soldier interrogated. McDonald, who had cooled off a bit, approached Askew and showed him the cap. "Tell me about this cap. Are these your initials, C.W.A?"

"Yes, sir. I gave the first sergeant one of my old caps," Askew said. "When we were at Fort Niobrara, we turned in our old caps for new ones. There was a box of old caps that was shipped down to Fort Brown, and when we got down here, they opened that box of old caps. They put it on the back porch. Some of those muchachos, I suppose, found them and got them and carried them away. I think that is the way they got the cap."

"So you think the Mexicans shot up the town?" McDonald said.

"I don't know who did it," Private Askew said.

Several other soldiers were interrogated, but they all denied knowing anything about the shooting. McDonald thought all of them were lying. Still furious at Macklin, McDonald rubbed his chin, peered intently at Macklin, and said, "You know, I don't believe you were sleeping. I believe you were out with them coons committing murder and trying to kill ladies and their children.

"And you, Penrose, when I came in here, you told me you couldn't find out anything. I've been in here less than an hour and I've found enough with what I got last night to warrant me charging a bunch of your men with murder. How do you explain that?"

"You haven't found out anything new," Penrose said.

"You crackers down here are dumber than the niggers." McDonald shook his finger at Penrose and Macklin. "You, as their officers, ought to be the first to hunt 'um out, instead of trying to hide 'um."

The next morning, Thursday, August 23rd, McDonald walked into Penrose's office, beaming with confidence. "Penrose! I have a warrant for the arrest of twelve of your men, charging them with conspiracy to commit murder." He handed him a bench warrant signed by Judge Welch.

"I will confine them to the guardhouse on post until I consult with my superiors," Penrose said.

"The hell you will. You're going to turn them over to me now."

Penrose refused. McDonald left in a huff, saying, "All right, big buddy, I'll be back."

As McDonald was walking out of the Fort Brown gate, he saw a sign that read, 'Telegraph office.' *That's where I need to go*, he thought. He went into the telegraph office, closed the door, slid the bolt lock in place and went directly through the swinging one-arm gate. The telegraph master reached for his pistol. McDonald put the shotgun to his neck. "Don't go for that. This is not a robbery. I am Captain McDonald. You will deliver to me every telegram sent to that fort." When the telegraph master turned around, he came face to face with the double-barrel shotgun.

"Can't do it. They are confidential."

McDonald jabbed him with the shotgun. "Got no time to argue with you. Do what I tell ya. Bring them telegrams to the sheriff's office."

"I propose to do my duty."

Penrose conferred with General William S. MacCaskey, Department of Texas. "I don't believe these men will have an unbiased trial here, in my opinion. An effort should be made to have them tried elsewhere. I also fear for their safety, if turned over to the civil authorities, in case of mob violence."

MacCaskey agreed and sent a telegram to the War Department saying, "We think it unsafe to leave the accused at Fort Brown with only one white company of forty-eight men to protect them. We also fear that turning them over to civil authorities now or in the immediate future would be disastrous to them. Train is now waiting at Fort Brown to take battalion, the 25th Infantry, to Fort Reno, Okla."

The telegram further recommended that the accused men be taken on the same train with them and dropped off at Fort Sam Houston in San Antonio. There they should be confined to the guardhouse until it was safe to turn them over to civil authorities. The rest of the battalion should continue to Fort Reno immediately. The recommendation was further delivered directly to President Roosevelt at Oyster Bay.

The president agreed. "I entirely approve of the action you propose to take. Act immediately."

Penrose received his orders by confidential telegram about five o'clock that evening.

At about the same time a man hurried into the sheriff's office, dropped a copy of the telegram on the Sheriff's desk and left. McDonald was there trying to get some men deputized to march on the fort to take the prisoners by force.

McDonald recognized the man as the telegraph master and thought, that's it. The sheriff reached to pick up the telegram, but McDonald slapped his hand down on top of the envelope, "It's mine!" He stepped to a corner of the office, read the communication and rushed out the door.

He brushed past the sergeant major's desk into Penrose's office, yelling, "Penrose! I want custody of them prisoners."

"I am directed by the president himself not to release these men," Penrose said. Gaining courage from an order issued to him directly from his commander-in-chief—a former soldier and colonel and the hero of San Juan Hill—Penrose added, "You get out of my office. Get off this post. Never come back!"

"Well, I'll see what Stan Welch got to say about this here shit," McDonald said and left for the judge's office.

As a courtesy to Judge Welch, Penrose went to his office that evening to inform him that he had a higher order from the president nullifying the warrant. He found McDonald already there and arguing with the judge.

Penrose showed Judge Welch the telegram. McDonald pretended that he had not already seen it, and argued that he be allowed to read it. Penrose refused. When Judge Welch nodded his head in agreement, McDonald turned against him.

"Judge, nobody gonna move them niggers from here. They are my prisoners. I'm gonna hold them. I'll wire the governor."

McDonald sprinted to the telegraph office where he wrote out a message and handed it to the telegraph master. "Send this!"

Brownsville, Texas, August 24

To Gov. S. W. T. Lanham, and Gen. John A. Hulen. Austin, Texas — The Military authorities are trying to take our prisoners from here for the purpose of defeating justice and will attempt to do so at once over my protest. Please send assistance to prevent this outrage. The officers are trying to cover up this diabolical crime that I am about to uncover and it will be a shame to allow this to be done. I turned warrants over to them in due form with the promise that they would hold prisoners in the guardhouse and then turn them over to me when called for. I propose to do my duty.

McDonald sent a telegram to Penrose, again demanding release of the prisoners to him.

Penrose responded by telegram. Again he refused, saying that the soldiers would be turned over to civil authorities when their safety had been assured. "After a most careful investigation, I am unable to find anyone or any party in any way connected with the crime of which you speak. I return to you herewith the warrants delivered to me yesterday."

Later that day, Governor Lanham replied to McDonald:

Austin, Texas, Aug 24–To Capt. W. J. McDonald, Brownsville, Texas. Have requested General McCaskey to prevent removal of soldiers charged with recent murder. Consult district judge and sheriff and act under, through them.

S. W. T. LANHAM, Gov.

McDonald went back to see Judge Welch and showed him the telegram from the Governor. "You see, the Governor agrees with me."

"I read no such thing in that telegram. You'll act under me."

"We got to hold that train!"

While Judge Welch firmly believed some of the soldiers had shot up the town, he began having doubts about the 12 men McDonald fingered. It didn't make much sense to him now that he thought more about it. It seemed that they were picked at random, so he pressed McDonald for more hard evidence. "You got to get me more evidence."

"Judge, the niggers did it."

"But which ones?"

"The ones we got."

Welch was losing patience with McDonald. "I want those warrants back."

"Judge, that means they'll take them murderers out of town! I must do my duty."

"I'm telling you, McDonald! Those warrants I gave you for the arrest of those men are abrogated. Get them back to me!"

McDonald turned on his heels and left Welch's office.

Within the next hour, Welch sent a telegram to McDonald, revoking the warrants:

Brownsville, Texas, Aug. 24–Capt. W.J. McDonald Sir, This is to direct you to immediately return to me without any further attempt at execution the three warrants of arrest placed in your hands by myself yesterday, wherein thirteen persons, twelve soldiers and one ex-soldier — were charged with murder and assault with intent to murder.

Given under my official hand this 24th day of August, 1906.

Stanley Welch, Judge

28th Jud. Dist of Texas.

McDonald pondered the order from Welch. He picked it up, looked at it, put it down, and shook his head. He re-read the Governor's telegram. The more he thought about it, the more furious he became. The governor seemed to be "shilly-shallying" around, passing the buck back down to Judge Welch and the sheriff. Worst of all, the governor had put him under the authority of those two men—the sheriff, whom he had no respect for, and Judge Welch, whom he suspected was caving in and personally moving against him. He was rapidly beginning to despise the judge. The nerve of him asking for those warrants back. *I won't give them back,* he thought. Got to be somebody around here to help me.

McDonald was in and out of the mayor's office, the district attorney's office, and the sheriff's office—but no one agreed with his position to hold the prisoners. He went to the train station and pleaded with the railroad officials to hold the troop train, which was scheduled to depart at midnight. They flatly rejected what the station master called a "crazy idea." He was just about exasperated when he visited John Gardner in his hotel room to get the congressman to use his influence. Gardner had come to Brownsville to check on "the mess" himself.

Gardner called Judge Welch. "We better call a meeting. McDonald is going off his rocker."

"All right, tonight's fine. If you see him again, tell him he damn sure better bring those warrants," the judge said.

McDonald was the last person to get to the meeting that night. Mayor Combe, the district attorney, Congressman Gardner, Attorney James B. Wells, and Judge Welch were patiently waiting for him in the judge's office. He walked into the meeting, gripping his automatic shotgun tightly while waving it up and down. "That train ain't leaving here with them prisoners. I'll shoot it out with the whole damn army. I'll stop that train, if I have to stand in the middle of the tracks."

Wells tried to calm him down. "You are zealous. You are a good officer, but if you attempt to interfere with those soldiers down there, this matter will break out anew, and we will lose a great many lives here."

"You all are being misled!" McDonald shouted. "We got to hold that train!"

Judge Welch stepped forward. "McDonald, Put down that shotgun. You no longer have the authority to hold those men. Give me those warrants."

"You can't change it now," McDonald said, "Them warrants are still good."

"They are abrogated."

Welch, the one-armed judge, the small pint-sized man, the patriot who lost one arm firing a cannon on the fourth of July, got up from his chair. His armless shirt sleeve stretched across his chest like a badge of courage. He unbuttoned the cuff end and a small snub-nose pistol slid into his hand. The two small men stood face to face—McDonald with his shotgun in one hand, his two pistols hanging from his belt on both sides—and the Judge, with his powerful derringer aimed at McDonald's gut.

Welch said, "You'll return those bench warrants to me."

McDonald did.

FOURTEEN

DEPARTURE FROM

Fort Brown

Sunrises are not for the walking dead

IT WAS EARLY SATURDAY morning, August 25th. The soldiers, their wives, and children were packed and ready to leave Brownsville. But they were not ready to leave Fort Brown. It was a sad day, a day that began without honor for the soldiers of the 25th Infantry. It was the first day of a long, bitter journey down the road of dishonor, disgrace, and shame. It was a day of heavy hearts, burdened with the specter of possible murderers among them, phantom raiders robbing them of their good names, their honor, and their livelihoods. The raiders must have been ghost soldiers, nobody knew their names. They came out of nowhere and shot up a community. Then they vanished into the night, leaving no trace of who they were or from whence they came.

The sun rose and so did the spirits of the people of Brownsville. Their hearts were gladdened. They had gotten what they wanted. However, nobody among the soldiers saw a sunrise. Sunrises are not for the walking dead.

Everything was in place for their departure. The police deputized a force of 50 to 60 hand-picked civilians to assist them. They stood guard along the route the soldiers would take to the depot. Mayor Combe and Major Penrose worked feverishly and secretly behind the scenes, unbeknown to Mc-Donald, devising a plan for the safe and orderly departure of the black soldiers.

It was widely circulated that the soldiers would leave at midnight, but the mayor advised Major Penrose against it. "If any person is unkindly disposed toward your command and wants to commit an act of violence, they can do it easily under the cover of darkness."

Penrose agreed.

The mayor issued instructions to the sheriff, "If any citizen makes any demonstration whatever, or interferes with the departure of the troops, arrest him. And if a citizen fires a shot, or anything of that kind, shoot him."

Combe met Penrose at the main gate. He marched at the head of his command, leading his troops out of Fort Brown. The mayor placed himself at the head of the column next to Major Penrose and fell in step. The two men marched side by side ahead of the troops toward the freight depot.

There was an eerie quietness, a silence disturbed only by the orderly, systematic sound of boots striking the dusty streets of Brownsville. Then, they heard a strange sound—the tolling of a church bell in the distance, as if it were mourning the fate of the soldiers. When Mingo Sanders heard it, he thought that bell was knelling the death of justice.

Was it a coincidence, as stated by the *Brownsville Daily Herald*? The newspaper reported, "By coincidence, a church bell was tolling as they left. Or was it the friendly hand of a Brownsville citizen, ringing the bell in some church belfry?"

They marched as if on parade while masking their grief. Heads were held high, shoulders snapped back—proud United States Army soldiers marched in unison. They carried

their colors, Old Glory, along with battle streamers signi-
fying victories in Cuba, Philippines, and Indian campaigns.
Their wives and children walked behind, masking the sorrow
they felt within. They refused to be transported in carriages.
Their heads were bent, some sobbed. A single soldier walked
behind with the dog, Trooper, who trotted along on a short
leash. It was not a holiday.

McDonald watched for his 12 prisoners. He wondered
where they could be. He stretched his neck forward and
looked up and down the column. He couldn't see them.

When the column of soldiers reached the depot, Major Penrose turned around and faced his command. Then
he marched backward for about three or four steps, raised
his hand and stopped the column. The special troop train
waited. The conductor shouted, "All aboard!" Mayor Combe
extended his hand to Penrose. The two men shook hands.

The soldiers, company by company, boarded the train.
Their wives and children followed. As the soldier with
Trooper started to board the train, Trooper broke away and
ran across the street, skidding to a stop in front of a policeman. The dog gnashed his teeth, growled at the man, and
grabbed his pants' leg. The policeman tried to kick the dog
away, then pulled out his pistol. When the sheriff saw what
was going on, he shouted, "Hold your fire, Garza!" The soldier retrieved the dog, pulling him back across the street, and
boarded the train.

When the last soldiers had boarded the train, the conductor shouted, "All aboard!" for the last time and took up the
train steps. McDonald still watched. He looked for guards
with prisoners and saw that everyone was on the train. The
train engineer yanked the cord and the whistle blew. A cloud
of steam shot out, the engine puffed black smoke from its

stack—and the train moved off slowly. Gradually, it began to pick up speed—going faster and faster—taking the soldiers away from Brownsville to El Reno, Oklahoma.

By now, McDonald was terribly confused. He walked over to the sheriff, looking mystified. "Where in the hell are the armed guards with my prisoners? I didn't see them get on that train. Did Penrose turn them over to you?"

"No," the sheriff said.

"You're lying," McDonald shouted in the sheriff's face. He flew into a rage, stamping his feet and waving his shot gun. "You dirty rotten Mexican! You half-wit! You been working with the niggers all along."

As the mayor walked back to his office, his heartbeat slowed and his nerves calmed. He began to feel good. He had saved his town from mortal conflict, but something still nagged at him. Something raised questions in his mind but he didn't know why. He thought maybe it had something to do with Garza. Why did that dog dislike Garza? He thought back to the night of the shooting and his encounter with Garza carrying the jammed rifle. What was Garza doing with that jammed Winchester rifle during the shooting? Upon reflection, Joe Crixell's explanation to him didn't make much sense. Why would Crixell's brother give Garza a defective rifle with the bullet so jammed that it couldn't be removed? When was it last fired? Could it have been fired that night before it jammed, and if so, by whom?

"Where is Holomon?"

Major Blocksom took a carriage back to Fort Brown from the depot. As the carriage rolled along, he rested his head back on the leather pillow of the seat, relaxing and feeling triumphant. The President had approved his recommendation and the black soldiers were on a train speeding away from Brownsville. He had averted a disaster. With that kind of success, the War Department would be pleased with him.

Then, he began to think bigger. Maybe the president would invite him to the White House. Maybe he would get a promotion out of this peaceful resolution. All he had to do now was find evidence to support his recommendation. That shouldn't be much of a problem, for this was his area of strength. He knew how to make any report perfect. He could justify anything. He was a red-tape officer, a consummate paper-pusher. He was the white glove inspector that the troops loved to hate. But Blocksom didn't care about that kind of stuff now. This situation was big, very big. He'd need to do more work. He'd have to talk to more civilians. His carriage pulled up in front of the Miller Hotel. He alighted from the vehicle, went to his room, and started to plan more interviews for his investigation.

Meanwhile, McDonald went back to his own hotel room. He spent much of the day talking to various people, trying to figure out who were involved in what he considered a conspiracy against him. As the day wore on, he had just about given up. That evening, he read the *Daily Herald*, looking to see how he fared with the press. Then a subtitle caught his eyes, "Prisoners Released and March out with Their Comrades." So that's how they done it. They done mixed up them prisoners with the rest of them niggers so they all look alike, McDonald thought.

The train trip to Fort Reno, Oklahoma, had been uneventful, boring, and tiresome for the troops, their wives and children. It had been an emotional roller-coaster ever since they first arrived in Brownsville just a few weeks before. Now that it was over, they found themselves numbed by their Brownsville experience. The only excitement came when the train stopped in San Antonio. There the prisoners were turned over to the military authorities, who were waiting in an ambulance to take them to Fort Sam Houston.

Major Penrose made an unusual decision at the outset after Judge Welch revoked the warrants. He allowed the prisoners to march with their units to the depot without armed guards. They could move freely aboard the train and associate with their wives, children, and friends. It lent ample opportunity for the noncommissioned officers or somebody to overhear loose talk that might give a clue as to who shot up the town.

All the prisoners came forward to disembark, except John Holomon.

"Where is Holomon?" Mingo Sanders asked his squad leader.

"He went back to the baggage car a few minutes ago."

Holomon had stepped into the baggage car with his hand in his pocket rattling his gold coins. A man who was hiding in the car peeped around a stack of baggage. Holomon handed him a letter and a bag of money. Holomon whispered, "Mail this letter to my son and put the money in the bank. Goodbye, my friend." The man took the letter and the bag and disappeared back into the freight car.

"Holomon, let's go!"

"I'm coming!"

"Get out here now!"

The prisoners said goodbye to their friends, saluted their officer, and were taken away to prison in an army ambulance to Fort Sam Houston. The troop train moved on down the track and arrived in El Reno, Oklahoma, at just past midnight on August 27. Penrose and his soldiers left immediately for Fort Reno, 25 miles away.

FIFTEEN

FORT RENO

Days of Forced March

MINGO SANDERS WAS UP early the next morning after their arrival at the fort. He poked around outside, looking over his new surroundings. *What a God forsaken place this is,* he thought. In every direction he looked, he saw some kind of disrepair and disorder. There were rundown buildings, peeling paint, trash, and abandoned junk lying around. In a perverse way, maybe it was good the place was in such a mess. There would be a lot of work to do. Something to keep them busy and keep their minds off of visiting the town. He was sure nobody was going into El Reno—Major Penrose had confined them to post. No soldier was permitted to enter El Reno for any reason whatsoever.

Sanders was not surprised when their officers ordered him and the other sergeants to conduct daily training drills. In fact, he considered it an effective way to get information about the shoot up of Brownsville.

The sergeants marched the men up and down the parade field and back again. Day after day, they made long, forced marches into the bleak area surrounding the fort. They marched up and up "Misery Hill," then down and out into the salt flats. The next day it was up and down "Agony Hill," and back onto the salt flats. There wasn't much relief at night following the marches. The sergeants conducted repeated surprise shakedown inspections, usually in the middle of the night. They rousted the men from their bunks, depriving them of sleep. Sanders hoped that sooner or later the punishing routine would break their will and somebody would talk.

A day of rain did not provide any relief. On a particularly sodden morning, they assembled the soldiers on the parade field. It was raw, windy, and rainy. The orders of the day were announced. "There's a change in schedule because of the rain," Sanders said, "We are going take the inclement weather schedule. I see some of you got your raincoats on. Take 'em off! You don't want to get your raincoats wet. The mud will be great for you today, nice and slippery. We're going back up Misery Hill again. Tomorrow it'll be hot, so we'll take a speed-march up Agony Hill. Let's go!"

Into the downpour the exhausted troops marched. They trod mile after mile along the road toward Misery Hill carrying full packs rolled up upon their backs. By the time they reached the foot of the hill, they were soaking wet. Streams of muddy water ran down the hill, washing more mud down the sides. The sloppy slurry swirled into puddles of thick, gluey muck that settled at the bottom of the hill around their boots.

Sanders gave the order to stack arms. They put their rifles in neat stacks in any place they could find free of mud. Sanders gave the orders, "Form a skirmish line, go!" As they turned to climb the hill, their boots stuck in the mud. When Sanders saw that the men were having trouble getting a foothold, he barked, "Get on your knees, crawl!"

As they struggled and moved a little way up the hill, he shouted. "Fall on your bellies, slither up the hill! Now get on your backs, scrub your way up the hill!"

On their backs, the men scooted farther up the hill. "Sit on your ass, butt walk!" Sanders yelled. "Now, get on your feet. Run!"

The men began running, slipping, sliding and falling all over the hill. Some of the old soldiers had difficulty. When one fell, a young one helped him up. When one wanted to quit, an old soldier grabbed him and pushed him forward. No man was allowed to give up.

Everyone reached the top of Misery Hill, sat down and watched as Mingo Sanders charged the hill as if he were in a real field action. Unlike the other soldiers who climbed the hill, Sanders carried his rifle. He darted here and there along the steep rise, falling to the kneeling position, then the prone. He rolled from side to side, all the time pointing his rifle at an unknown enemy. One time he fell and couldn't get up. He thought he wouldn't make it, but then he heard the men cheering. He got up slowly—and stumbled to the top of the hill.

After Sanders got his breath, all the soldiers ran down the hill together as fast as they could and started back to camp. It was late. Their faces were dirty and grimy. Their uniforms were muddy, some in tatters. Their bodies were worn out, but their backs were not broken. Their *esprit de corps* was intact. They were not a straggling horde. They marched at an easy gait with their flag and their battle streamers flying high.

Morale was so high after the Misery Hill march that the men felt they had earned the right to go into town. Dorsie Willis, an 18-year-old soldier from Mississippi, yelled, "Hey, Sarge, we did good! See if we can go into town."

"Yeah. Sarge, go see Major Penrose," Boyd Conyers said.

Penrose had set up an extended open door policy for any soldier to come in and talk to him freely without going through the chain of command or getting permission from any one. Thus, he hoped to gain information, and perhaps gather some clues about the shooting. Weeks went by and no soldier came to his office.

When Penrose learned that Sanders wanted to speak to him, he was excited with expectations that Sanders had found out something. Penrose set up a plan to have special trusted soldiers listen in on conversations and report back any clues about the shooting. He called these soldiers the listening posts.

As soon as Penrose heard Sanders talking to the sergeant major in the outer office, he eagerly got up and met Sanders at the door. "Come in, Sergeant Sanders. What have you got for me from the listening posts?"

"Nothing yet, sir."

"Nothing?"

"We're still listening, sir. I want to talk to you about something else."

"About what?"

"We've been here for weeks. Nobody has been allowed in town. You know, sir, soldiers are soldiers. The young ones are not married. They need to get to town."

Penrose knew what Sanders was trying to tell him—he couldn't keep soldiers locked up in compulsory chastity for too long. Somebody would break out eventually, and that was just what Penrose wanted some soldier to do. He might be able to get the information he wanted then.

"Tell them to bring me some information and I will remove the 'off limits' signs in El Reno."

"Suppose they don't have anything to tell us, sir? How can we make them tell us something they don't know? How can we do that, sir?"

Penrose was startled by Sanders' logic and directness. He reflected on Sanders' words for a moment, then said, "Well, Sanders, you got a point. But how do you explain those empty cartridge shells found in the streets?"

"I don't know, sir. But, sir, did you smell those empty shells?"

Penrose was shocked and embarrassed that Sanders hit upon something he and Captain Macklin failed to check. They didn't smell the empty casings for the tell-tale smell of sulfur. It would not have dissipated by the next morning when the empty shells were picked up in the streets of Brownsville.

Penrose sighed. "Come to think of it, we didn't." He rested his chin in the palm of his hand with his elbow on his knee and frowned. "How could we have missed doing that?"

"I don't know, sir, but, it's too late now."

Sanders passed word to the other sergeants that Major Penrose refused to lift the 'off limits' restriction—and they passed the bad news on to the men. That same night some men began to sneak into town. Five were caught and charges were prepared against them.

Penrose offered each man the same deal. "I have but one rule in these matters, and that's charges. But, if you will tell me any man, or if you can find out any man, or if you can get me any clue that will lead to the identity of any man connected with the deed in Brownsville, I will tear up these charges. They will not be preferred against you." Each man denied any knowledge about the shooting.

One man begged to get out of it. He pleaded with Penrose to allow him to stay in the service and said as tears ran down his cheeks, "I swear before almighty God, I don't know anything about this thing." Shortly afterwards, Penrose court-martialed him and the other four men, and the court gave them dishonorable discharges.

As time went by the men grew suspicious of each other. They ate their meals almost in silence and talked only when dictated by necessity. "Pass the potatoes, the beans, the salt, the pepper." They glared at each other across the aged and notched oak dining room tables.

Sanders sat alone at the noncommissioned officers (NCO) dining room table. He did not go to his quarters to eat supper with his wife. To learn anything about the shooting, he felt he must eat with his men. But he found it getting harder to eat. He stared into space, his hands lying limp along the edge of the table. Then, his fingers began trembling. It disturbed him that the men seemed to be counting the notches. When he reflected on what the notches meant, it saddened him. They were carved by soldiers like him not too long ago. They indicated how many Indians they killed as they drove the Red Man into Oklahoma and beyond.

He tried to stop the uncontrollable twitching of his fingers, but he couldn't. His thoughts troubled him. He was frightened for one of the few times in his life, when he was not facing an enemy. He now faced one he couldn't see, couldn't shoot—one he knew nothing about. Soldiers needed something to shoot, something to kill, something to keep them edgy and ready for battle.

His men told him nothing. The other first sergeants got nothing from their men either. He repeated to himself what he suggested to Penrose. *My men aren't telling me anything, because they have nothing to tell me.*

Had he done all he could do to find out who did the shooting? He thought he had. Nothing added up. What should he do? Who would point the finger of blame at him? Who would say he did it? Who would say he knew who did it while looking at him? Who would try to save himself by lying about him? Who would start another ring of notches, and count him among them?

Sixteen

JUDGE PARKS FAILS TO KEEP

His Appointments

A night of poor judgment

JUDGE PARKS CONFIDED IN Mayor Combe that he hadn't felt well since the night he sat in the window at the Leahy Hotel and watched the raiders tear up the town of Brownsville. Something worried him. It ate at him. This thing tore his legal mind apart—and he couldn't put his finger on it. He surmised that it had something to do with Major Blocksom's investigation. It got so bad that he scheduled an appointment with Combe to talk to him in confidence about it later that evening. The judge also told Combe that he was going to meet with Blocksom early the next morning to discuss a sensitive matter.

Hours before the meeting, Judge Parks decided that maybe he didn't need to see the mayor after all. Maybe he needed to skip across the border to Matamoros and have a little fun. Maybe that's all he needed. He was not sure he should confide his misgivings about the shooting incident to Fred Combe. So he went to Matamoros. He met some friends, had a good time—and completely forgot about his appointment.

Mayor Combe waited for the judge for over an hour, but Parks did not show up. He missed his appointment and

Combe had to go. He was worried. It was unusual for Judge Parks to break an appointment.

Later that evening, Katie Leahy saw Judge Parks stumbling up the stairs, going toward his room, "He smelled like a busted whiskey keg." Apparently he had just returned from Matamoros. He was last seen sitting in the same window at the Leahy Hotel, trying to cool off.

The boarder in the next room said he heard Judge Parks come into his room, but he also heard footsteps climbing the stairs a minute or so behind him. Someone else entered the room. Then, he heard a voice say, "What do you want? God, a man can't get any peace, anywhere?" The next morning Katie Leahy found him lying dead on the ground beneath the window. It was the same night the troops arrived at Fort Reno—August 27.

Seventeen

A CONSPIRACY

Of Silence

Black over White Won't Go

MAJOR BLOCKSOM HAD JUST finished packing his bags and was about to go to the depot to catch a train for Fort Reno. He had given up on meeting with Judge Parks. He would complete his final report without whatever Parks wanted to see him about. He picked up his bags and was about to go out the door when Mayor Combe walked into his office at Fort Brown. "Major, Judge Parks is dead," Combe said softly. "Katie Leahy found him this morning lying on the ground at the bottom of his window."

"Do you know what happened?"

"Sort of. I found out he went to Matamoros. Probably imbibed too much and fell out the window. That's all there is to it, I guess."

"Poor fellow. Thanks for letting me know. I've got to catch a train."

Blocksom settled into one of the hard-backed leather seats on the train. Ten days after he arrived in Brownsville he was on his way to Fort Reno to finish his investigation. It was August 27. He had to write his final report. He opened his rawhide case and searched for his notes on Judge Parks.

Who was Combe trying to fool, saying, 'That's all to it?' There had to be more to Parks' death, but what was it? There was Parks' story of what he said he saw. He said he saw the whole thing from his window in the Leahy Hotel. He saw men shooting, but never said he recognized them as black soldiers. Did he tell anybody else this? What else did he see? Katie Leahy stood in the same window and told Blocksom that Judge Parks couldn't have recognized them because he didn't have on his glasses. Well, whatever Parks had to tell him, he would carry it to his grave.

Blocksom had talked to many people who represented themselves as eyewitnesses, but most were gossipers, story-tellers, barflies, politicians, and loafers. The saloon keepers, policeman, Miller Hotel residents, and many citizens also claimed the black soldiers shot up the town. But which ones did the shooting? How could he explain the contradictory testimony between the civilians and the soldiers?

The soldiers denied that they had anything to do with the shooting or knew who did it. They denied that they held any animosity toward the citizens. Where is the motive? He was perplexed and conflicted. Who was lying?

He wanted to believe the soldiers. After all, he was a soldier. We all wear the same uniform. *That's what connects us*, he thought. The battalion had an excellent reputation up to the 13th of August. But this stain was the worst he ever saw in the Army. How could the old soldiers not know? How could the sergeant of the guard not know? Or, harder to believe, how could the guards walking their posts in the barracks area not know? Worse yet, how could Company B's noncommissioned officer in charge of quarters not know?

He took out a pen and began to jot down some of his thoughts. They came rushing out on the paper, though the bumpy ride made it difficult for him to write them down.

How could sixteen to twenty men jump the wall, break out of the fort, shoot up the town, and sneak back in undetected by the guards? And then, how could they fall into formation and answer to their names without some of the soldiers not knowing? Impossible! Surely somebody must have seen them and have knowledge of the guilty parties. They had to be tacitly cooperating in a conspiracy of silence to protect their race. That was it! To protect their race, they lied, he thought. They had to be lying.

He concluded that if the old soldiers didn't disclose their knowledge, or if any of the black soldiers didn't disclose what they knew, they should be made to suffer with others who were more guilty, and suffer as far as the law will permit.

That thought was so powerful to him that he dropped his pen.

The men Captain McDonald fingered as the actual raiders were probably guilty, he concluded, but how could that be proven in a court of law or by military court martial? He reasoned that there was little prospect of conviction on evidence produced so far.

Who was he kidding? He knew there was evidence on the other side in favor of the soldiers which he must deal with if his final report was going to be accepted.

That post scavenger's story—he didn't see any soldiers shooting from the porch of B Company and he didn't see any soldiers shooting at all—would be hard to controvert since he had been in the best position to see. He must have seen them. Why was he lying?

He might have known Wilbur Voshelle would lie to protect his job. He was the corral boss at the fort, a post employee. But he seemed to be an honest man with nothing to hide. Why did he tell him that fantastic story that when he heard the shots he was sleeping in town, got up, hastily dressed and went down to the corral at the post? He didn't see a single soldier on the streets. He saw only two policeman and four citizens with arms talking about soldiers. When he got to the fort, he went to bed in the corral with the horses. Before he fell asleep, he heard about six shots fired in town again. That sounded like a big lie to Blocksom. Why was that white man lying to protect those colored soldiers?

Blocksom had to admit to himself that he had uncovered a mixture of contradictory information. In addition to that evidence, both Mayor Combe and Major Penrose told him that the first shots heard were pistol shots, then high-powered rifles. Where did the soldiers get pistols from? Penrose assured him that only the officers had access to pistols.

Now that he thought more about it, doubts began to surface about the evidence. It was too late now, though, for him to change his first recommendation that the soldiers did it. He must go with it. He must make it stick. But only eight witnesses could qualify as having actually seen the raiders, and the soldiers denied it. It was a dark night and the streets were poorly lit. That fact would not escape General McCaskey, old 'Eagle Eyes.' He needed to bury it somewhere in his report.

He stopped writing, shut his case, lay his head back and closed his eyes. But he could not sleep. He agonized.

Who would the top generals believe? Who would the politicians believe? Who would the president believe, and who did he believe — eight white people or 167 black soldiers?

The answer became clear to him. He knew what it was even though it was buried deep in his subconscious, created by his teachings, his experience, and his upbringing. The answer was so deeply entrenched in his soul that it easily answered the question. No matter how hard he tried to believe the soldiers, no matter the evidence, something in him wouldn't let him go. And it wouldn't let him believe black soldiers over white citizens.

Upon arriving at Fort Reno, he went directly to see Major Penrose to find out if he had uncovered any more information. The expression on Penrose's face spoke for itself. He hadn't.

Blocksom set himself up in a local office and wrote his final report on August 29.

"That the raiders were soldiers of the 25th Infantry cannot be doubted. The evidence of many witnesses of all classes is conclusive. Shattered bullets, shells, and clips are merely corroborative."

From all he had heard and seen of the evidence and from his analysis, Blocksom didn't believe the individual criminals ever would be identified. So he must come up with something extraordinary. His second recommendation must be conclusive and final. All along he was formulating his conspiracy of silence theory as the foundation upon which to base his final recommendation.

He finished his recommendation saying that if the black soldiers didn't come forward with the evidence to convict somebody, that "All enlisted men of the three companies present on the night of August 13 be discharged from the service without [honor] and debarred from re-enlistment in the Army, Navy, and Marine Corps." That included all the black soldiers and the sick men in the hospital under the care of white hospital corpsmen.

He ended his report with these words:

> *It must be confessed that the colored soldier is much more aggressive in his attitude on the social equality question than he used to be.*

Taft accepted Blocksom's report even though he had doubts about it and thought it was sweeping, drastic, and excessively punitive. Nevertheless, he sent it directly to President Roosevelt, who approved it. But first, Taft thought the Army should try the 12 soldiers being held in the guardhouse at Fort Sam Houston by military court martial before they announced the decision. Military charges and specifications were promptly prepared. Lieutenant Colonel Leonard A. Lovering was sent to Fort Reno to collect evidence for the trial.

EIGHTEEN

THE GRAND JURY

Investigates

"You don't know who in the hell did this."

WHEN JUDGE STANLEY WELCH heard the news of the mysterious death of Judge Parks, he was in his chambers preparing to preside over the Cameron County Grand Jury investigation of the Brownsville raid. Welch wasn't a friend of Judge Parks. Parks was a bit too liberal for him—and worse than that, he was a Republican. But Welch considered him a fair judge, and thought his death untimely, tragic, and somewhat puzzling. He had wanted Parks to testify before the grand jury. He needed credible witnesses—and he wasn't satisfied that Parks simply got drunk and tumbled out the window. So he asked the district attorney to look into the circumstances surrounding Parks' death. After all, it happened in his judicial district.

A week later, Welch was walking back to his hotel late one evening, when he felt certain he was being followed. When he turned around to see who it was, a shadowy figure bent down behind a water barrel on the street. A muffled voice called out, "Stanley, let it go."

He didn't recognize the voice. Welch walked back toward the barrel, fumbling for his pistol in his sleeve, but the man darted into Cowen Alley and disappeared. Welch figured that he had better keep this incident quiet. Nobody should think he could be intimidated.

Welch convened the grand jury in the early part of September without Parks, but there were plenty of other witnesses. He also had the report of Bill McDonald, the tough-talking, shotgun brandishing, double-hip-pistol-toting Texas Ranger. But he didn't think McDonald's report had much credibility. He wished Parks were still alive.

That morning, when Welch opened the grand jury session, he was in a sour mood. While addressing members of the grand jury, he excoriated the soldiers:

> ...[the] unprovoked, murderous midnight assault committed by the Negro soldiers, their fiendish malice, and hate-showing hearts' blacker than their skins, was evidenced by their firing volley after volley from deadly rifles into and through the doors and windows of family residences, clearly with the brutish hope on their part of killing women and children, and thus make memorable their hatred of the white race.

Judge Welch put the witnesses under oath, subject to the penalty of perjury. Day after day, week after week, witness after witness, irate white citizens testified that the soldiers shot up the town. After hearing much rehearsed hearsay and repeated stories, Judge Welch grew weary and began to question his own assumptions about the soldiers as well as his own judgment.

Why did I allow myself to be suckered in on such flimsy evidence about the prisoners? he thought. He was disgusted with himself. He prided himself on his fairness and objectivity. As he was accustomed to saying, "Every dog, every Indian, every Mexican, every nigger, every Chinaman, gets justice in my court."

After hearing a few more witnesses, Welch hung his head low on his chest for a moment. Then he raised his head and said to the lawyers and jurors, "I haven't heard a damn thing that would indict anybody. You haven't uncovered a clue. You don't know who in the hell did this. You are no further to the truth than when you started. I am not going to let this thing go on any longer. Wrap it up." Welch dismissed the grand jury, saying, "You didn't indict anybody, not even a ham sandwich."

He issued an order notifying the military authorities that the soldiers now being held in jail were entitled to go free.

Welch became a pariah.

The district attorney later pointed out that the "evidence did not point with sufficient certainty to any individual or individuals to justify or warrant them in bringing in an indictment."

Later, Welch wondered why the War Department and President Roosevelt still insisted on keeping the soldiers locked up. Why were they violating his order, and why in the world did they still believe that McDonald was right in selecting those men as the raiders in the first place?

When Welch learned that the Army was sending Lieutenant Colonel Leonard A. Lovering to Fort Reno to collect evidence for a court martial, he rationalized that maybe the grand jury missed something. Maybe he was too hasty in dismissing them. Suddenly, he felt exposed.

Colonel Lovering arrived at Fort Reno in early October to collect more evidence for the court martial of the 12 prisoners. He found none.

General McCaskey had doubts even before he dispatched Lovering:

The reasons for the selecting of these men, or the manner
by which their names were procured, is a mystery. As
far as known, there is no evidence that the majority of
them were any way directly connected with the affair.
It seems to have been a dragnet proceeding.

Hearing about Lovering's report, Welch was relieved and
felt vindicated. The charges were dropped, but the 12 men
were still kept behind bars. Welch wondered why the War
Department was keeping those soldiers locked up. *Must have*
something to do with politics, he thought.

Welch's dismissal of the grand jury and the charges against
the 12 soldiers further enraged McDonald. He was back at
his Corpus Christi Ranger Station plotting how he could get
even with Welch. Again, he felt betrayed by the judge. He
was also incensed that the Texas authorities gave up so easily,
especially when he believed he was about to disclose a bigger
conspiracy that involved the white officers. It seemed to him
that this was about politics. Welch and the mayor sold out
to the Republicans who just wanted to keep the peace. Once
they got the black soldiers out of town, that's all they cared
about. That last trick they played on him at the depot was
too much for him to let go. He had paid the price in mental
anguish for weeks. He had been tricked and outwitted.

A life-long Democrat who had attended almost all of the
Democratic conventions, McDonald had fought Republicans
all his life. His only political lapse was the time he went
wolf hunting with Teddy Roosevelt in Oklahoma. Roosevelt
didn't forget that wolf-hunting trip. Roosevelt believed him.
Politics always wins, he thought. *That's the reason them niggers*
are still in jail. But locked up in a military jail wasn't good
enough for McDonald. He wanted them behind bars in a
Texas prison, waiting to be hanged by Texans. Welch was a

turncoat, McDonald was more certain of that now than ever. Texas had a way of taking care of turncoats. It was a damn good way of settling political squabbles. He hated Welch. Politics would take care of him, he was sure.

In early November, Judge Welch went to Rio Grande City, a town not too far from Brownsville, to talk to the Brownsville District Attorney and take care of some political business. He met with the district attorney in a local hotel and told him the strange story about his encounter with the muffled voice in Brownsville. "Tonight, on my way here to meet you, again I felt that I was being tailed. I turned around and heard the same voice, this time coming from a side street. 'Stanley, I told you to let it go. Now it's too late.'" I asked, 'Who in the hell are you? What do you want?'"

The voice said nothing else, but Welch heard the sound of someone running down the side street.

"Who did you tell about our investigation into Parks' death?" Welch asked the DA.

"Nobody, but the sheriff, and the police chief," the DA said.

Welch and the DA took separate rooms at the hotel at the hotel Casa de los Abogodos in Rio Grande City. The next morning, Judge Welch was found murdered in his bed with the door still locked from the inside.

Judge Welch's murder shocked the citizens of Cameron County, and particularly Mayor Combe. Was it connected to his dismissal of the grand jury?

Attorney Wells wired the governor asking that the Texas Rangers investigate the murder. He also advised him to send anybody but Bill McDonald. The governor ignored the advice and sent McDonald.

Nineteen

THE ULTIMATUM

"So help me God, I don't know."

Things were not looking good from a legal stand-point for the War Department and Roosevelt. The Cameron County Grand Jury returned no indictments. Colonel Lovering found no evidence to indict anyone, and the Citizens Committee failed to identify the guilty parties. Worst of all, the lawyers in the judge advocate general's office privately considered Blocksom's report worthless since it contained no sworn statements and too many contradictory witnesses. But the president had already approved the report, and he didn't want to go into it any deeper.

But Roosevelt wasn't finished with the matter. On October 4, 1906, he ordered General Ernest A. Garlington, the Inspector General of the Army, to go to Fort Reno and Fort Sam Houston to conduct still another investigation.

Roosevelt never doubted Blocksom's report that some of the soldiers were guilty, but he wanted to know which ones. Yes, he had approved it. And he knew it prescribed drastic punishment, if the guilty ones were not discovered. But he needed to have a valid justification for such a harsh decision. So he went one step further and directed Garlington to issue an ultimatum that unless the enlisted men who had knowledge of the incident came forward and identified the guilty parties, "every black soldier stationed at Fort Brown would be discharged 'without honor' and would be forever debarred from reenlistment as well as from employment in any civil capacity under government."[1]

General Garlington was a native of South Carolina, the home state of "Pitchfork" Ben Tillman. Tillman was the fiery senator from South Carolina who blasted Roosevelt for inviting Booker T. Washington to the White House for dinner in 1901. "The action of President Roosevelt in entertaining that nigger," he predicted, "will necessitate our killing a thousand niggers in the South before they will learn their place again."

Garlington welcomed the task Roosevelt assigned him. In fact, he thought he was uniquely qualified to identify the culprits. "I lived with them, played with them as a child, was brought up on a large plantation with them."

He arrived in Oklahoma City on October 8, 1906. He immediately consulted Major Blocksom whom he considered had made an "exhaustive investigation." He was briefed by Blocksom, listened to the talk about the "niggers" breaking out of the fort, absorbed all of the "evidence" McDonald collected on the 12 prisoners and agreed with it absolutely. He reviewed the personnel records of the 12 prisoners and went over them again and again until he felt that he knew everything about them.

He obtained a copy of Colonel Lovering's report and reviewed the sworn testimony Lovering took. He was disappointed that Lovering gained no evidence from the soldiers. All he got were denials that they participated in the raid or knew who the raiders were.

---

1 Earlier Roosevelt had softened his order by allowing each soldier to apply to for reinstatement provided he could prove his innocence.

THE BROWNSVILLE TEXAS INCIDENT OF 1906

Garlington got back on the train and headed for Fort Sam Houston to interview the 12 soldiers McDonald accused. For more than a month the 12 men languished in the guardhouse, wasting away and not understanding why they were still being held behind barbed wire after Judge Welch had urged their release.

Military escorts met Garlington at the San Antonio depot and carried him away in the Commanding General's carriage to Fort Sam Houston. As was customary for an IG visit, Garlington was shown great deference—and even more so than usual for this man from Washington. He was greeted with much saluting, bowing and heel-clicking, and a lot of "Yes, sirs!"

Every soldier knew he could go directly to the IG, without going through the chain of command, to get his grievances redressed without fear of reprisal. So the 12 Brownsville prisoners looked forward to meeting General Garlington. They believed he would be fair. He would get them out of jail and back to their unit where they would be reunited with their friends, wives, and children. And for Holomon, get him back to his business interests.

The carriage reached the entrance to the guardhouse grounds and stopped at the foot of the hill. Garlington stuck his head out and looked up the Hill. He saw the guardhouse, a low, bubble-like building with thick adobe walls, squatting on a low hill. It was protected by a barbed wire fence, which began at the bottom of the hill and encircled it with concentric rings of wire. Each ring became smaller and smaller as the fences went up the hillside, until a small ring at the top choked the neck of the hill.

The guardhouse was all that was left of an old fortress with heavy masonry fortifications. These were embedded with old guns, which used to provide 360 degrees of coverage. Narrow windows at the top, now reinforced with short iron bars, provided observation but discouraged any escape plans.

Two guards standing at the door of the guardhouse came to attention and saluted. The commandant greeted Garlington and led him inside the guardhouse. The inside walls were bare, rough slabs of crumbling sandstone, reaching up to the ceiling like giant tombstones. Each cell was a square cage formed by zig-zagging barbed wire.

Garlington met the 12 men as a group. First he tried the friendly approach, a folksy manner, the southern gentleman's approach:

"Where are y'all from, boys? I am here to get you out of this mess. Ain't this place horrible? This is the ugliest place I ever laid my eyes on. Are they treating you all right here? Are you getting enough to eat?

"I know that some of your buddies got all liquored up and jumped that wall, went into town and did a little shooting. Now they really didn't mean to hurt anybody, but wild shooting sometimes can kill folks. Somebody is guilty as hell. Not all of you, but some of you know who the rascals are. You got to tell me who these criminals are. Now you just tell me, and every thang gonna be alright. I'm gonna talk to y'all in private. Who's from South Carolina?"

"I am," Private James Newton answered.

"I'll talk to you first." Garlington turned to the commandant. "Let these here other boys out in the yard to get some fresh air. It's stuffy in here."

Having said that, Garlington and Newton went into the visitors' room and continued the interview.

"Oh, so you're from South Carolina? What part?"

"Greenville."

"Oh, Greenville. Mighty fine town. Now that's some co-incidence." Garlington grabbed Newton's hand and shook it vigorously, pumping it like a politician looking for votes. "I'm from South Carolina, Greenville! I know you are a good boy. You don't belong in here. Who are your folks? I may know them."

"The Newtons."

"Why, yes, I know'um. Mighty fine family." Garlington was pleased with this discovery.

But Newton noticed the general's hand was cold. It felt like a fish freshly-caught from Greenville Creek. *His hand should be warm from all this hand-shaking*, Newton thought, *but it's icy.* He remembered what his mother used to tell him, "Deceit in a man's heart chills the blood flowing to his hand."

"Now that man that knocked you in the head with his pistol, he was wrong, shouldn't of done it. Didn't you wanna git back at 'im?" Garlington said.

"Yes, sir, but after a day or so, and a few beers, I forgot about it."

"You forgot about it!"

"Yes, sir."

"You didn't feel any animosity against him and the people in Brownsville?"

"No, sir."

"Now, Newton, tell me what you have heard about this shooting."

"I don't know nothing about it. I didn't do it."

"Newton, I have the power to get you out of here if you tell me who did it."

"I told you, sir," Newton said, shaking his head. "So help me God, I don't know."

A Conspiracy of Silence

John Holomon, the money lender, was of special interest to Garlington. "Send John Holomon in here!"

Garlington had read McDonald's report before he left Washington. McDonald speculated that Holomon was the ringleader of the raiders and the real leader of the enlisted men. After all, Holomon was captain of the B Company's baseball team and ran the saloon. Everybody owed him money and nothing could be planned or done without Holomon knowing about it. McDonald wrote that Holomon held a business grudge against John Tillman, the owner of the Ruby Saloon, and wanted to run him out of business.

Holomon walked in with his hands buried deep in his pockets, eyes fixed, defiant, distrustful. He had lost weight and looked almost emaciated. His uniform hung on his body like a sheet. His once bulging baseball arms were shriveled, his once broad chest, shrunken. His face was hollow.

Garlington was unnerved by the appearance of this soldier. He looked like a ghost. Garlington reached out to shake his hand.

Holomon looked down at the stars on the general's shoulders, removed his hands from his pockets, snapped to attention, saluted, and said, "Private Holomon, reporting, sir! I have a complaint to make."

Garlington withdrew his hand and returned the salute. "At ease, soldier. Sit down."

"I have a complaint to make," Holomon repeated.

"You damned right you gotta complaint. They haven't been feeding you, have they?"

"No, sir."

"Well, they are gonna feed ya!"

"Yes, sir, there's plenty of food."

"Boy, I don't understand you. You say, 'No, sir.' when I asked you if they've been feeding ya, and you say, 'Yes, sir, there's plenty of food.' Which is it?"

"Sir, I don't wanna talk about eating. I want to get out of here. I got a son to take care of. I got to get hold of him."

Garlington thought he had better get straight to the point with Holomon. "You are a good businessman, I hear."

"I'm a better soldier, sir."

"You ran the Holomon Saloon?"

"It was called Allison's Saloon, but I owned it."

"What time did you close the saloon on the night of the shooting?"

"About 7:30 that evening."

"That was early, wasn't it.?"

"Yes, sir. We had a curfew. We had orders to be in by eight o'clock."

"Were the troops liquored up?"

"I didn't sell whiskey. I sold beer."

"Well, were they juiced up?"

"I didn't see anybody drunk."

"Okay. Do you know a saloon keeper called John Tillman? He runs the Ruby Saloon."

"I met him when we first came to Brownsville."

"The Ruby Saloon was competition with your saloon, now, wasn't it?"

"I wouldn't say it like that. Most of the men never went to the Ruby Saloon. My saloon had most of the soldier business."

"Boy, you had a grudge against the Ruby Saloon, now, didn't ya? You know a soldier named John Brown, don't ya? You, John Brown, and your buddy Allison planned the whole damn thing. You did, didn't ya? You got whiskey from San Antonio, you fed a few boys liquor, you went into town to put the Ruby out of business, to scare 'em. Didn't ya? You figured a little shooting wouldn't hurt anybody, but it got out of hand, didn't it? You fed 'em too much whiskey. Didn't ya? You did it, didn't ya?"

Holomon appeared amused. He tried to compose himself. A faint smile broke out around his lips and he looked the general dead in the eyes. He started to snicker, chuckled a little—and tried to hold it back. Finally, he couldn't hold it back any longer. He placed his hand over his mouth and burst out laughing.

"What's so funny? What're you laughing at? Don't you disrespect me."

"I'm not disrespecting you, sir. You asked if I knew John Brown. I know 'im."

"He was absent when the roll was called, wasn't he?"

"He was over at the bake shop, baking bread, when the shooting was going on."

"He was in on it with you, wasn't he?"

"Sir, if I had any intention of committing a crime," Holomon said, "John Brown would have been one of the last men in the world I would have selected to carry out a deed like that."

"Why not?"

"He is the dumbest man I ever met. That man put in about six years without learning to right shoulder arms. He's dumb and stupid. You couldn't learn him anything."

"Is John Brown too dumb to bake bread?"

"That's about all he can do."

There was a knock at the door that interrupted the interview. The commandant came in and handed Garlington a note that read:

This prisoner puts himself on bread and water for days, some days on, some days off. Some kinda protest.

Garlington realized that he wasn't dealing with the average soldier, but a shrewd manipulator. He thought he had better make a deal, a money deal, if he were to get anything out of Holomon. "Son, did you leave any money in the bank in Brownsville?"

"No, sir, I got it out before we left."

"Oh?"

"Yes, sir. I got it all out."

"Well, maybe you weren't in on it, but you must know who was. You tell me and I'll see what I can do to get a transfer for you to the Ninth Cavalry or the Tenth Cavalry. You can still open a saloon and carry on your business. You can still make money. How's about that? You just tell me, son."

Holomon hesitated as all kinds of thoughts ran through his head. Money was uppermost in his mind. He also thought of his money lending business, opening up another saloon, his son, his army career, and even an escape from the gallows, if they somehow managed to pin this crime on him. This angle was his way out. He could lie, but he never liked lying. Lying was like cheating, and he never cheated on anybody except his wife.

He hesitated so long that it encouraged Garlington. "Come on now, son, tell me. It'll be all right. Leave it to me. I'll take care of it."

Finally, Holomon said, "Sir, if I had any previous knowledge of any crime contemplated by the soldiers, I would have done everything in my power to stop it."

"Why would you do that?"

"If for no other reason, to protect my financial interest. And I have another reason, my son Robert. He's nine years old and lives in Macon, Georgia, with my wife. My marriage is in the shithouse, it's over. I want my son with me. I had planned to bring him to Brownsville. I haven't seen him in a long time. I just rented a house across the street from my saloon, on Garrison Road."

Holomon reached in his pocket, pulled out a receipt, handed it to Garlington, and said, "See? I paid three dollars for one month's rent for the house. I shipped my household goods to Brownsville. I bought a dining room set on the same day of the shooting. I planned to set up a home for my son."

"How were you gonna do that?"

"I had a housekeeper in Valentine, Nebraska. I was going to bring her to Brownsville to care for my son."

"What was the woman's name?"

"Stella Harris."

"Well, maybe we can still work it out."

"I don't think so, sir."

"Why not?"

"You want me to lie."

"You're lying now!"

"I want a court martial. They will know I didn't do it. I want my day in court, sir. I don't know who did it."

"You're dismissed."

In succession, Garlington interviewed the rest of the 12 prisoners without success. He assembled them in a group again and said, "You all have until 5 o'clock to tell me who did it. I know beyond a reasonable doubt that somebody in the 25th Infantry fired into the houses of Brownsville. I told you the president sent me here to give you all a last chance to identify the guilty culprits. You all didn't tell me anything, and if you all don't by 5 o'clock, you will all be kicked out of this army without honor."

Garlington waited until 5 o'clock rolled around. No soldier showed up. He departed for Fort Reno, Oklahoma, empty handed.

Garlington reached Fort Reno and, to his chagrin, learned that Penrose and his officers hadn't found out anything new from the soldiers either. Thus far, Penrose had failed. And so had he. He didn't know what else to do.

Garlington rationalized the reasons why he didn't get anything from the men in the guardhouse. They had to have known who was guilty. They must have been in on it. They were the real guilty ones. No soldier could have jumped that wall, shot up the town, and returned without those key people knowing about it, seeing it—and perhaps participating in it. They were hardened criminals, not amenable to reason.

Some of the old soldiers who had a lot to lose still might be induced to talk. He would remove some formality. He would examine some of the men under oath, others he would not.

He questioned about 28 men, restricting them to answering a narrow range of questions:

Who was engaged in the shooting? Didn't you participate in the riot? Wasn't Holomon the ringleader?

Garlington refused to listen to any answers explaining where they were, and to conditions which made it impossible for them to have knowledge of the rioters' identities or any details. When a soldier tried to explain that he was sick in the hospital or that there was some other situation which could exonerate him, Garlington refused to hear it. He would interrupt, "I didn't ask you that."

Every man insisted that he had no knowledge, that he had not taken part in any shooting and that he didn't know anybody who had. As each man denied the accusations, Garlington became more and more convinced that Blocksom was right—all of the soldiers had entered into a conspiracy of silence.

Garlington became so exasperated that his true feelings began to surface during the interviews. "Now, sergeant, don't you know that your people are always sticking themselves into some place where they are not wanted?" he asked Sergeant Walker McCurdy.

"Sir, I don't know anything about it. I only follow orders."

After Garlington asked Sergeant Luther T. Thornton a few questions, he said:

Now, sergeant, I am a Southern man myself, and naturally, what I speak I speak from experience. Have you noticed that in the South, when the colored people get into trouble with white people, a class of colored people place themselves in a position of authority where they had no business to be, and when a colored man commits a crime, he is protected by all the rest of his people?

Luther responded:

Sir, I was born in the North. The only experience I had
with Southern white people was while in the Army. Their
attitude toward colored soldiers was one of disrespect
for the man wearing the uniform, and not a charitable
feeling for the man of color.

They Might Even Lie About the Weather

On Friday morning, Garlington and Penrose walked
along a small trail in the back of the officers' quarters, heads
down in deep conversation. Since nothing had worked to get
the soldiers to produce any information about who shot up
the town, Garlington decided to use his last, most powerful,
and most draconian tactic. He would issue an ultimatum
which had been recommended by Blocksom and directed by
Teddy Roosevelt.

"Major," he said to Penrose. "Your men are lying to me.
They are telling me that they have not heard any barracks'
talk about taking revenge against the white people in town.
That was their motive. Revenge. God dammit! Somebody
heard something and I'm gonna get it out of 'em!"

"Yes, sir." Penrose racked his brain, trying to think of
something to add. He looked around and saw that it was a
beautiful autumn day without a cloud in the sky. "Sir, I have
heard you say many times that you are a Southern man. Do
Southern white people believe colored people are truthful?"

Garlington bristled at Penrose's question. "I don't know
about all Southern white people."

"What about you, sir?" Penrose asked. "Do you believe
colored folks tell the truth?"

Garlington moved closer to Penrose and faced him squarely, "No! I don't believe colored folks are generally truthful."

"That's why you don't believe that any of my men—even the ones you put under oath—are telling you the truth."

"I told you, Penrose, colored folks just don't tell the truth."

The two men began walking slowly, heads down. "You think a colored man might tell the truth about the weather, but not about a crime, sir?"

"He might have a problem in telling the truth about the weather," Garlington said.

Penrose was devastated by Garlington's cynical admission. He was still conflicted. He knew his soldiers had been truthful with him before the shooting. Why would all of them be lying now? What was he to believe? Who was he to believe? He was deeply saddened. He felt that no white officer, not even his commander in chief, the president, would take his soldiers' word over that of a white Brownsville citizen. But why did he want to believe his men?

"Major Penrose, tomorrow morning at ten o'clock, assemble all of your men and officers on the parade field in an informal horseshoe formation. I'm gonna make one more appeal, then I'm gonna give 'em the president's ultimatum."

"White officers, too?" Penrose asked.

"No, Penrose, just the colored men."

"What about the men in the hospital?"

"All of 'em, Penrose!"

You Have Until Nine O'clock Tomorrow

It was Saturday morning. By ten o'clock the fog should have lifted, but a heavy cloud still hugged the ground. Garlington stood in the center of a horse shoe formation. He noticed that Penrose had assembled his men without the flag and without the battalion colors. He yelled at Penrose, "Major, get the flag and the battalion colors out here!"

The request was soon fulfilled and Garlington addressed the troops:

It has been established by investigation that certain men of your battalion have committed the crime of killing one man, wounding another, and shooting into houses containing women and children. I have been sent here by the president of the United States to endeavor to discover the guilty men. You men have fought for that flag.

He pointed to the flag behind him.

I appeal to your pride in your regiment and your individual service to this Army to come forward and take this stain from your regiment. Keep it out of your personal records. It will be a blot on your records, a blot on your race. You must come forward now. Tell me who did this horrible thing.

No soldier stepped forward. No soldier said anything.

Many of you old timers have long service. You have too much to lose. Think of your pensions. You are too close to retirement. Don't throw it all away. Don't let the criminals among you damage your good service. Throw them up! Cast them out from among you! Step forward! Tell me who did it!

No soldier moved forward. There was not even a cough. No one even cleared his throat.

Men, think of your families, your women, your wives, and your children. Don't let this hurt them.

When no one came forward, Garlington issued the president's ultimatum.

Unless you men with guilty knowledge come forward and identify the guilty parties, you all will be discharged 'without honor' and will be forever debarred from re-enlistment, as well as from employment in any civil capacity under government. There, you got it! Do you understand? Do you hear me? You better come on up here this very minute!

There was a long silence and a seemingly longer wait. Garlington continued:

I'm gonna give you one last chance. You have until nine o'clock tomorrow morning. I'll be accessible until then for any man who desires to give me information.

By Sunday morning, no one had showed up. Then Mingo Sanders walked through the door, stood ramrod straight, saluted the General. He then laid his military records out on the desk and said, "Sir, I have talked to every man, and ..."

"Wait a minute there, Sergeant. You mean to say you talked to every man in this outfit?"

"Yes, sir! Not all last night. I started talking with them in Brownsville, on the train up here and since we been here in Oklahoma. I spent all last night talking. I finished talking to the last ones early this morning. That's why I got here the last minute."

"Well, I hope you got something to tell me."

"All the men deny it. I'm convinced that no man in the 25th Infantry did this. Sir, I believe that they don't know anything to tell you. That's why they are not telling."

Garlington pounded the table with his fist. "You're a liar. You are lying, sergeant!"

"I beg your pardon, sir. Why would I lie to protect a criminal? Why would any of the men lie to protect a murderer?"

"You people lie to protect your race."

"Sir, I'm telling you the truth. I believe the men told me the truth."

"So, sergeant, you are speaking for all those liars. Yeah, I believe you're talking for 'em all. Sergeant, you are a part of this conspiracy of silence."

"Sir, those are big words for me. I'm a lowly sergeant. I don't understand what you are saying. Are you saying I'm part of some kind of clique?"

"Yeah, more to the point, Sergeant, a silent gang."

"I'm not part of any gang. I brought my enlistment records. My records show, 'Character excellent, a faithful and reliable soldier.' I'm fifty-years old. I have served twenty-five years, six months and seven days. I fought in Cuba and the Philippines and I was continually on the firing line. On the 25th day of June, about nine or ten miles from Siboney in Cuba, Theodore Roosevelt came to me, and at my special request, my company shared our supply of hardtack with his command."

Garlington became uneasy and shifted around in his chair. "Hold on there, sergeant," he said. "You are talking about the president. That's a serious accusation you are making. Do you understand what you are saying? Do you know what you're talking about? You are slandering Colonel Roosevelt. You are speaking ill of the president. You're telling me he outran his supply lines? And you had to give them some of your biscuits?"

"I don't mean any disrespect. President Roosevelt knows me and some of the old timers who fought with him in Cuba. He knows we are honorable soldiers. Tell 'im you talked to me. He'll know. We helped him out at the battle of San Juan Hill. We captured El Caney. We are in a tight spot now. We need his help."

"You have anything else to say?"

"Yes, sir. You know many of us don't have much longer to serve to get our pension. We don't want to lose that."

"I told you that."

"I have only two and a half years to go. Now, I am a poor man. I served honest and faithful for the government."

"I understand, sergeant, but you all are standing together to resist the detection of the guilty. Therefore, you all should stand together when the penalty falls."

Garlington completed his investigation on October 19, 1906, and agreed with Blocksom's theory that the men had joined a conspiracy of silence. His recommendation, All of them must be punished and discharged without honor.

Mingo Sanders still had faith in Colonel Roosevelt. "He will not let us down," he told Sergeant McCurdy. "We shared our rations with him. We helped him. Now he will remember and he will help us."

"Will he?" McCurdy said.

TWENTY

PRESIDENT ROOSEVELT

Makes His Decision

Turkey Hunting in Virginia

BY OCTOBER 22, 1906, Garlington's report had passed through the military chain of command and reached the War Department. It immediately caused a legal stir and a debate among the War Department lawyers. Judge Advocate General George B. Davis opposed it and went directly to William Howard Taft to lobby against it. Davis had hoped that Garlington would bring back a tighter legal case and he sat down with Taft to discuss it. He told Taft he was disappointed in the report and considered it just a warmed-over Blocksom report. It had no hard evidence or even a factual basis for its conclusive findings that, beyond a reasonable doubt, the men of the 25th Infantry committed a crime. Davis laid the report on Taft's desk directly in front of him.

"Mr. Secretary," Davis said, "you can't let this report get to the president without more evidence."

"Hold on a minute," Taft said, "I'll get my copy."

His secretary brought the report to him. Taft said he had been studying it and flipped to a page that he said had been giving him a headache. "This part is categorically blaming. It faults all of the soldiers for refusing to tell something that nobody has shown they knew anything about in the first place, 'to tell all that it is reasonable to believe they know concerning the shooting.'"

"If this thing is ever implemented," Davis said, picking up his copy, "it'll be harsh and sweeping in its effect. It'll take away their uniforms, which you know soldiers love so much. It'll take away their honor, which the record shows they have earned, humiliating them. It will take away the pensions of the long-service men. And Mr. Secretary, look at this paragraph," Davis pointed to a certain section. "It takes away their employment possibilities in any capacity with the government, even as garbage collectors." He paused for a second. "You know something, Mr. Secretary? I don't believe the president has the power to take away their future employment."

"Well, he may not have the power to do a lot in this report, but he'll demand that we find a way to get it for him," Taft said.

"Just think about this," Davis said. "This paper would punish everybody, even the men who were in the hospital during the shooting. And worst of all, Mr. Secretary, it punishes all of them without due process, all without a trial. There is no constitutional basis for this drastic recommendation without giving those boys a trial. We just can't let this get to the president."

"I'll talk to him about it before I send the report," Taft said.

Davis picked up his copy of Garlington's report and left. Taft went to lunch leaving his copy in the middle of his desk.

Taft sat in his private dining room nibbling at his food, distracted by the troublesome legal issues Davis raised. Did he really think Roosevelt would change his mind? Taft knew he couldn't change Roosevelt's mind if he had already made it up. Everybody knew that. He had already made up his mind when he gave Garlington the authority to issue that ultimatum. If not, why did he do it? Still, he must find a way to get Roosevelt to pull back on this thing, or at least delay it until after the November off-year election of the new Congress.

When the report reached President Roosevelt's desk, he delayed action on it. He went turkey hunting in Pine Knot, Virginia. He held it on his desk for days, waiting until after the elections.

Mingo Sanders waited patiently to see if his former brother-in-arms, now his commander-in-chief, would support him in affirming his innocence. He hoped he would not forget him. Sanders felt that Roosevelt was still their best hope for getting out of "this mess."

Sergeant McCurdy was still doubtful.

A Crime 'Blacker than Black'

It was Monday, November 5, 1906. Roosevelt was ready to make his decision. He sent for Taft. They met briefly and discussed Garlington's report. Roosevelt accused the soldiers of shooting up the town, perpetrating a crime "blacker than black," calling them murderers, midnight assassins, criminals. He further accused all of them of engaging in a conspiracy of silence to shield the guilty.

Taft, a lawyer by profession, made a legal argument against it. Roosevelt, not a lawyer, didn't want to hear the legal details. He pointed to the paragraph in the report which obviously impressed him, and perhaps was the overriding reason for his decision. Garlington had emphasized that his recommendation was designed as a deterrent, "a forceful lesson" for other soldiers, and a vow to the citizens of Brownsville and other citizens that "men wearing the uniform of the U.S. Army are their protectors, and not midnight assassins."

Roosevelt made his decision. He directed Taft to implement Garlington's recommendations, but to delay public announcement until the next day.

Roosevelt did not hang around Washington for long after he made his decision public. He went aboard the presidential yacht and headed for the Panama Canal Zone to see how construction was progressing. The next day, Friday, November 9, 1906, the War Department issued Special Order 266.

Figure 15. President Theodore Roosevelt
SOURCE: American History Illustrated, Volume xxi, Number 6, 1986,
Historical Times, Inc. Harrisburg, PA
Culver Pictures, New York City

TWENTY ONE

A PUBLIC

Outcry

A New Hope

IT WAS LATE TUESDAY evening, November 6, 1906, after the off-year elections when Roosevelt's decision was publicly announced. Almost simultaneously with the public announcement of that decision, there was a huge public outcry against the decision. After having secured overwhelming black support for the Republicans, the election of Charles Evans Hughes and a Republican Congress, which included the re-election of his son-in-law, Nicholas Longworth, from Ohio, Roosevelt could now make his decision known to key black leaders. This, he did. But Roosevelt gave his loyal Republican friend, Dr. Booker T. Washington, the founder of Tuskegee Institute in Alabama, advance notice of his decision before it was made public that day. It was still a *fait accompli* and he was not about to change his decision, notwithstanding Dr. Washington's best efforts to talk him out of it. Washington pleaded with him, urging his good friend and the best white friend of the Negro race (in Washington's opinion) to change his mind. When Roosevelt refused, Washington candidly characterized the decision as a "blunder."

But the other influential black leader—educator, sociologist and activist, Dr. W. E. B. Du Bois—got no advance warning from Roosevelt. When he got word of the decision, he was less charitable in his characterization of Roosevelt's decision. "It was a cowardly act," he said, and he denounced Roosevelt as a "coward." Du Bois even went further. He threatened to break ranks with the Republican Party and to support the Northern Democrats. He began to openly court William Jennings Bryan for president even though the presidential election of 1908 was two years away.

Like Du Bois, some of the black press was not charitable in their depiction of Roosevelt's decision and the timing of its announcement. *The Washington Bee*, a black-owned newspaper, made this observation: "Negroes are not fools, at least not all of them, and this after-election order is well understood by them."

The *Waterville Maine Sentinel* made a direct challenge to Roosevelt's bravery, just as Du Bois had done:

The picture of the president, whose chief merit is supposed to lie in his fearless bravery, dodging an issue like this one until after the votes are counted, is not pleasant to look upon, even though it stamps him as a clever politician.

The black press was not alone in its criticism of Roosevelt. White newspapers, notably the *New York Times* and the *Washington Post*, joined in the public outcry against the president. While the press railed against Roosevelt and black ministers excoriated him in their pulpits, all without any effect, the Constitutional League swung into action to offer direct help to the soldiers.

The Constitutional League (the League) was a civil rights organization financed by John Milholland, a white millionaire. He was sitting in his office, reading the *Wall Street Journal*, checking his stocks and bonds when his telephone rang. The caller was Gilchrist Stewart. A tall and leathery-faced man, Stewart was a black lawyer who was active in the League's pursuit of justice. "John, did you see what our friend Roosevelt did to the colored soldiers? If these were white soldiers, he wouldn't have done it."

"Wait a minute, Gil," Milholland said, "you're jumping at conclusions. He hasn't done anything yet. This is just a political thing right now. Taft put the order out. He wants to be president. There are a lot of black voters in Ohio. He needs Ohio in the presidential election in 1908, and he's starting early. He is out on the campaign trail right now. He'll change that order. If Roosevelt is serious about actual implementation of that fatuous order, and I don't think he is, we'll stop him. We've got the U.S. Constitution on our side. Believe me, it won't be a problem—he'll change that order. We should not be too quick to bring race into it. We'll do better without using race. Let's just get facts."

"Now, John, you know race prejudice is pervasive throughout the Army. I tell you, it's ripe with racial bigotry, just as the French Army is with anti-Semitism. You know what the French Generals did to Captain Dreyfus just a few years ago," Gil responded.

"You know I know. Dreyfus was set up just because he was a Jew. They framed him."

"That's exactly what the Army is doing to these soldiers, except they are doing it 167 times. There are 167 Dreyfuses. Nobody is helping them. There is going to be a lot of hand-wringing and talk, but nobody is going to do anything about it except talk it to death. We must get involved."

"So you want to be Emile Zola? All right, why don't you go to Texas and talk to the soldiers?"

Time was running out, and Stewart knew it. He packed his bags and took the next train to Oklahoma City, where he continued by hack to Fort Reno about 23 miles away. There he found the soldiers in a desperate situation. They were still cooped up in virtual house arrest. Dispirited, they were now feeling the full impact of the public announcement of the order. They were overwhelmed by a heavy sense of helplessness, abandonment, and betrayal by their commander in chief.

Stewart asked Penrose to get the men together in one group. Penrose assembled the black soldiers in the same horseshoe formation used by Garlington. When all the men were assembled, Stewart addressed them as a group. "My name is Gilchrist Stewart. I'm a lawyer from New York representing the United States Constitutional League. The League, as we lawyers call it, is a civil rights organization. It sent me here to help you secure your constitutional rights to due process, and to get a fair hearing and a fair trial.

"At this time, this moment, this day, you should know that our Constitution considers all of you innocent until proven guilty in a court of law. I'm going to hear your side of the story. All you have to do is tell the truth."

Private Boyd Conyers raised his hand and got Stewart's attention. "Sir, that's what we've been doing. Nobody will listen to us. Major Blocksom and the general from Washington wouldn't let us tell our side of the story. They tried to force us to tell who did it. We don't know who did the shooting. If we don't know who did it in the first place, how can we tell anybody who did it? We can't tell what we don't know, even if we wanted to."

"That's a good point. You can't tell me or anybody else anything you don't know. But you can say what you want to say or say nothing. I'm going to ask all of you to make sworn statements. I can't tell you what to say, because I wasn't there the night of the shooting, and I am not allowed to tell you what to say anyway. You don't have to make any statement, if you don't want to, but I strongly encourage each and every one of you to do so."

The League formed a "commission of inquiry" and hired George H. White, a prominent lawyer, as counsel. The League sent more lawyers to Fort Reno, Oklahoma, Fort Sam Houston, Texas, Fort Brown, and Brownsville. In the days that followed, morale among the soldiers began to rise as they saw visible activity of the League lawyers, counseling them on their rights, taking affidavits, talking to Major Penrose and the others officers.

"Republicans will pay for this."

It was Saturday morning, November 17, 1906. Mary Church Terrell, a black woman, civil rights activist, and president of the National Association of Colored Women, had just returned to her home in Washington, D.C. from a trip to Boston. Her telephone rang and on the line in New York City was John Milholland, the white financial sponsor of the Constitutional League.

"Mary, I want you to go over to the War Department and talk to Taft about that order. Get him to delay it till we get the facts. The League has a lot of lawyers running around in Texas and Oklahoma, trying to make sense of this thing."

"I heard the rumors floating around Washington for several days before I left for Boston," Mary said, her voice shaking. "I didn't believe our friend Roosevelt would take such drastic action. In fact, few of the people I talked to believed he would do so. All right, I will go see Secretary Taft."

"See him today. He's supposed to be back in Washington. We don't have much time."

Secretary Taft was sitting at his desk at the War Department, wading elbow deep in a pile of letters, petitions, resolutions, telegrams and newspaper articles, all concerning Roosevelt's Brownsville decision. Most of them blamed him and he didn't like it.

A military aide to the secretary stepped into Taft's office and saw that Taft was extremely busy. He turned around and started to leave, when Taft raised his head, "What is it? I hope there are no more papers on this subject today."

"There's a colored woman outside. She stopped me as I was walking through the lobby and asked me to tell you she's been waiting all day to see you. Says she knows you. Your secretary says the woman doesn't have an appointment."

"What's her name?"

"Mrs. Mary Church Terrell."

"Tell my secretary to show her in right now." Taft was concerned that a powerful, influential black Republican like Mary Church Terrell, who could influence so many black voters across the country, had been kept waiting outside his door like a servant.

Pushing down on both arms of his chair, Taft slowly lifted his massive bulk and moved from behind his desk. He was standing when his secretary ushered Mrs. Terrell into his office. "Mary, have a seat over here," he stretched out his beefy hand toward a leather couch along the mahogany wall under an oil painting of General Ulysses S. Grant. "Sorry they kept you waiting." He sat down again.

"Mr. Secretary, I've come on behalf of the colored soldiers."

"What do you want me to do about it? President Roosevelt has already dismissed them and he has gone to Panama. There is nothing I can do."

"All I want you to do, Mr. Secretary, is to suspend the order dismissing the soldiers until an investigation can be made."

"Is that all you want me to do, Mary?" Taft said, with a patronizing smile.

"For now, yes. I'll always ask for more till we get the same rights.'

"So all you want me to do for now is suspend an order issued by the president of the United States during his absence from the country."

"I want you to do what's morally right and what's politically right, and they are the same in this situation, Mr. Secretary."

Taft understood well what Mary Church Terrell was talking about. The political cost might be high. It might mean the difference between winning the 1908 presidential election and losing to William Jennings Bryan, or any other Democrat. Taft stood up indicating that he had gotten the message. "All right, Mary, no promises. I'll think about it."

"Thank you, Mr. Secretary."

Political pressure was building against Roosevelt's decision, and Taft felt it. On Sunday morning, November 18, 1906, black ministers shouted from their pulpits that the Republican Party had sold out to the Southern Democrats, that the United States Constitution was being lynched in Texas along with the black soldiers. They cried that Roosevelt had betrayed the race, and that Taft would pay in '08 if the order was not suspended.

Taft Has Cold Feet

Taft was on the train on his way to New Haven, Connecticut, reading the Sunday Morning newspapers, when the pressure became so overwhelming that he stopped first in Baltimore and again in Philadelphia's West Philadelphia station to call his private secretary. Taft instructed him to cable the president that the implementation of the order had hardly begun and that the order could be suspended. But Roosevelt had left Panama and hadn't received either of the messages.

By Sunday's end, the pressure had become too great to ignore. Taft suspended the president's order, an act unthinkable to him before Mary Church Terrell's visit.

Two days passed and Taft had heard nothing from Roosevelt about his decision. Taft grew uneasy, worrying that perhaps he had done the wrong thing and that Roosevelt would think he had crossed him. It was not like Roosevelt to keep quiet about the suspension. He should have gotten at least one of the messages sent to him by now. Furthermore, several newspapers had carried the story in bold headlines on their front pages.

Anxiety finally got the better of him and he lifted the suspension of the order, directing the discharges without honor to be executed.

It was a good thing he did, because when Roosevelt got news of the suspension in Ponce, Puerto Rico, he fired back at Taft on Wednesday, November 21, 1906:

> *Discharge is not to be suspended unless there are new facts of such importance as to warrant your cabling me. I care nothing whatsoever for the yelling of either politicians or the sentimentalists. The offense was most heinous and the punishment I inflicted was imposed after due deliberation.*

After Taft read Roosevelt's telegram characterizing the alleged offense as most heinous, the fear that the black soldiers would mutiny troubled him. He feared that they might cause a nasty incident at Fort Reno that would get beyond the control of their white officers. To prevent such an occurrence, which was indeed probable in his mind, he secretly ordered a battalion of white soldiers to Fort Reno to quell any revolt. And considering the potential consequences to his actions, which could be perilous, he decided to make all the evidence public. He released the essential elements of facts contained in the two reports by Major Blocksom and General Garlington, the inspector generals. The newspapers had a field day criticizing the reports.

When the news of Taft's cancellation of the suspension of the order reached Fort Reno, hope began to fade. The Constitutional League had not finished its investigation. Stewart had not completed taking sworn statements from the soldiers. However, he had gathered sufficient facts to reach two significant conclusions—the soldiers were not in a conspiracy, and the soldiers had not been allowed to present their side of the story to General Garlington. Stewart wired Taft and told him of these important, and possibly game-changing findings. But it was too late.

TWENTY TWO

WITHOUT HONOR,

The Drumming Out

"Collect the rifles and secure them."

WINTER SEEMED TO BE coming early to Fort Reno. A few snowflakes had been dropping all night, and in the middle of the afternoon, a light snow had begun to fall. In the back of the narrow dining-room kitchen, Dorsie Willis sat outside on the back steps, peeling potatoes. The falling snow made that simple task difficult. His fingers were growing stiff—but never mind that, he would get the job done.

Using a sharp knife an Indian friend gave him when he was growing up in Oklahoma, he peeled them quickly, cutting off long strips of skin. When they were peeled, he tossed them into several buckets of water. *Why so many today?* He soon got his answer.

Along the road leading into Fort Reno, Willis saw a long line of soldiers marching through the main gate of Fort Reno. Through the falling snow he couldn't quite make out who they were. He stood up and gazed intently at the line of soldiers. It was Company A! He sure was glad to see them. The soldiers of Company A, their sister company, had been left in Montana to protect the settlers. They were supposed to join them later in Brownsville. Now they were coming to Fort Reno, he could see them.

But there were too many soldiers coming through the gate to be Company A. It looked like a battalion of soldiers—three times the number of men in Company A. He looked at the battalion colors and streamers as the column came closer. Then he made out the unit designation. It was the 26th Infantry. *That's not our regiment*, he thought. As they marched closer and closer, he could see that they were white soldiers.

He dropped his knife and he took off running as fast he could, telling everybody he met, "White soldiers are coming! White soldiers are coming! They're going to drum us out!"

Mingo Sanders stood at a window and watched as the new troops marched onto the parade field. It was an unhappy sight for him. Other black soldiers stopped what they were doing and glared at the newcomers as if they were foreign soldiers who had no business at the fort.

Penrose went out on the parade field to meet the new troops and their commander.

He knew they were coming, but he was caught by surprise when he saw their commander. "So they sent you, C.T."

"My orders were secret. Glad to see you, but I've got to say, not like this."

Major C.T. Clarke, the commander of the white troops, was an old friend of Major Penrose. They had attended high school in Detroit and hadn't seen each other since graduation.

"Been an ugly job for me," Penrose said, "Now it's an ugly one for you."

Major Clarke hastily moved his troops into their quarters and prepared to supervise the unpleasant business to come.

Starting at the noon assembly formation, the black troops were ordered to assemble with their rifles. All the black soldiers of companies B, C, and D, without any exceptions, were to attend—sergeants, corporals, privates, cooks, mechanics, musicians, coral masters and orderlies. After all the men were in formation, the ceremony of surrender arms began. The battalion of white soldiers with loaded guns marched onto the parade ground and surrounded them.

The commands were given by Major Penrose to his company commanders, "Have your musicians, buglers, and drummers, come front and center and surrender their instruments!"

Each company musician marched to the center of his company with his musical instrument and laid it down on the ground in front of his company commander, never to be raised again by that musician to blow reveille, assembly, "Retreat," tattoo, taps or sound call to arms.

"HAVE YOUR MEN TAKE TWO STEPS BACKWARD AND SURRENDER," Penrose ordered.

This came as a terrible shock to Mingo Sanders. He believed that such a dishonor would not come to him. Somehow he believed Roosevelt would not let it happen to him. After all, he had helped Roosevelt when he came begging him for bread for himself and his Rough Riders, when they first met in Cuba. He realized he had not faced the harsh possibility that the unthinkable could actually happen. Sanders stepped forward two steps and laid his rifle on the ground. Unlike Sanders, the other soldiers took two steps backward, and came to "port arms," a position that made it easy for the officers to take their rifles.

Lieutenant Lawrason strode up to Mingo Sanders. "Sergeant Sanders, what's the matter with you? Didn't you hear the command?"

"Yes, sir. I heard the order to surrender arms. To me, surrender arms means to lay down your rifle. I've done that. I cannot shoot anybody, because I don't have a gun in my hands, and I can't hit anybody with the butt of my rifle, because it is not in my hands."

"Lieutenant Lawrason!" Penrose shouted. "Don't push Sergeant Sanders! He's doing the best that he can to avoid violence. Get out of his face. Go back to your position!"

Lawrason didn't move. Penrose knew Lawrason had a temper. Penrose also knew Sanders was a natural leader. He might lead a revolt and the men might follow him. Penrose could have a mutiny on his hands and a lot of bloodshed. Why didn't he do more to get an exception for Sanders from Garlington? He reflected on the raid. *Were the rifles really unloaded? Had the officers checked?*

Major Clarke, sensing the mounting crisis, rushed over to Major Penrose and whispered something in his ear. Penrose nodded, the two men exchanged salutes, and Major Clarke trotted back to his command.

Speaking in a normal tone to Lieutenant Lawrason, Penrose seemed somewhat relieved. "Lieutenant, return to your position. Sergeant Sanders is right. The correct command is, 'Take two steps forward, and lay down your rifles, then take two steps backward to return to your position.'"

When Lieutenant Lawrason returned to his position in front of Company B, the company commanders repeated the new command. Now having heard the new command, the soldiers took two steps forward, laid down their rifles, and took two steps backward to their original positions.

Lieutenant Leckie, a white officer, was standing on the parade field observing the ceremony. He whispered to Lieutenant Grier, "Looks like they are taking it awful hard. Look! The old soldiers have tears in their eyes, even Mingo Sanders. You know, giving up their rifles today means giving up their pensions later. I feel sorry for them from the bottom of my heart. I know they are innocent of any wrongdoing, and it looks pretty hard on them. I'll do whatever I can to prove they didn't do it."

"You're a little late, aren't you?" Lieutenant Grier said.

"No! It's never too late to stand up for justice," Leckie whispered back.

When the black soldiers had cleared the parade ground, Major Clarke walked over to Major Penrose, and said, "That was no ragtag group of soldiers. They were very neat, orderly and soldierly. How is it that they could have shot up Brownsville?"

"I don't know. It's still a mystery to me. Please have your soldiers collect the rifles and secure them in the armory."

The Day the World Changed

Mingo Sanders hadn't slept at all that night. Now it was early in the morning on November 20. It was his last day in his beloved Army and the day the drumming out of the soldiers was to begin. It was a gray morning, and with low-hanging clouds already in the sky, no one would see the sun. It looked like it might snow. The wind was sweeping low along the ground across the parade field, like a giant broom. Little corkscrew-like whirlwinds followed the sweep of the wind, jumping across the field like spinning tops, picking up little balls of weeds and spinning them round and round. As a small boy growing up in South Carolina, Sanders had been fascinated by the little dust-devils churning across the dirt yard. He chased them about the yard and wondered what made them spin.

Today was the day he never dreamed would come for him. He had seen soldiers drummed out of the regiment before. He had heard the reading of the orders, the charges, heard the roll of the drum. He had seen buttons cut off the uniforms, regimental crests removed, regimental coat-of-arms buttons and insignia of rank ripped off. But it was the image of the final humiliation that disturbed him most, when at the roll of the drum, the soldiers would be marched across the center of the parade field, followed by a lone drummer beating a slow, mournful drumbeat, then marched to the main gate and booted off the post. He could under-stand those cases where the men were guilty of some serious infraction. He had never seen this happen to an innocent man. And he still found it hard to believe that his friend, President Roosevelt, would let this happen to him.

A little before noon, company commanders marched the black soldiers onto to the parade field. They stood at at-tention in their usual positions and were ordered by their company commanders to stand at parade rest, a semi-relaxed position. Each soldier stood with his arms behind his back and his hands clasped together at the small of his back.

From four directions, white soldiers simultaneously marched onto the field, encircling the entire formation. Ev-erything was ready, except that Major Penrose and Major Clarke hadn't come onto the field. They hadn't left Penrose's office. Everybody was waiting for them.

Lieutenant Grier was concerned. He was the battalion ad-jutant. It was his responsibility to read the order, get the men paid and handle the discharge paperwork. It seemed strange to him that Major Penrose would hold up the discharge ceremony. Penrose was always prompt, never late. Grier looked toward the administration building and through the window, he could see the two men talking. Penrose appeared to be making defiant gestures.

From the black soldiers' perspective, with their backs to the administration building, the delay took on a hopeful sign. Maybe the whole thing was going to be called off. Maybe a last minute reprieve had come through.

But the reality was different. The two officers were standing in Penrose's office in a heated discussion. An argument had broken out between the two friends about the use of the drums in the discharge ceremony and the interpretation of Clarke's instruction from the Military Department at Fort Sam Houston, Texas. Penrose was animated, anxious, and angry. "We don't have to use the drums," he said.

"My orders were to go to Fort Reno, prevent any disturbance and drum 'em out," Clarke growled, "Penrose, why are you resisting this? The authorities in Texas want these soldiers drummed out. I've got the power to do it."

"Where are your written orders? I want to see them."

"They were verbal and secret. Somebody at headquarters thought you might not be up to the task of carrying this thing to conclusion. I am empowered to do it. You can witness it or you can leave the fort now. Don't make this harder than it is, my friend. Believe me, it'll come back to hurt you. Don't blame me. Let's get this over with." Having said that, Major Clarke turned on his heels, walked out, down the steps and onto the parade field. At the same time, he raised his saber giving the signal for his drummers to play a drum roll and then take their positions.

Two drummers from the white battalion gave a drum roll standing in place. After that, they went onto the field playing a marching drum beat as they stepped across the front of the formation to the opposite ends of the field and took up positions at each corner of the parade ground.

By the time the drums stopped, Major Penrose had regained his composure and mustered up enough nerve to take charge of his command. He walked out of the administration building, took his command position and called his battalion to attention for what he knew would be the last time.

"Battalion attention!"

The soldiers snapped to attention smartly, as always.

"Adjutant, publish the orders," Penrose said softly.

After a brief drum roll, Lieutenant Grier stepped forward with a sheaf of papers in his hand.

"Attention to orders!" he said. Then he read the order:

Special Orders No.266, War Department. Washington, November 9, 1906. By direction of the president, the following named enlisted men who, on August 13, 1906, were members of Companies B, C, and D, 25th Infantry, certain members of which organizations participated in the riotous disturbance which occurred in Brownsville, Texas, on the night of August 13, 1906, will be discharged without honor from the Army by their respective commanding officers and forever debarred from reenlisting in the Army or Navy of the United States, as well as from employment in any civil capacity under the Government.

The adjutant paused and looked up at the sky. It had been threatening snow all morning, but had not begun yet. It was so heavily overcast that the clouds appeared to be descending to the ground, threatening to engulf the parade field in darkness even though it was just past noon. The adjutant continued reading, calling off the name of the first company to be dismissed.

"Company B, 25th Infantry," then he read the name of the first soldier on the list.

"First Sergeant Mingo Sanders. Discharged without honor. Quartermaster-Sergeant Walker McCurdy; Sergeants James R. Reid, George Jackson and Luther T. Thornton."

Hearing the sound of his name called out for dishonor jolted Sanders. He stiffened and stared straight ahead. He showed no outward signs of emotion, but the words "without honor" tore him apart inside. Feelings of shame and sadness overwhelmed him. It was a new kind of shame and sadness he had never felt before. He had felt the cruelty of war. The shame of it seeped into his sorrow and surfaced into his consciousness. It caused him to call into question his heroic exploits in battle. He became confused and a moral divergence crept into his soul. Were all the killings he had seen in war with or without honor?

Images of past battles clashed painfully through his mind. He felt as if he were fighting fragments of those battles over again. But this time, the battles seemed to be collisions between right and wrong. With honor? Without honor?

The image of Colonel Roosevelt came floating into his mind and sat on the front steps of his memory. It was June 25th, 1898. Colonel Roosevelt was no longer a supplicant, begging for food for himself and his men. His countenance had changed inexplicably from friendly to unfriendly, his eyes from kind to cold and his lips from a smile to a smirk. Like the portrait of Dorian Gray, he had evolved into something darkly unsavory. Roosevelt had a scowl on his face and was aggressively belligerent. He was not asking for food, he was taking it.

Why did soldiers end up killing so many people in battle like the Sioux Indian campaigns of 1890 and 1891? He remembered the dead Sioux covering the ground at the battle of the Pine Ridge Reservation, later known as Wounded Knee. Why did he care now?

The battle for El Caney, Cuba, the first of July, 1898. The assault on the block house perched on top of the hill was dreamlike. It was nine o'clock in the morning and he was fighting that battle all over again. The 25th Infantry was ordered into the fight to protect the flanks of the Second Massachusetts Volunteers as they moved up the hill to capture the block house. Sporadic exchanges of gunfire between the Spaniards, the Second Massachusetts Volunteers and the 25th Infantry signaled a standoff. Colonel Roosevelt and his Rough Riders were bogged down at the base of San Juan Hill [Kettle Hill]. They couldn't advance until the block house was captured.

It was now about two o'clock in the afternoon. The Second Massachusetts Volunteers were ordered to make a frontal assault and take the block house. As they began the final assault, the Spaniards laid down a hail of heavy fire against them. Second Massachusetts collapsed under the barrage and executed a full-scale "Retreat" back down the hill.

"Move up! Advance!" The 25th got the order to move to continue the frontal assault abandoned by the Volunteers.

"You might as well turn back," shouted a bloodied straggler as he staggered down the hill.

"If anybody can take the block house, we can," Sanders shouted back.

Taking advantage of the lush vegetation, Sanders and his men concealed themselves as much as they could. They moved closer and closer toward the block house, holding their fire as they went. When they were within 100 hundred yards of their objective, a bugler blew the charge. Bayonets fixed and guns blazing, the black soldiers of the 25th Infantry caught the Spaniards by surprise. They overwhelmed them and continued the attack. They went on to take the town of El Caney and pulled down the Spanish flag in celebration.

The sounds of dead men moaning, groaning and asking for mercy passed through Sanders' mind as he half-listened to the drone of the adjutant's voice. The names of the other discharged soldiers were being called. "Boyd Conyers, John Amos Holomon, Carolina De Saussure, and Winter Washington...."

He heard a woman's voice coming from the edge of the field where the wives of the soldiers and the officers had quietly gathered. It was a soft voice, sobbing, weeping. "No! No! No! Don't do this. Don't do this," she cried.

Sanders recognized that voice. He had heard those sounds before. The sobbing and weeping were the sounds that always accompanied his being shipped off to war—Cuba, Philippines, India campaigns. It was the voice of his wife.

A powerful urge griped him. He wanted to break ranks, go to her and take her in his arms and comfort her. That he could not do. Military discipline would not let him go. He could not break ranks and leave the rest of his men standing there alone. That would break the bonds of unity, allow fear to creep in, and ultimately crush the goals of discipline he had worked so hard to achieve. No, he could not go to her. He was still a soldier. Even though he was being dishonored and his status as a soldier had just been taken from him, he felt he must still maintain discipline.

The adjutant continued down the list until he reached the name of the last man in Company D—Dorsie Willis.

There were three other names on the list from other units who just happened to be on temporary duty at Fort Brown.

Having completed publishing the orders, the adjutant completed the instructions:

> *Now listen up! You are not out of the army yet! You must come to the administration building. You will be given your discharge without honor certificates, and your pay. You must remove all rank of insignia, buttons and units' crests from your uniforms. If you don't, they will be ripped off, and then, and only then, will you be paid. You must leave immediately. You will be escorted out the gate in small groups beginning today, and continuing until all of you are gone.*

The adjutant did an about face and saluted Major Penrose, "Sir, it's your command."

Major Penrose wanted to say something to his troops, but he didn't know what to say. He couldn't praise them, and he couldn't condemn them. He was still unsure of their guilt or innocence. He was choking on indecision.

Their innocence had been impossible for him to prove. Had he tried hard enough? Then he remembered something about the empty shell casings. *Yes*, he thought, *two of the empty cartridges that Mayor Combe gave him seemed peculiar.* What was it about them that didn't ring true? Yes, Yes, Yes. The markings on them didn't have the date of manufacture imprinted on them. His heart was racing, beating out of control. He had to steady himself. He was still unsure.

That was it! All bullets made by Union Metallic for the government by contract had to have the date of manufacture imprinted on them. Bullets made for the civilian market didn't have those markings. His men didn't have access to that kind of bullet. What did it mean? It could mean that some of the citizens of Brownsville fired those shots. Maybe his men were innocent after all. Was that enough proof? Should he suspend the discharge of his soldiers until the new evidence could be investigated or was it too late?

His stomach was churning. He felt sick and nervous. He felt the urge to move his bowels. The old dysentery was coming back. He started to speak, but couldn't. The right words would not come. His resolve to say something of importance relevant to the plight of the men began to weaken. Then he looked straight ahead and saw Mingo standing there like a ramrod. His face belied his military posture. It was washed with sadness. His eyes spoke of betrayal, Penrose's betrayal, the Army's betrayal, President Roosevelt's betrayal. There was no one who would speak for him or them.

Finally Penrose said, "Company commanders, take charge of your companies." He turned to Major Clarke and said, "There go the best men, the best soldiers and the best battalion, in the Army." Desperate to be alone, he rushed from the field.

Some of the soldiers didn't even have enough money to buy a suit of clothes. Later, John Holomon wired some of them money to buy clothes, and when he got into town from San Antonio, he arranged credit for others.

They were already packed. They left Fort Reno and the Army with their wives, and children. While they were leaving, they were orderly, peaceful and soldierly. Their carriage was one of a silent dignity. When they arrived in El Reno, they didn't cause any disturbances or trouble of any kind. No one was arrested for drunkenness or lawlessness. They refreshed their long, three-month drought with beer and then slipped away quietly and separately into their new world.

TWENTY THREE

THE GRIDIRON CLUB

Dinner Debate

A New Investigation

WHEN PRESIDENT ROOSEVELT RETURNED to the White House on Tuesday morning, November 27, he declared the Brownsville matter closed to Booker T. Washington's emissary, Emmett J. Scott.

But it wasn't closed. After reading the president's 1907 message along with its attached investigative reports, Ohio Senator Joseph Benson Foraker found them legally insufficient for the action Roosevelt had taken. Foraker criticized Roosevelt's order dismissing the soldiers on the Senate floor and introduced a Senate resolution calling for a full investigation into the Brownsville affair.

All along, the lawyers in Roosevelt's cabinet, as well as the Judge Advocate General (JAG) in the War Department, were unhappy with Blocksom's report. In response to Foraker's criticism, they advised Roosevelt to send Milton D. Purdy, an assistant attorney general, and Blocksom to Brownsville to take sworn testimony to refute Foraker. Purdy and Blocksom arrived in Brownsville the day after Christmas and started another after-the-fact investigation.

Purdy and Blocksom took 63 affidavits. They collected a host of items that had been picked up in the streets of Brownsville—33 empty shell casings, seven ball cartridges, a bandoleer and four clips. Roosevelt then rushed the resulting report to the Senate mid-January 1907, still confident that the black soldiers were guilty. He made a point of saying so and challenged anyone who took a contrary view. The additional evidence, he said, "renders it impossible to question the conclusion on which my order was based."

Foraker wasn't buying it. He took to the Senate floor and verbally ripped Purdy's report apart, saying that it was taken behind closed doors and was all "ex parte," since the soldiers had no opportunity to meet their accusers. He called again for adoption of his resolution for a Senate investigation of the Brownsville Affray.

"I want these men who have been accused of murder, mutiny and treason to have their day in court, where they will have a chance to defend themselves," Foraker said.

A running debate ensued between Roosevelt and Foraker. Roosevelt defended his action as if he were acting on the divine right of kings, while Foraker hammered him with eloquent, scholarly legal speeches from the senate floor.

"The men have been condemned without a hearing, and that is contrary to the spirit of our institutions," declared Foraker. "It is our duty to undo the wrong by giving them a chance to face their accusers."

Roosevelt was outraged. When the Senate adopted Foraker's resolution to authorize a senate investigation on January 22, 1907, Roosevelt set out to get revenge. Working behind the scenes, he set up surrogates in the senate to attack Foraker. In this volatile political climate, Roosevelt and Foraker were destined to collide at the famous annual Gridiron Club dinner hosted by the Washington newspapermen.

A Fine Speech

A kind of wet snow had been falling most of that day in Washington, and the accumulation was getting deep and mushy as Senator Foraker made his way toward the Willard Hotel where the dinner was being held. It was Saturday night, January 26, 1907, just a week or so after the senate had adopted his resolution to hold hearings on the Brownsville affair. He hadn't expected anything serious at the dinner—nothing but a good old fashioned stag party, a lot of fun, ribald humor and good food.

Foraker didn't know the president was to attend until he saw him sitting at the head table next to Samuel G. Blythe, the club president. Tables were arranged to form the gridiron, and the banquet room was packed with the powerful and the elite—business men, senators, congressmen, cabinet officers and federal judges. Reporters were there in force, too. Foraker took his seat at the first table on the immediate left of President Roosevelt. Foraker glanced over at Roosevelt and thought he appeared tense, grim, and worried.

A minstrel clown in blackface shuffled onto center stage. "I wants to see de president. I'se an old nigger from down Tuskegee way. I was up here and heard the president was here, so I came in here to see him. I'se surely interested in dat man. I had a boy in dem colored troops down in Brownsville, but I 'spect he's own his way home now."

Roosevelt smiled.

By protocol the president always spoke last. At this dinner, however, Roosevelt asked to speak first. He was called to the podium. The president of the Gridiron Club introduced Roosevelt.

Before he began his speech, he opened the souvenir booklet and saw a spoof attributed to him, which read in part, "All coons look alike to me."

Roosevelt frowned. Then he launched into his speech.

I want to set a few things straight here tonight. The domination of this nation by big business is over. The time when a few plutocrats could get together behind closed corporate doors, set the policies of this government, rule this government and fleece the people ended with my administration. Some of you sitting right here in this room tonight better get used to it. You should be thankful that my railroad and corporate reforms were put in place by my conservative Republican administration. If not for this administration, you plutocrats would have had to swallow more drastic, punitive and distasteful measures forced on you by the spirit of the mob. The Mob! The Mob! The Mob!

The government ought not to conduct the business of the country, but it ought to regulate it so that it shall be conducted in the interest of the public. You can bet on it. I'll damn sure do that.

Then he leaned over the podium. He made his remarks personal. He shook his fist at J.P. Morgan, the Wall Street financier, and at Henry Rogers, the vice president of Standard Oil. "You boys better correct your ways," he warned them. "You better not try to block my reforms. Your time is thoroughly over."

Then he raised his head, looked around the banquet room and said softly, "No man in this country is so high or so low that I would not punish him, if I could, for violating the law. No man is so high or so low that I would not give him the full protection of the law if innocent of offense against the law."

The guests at the dinner couldn't believe it. Mouths fell open, eyebrows were raised. People squirmed in their seats and looked around at each other as Roosevelt continued to pour it on. They had expected friendly banter, not an hour-long sermon, and certainly not a self-righteous diatribe. J.P. Morgan sat there stone-faced, angrily glaring back at Roosevelt.

Foraker was not mentioned by name. Nonetheless, he was attacked. Roosevelt chastised the opponents of his railroad regulations and dismissed the senate debate on Brownsville, characterizing it as an "academic discussion." It just happened that Foraker was the chief opponent of Roosevelt's railroad regulations and his nemesis on Brownsville. As to his constitutional power to dismiss the soldiers, he said it was not subject to review by the legislative branch of government.

Roosevelt seemed to be in the same frame of mind he was in just before Christmas, when he said he would even refuse to obey the law if Congress passed legislation over his veto reinstating the black soldiers. "I would invite impeachment," he said.

Roosevelt ended his speech with words he probably thought wouldn't get reported by the press. "There may have been but two companies of that regiment engaged in that unwholesome business, but all coons look alike to me."

The Washington Post reported that "All coons look alike to the president" on the front page, Monday, January 28, 1907.

No one usually was allowed to speak after the president, but in this case Roosevelt had opted to speak first, leaving the toastmaster no choice but to allow Foraker to speak, since he had been the main target of Roosevelt's speech.

After being called to the podium, Foraker hesitated. He was reluctant and his first thought was to refuse. He had not expected to speak, had not prepared a speech and didn't feel equal to the occasion.

Calls came from the floor, "Speech! Speech! Speech!"

The toastmaster shouted, "Let the bloody sarcasm begin."

Hearing those words, Foraker knew he could not refuse. He took the floor, making a striking appearance. He was tall, over six feet, slim, with a shock of iron gray hair and a well-trimmed gray mustache. He was a patrician-looking, handsome man who now looked like he had been wounded. His face was ashen white, and he didn't appear ready to do verbal combat with Roosevelt.

After looking directly at the president for what seemed like a long, reflective moment, Foraker began slowly. "I, too, like you, Mr. President, favor governmental supervision and regulation of railroads and corporations. The only difference between us is the character of the legislation that should be enacted to accomplish it. My opposition to the rate bill had been because I thought it unconstitutional."

As to his votes, he said he was only responsible to his constituency and nobody else, and he denied the right of anybody there or any place else to tell him how he should vote on great constitutional issues.

Not lingering long on esoteric corporate law, anti-trust law and regulations, he moved on to the Brownsville debate. It was his favorite passion, and he challenged Roosevelt's assertion that it was merely "academic" because all power was vested in him. Then Foraker quoted from one of his earlier speeches.

"Where a soldier is charged with a crime and denies it and stands upon his rights, he has the right to a trial, and without it there is no power lodged anywhere to say he is guilty and order him dismissed; there is no power lodged anywhere to indict a man by order; convict a man by order; and then punish him by order."

Foraker continued to lecture the President. "That, Mr. President, has been the law of the world since civilization... No man shall be convicted of a crime until he has been permitted to face his accusers and cross-examine the witnesses."

When Roosevelt made that eloquent remark in his speech about his policy toward corporations—"No man is too high or low too be punished or to receive justice"—Foraker saw in that statement the ultimate contradiction when that standard was applied to the black soldiers, and he stated this view to the president.

"Mr. President, you have failed to apply that standard in the Brownsville case, where, according to your own statement of it, there were doubtless many men with splendid records as soldiers, absolutely innocent, yet you branded them as criminals, and dismissed them without honor."

"That's not so," Roosevelt said in a low voice, but loud enough for some of the guests to hear.

Foraker started to speak about the illustrious record of Sergeant Mingo Sanders and how badly he was treated. "Sergeant Mingo Sanders had twenty-six years of service, and a record of bravery in battle ...."

"That's not so." The President gritted his teeth while shaking his head.

"He was turned out when he was nearing the time when he would have had a right to retire," Foraker said.

"I'm going to answer that," Roosevelt balled up his fist, and started to rise from his seat.

Supreme Court Justice Harlan reached over and laid his hand on Roosevelt's shoulder, "No, please."

Foraker felt the pressure from the interruptions of Roosevelt. He struggled to continue his speech. "He would have a right to retire on pay, but he was stripped of all his valuable rights, and disgraced."

"I'm not going to stand for it." Roosevelt started to get up again, but was restrained by the justice again.

Foraker came to the end of his speech. "When legal and human rights are involved, all persons look alike to me." Foraker completed his speech with a brave assertion of his high duty as a senator. "I didn't come to the senate to take orders from anybody, either at this line or the other. Whenever I fall so low that I cannot express my opinion on a great question freely, and without mental reservation, I will resign and leave my place to some man who has the courage to discharge his duties."

Those words brought thunderous applause from the guests. Foraker finished his speech and was about to return to his seat, but he hesitated and appeared to reflect for a moment. Then he addressed Roosevelt directly with outstretched arms, as if he were welcoming him into his embrace in respect for some great occasion.

"Mr. President, there was a time, which you well know, when I loved you as though you were one of my own family. There was nothing legitimate or honorable that I wouldn't do for you. I supported many of your programs—not all. Yet I didn't feel that my love stood in the way or that I had any right to allow it to stand in the way of my differing from you when, in my judgment you were in error. So as it was in the past, so it will continue in the future."

The crowd rushed the podium before Foraker could take his seat. He was mobbed by cheering guests and reporters, wishing him well and telling him what a great speech that was.

Roosevelt stood up, and tried to quiet the crowd, saying that he was entitled to have the last say. And he was, by club protocol. He made it back to the podium and said, "Some of those men were bloody butchers. They ought to be hung. The only reason that I didn't have them hung was because I couldn't find out which ones did the shooting."

THE WHITE HOUSE.

WASHINGTON.

November 27, 1906.

dear Mr. Secretary:

The President directs me to call your attention
to the enclosed clipping of an interview with Major
Penrose appearing in this evening's Star.   The President directs that you wire Major Penrose this evening
asking what explanation he has for giving out such an
interview or any publication whatever in reference to
the dismissal of the three Companies of the 25th Infantry.   The President desires an immediate and full
explanation of what he has said and his reasons for
saying it.   If this interview was authentic the
President wishes by wire an immediate and full statement in justification or explanation of it.

Very truly yours,

Secretary to the President.

Hon. Wm. H. Taft,
    Secretary of War.

Figure 16. Letter from President Roosevelt's Secretary
to William Howard Taft, 11/27/06
The President demands an explanation from Major Penrose
for making laudatory comments to the *Evening Star*
about the discharged soldiers.

TWENTY FOUR

THE LAST

Investigations

The Con Artist

THE SENATE BEGAN ITS investigation on February 4, 1907, just a few days after the Gridiron dinner debate. Roosevelt had vigorously opposed the investigation. After that debate and the start of the senate probe, the social and political relations between the president and Foraker were, for all practical purposes, broken. Foraker had hoped the wounds inflicted in that debate would heal with the passage of time, but Roosevelt began maneuvering socially and politically against him. He never invited him again to the White House for social or political events. Roosevelt also denied federal judgeship appointments and other patronage jobs to Foraker's recommended candidates.

Secret Service agents stood near Foraker's home and watched the comings and goings of guests to such an extent that old friends and political allies, fearing Roosevelt's political retribution, virtually stopped visiting him and his wife. Their mail was opened and tampered with. It got so bad that Foraker felt that Roosevelt wanted to oust him from political life altogether.

As Roosevelt mounted the political pressure against him, Foraker became more and more passionate in his defense of the soldiers. He pounded Roosevelt in speeches on the senate floor at every opportunity he could get.

Then, one Saturday night in April, Herbert J. Browne, a former newspaper editor, came to Foraker's home and gave him some startling information. He said he had it on good authority that seven white civilians had shot up the town. Four of the raiders were willing to talk, if offered immunity from prosecution. The other three men, however, had left town without a word. Browne volunteered to go to Brownsville, take the testimony of the four men who were willing to talk and make it available to the senate. All he wanted were expenses and a small fee for his services. Foraker gave Browne $500 of his own money to get the venture started.

Browne arrived in Brownsville by train on Wednesday, April 24, 1907. Arriving at a quick conclusion after interviewing several citizens, he wrote Foraker on April 29 that Louis Cowen was the 'head devil' in the whole business. He also noted that Cowen was really a renegade Russian Jew who had changed his name from Cowajiian to Cowen. To get additional information from Cowen and "his gang," he was going out hunting with them.

By early May, however, Browne had completely flip-flopped. He reported to Foraker that he had discovered the true answer, "The Negro troop had shot up the town. I can name four of them."

How could he have let himself be fooled? Foraker realized that he had been victimized by a con artist.

But the unfortunate con was just the beginning of a series of setbacks for Foraker and his ardent support of the soldiers. The senate committee ended its investigation a little over a year later in March 1908. Its finding was a bitter disappointment for Foraker. A majority of the committee members voted against the soldiers, confirming Roosevelt's position that some of the soldiers had shot up and terrorized the town. They still couldn't identify which ones, though.

After having bilked Foraker out $500, Browne must have thought there must be other suckers out there waiting for him to lift their wallets. So about a year later, Browne wrote Taft a letter bragging, "I spent three weeks in Brownsville last April and became thoroughly satisfied that, following a conspiracy, fourteen or more soldiers of B Company shot up the town."

Taft wanted to see him right away and did. Browne brought William J. Baldwin with him to the meeting. Baldwin was a detective from Roanoke, Virginia. The two men presented their credentials, which impressed Taft so much that he immediately offered them a $5,000 contract to find and identity the Brownsville terrorists. He wouldn't sign it, however, until he had a chance to consult with Roosevelt and check out their credentials.

Taft didn't have to do much to convince Roosevelt, even though he had won some sort of a victory when the senate investigation agreed with him. However, Foraker had written a strong dissent backed up by several senators, and there was a bill before Congress to reinstate any of the soldiers who could prove their innocence.

After Taft satisfied himself that Browne and Baldwin were "competent, earnest, and reputable men," Browne and Baldwin formed a team, hired eight other agents, and began working for the War Department on April 28, 1908. They had a deadline of June 15 to finish their investigation.

Browne went undercover as a newspaper reporter, pretending he was interested in writing a sympathetic story about the injustice meted out to the Brownsville boys. Using this ruse, he obtained the home addresses of many of the men from a black lawyer who was a staunch supporter of the soldiers. Browne hid the fact that he was now a part of the Browne & Baldwin Detective Agency.

Browne & Baldwin detectives spread out across the country, hunting down the soldiers, interrogating, bribing, and threatening the former soldiers to try to extract confessions from them.

Browne missed his deadline, but sent in several progress reports over eight months to the JAG in the War Department. Finally on December 5, 1908, Browne reported the good news that ex-private Boyd Conyers of Company B, living now in Monroe, Georgia, had confessed that he, John Holomon, John Brown and Carolina De Saussure were the leaders in the raid and that they had shot Police Lieutenant Joe Dominguez and the bartender. Conyers' confession was supposedly made to William Lawson, one of Baldwin's detectives. When Conyers found out that he had made his statement to a detective, he tried to commit suicide.

Browne continued, "We have located over 130 of these ex-soldiers and have been in thirty states in quest for information." He concluded that there was a "general knowledge on the part of the ex-soldiers that the raid came from inside the fort," and he fastened the guilt on B Company. Browne claimed Conyers identified 14 of the raiders by name.

"I have…sufficient evidence, circumstantial and direct, to indict, convict, and hang under the laws of Texas four ex-soldiers…for the murder of Frank Natus," Browne reported.

Upon receipt of Browne's good-news report, Roosevelt quickly got out a Special Message to the senate on December 14, 1908:

This report enables us to fix with tolerable definiteness at least some of the criminals who took the lead in the murderous shooting of private citizens at Brownsville....

Roosevelt, however, reminded the senate that the detectives' work had not been completed and would continue until all the criminals were brought to justice.

When Senator Foraker read the Browne & Baldwin report in Roosevelt's Special Message, he was more than skeptical. He was horrified. He didn't believe a word of it, and he set out to prove on the senate floor that Conyers' alleged confession was an out-and-out fabrication.

Unknown to Browne & Baldwin and to Roosevelt, Conyers kept Foraker informed in detail of all the contacts the detectives had with him. Foraker had a stack of letters from Conyers detailing the interrogations, bribes and threats made by Browne & Baldwin agents. Those letters would be crucial for Conyers. For if that confession couldn't be proven false, he was headed straight for the gallows in Texas.

Again, Foraker defended the ex-soldiers. On January 12, 1909, he took to the senate floor, and based on Conyers' letters, he gutted Browne's report, laying bare the elements of its fiction starting with Lawson, Baldwin and Browne. Detective Lawson had traveled to Monroe, Georgia, the hometown of Boyd Conyers. There he took a room in Ester Crews' boarding house, posing as a traveling salesman and struck up a friendship with another roomer named Parker. As the friendship grew closer, Lawson asked Parker if he would write his detective reports for him about Brownsville, confiding to him that he couldn't read or write.

Later, the friendship soured when Lawson accused Parker of stealing a suit of clothes from him. Parker didn't want to tangle with a Washington detective, so he fled. But on his way out of town, he sent a warning to Mrs. Conyers, urging her to tell her husband that Will Lawson was not what he pretended to be. He was a detective gathering information about the Brownsville shooting. At that time Conyers was out of town, working at the National Guard Armory in nearby Chickamauga.

As Conyers related the story, when he got off the train, returning home from Chickamauga, his mother-in-law was at the station waiting for him. She told him that Will Lawson was a detective, and that the word was out that he, Conyers, had confessed to shooting a white man in Brownsville.

When Conyers spotted Will Lawson on the street the next morning, he went to Sheriff Arnold and asked him to find out what Lawson was up to. Sheriff Arnold called Lawson in and demanded to see his papers. Lawson produced a letter satisfying the sheriff that he was indeed a detective working for Browne & Baldwin.

Sheriff Arnold later swore that Conyers denied that he had ever spoken to Lawson about Brownsville in his presence, and said Conyers called Lawson a liar to his face.

As Conyers related the story in his letters to Foraker, he had only a brief encounter with Lawson before he confronted him in Sheriff Arnold's office, and that Will Lawson had said nothing about Brownsville. "I am just as innocent of taking any part in that trouble that night as God is on high."

A few weeks later, a white businessman calling himself Wallace L. Gray turned up in Monroe, Georgia from Roanoke, Virginia. Several months ago this same man had written Conyers a letter offering him a job paying $60 to $70 a month if he would move to Virginia. Conyers had declined the offer because he said his wife was too sick to move.

Sheriff Arnold asked Conyers to meet Mr. Gray and him in his office that night for an agenda not made known to Conyers. When Conyers stepped into the sheriff's office, to his surprise he learned that Mr. Gray was a detective named William G. Baldwin and that Will Lawson worked for him. Baldwin interrogated Conyers, but Conyers denied any participation in the shooting. Baldwin asked Conyers, "Now what about that Negro Lawson I sent down here to talk to you. What did you tell him?"

"Sir, I didn't even have any private talk with him."

Baldwin returned to Washington and told Browne that Conyers denied having a private talk with Lawson and that the alleged confession was shaky.

Realizing that he had a weak case with a confession produced by an illiterate detective who signed his name with an X on an affidavit attesting to the authenticity of the confession, Browne decided he had better go talk to Conyers himself. So several weeks later another white man, a stranger to Conyers, arrived in Monroe and conducted a full press interrogation of Conyers in Sheriff Arnold's office.

Sheriff Arnold joined the interrogation, all the time hoping to collect the reward money. He had always believed that some of the soldiers shot up the town, and for that reason he was happy to have an opportunity to be able to help solve the mystery.

Again, Conyers denied any part in the shooting.

Browne said, "We have been able to prove B Company men did the shooting, and what I want you to tell me is just the men that did the shooting. I know you can, if you will. We already know three men that did it, but we want the whole gang. The three are you, John Holomon, and John Brown. Now suppose you dream on it, and come back here in the morning and tell me and Sheriff Arnold about it. We will see that nobody hurts you, if you were in on it."

"Mr. Browne, what do you want me to do—tell a lie?" Conyers said. "Pick out this man and that man and say they were in on it? It's impossible for me to do that."

Browne caught a train to Washington the next morning and didn't return to Monroe until October 6. He really tore into Conyers that time. Again Sheriff Arnold participated, locking his door so they wouldn't be disturbed.

Browne and Sheriff Arnold kept Conyers under "the most severe" cross examination until 11 o'clock that night, but failed go get anything out of him. Browne asked Conyers if he had a picture of the B Company baseball team. Conyers retrieved his copy from home and showed it to Browne, who quickly copied down the names of the players. Except for the names of the baseball players, Browne went back to Washington empty handed.

Browne returned to Monroe on October 11, feeling desperate. Again Browne and Sheriff Arnold put Conyers under another rigid interrogation, but this time they promised him monetary inducements and pardons. Then they threatened him with death by hanging in Texas. Conyers said, "Let God's will be done." He would not lie to save himself from the scaffold.

Sheriff Arnold read Herbert J. Browne's version of what happened in his presence with Conyers and swore, "It's the most absolutely false, the most willful misrepresentation of the truth, and the most shameful perversion of what really did take place between them that I have ever seen over the signature of any person."

So after paying Browne & Baldwin thousands of dollars from a military contingency fund, Roosevelt and Taft got nothing for the government's money except a worthless, fabricated report.

Figure 17. Company B's Baseball Team

1. Harry Carmichael
2. Jas. Johnson
3. Edw. Daniels
4. Henry Jones
5. Geo. Mitchell
6. C.E. Cooper

7. Mingo Sanders
8. Isaiah Raynor
9. Wade Harris
10. John Holomon
11. Jonas Allen
12. Joseph Wilson

The last government investigation during that time came at the urging of Senator Foraker in December 1908, near the end of his senate term. Roosevelt had crushed the Ohio senator's political underpinnings and he lost his re-election bid. But even though he was a lame duck, Foraker introduced a bill that, if passed, would have created a tribunal. The tribunal would have allowed the men to face their accusers, testify in their own behalf and present witnesses and evidence—all under the presumption of innocence. He proposed that all the ex-soldiers should be allowed to re-enlist if the government didn't show affirmatively that they were guilty of the charges. In other words, his bill would place the burden of proof on the government.

Roosevelt campaigned against Foraker's bill, stating in a personal letter to Senator Warren, "Senator Foraker's bill amounts simply to a proposal to condone murder and perjury in the past [and] puts a premium upon perjury in the future...."

Foraker's bill failed. Senator Nelson W. Aldrich submitted a substitute bill designed in favor of Roosevelt and Taft. It was signed into law by President Roosevelt on March 3, 1909, creating a military court of inquiry—not to be confused with a military court-martial or any other duly constituted judicial court. Under the court of inquiry, the ex-soldiers were presumed guilty and required to prove their innocence.

The court of inquiry, composed of retired generals met from 1909 to 1910, heard 82 of the ex-soldiers. They allowed them to appear and testify, but denied the other 85 who wanted to be heard. They were denied for no apparent reason except that the old generals were probably tired and worn out from the tedious proceedings of witnesses testifying, presentations of technical evidence and arguments by lawyers over such a long period of time.

The court adjourned on March 28, 1910. It concluded that the soldiers shot up the town as charged, but it allowed 14 men to re-enlist without giving any reasons why.

THE WHITE HOUSE
WASHINGTON

February 7, 1909.

To the Secretary of War:

I have received your letter of February 6th and the accompanying report of Mr. Brown on the Brownsville raid. I agree with you that it is not necessary to send this report to Congress. Mr. Brown clearly establishes, however, by the testimony of the colored men themselves that the shooting was done by colored soldiers and in all human probability by the men he mentions. He also shows clearly that First Sergeant Mingo Sanders, in spite of his reputation for personal courage, was as thoroly dangerous, unprincipled and unworthy a soldier as ever wore the United States uniform, and that under no conceivable circumstances should he ever be allowed again in the army. The testimony is clear as to the part of Hollomon also. If the Senate legislation passes this letter of mine and the accompanying documents will be put befor

the board of officers who are to consider the question of what men, if any, are to be reinstated; and they will also be put before the President if the board decides that any of the men shall be made eligible for reinstatement.

Theodore Roosevelt

Figure 18. This letter shows that the President believed the fraudulent report of detective Herbert Browne. It also shows Roosevelt' animus toward Sergeant Mingo Sanders.

BOOK II

—∞—

YEARS LATER

My Quest to Exonerate the Innocent

TWENTY FIVE

THE PENTAGON

June 1972

The Odyssey Begins

YEARS LATER, AFTER I witnessed the tragic death of the
old man, how strange—yet fortunate—that I should find
myself as a staff officer at the Pentagon with the opportunity to reinvestigate the Brownsville Incident. How fervently
my grandfather had believed in the innocence of those soldiers! I had not forgotten. And I will never forget the old
man and the quaint wide-brimmed hat he wore. His death,
the stories my grandfather told me about Brownsville, and
that telephone call from Colonel Harry Brooks that sent me
scrambling all over my office looking for the Brownsville file
were the roots that grew into a personal odyssey.

Time was of the essence for me. I needed to stop, reflect
and take a good look at the origin of the trouble at Brownsville. The time pressure urged me to take the road followed
by William Howard Taft, Secretary of War under President
Theodore Roosevelt. Taft was a good man who would stand
up to President Roosevelt for what was right. He would acknowledge the moral imperative, when it was in conflict
with the legal. Or, so I thought.

"What in hell do you want from me?

That journey began early on the morning of June 1, 1972, when Colonel Harry Brooks assigned me to work on the Brownsville project—after I volunteered. Congressman Hawkins had introduced a bill that would require Secretary of Defense Melvin Laird to rectify the injustice of Brownsville. The Judge Advocate General opposed enactment of the bill. And the Army General Staff not only refused to intervene—but to my grief, concurred with JAG. Previous overtures to get JAG to change its position were fruitless. I had high hopes for passage of the legislation, if I could just persuade JAG to drop its opposition. I set out to do that. My job was to write a non-concurrence position paper against JAG's opposition. Once the Secretary of the Army heard my argument, I believed he would support the bill. But before I did that, I decided to make one last appeal to Colonel Wade Williamson whom I understood was the lawyer leading the charge against the proposed legislation.

As Bob Dews and I left Harry Brooks' office, Dews cautioned me, "Williamson is a good man. He's no bigot. He is a very capable lawyer. He has the reputation of being the most brilliant lawyer in the JAG's Office, but I understand he is a very religious man who sometimes mixes his religion with the law. He says all the time that he believes in the right as God has given him the wisdom to do."

While walking over to Williamson's office, I began to wonder why Williamson had agreed to see me. Was it just out of courtesy for Brooks, his friend? Or, was he afraid of the formal non-concurrence? If so, why? Did JAG have something to hide? If so, what? Williamson knew the strict rules for writing a non-concurrence—you write one at your own peril, and you damn well better have your facts right. On the other hand, he knew the rules for overcoming a non-concurrence were tough, rigid, and uncompromising. You must write a concise formal statement not to exceed one page, debunking every allegation and every theory with facts.

The non-concurrence was a powerful administrative tool, and the only sure way of saying "no" to a great many plans. It was used to kill all sorts of programs, proposals, ideas, innovations, and so on which arose almost daily at the Pentagon, and were passed along for agreement by the general staff. Many of them arose from on high, endorsed with high-level signatures. Some originated from Congress in the form of bills and proposed legislation. These documents usually demanded extraordinary care and review—and had to be handled carefully and with utmost caution. But not Hawkins' bill. Maybe it was because Hawkins was a member of the Congressional Black Caucus and a liberal from Cal-ifornia. He was also a close associate of Congressman Ron Dellums who was considered a notorious persona non grata by some military officers in the Pentagon because of his open opposition to the Vietnam War.

A few ideas were daring, innovative mold-breakers, capa-ble of garnering consensus or final approval. Sometimes ideas were rejected for no good reason, except that they challenged the status quo or threatened to create precedents, either good or bad. The worth of the ideas didn't matter.

As I walked into a wide, spacious office, there was no doubt that I was in the domain of the legal profession. Heavy leather chairs were everywhere, law books lined the shelves along the walls, and a lush, heavy carpet gleamed on the floor.

A short, stocky, white military officer with broad shoul-ders, square jaw, and prematurely graying hair cropped close to his head stood in the middle of the room. He wore a green military uniform. Military ribbons decorated his chest. He was talking to a tall, slightly overweight, white man with curly, sandy-brown hair. The man wore an expensive-looking, blue pin-stripe suit and black wingtip shoes, giving the impression that perhaps he was an attorney. A woman sat at a typewriter off in a corner of the room, tapping away. From the manner in which the officer stood, confident and squared off like a boxer, I guessed he was Colonel Wade Williamson.

The other man seemed tentative and unsure of himself. I heard him say, "I'm not sure General Bowers will support you. Who agreed to this in our office?"

"Jessie Wheeler," was the answer. Wheeler was General Kerwin's chief of staff. Kerwin was a powerful man in the Pentagon. He was a three-star general, the deputy chief of staff for personnel—and our superior officer.

Extremely agitated, the other man said, "Jessie Wheeler doesn't work for General Bowers. He works for General Kerwin."

They still hadn't noticed me until another man came through the door and said to me, "You must be Major Baker. I am Captain Jim Murdoch, Chief of the Legislative Team. I work for Colonel Wade Williamson."

"Glad to meet you." Feeling a little awkward, I extended my hand for a handshake, trying to cover my eavesdropping on the other men's conversation.

"Major Baker, I see you are here. I'm Burt." The man I had guessed was Colonel Williamson addressed me, dropping his rank and surname. "This is Mr. Richard Belnap, the special legal advisor to the adjutant general. I see you have already met Captain Murdoch. He is a fine lawyer. Well, he has got to be since he's working in the Pentagon for Wade

Williamson. He's tough man to work for, and Wade works for me."

Murdoch seemed somewhat embarrassed by the praise. He shook his head in feigned disagreement, walked up to Colonel Williamson and handed him a manila folder. "All the papers are in here, sir. I'll stand by in my office. Call me if you need me."

Belnap stood there blankly. He looked as if someone just handed him a problem that he didn't know what to do with. He appeared anxious to leave, or better yet, flee. He also seemed surprised to see that I was standing there, or maybe surprised that I was black. Black officers were a rarity in the Pentagon. He looked at me with an expression that implied, *You've been listening. How long have you been standing there? How much did you hear?*

But as we shook hands, I felt a genuine warmth flow between us. It triggered a unique recognition of deep, buried roots going back centuries. These roots were ancient, reaching long before the civil rights movement and its Jewish participation. They reflected shared misery and deprivation arising from our long struggles with and flights from persecution and slavery.

I also had to admit that I felt a sense of estrangement. Jews had always supported black civil rights in the past, but where had they gone? Had the emerging rise of black anti-Semitism and affirmative action chased them away? As the handshake ended, these conflicting thoughts vanished. I hoped Belnap had not forgotten the old alliances between our peoples. I hoped he had not forgotten our common enemy—the real anti-Semites, the real bigots.

"Hi," Belnap said, as if he knew something he wanted to tell me, but couldn't. "General Verne Bowers asked me to sit in on this meeting, if I thought it necessary. After talking with Colonel Williamson, I don't think it is."

Belnap then left and Williamson welcomed me into his office. "Come into my office, Major Baker. Do you take coffee or tea?" But before I could answer, he stepped to the door and asked his secretary to bring both coffee and tea. Once we were seated around a long mahogany conference table in the colonel's inner office, he asked me, "What do you want, Major?"

The directness of the question and the blunt nature in which he asked it caught me by surprise. Colonel Williamson had made a complete metamorphosis from the friendly "Wade" to a stern-looking man, a hanging judge. He made me feel as if I were guilty of some crime. But then I realized who and what I was dealing with—a superior officer who was using his rank to intimidate me and scare me out of his office.

I stood my ground as respectfully as I could and reverted to military formality. "Colonel Williamson, sir, I want to know why the JAG is opposing Congressman Hawkins' bill."

"What do you mean by the JAG? Don't you mean the Office of the Judge Advocate General?"

"No, sir, I mean Major General George S. Prugh, the Judge Advocate General. Not the office, the general himself, sir. Why is he opposing it?"

The subtlety was not lost on Williamson. He knew exactly what I was getting at. I was making a distinction. I was deliberately separating the man from his office and subordinates, and kicking the responsibility upward. The buck was to stop right in General Prugh's lap. And the core question was:

*Was General Prugh aware that his name had been used
to oppose a major piece of legislation? Did he know that
his staff sent a letter across the Potomac River to the
Nixon administration without his knowledge?*

Williamson stared at me, bit his bottom lip, and turned
his head away in contempt. He picked up his telephone, held
it for a second or two, then put it down, and turned back to
me. "Major, you have made it clear that you know the difference between the JAG and the Office of the JAG," he said,
"Now what in hell do you want from me?"

"All right, sir, with all due respect to you, why are you
opposing this bill?"

"Harry Brooks sent you over here to talk with me about
the non-concurrence. I told Dews yesterday that we were
opposing that legislation. That's JAG's position. We are not
about to change. Dews told me yesterday he was going to
write a non-concurrence. Now are you writing it, or Dews?"

"Sir, the rules require us to try to resolve the matter first."

"Don't you lecture me. I know the god damned rules.
There's nothing for Dews to do but drop that stupid idea
about writing a non-concurrence. If Harry hasn't gotten that
through Dews' head yet, I know he will."

"Sir, I don't think we are at loggerheads yet. The way I
see it, we don't have a basis for writing a non-concurrence,
or writing anything, until we find out why you are objecting
to this bill."

The colonel's mouth cracked slightly open, his lips
stretched back on both sides of his mouth showing his teeth.
Leaning his square head forward across the table, he glared
at me intently and said, "All right, you want to know, I'll
tell you." Shuffling the stack of papers on the table in front
of him until he came to Hawkins' bill, he picked it out and

hurled it across the table at me. "That's crap, that's crap, a piece of worthless shit. Have you read it?"

He launched into an attack on Hawkins' bill, ripping it apart with such vehemence that it seemed he even hated the paper it was written on. Pointing to a copy of the bill lying in front of him, he said, "It was sent over here naked, stark naked, without any legal arguments attached to it, no new facts, no re-investigation, no nothing. Just assertions."

To him, Congress was without authority to direct the Secretary of Defense to change the discharges from 'without honor' to 'honor.' He invoked the name of Teddy Roosevelt and quoted him, "President Roosevelt said, 'The order was within my discretion under the Constitution and the laws, and cannot be reviewed or reversed save by another executive order.'"

"Just a minute, sir," I interrupted, "Do you mean to say that Congress doesn't have the power to reverse Teddy Roosevelt's decision."

"That's exactly what I mean."

"For the sake of argument," I ventured to say, "suppose the bill passed, and ...."

"Then President Nixon would be obliged to veto it, if for no other reason than to preserve executive privilege," Colonel Williamson was quick to point out.

"Well, then suppose the veto was overridden by Congress?"

"Then we would have a Constitutional crisis. It would have to be settled by the U.S. Supreme Court."

"Then, sir, would you agree with me that President Nixon has the power to reverse that decision?"

"Well ..., well, I don't know. I'm not a constitutional lawyer," Williamson stammered. "By the way, where did you get your law degree?"

"I don't have one. I didn't go to law school."

"What!" Williamson raised himself halfway up from his chair. He leaned over the table toward me, obviously annoyed that he had been discussing law with a non-lawyer.

"That's right, sir. I'm not a lawyer."

"Well, that explains your god-damned ignorance." He looked me over as if I were some new kind of animal he had never seen before. "I hope you're not one of those left-wing, shit-headed sociologists."

"I'm a technical service officer, sir, Signal Corps."

"Well, I reckon you got half a brain just like me. You know JAG is somewhat of a technical service. I got some respect for you."

Watch out, I thought. He's trying another tactic. He's trying to soften me up.

"Are you a poker player?"

Why did he ask me that? What in the name of heaven was he getting at? What's poker playing got to do with this? "I never played poker, sir. I grew up a Missionary Baptist. Gambling was considered evil. Why do you ask?"

Appearing somewhat disappointed that I was not a poker player, he said, "Well, I grew up a Southern Baptist, and I still go to prayer meeting on Thursday nights when I can. But hell, I don't think a little poker game will keep me out of heaven. Anyway, what will be, will be. That's what the Good Book says." Ending the conversation, he said firmly, "You're holding a losing hand."

What I didn't tell him was that I had worked at BRL, the United States Ballistic Research Laboratories. I was a ballistic research and development coordinator at BRL, and an operations research systems analyst in the Weapons Systems Laboratory. I had learned and practiced war game theory there and was familiar with the techniques of winning and losing. Telling him that wouldn't have made any difference to him anyway. It was better that he thought that I was nothing more than a lowly staff officer doing his stint in the Pentagon who was just punching his military ticket and enhancing his career. I wouldn't do anything to disabuse him of that idea.

He looked at his watch and said he had another meeting scheduled. He began looking through the papers Captain Murdoch had given him and said, "Oh, here it is." He was talking about the letter to George Shultz, prepared by Captain Murdoch and approved by himself. He began talking, reading, skipping through most of it until he came to the part about conspiracy of silence. "You know, those black soldiers committed an atrocious crime, and all of them covered it up with their cowardly conspiracy of silence. There were several investigations and all of them concluded that the black soldiers did it."

"What investigations, sir?" Certainly, I had read about the investigations in the file, but I wanted to hear from him. Maybe he knew some that I hadn't read about.

"Don't you know? You mean you came over here unprepared, wasting my time? And don't tell me what your grandfather told you, I've heard that from Dews. All right, I'll tick them off for you." He started to read from a card, and then he thought better of it. "I'll have my secretary make a copy for you."

Then he started reading again from the letter. "It was the president's opinion that a heinous crime had been committed...and that another crime only of slightly lesser magnitude supplemented it in the shape of a successful conspiracy of silence, and the duty to come forward, that in fact was the basis for discharge of all of the participants. There was overwhelming evidence to support that conclusion by the inspector general.

"That's my reason for opposing that bill," he said, "and I won't change. I told that to Dews, now I've told it to you, and I'll tell Harry. There is nothing for your office to do except join me in opposing that bill. You should drop this non-concurrence nonsense."

"All right, sir, I hear you. May I read the JAG's legal opinions on the case?"

"You may not," Williamson said.

"You have them in that folder, don't you, sir?"

"Yes, but you can't see them."

"Where can I get information on the case, sir?"

"You can start with the Law Library."

"Thank you, sir. When can I talk with you again?

"When you are ready to concur with my position. Anything else?"

"Yes, sir. May I have a copy of the letter from Attorney General Kliendienst?"

"Yeah." He rustled through the file folder looking for it, then he looked up. "Can't find it here. I'll have Murdoch get you a copy."

It seemed incredible that Colonel Williamson wouldn't let me see JAG's legal opinions on the Brownsville case while admitting that he had them. It made me suspect that things might not be entirely on the level. There was something wrong here. I sensed JAG wasn't holding the winning cards, and that Wade Williamson was bluffing.

TWENTY SIX

SEARCH FOR EVIDENCE

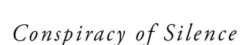

Conspiracy of Silence

Fighting the Alligators

AFTER THANKING THE SECRETARY for copying the list of military investigations for me, I hurried to the Law Library on the A corridor. I skipped the card catalog and went directly to the military documents reference librarian. When I showed her the list of military investigations I wanted, she didn't need to check the card catalog. "Come with me," she said. She got up and headed for the reference stacks. She acted as if she had been expecting me. Had someone called her and told her that I was coming?

Opening up both of her arms in a wide gesture as if she were going fly off a hill top, she said, "You see all of these books here? They are reference books on the Brownsville Affray. The red and yellow-bound volumes are the senate documents, which include reports of the Senate Committee on Military Affairs Investigation. The red bound volumes are Court of Inquiry. Some of the smaller volumes are messages from the president, reports from the secretary of war and there are other documents."

My heart sank as I surveyed the overwhelming volume of reference materials. There were volumes and volumes of stuff—daunting for any reader to take in over a long period of time—and I didn't have much time. "Can I check out some of these materials?" I knew full well the answer would probably be 'no,' and that's what I got, a polite, 'no.' Then, she reminded me that the library was open all night and went back to her desk.

After thumbing through a few pages of the neatly bound green senate reports, I saw that there were more than 3,000 pages of testimony, numerous exhibits, maps, pictures, and charts. I quickly moved along the shelves to the red volumes which were the reports of the Court of Inquiry Investigation. I looked at the first and last volumes. They were even more lengthy with more than 13,000 pages of testimony and exhibits. And then there were the Congressional Records. These thick tomes stood all by themselves, taking up a lot of shelf space.

I went back to the reference librarian, and said, "Ma'am, I want the specific reports of these officials—Major Blocksom, Colonel Lovering, General Garlington, Assistant Attorney General Purdy and the messages from President Roosevelt."

She looked at my list again, which was the same list I showed her earlier. Then she went somewhere in the back and came out with five investigative military reports. They were moderate-size books, some even pamphlet size. She spread them out on her desk and asked me if those were the books I was looking for. Glancing at the texts, I saw that they were indeed the ones I wanted. I took them to a table set back in a corner of the library and set up shop. With the official military reports spread out in front of me, I perused all of them, leafing through them quickly. I looked for key words and phrases that I had found in JAG's letter to George

Shultz, such as 'conspiracy of silence,' 'due process,' 'presidential authority,' 'without honor,' 'evidence' and so on.

After that, I knew that I had to set up a conceptual framework or a methodology to guide me. With my elbow on the table and my chin cupped in the palm of my hand, I began scratching the side of my face. I became downhearted as I tried to figure out where to start. Then something came to mind, a dictum straight from the head of poet and writer, Edgar Allen Poe. I scrawled it on a yellow pad, "Eliminate the impossibilities, and what remains must be the truth."

Then I remembered what Doctor Holmes, my philosophy professor at Howard University, used to caution, "Re-examine your assumptions," quoting the French philosopher, Rene Descartes. So I wrote down "Re-examine their assumptions." Still more direction came from Professor Holmes, "The difficulty in proving a negative." It was a quote from the Scottish philosopher, David Hume, and it reminded me that I had a tortuous path in front of me.

Finally, I wrote on my yellow pad the words inscribed on the little sign that Colonel Brooks kept on his desk, "REMEMBER THE MISSION IS TO DRAIN THE SWAMP–NOT TO FIGHT THE ALLIGATORS."

Being acutely aware of my deadline, and after I established a generalized conceptual framework, I set up a plan with a few simple rules to follow. I thought that they would allow me to move through the prior investigations rather quickly.

I started my review with Major Blocksom's "Report of Investigation" which included a series of earlier reports. I learned from reading the panic-stricken telegrams that he sent to Washington starting on August 20, 1906, that he was afflicted by the same fear that gripped Brownsville. On

August 20, 1906, just two days after his arrival, he recommended that the soldiers be moved out of Brownsville.

Based upon that recommendation, President Roosevelt ordered the soldiers removed from Fort Brown. They had arrived at Fort Brown on July 25, 1906, and were removed on August 25, 1906, whereupon they arrived at Fort Reno, Oklahoma, on August 27, 1906. My goodness, all of this happened in about one month, from arrival to kick-out!

I examined Blocksom's major conclusions—that nine to 15 soldiers, possibly more, jumped the garrison wall and attacked the town. He also concluded that all the other soldiers who didn't join the attack knew who did. Upon re-examination, which Blocksom should have done, I found his conclusions to be nothing more than assumptions of guilt. These conclusions were based on flimsy, unsubstantiated evidence. In some cases, they were complete fabrications.

What bedeviled me most of all in my review was the empty cartridge casings and empty magazine clips found in the streets of Brownsville. How was I going to deal with that seemingly incontrovertible evidence? I decided to come back to it later.

As I continued to analyze Blocksom's report, I found references to a Captain Bill McDonald of the Texas Rangers and the 12 soldiers and one civilian he had arrested. I didn't find any evidence against them. Incredibly, Blocksom admitted to not having any evidence, yet relied on Bill McDonald's word. Here is what Blocksom said in his report, "Almost no evidence against men arrested, though [I] believe majority more or less guilty."

'Conspiracy of silence' was the linchpin of JAG's opposition to the bill, and I determined that it was Blocksom who concocted that theory. I examined and re-examined his assumption that the old soldiers must know something but weren't telling. I searched his report for verifiable facts, but found none because he had found none. He assumed facts that he had not discovered, then used them to support his conclusion.

I moved on to the next military report, the investigation conducted at Fort Reno, Oklahoma. It was led by Lieutenant Colonel Leonard A. Lovering, Inspector General from the Southwestern Division, the superior headquarters for Fort Reno. I subjected it to the same tests and found the results quite revealing in an amazing way. Lovering's investigation began on September 24, 1906, and was completed on October 4, 1906. Viewed as a whole, the preponderance of his evidence supported the innocence of the soldiers. Writing such a report was a remarkable act of courage. He must have known that his report would be unpopular and perhaps the kiss of death for his career. Lovering invited attention to soldiers' testimonies suggesting that the town was shot up by parties other than the soldiers. "Testimony as to the expression heard while the firing was going on—'Black sons of bitches,' etc.—on the town side of the garrison wall."

He didn't mention anything about a 'conspiracy of silence.' Instead, he simply presented sworn testimony of the soldiers denying any participation in the shooting and having no knowledge of who did it. Embedded in his report was evidence debunking the 'conspiracy of silence' theory. But Lovering left the evidence raw and undigested. He never even wrote an interpretation of it in his report, and I knew why.

It is common knowledge among military officers that when an inspector general finds evidence contrary to what his superiors want him to find, his report sometimes evokes the expression, 'That's not what I want to hear.' This happens at times when higher headquarters have assumed wrongdoing by individuals or units without evidence, or when the IG has been expressly told to go down and get evidence on the 'guilty' parties.

I found that Lovering's investigation completely supported the innocence of eight of the 12 men implicated by Captain McDonald, including John Holomon. His report simply stated, "The following men of the 25th Infantry, now prisoners at Fort Sam Houston, can apparently prove an alibi."

I was not at all surprised when I learned that Major Blocksom attached rebuttal notes to Lovering's report. Blocksom attacked the sworn statements of the soldiers, stating among other things, "I heard nothing of the expression 'black sons of bitches.'" In an attempt to further discredit Lovering's findings, Blocksom discounted sworn statements by a number of soldiers who were positive that shots were fired toward the post. Blocksom then concluded erroneously that because he could find no evidence of bullets striking the post, that none were fired toward or over the post. And from that reasoning, Blocksom missed the point that the raiders may have intended to fire high. Perhaps they didn't want to hit anything, but wanted to manufacture a crisis and create a deception for a frame-up.

Then I turned to the report of the Inspector General of the Army, where I continued my review. It didn't take me long to realize that Roosevelt sent Garlington to Texas and Oklahoma to break the so-called 'conspiracy of silence.' That was his real mission. His orders to Garlington were front-end-loaded with an assumption of guilt on the part of the soldiers. I read the first line and became painfully disappointed. Finding the soldiers guilty was actually the goal of Roosevelt's investigation:

> *The President directs that you proceed to the places named…and endeavor to secure information that will lead to the apprehension and punishment of men of the 25th Infantry believed to have participated in the riotous disturbance which occurred in Brownsville, Texas…*

However, more disturbing to me was the president's assumption of a 'conspiracy of silence,' Major Blocksom's theory that all of the soldiers must have entered into a tacit understanding to protect the guilty. He had 'reasoned' that they must have guilty knowledge of who did it, and, therefore, all of them must be punished for not telling. This meant to me that President Roosevelt was persuaded by Major Blocksom's specious reasoning.

A Search for Evidence

I further reminded myself that I had to persuade Colonel Williamson and JAG that a 'conspiracy of silence' had not existed to have any chance of getting them to drop their opposition to Hawkins' bill.

So I looked for unbiased, hard evidence in Garlington's report of a 'conspiracy of silence.' What I found both shocked and delighted me. Garlington admitted that he found no evidence of a conspiracy of silence.

> *The uniform denial on the part of the enlisted men concerning the 'barrack talk' in regard to these acts of hostility upon the part of certain citizens of Brownsville indicated a possible general understanding among the enlisted men of this battalion as to the position they would take in the premises, but I could find no evidence of such understanding.*

After I finished reviewing Garlington's report, it was clear to me that the general discredited his report by his own words, perhaps unwittingly. He did so by arriving at a conclusion unsupported by evidence, evidence he admitted he didn't have. But he still blamed the soldiers. Any way you looked at it, Garlington admitted failure.

First, he admitted that he read Judge Stanley Welch's decision dated September 28, 1906, which stated that the Cameron County Grand Jury found no evidence against the 12 soldiers, had not indicted any of them and "therefore [they] are entitled to release." But Garlington still found the men incarcerated at Fort Sam Houston, Texas, when he arrived there. When he questioned them about the raid, they denied participation in it and denied having any knowledge of it.

"As soon as the trouble at Brownsville was introduced, the countenance of the individual being interviewed assumed a wooden, stolid look...," according to Garlington.

From Fort Sam Houston he went to Fort Reno, Oklahoma, where he encountered failure again and again as he questioned all of the officers. Again he had to state that Major Penrose and the other officers found nothing:

I found that absolutely nothing had been discovered; that they had found no enlisted men who would admit any knowledge of the shooting or any circumstance, immediate or remote, connected with the same.

Learning that the officers came up empty, Garlington tried his hand at questioning the men, but uncovered not a thing, not even a motive.

...[I] could discover absolutely nothing that would throw any light on the affair; and received the same denial that any feeling of animosity or spirit of revenge existed among

THE WHITE HOUSE.
WASHINGTON.

December 1, 1906.

My dear Mr. Secretary:

The President would like to have you look up
any precedents (Lee's or others) for the action
taken in discharging the battalion of the Twenty-fifth
Infantry, and if there exist any such, send them to
the President.

Very truly yours,

Secretary to the President.

Hon. William H. Taft,
Secretary of War.

Figure 19. Letter from Roosevelt's Secretary to William Howard Taft
12/01/06
President Roosevelt seeks precedents for his decision against the soldiers after the fact.
U.S. Archives, AG file 1135832

the enlisted men of the 25th Infantry against the citizens of Brownsville on account of discrimination against them in the way of equal privileges in saloons or on account of the two acts of violence against their comrades.

And like Blocksom, but worse, he chose to blame his failure to find evidence on a 'conspiracy of silence.' He blamed not only the soldiers, but also the entire Black race. Instead of attacking the logic of the soldiers' argument, he chose to make an *ad hominem* attack on the presumed "secretive nature of the Black race:"

The secretive nature of the race, where crimes charged to members of their color are made, is well known. Under such circumstances, self-protection or self-interest is the only lever by which the casket of their minds can be pried open.

While I don't intend to be disrespectful, even to a dead general, and I surely don't know what he had in his mind when he took that metaphoric leap that he called "casket of their minds," I do know that the only dead mind was the seat of his reasoning.

Probing the Mind of a President

By this time I had spent three days and two nights in the law library and time was running out. I had barely scratched the surface of the materials lined up on the shelves. Starting with the Senate documents, I pulled out volume after volume, skimmed the tables of contents, and slid them back on the shelves again. There were over three thousand pages of testimony and numerous exhibits, maps, charts, affidavits and so on. The books were thick and heavy, so I began just piling them up on the table and then sat down. I hadn't spent 15 minutes skimming the tables of contents before I soon found myself drawn hopelessly into the details of the books. I found the information, stories, testimony, and analyses so interesting and riveting that I deviated many times from my original plan. Skimming turned to scanning, scanning to reading, and reading to methodical study.

I found it hard to believe that President Roosevelt took such drastic action based only on the reports of Blocksom and Garlington. How could the President, the attorney general, and the secretary of war have scrutinized these investigations without concluding that the soldiers' guilt couldn't have been reached based upon the evidence thus far adduced? Surely there must be more, something that so far, I had missed. Maybe President Roosevelt found more in the reports than I did.

My answer came when I read the reply of President Roosevelt to a Senate resolution dated December 6, 1906. The document concerned the discharge of the three companies offered by Senator Joseph Benson Foraker, Republican from Ohio, directing the Secretary of War to send to the Senate all information in his possession on the subject.

President Roosevelt responded quickly, vigorously and intemperately on December 19, 1906. To my chagrin, he had not only accepted completely and without questions the reports of Blocksom and Garlington (including copies of those reports in his reply), but to my amazement, he added nothing new, nothing from the investigations of the Secret Service he dispatched to Brownsville and nothing from the assistant attorney generals in Texas.

Included in his reply to the Senate were memoranda citing "plenty of precedents for the action taken" to support his decision. After reading those precedents, they appeared to be powerful arguments, and I made a note to search the historical records for each precedent to determine the facts and circumstances involved. Where in the world would I find any facts on those precedents? It sounded like a master's thesis in history to me, and I was no historian.

Curiously, in an apparent contradiction, Roosevelt accepted Colonel Lovering's report, which did not support Blocksom's findings, but tended to support the innocence of the soldiers.

Even though the President said that he was "glad to avail" himself of the opportunity to answer the resolution, his whole response was one of righteous indignation. His constitutional authority was being questioned. His fairness to the soldiers and yes, to the Colored race was being questioned. And the objectivity of General Garlington was being questioned because he was a Southerner.

Here are some of his characterizations:

[I] lay before the Senate the following facts as to the murderous conduct of certain members of the companies in question and as to the conspiracy by which many of the other members of these companies saved the criminals from justice, to the disgrace of the United States Uniform.

...the evidence proves conclusively that a number of soldiers engaged in a deliberate and concerted attack as cold-blooded as it was cowardly, the purpose being to terrorize the community and kill men, women, and children, in their homes, in their beds, and on the streets.

He spoke so confidently, and with so much praise for Major Blocksom's investigation that I realized that something else must have been operating in Roosevelt's psyche. There must have been something deep-rooted and, in particular, race-driven, driving his thinking. It was the base notion of the dispensability of the black soldiers. It appeared to me that this throw-away attitude operated just below his subconscious, surfacing under certain conditions of conflict (real or imagined), when it came to certain perceived God-given rights.

Roosevelt, who was such a brilliant man, a Harvard University graduate and a man who had read many books, had to know that both Blocksom's and Garlington's reports offered no evidence of a 'conspiracy of silence.' He had to know that General Garlington admitted as much. He knew the 'conspiracy of silence' was a lie. There was no euphemistic way of putting it. It was, in fact, a lie. But Roosevelt embraced it. Why? My speculations will come later, but first, here is how Roosevelt praised Blocksom's report:

> *...most careful, is based upon the testimony of scores of eyewitnesses —testimony which conflicted only in non-essentials, and which established the essential facts beyond chance of successful contradiction.*

If I could find the fallacies in Garlington's reports as well as Roosevelt's apparent complicity in embracing them (for Roosevelt was not a gullible or easily-deceived man), then other objective observers must have found the holes, too. And certainly some of the newspaper pundits must have as well. But it wasn't enough evidence to give me the confidence to return to JAG and confront them with what I believed they already knew. For some unknown reason JAG continued perpetuating this myth of a 'conspiracy of silence.' But did not one of the soldiers shoot up the town? My objectivity required me to withhold judgment until I did more research and analyzed more evidence.

From the Law Library at the Pentagon, I called the Library of Congress, and learned that there were many old newspaper articles about the Brownsville Affray. I spent all day Saturday at the Library of Congress, researching and reading old newspaper accounts about the incident. To my comfort, several newspapers arrived at much the same conclusion that I reached some 66 years later—that the reports of Blocksom and Garlington's investigations, and Roosevelt's curious use of them in his reply to the Senate, adduced no evidence of a 'conspiracy of silence.'

Most comforting to me was the conclusion of the *New York Times*, November 22, 1906, which was just what I was looking for. "Their contents proved surprising. It was found that no evidence had been gathered to prove a conspiracy of silence on the part of the members of the battalion.[black soldiers] The whole proceeding in fact was based on the assumption of the officers who made the inquiry that those who did not take part in the riot at Brownsville 'must know' who did."

Speaking less charitably of Garlington's report, the *New York Times* characterized it as:

> *Extraordinary...Not a particle of evidence is given in the 112 pages of the document to prove that any enlisted man had certain knowledge of the identity of any participants in the riot.*

I had found enough evidence that I believed would persuade JAG to drop its opposition to Hawkins' bill.

TWENTY SEVEN

THE NONCONCURRENCE

FEELING THAT I HAD found enough evidence to prove the conspiracy of silence theory was unsupportable by Roosevelt back then, and certainly untenable now by JAG, I was ready to confront JAG with a written nonconcurrence. I went back to my office and typed out a draft. As I was leaving to go to Colonel Williamson's office to discuss it with him, the secretary called out to me, "Major Baker, you have a call from the White House. Mr. Paul Lavarkis wants to speak to you."

"Tell him to call me in five minutes at extension 53614."

When I walked into Colonel Williamson's outer office, I asked his secretary to tell him that I needed to speak with him right away. Hearing my voice, he said, "Where have you been all of this time, Major? Did you get lost in the Law Library or somewhere? You've had enough time to educate yourself. Don't you think you should agree with our position now?"

"With all due respect, sir, I have to tell you that JAG's position is wrong, and it has been wrong for 67 years. There's no evidence of a 'conspiracy of silence,' and I think you know it. Nowhere in General Garlington's report does he say that he found conclusive evidence of a 'conspiracy of silence.' To the contrary, he said just the opposite, that there was no testimony whatsoever, and I would add facts. You know what I think? You folks've been hiding this for many years. Something like a historic cover-up."

Williamson bristled. "What do you mean? What are you talking about? You get the hell out of my office, now!"

Pushing back my chair and about to get up and leave, I cautioned, "Sir, I think you ought to hear me out."

"When I say get out, I mean get the hell out," he said.

His secretary came to the door, and said quietly, almost in a whisper, "Major Baker, there is a call from the White House for you. Mr. Larvarkis has been waiting on the phone for you."

After thanking the secretary, I picked up the phone in the outer office. I answered a few routine questions from Larvarkis and went back to my office, stopping at a copying machine along the way to make copies of my draft of nonconcurrence.

No sooner had I sat down at my desk than I received a call from Colonel Williamson's secretary, stating that the colonel wanted to see me. I needed a little time to think, so I told her that I would be there in about 15 minutes.

I began to re-examine my strategy, arguing with myself as to whether I had adopted the right game plan for winning. And No. 1, where did I made my mistake in dealing with Colonel Williamson? Had I been too direct with him? Maybe I shouldn't have said he knew that there was no conspiracy. Maybe he didn't know. Maybe just the staff lawyers knew. But somebody in JAG had to know other than Captain Murdoch.

What did I know or had observed about the colonel? I knew that he was a brilliant lawyer. As I understood it, he sometimes mixed his religion with law. I needed to get into his head and determine what he was thinking, but that was impossible. But wait! He once told me that he was a poker player. What did I know about poker? Not much. But I did know that it was a zero-sum game. One player must win and one must lose. It's impossible for both players to win, and also impossible for both players to lose. In other words, there must be a winner, and there must be a loser, and there was a value to every zero-sum game. My mind brushed back through Von Neumann's theory—and all of this was classic Von Neumann. If one assigned a value, say, +1, to one player, and a −1 value to the other player, the value could be calculated. And no matter what strategy each player used, the sum would always equal zero.

It was likely that in Williamson's mind, he considered himself in a zero-sum poker game with me. All of his actions towards me indicated this approach. Thus, he knew he could maximize his winnings by bluffing and being unpredictable. I knew this too. I imagined he considered himself in a struggle with me where one of us had to lose. He determined that he would not lose, even if he had to end the game by throwing me out of his office. Throwing me out was supposed to be a power move. Instead, it showed his irascibility. It was a weakness, because he got rid of me without hearing me out and therefore didn't know what else I had to say.

The truth of the matter, though, was that we were not in a poker game or a zero-sum contest. I must convince Colonel Williamson that both of us made a mistake by trying to notch a win. I had to change the paradigm to a cooperative game so that the outcome would be a win-win, especially so that the colonel could see that he wasn't losing.

While thinking about it, I hurried back to Williamson's office and found him standing at a stand-up desk, writing out something on a yellow pad and rapidly turning the pages of General Garlington's report. Raising his head briefly to acknowledge me, he motioned me to sit with a curt, "Be with you in a second, Baker."

Waiting for him to finish what he was doing gave me time to re-examine my assumption that he knew that Garlington found no evidence of a conspiracy. Seeing him with that report made me realize that perhaps he really didn't know.

He continued to flip back and forth through the documents he was reading. Then the rustling sound of the turning pages stopped, his neck swelled and turned red. The veins in his neck bulged as he muttered, "Ah." Then he sat down with an air of resignation and looked at me in disbelief. "I think I know now what you found out."

"Then why did you send for me, Colonel Williamson?"

"Let's have it," he said, "You know something else, too."

What else should I have found out? Did I miss something? Now, I didn't know what he was talking about. So I deflected his question.

"What does it matter what I know if we proceed with the assumption that you and I are in a poker game where one of us has to lose?" I replied. "But first I want to admit that I made a mistake in saying you knew that there was no evidence of a 'conspiracy of silence,' and I apologize to you for that. However, I am not backing away from the assumption that some of your staff lawyers knew it. Before I go further, I want to say that I want to start all over."

"Start all over?"

"Yes," I said, "I've already apologized for my impertinence. I meant no disrespect. However, for whatever reasons we want to ascribe to it, we have been in a non-cooperative posture, and if we continue in that vein, it will lead to disaster for one of us and a Pyrrhic victory for the other. We should move to a cooperative mode so we can obtain the best solution for the Army. If we do this, we will arrive at a cooperative solution that will put us in a win-win situation. That's the only rational outcome for the Army. It's the path that will lead us to an outcome so we both will be better off, or at least neither one of us will be any worse off. We've got to cooperate."

"Baker, drop the abstract bullshit. Come to the point. I know what you are talking about. I guess I have been a little rough on you."

Having reached a truce, I addressed several delicate points. I brought up the specter of a "perceived cover-up" in JAG, a cover-up of the truth now and over many years. I brought to his attention that JAG had already sent a letter to OMB with half-truths and historic lies, and had shamefully withheld exculpatory evidence favorable to the soldiers. And now JAG was about to send another letter with false information to OMB. I cautioned him that the Justice Department would unveil the cover up, and discover the truth. And if the attorney general found it, surely Congress would, if JAG persisted in its opposition to H.R.6866.

"Have you written a nonconcurrence?"

"Yes, sir, I wrote a draft." I handed him my yellow pad notes, which he started to read:

For the reasons summarized in the following discussion, the Deputy Chief of Staff for Personnel non concurs with the Judge Advocate General's position opposing H.R. 6866, Congressman Hawkins' bill to 'rectify certain official action taken, as a result of the Brownsville Raid, 1906.'

1. JAG erred in stating that its opposition to Hawkins' bill was not controversial within the Department of the Army. JAG made that statement in its transmittal

*memorandum, which was signed by Captain James W.
Murdoch for Major General George S. Prugh, the Judge
Advocate General. This memo was submitted to the Office of Congressional Liaison (OCLL). See Exhibit "A"
attached hereto. Attached to this memo was a proposed
letter, written by JAG, to the Honorable F. Edward Hebert, Chairman, Committee on Armed Services, which
has been further submitted to the Office of Management
and Budget (OBM) for the Nixon administration's approval, which is required before it can be submitted to
the Congress. JAG assumed facts relative to the so-called
'conspiracy of silence' which were not found by any of
the military investigators and which were not included
in their reports.*

*2. JAG erred in assuming there would be no objection
from the Nixon Administration in presenting its opposition letter to the Congress when it advised Congressman
Hebert that there would be no objection. As was clearly
stated by OMB, the Justice Department objected to JAG's
opposition report.*

*3. JAG's proposed letter to the Honorable George P. Shul-
tz, office of Management and Budget, contains factual
errors with respect to the 'conspiracy of silence' theory.
But more egregious is the fact that JAG's staff lawyers
should have known when they prepared the letter that
the military investigators found no evidence of such a
theory, and if they didn't know it when they prepared
the letter, they surely know it now, for Major Baker has
presented the evidence to them. Nevertheless, JAG per-
sists in submitting false evidence to OMB, which might
eventually end up at the Congress, and if it does, the
falsity of that letter will certainly be discovered, and it
will be to the total embarrassment of the Secretary of
Defense, Mr. Melvin R. Laird, and to the Chief of Staff
of the Army, General Creighton W. Abrams.*

4. It is recommended that the Army drop its opposition to H.R. 6866.

"Have you shown this to anybody else?"

"No, sir. And I have not discussed it with anyone."

"Why? Why haven't you shown it to Harry, if you are so sure of yourself?"

"I wanted to talk with you about it, first. I want you to drop your opposition to the H.R. 6866. That's my job, to get you to change your mind."

"Baker, aren't you really afraid General Kerwin will not back you? If he did, he would have bucked the JAG, and this time I mean General Prugh. He's got the finest legal mind in the Pentagon."

"When I lay out the lack of evidence of a 'conspiracy of silence' by the former investigators, and show the possible perception of a historic cover up in the JAG, and the likelihood of discovery by the Justice Department, I have confidence that Colonel Brooks and General Kerwin will back me," I said. "They will take the issue to the Chief of Staff if need be, that is, if JAG doesn't back down. On second thought, I don't believe General Prugh would let it go that far, even now, if he had knowledge of the truth."

"You're talking pretty high and mighty, aren't you, Baker? You think you're holding the winning hand, don't you?"

"Sir, we are back where we started, back at winning and losing, playing a game of poker, zero-sum. We are repeating ourselves." Then, I realized that I had spoken too quickly when I saw a sardonic smile creep across his lips. He was thinking of something else.

"Son."

Colonel Williamson called me "son." *What the devil was he getting at now?*

He lowered his head and chuckled, almost to himself, as if he had gleaned some heretofore hidden insight, and as if he weren't even in the room with me. Then, looking up straight into my eyes, he said, "Baker, you are naive. You're putting your career on the line, and for what?" His voice got louder. "That bill will never see the light of day. It hasn't got a snowball's chance in hell in getting out of committee, let alone passing in the House. If it's lucky enough to get passed in the House, it will be defeated in the Senate. Big John Connally—you know who he is, don't you? He is the former Governor of Texas. He's got political clout on the Hill and with the Nixon administration. You know the election is coming up in November. And don't you forget, there are powerful forces in this building that you don't want to cross.

"Don't ruin your career, son. You have a great career ahead of you. Look at where you are and where you have been. Look at all those ribbons on your chest, two bronze stars and three commendation medals. Look at your war campaign ribbons. You are on the promotion list for lieutenant colonel. You are going places. Don't throw all of this away for a bill that's doomed to failure anyway. Tear up this nonconcurrence."

This time I didn't believe that Colonel Williamson was bluffing. He was alluding to the powerful forces in the Pentagon that could be brought to bear on my career if I threatened the power of the establishment—in particular the historic precedents that the Army deemed sacrosanct. The bottom line was that my career might suffer if I submitted the nonconcurrence.

Of all the things he said or hinted at, the most worrisome was his certainty that I made the wrong assumption that Congressman Hawkins' bill would pass.

My blunder was that I assumed that if I could get JAG to drop its opposition to H.R.6866, that would be the end of it and the soldiers would be exonerated. Failing to re-examine my assumption, or worse, not realizing that I had made it, led me to focus on an intermediate objective, which, even if achieved, would fall short of achieving my ultimate goal of restoration of the soldiers' honor.

"Well, Baker," Williamson said, "I see you're perplexed, you're undecided, and you're unable to make up your mind. Why don't you sleep on it? Let's talk about it again early tomorrow morning. It's Saturday. It'll be quiet in the building. You said you haven't shown this thing to anyone. You haven't talked about it with anybody. Is that true?"

"That's right, sir."

"Good!" He smiled as he ripped up my yellow pad notes with relish, and threw the scraps of paper in his wastepaper basket.

For a moment, I felt as if the truth had been torn into scraps of paper, and yet I found comfort in my belief that it would not be lost forever. The truth would always be there—waiting to be uncovered and for someone to speak it.

Walking out of Williamson's office, I sensed Williamson's motives weren't all that altruistic about my needing to sleep on it. He also needed time to think about the possibility of the facts contained in the nonconcurrence leaking out.

When I got back to my office, I found my other staff work piled up. I worked another three hours, clearing it away. Amongst that paperwork, I found a copy of the letter from the Department of Justice that Captain Murdoch sent me. I noted that the Acting Attorney General, Richard G. Kleindiest signed it. I knew from reading the *Washington Post* that he was a prominent conservative, a brilliant legal mind, and a Phi Beta Kappa undergraduate. I also knew that the Justice Department opposed the Army's report. I knew this from reading JAG's letter to OMB, but why was the Justice Department opposing the Army's report? Probably just to get black votes in November, or to get more blacks to take sub-cabinet posts in the Nixon administration. He was having difficulty getting minorities to serve in his first administration. And after the November election, Brownsville would probably be forgotten.

I was tired, beat, in no mood to read anything else, and unable to make up my mind about anything. It was late on a Friday night, so I packed my briefcase, went to the Pentagon parking lot, got into my car and drove toward I-95 south.

Traffic flow down I-95 wasn't that bad for a Friday night, but for some reason, driving down I-95 was difficult for me that night. I didn't feel well, and had more than just a headache. I was driving too slowly in the wrong lane, holding up traffic. The honking started and continued until I pulled into the extreme right lane. One motorist rolled down his window and gave me the finger. I felt a little dizzy. Cars in front of me seemed to be getting smaller and smaller, and at a greater distance from me than they really were. Disturbed by this, I looked to the side of the road to check stationary objects, and when I looked to the side, those objects appeared farther away from me than I knew they actually were. When little stars began blinking and twinkling before my eyes, I realized that I had to pull off. At the next exit I got off, rested for a while, got back on the road, and drove into the Springfield Shopping Center.

Since I was getting home unusually late for a Friday night, I thought I would stop at the Giant Super Market and get flowers for my wife, Bettye. After picking up a vase of flowers that I considered to be spectacularly beautiful, I started through the checkout line. For some reason, I felt that I needed confirmation of their beauty. So I asked the cashier, who was of Chinese descent, what she thought about the flowers. In broken English, she said something to me that I didn't quite understand. Seeing that I wasn't catching on, she rubbed her hand delicately over the flowers saying, "feke, feke, feke." As I still wasn't getting it, I paid and went home.

When I handed Bettye the flowers, she said, "Oh, Bill, thanks for the beautiful silk flowers."

"Glad you like 'em. I thought they were real." The sound of my voice upset me, made me tremble—made me nervous. The thought that I bought artificial flowers thinking they were real upset me even more. Artificial flowers? I never liked them, and yet I liked these. Why didn't I dislike them now? What was happening to me? I wasn't listening to that cashier. She was trying to tell me the flowers were 'fake.'

That cashier read something in my eyes. She knew I made a mistake. She knew I intended to buy real flowers. But how could she know? I hadn't told her.

Needing to settle my nerves, I fixed myself a bourbon and ginger, went out on the brick patio, and took a sip. It was bitter, so I spat it out. I lit a cigarette and took a draw but it tasted nasty. I threw it down and ground it out under the heel of my shoe. I must be firm when I meet with Williamson tomorrow or he will crush me under his heels just like I crushed that cigarette, I thought.

When I came back into the house, Bettye looked me over. "Bill you look awful. You're losing weight. Let's eat dinner, and then you should go to bed."

Barely touching my food, I took my wife's advice and went to bed, but I had difficulty falling asleep. I was hypersensitive to sound that night, even to the usual noises about the room—the ticking of the grandfather's clock down the hall, the cracking sounds of the settling house, and outside noises around the house. Every little noise disturbed me, and traffic on Old Keene Mill Road seemed louder, roaring like a diesel engine rushing toward our bedroom, causing me to jerk and dodge as if escaping an oncoming train.

I turned over and over again in the bed. I lay on my stomach for a while, then rolled over on my back, curled up in the fetal position on my right side, and rolled over on my left side. My heart pounded furiously. I started to wake up my wife, but I knew she would call 911. I would feel foolish if I got to the emergency room and the doctors found nothing physically wrong with me except a bad case of the jitters.

What I needed was a good shot of Jack Daniel's whiskey. *Maybe that will settle my nerves and bolster my courage,* I thought. I got up, went to the kitchen, changed my mind—and drank a glass of water. Instead of quenching my thirst, it made me thirstier. So I drank another glass of water, and another, and another, until I lost count. A strange uneasiness came over me.

I was afraid, but why? And of what? Certainly not the harmless noises I was hearing. After all, they were real, not in my head. I wasn't cracking up, I reasoned, and I went back to bed.

Still unable to sleep, I began thinking about what Williamson said about my career. That was one thing I was sure wasn't bothering me, for I had always been a risk taker. I was confident in my skills as a technical officer and there was a shortage of officers in my specialty. I could always go back to that—and moreover, I had several job offers in the corporate world. Some of my civilian friends thought that I was stupid to stay in the service when I could make more money out-side. Why I stayed was simple. I loved the Army.

But I often wondered why they brought me to the Pen-tagon to work as a personnel action officer, a soft skill. Well, so I had thought, until I ran into the myriad intractable human relations problems involved with equal opportunity. My calculator never argued back.

It wasn't the perceived career threats, though. It was something else, real or imagined, that gave me pure hell that night and caused me to react irrationally. But it wasn't going to stop me from submitting that nonconcurrence. I resolved to take it to the end, wherever that might be. I would just have to get over these damn jitters. Why should I be afraid to disclose the truth to rational men? But what if they weren't rational? Military men were supposed to be given to abso-lute rationality.

All of that water I drank forced me to get up. When I entered the bathroom, I caught a glance of my face in the medicine cabinet mirror. Looking back at me was the face of a frightened man. *Where did I go wrong?* I felt warm, un-comfortably warm. I opened the medicine cabinet, took out the thermometer, put it under my tongue, and took it out after a few seconds. I looked at it. My temperature was in the normal range. Knowing that brought me back to reality.

I put my hand on my forehead. It was no longer warm. Moving closer to the mirror, I looked into my eyes. Fear was still there, but it had become definable. Simply put, it was the fear of failure, fear that even if JAG dropped its oppo-sition to the bill, it still might fail in Congress. That's what Williamson was telling me. In fact, he was telling me that he was certain that it was doomed to failure and that's what upset me. But more than that, it was the probable defeat of justice for the soldiers that was eating me up. Not what might happen to my career, not a waste of my time, or damage to my career on a lost cause, but that perhaps the last chance for those men to be exonerated, while some of them might still be alive, would fail.

Where did I go wrong? I'd failed to reexamine my assumption that H.R. 6866 would pass simply if JAG didn't oppose it. Upon re-examination, I saw that assumption was open to question. Exonerating the soldiers was an even higher hurdle. Blocking JAG alone should not be my goal. I needed to do something else, but what?

There was something I wasn't seeing. JAG knew what it was, but they were hiding it. Williamson refused to allow me to see JAG's past opinions on the incident. I had a hunch that written in those documents were facts I hadn't discovered when reading the prior investigators' reports. There must be something else that would show they were suppressing evidence.

My mind wandered, but I began to feel better. I sat down at the kitchen table. My thoughts jumped from one thing to another. Assuming that the nonconcurrence would accomplish my goal was a mistake. I had not yet found the right means to the end I sought, which was the exoneration of the soldiers. I had confused the means with the end itself. Such sloppy thinking could cause me to stop before I reached my goal.

Not wanting to make any more mistakes, I began to think more carefully. My thoughts jumped to the assumed rationality of military men. That was an assumption I had to be careful with when trying to predict how Williamson might behave tomorrow morning when I met with him. First of all, I didn't believe he gave a damn about anything in connection with Brownsville, except protecting the honor of the JAG—and his honor. If he were to achieve that, he must not do anything dishonorable, or at least anything that could be construed as dishonorable, or had a high probability of being uncovered. So if his goals were as I speculated, he should behave rationally to achieve those ends. Mind you, I was not ascribing any laudability to his goals. Rationality means, in this instance, only that he should choose the right means to accomplish those ends. And that leads to the conclusion that he should cooperate with me and drop his opposition to H.R. 6866. But that still didn't give me any assurance that I would reach my own goal. Finding the missing link, a pointer to the solution—that was my problem.

I wished I could call on God to help me, to make the connection, and point the way. Like a sinner in his hour of distress, I needed Him to rescue me from my delirium of irrationality, but that was impossible. Earlier in my youth and throughout my life, I sought Him through rationality and found nothing but contradictions.

I often saw people doing good and trying to do good, and some doing evil and trying to do evil, all without God's intervention. But goodness seemed to be winning out. Empirically, there seemed to be an evolution of goodness and a diminution of evil. Thus, by my calculations, goodness was a trend line moving upward.

My observations allowed me to further surmise that since goodness comes from people, goodness must be buried somewhere in people and that goodness must be God. But that God is imprisoned and must be freed. When He is released, He takes the form of Goodness and that is the only way good can happen—by the God within.

I realized that my notion—that God was passive and incapable of any acts of goodness unless released by the acts of people—might not be an acceptable belief to Williamson. I had to approach him carefully, if I were to persuade him to release the goodness I believed he possessed. Otherwise, he might think that it was God's will that President Roosevelt punished the soldiers, and that it was his duty to uphold it.

Thus, I hoped to convince Williamson that it was the goodness in him, his God within, that demanded the truth. He should uphold justice because God demanded it. He should cooperate with me to rectify the injustice of the Brownsville incident, because it was the good and godly thing to do.

That was a tricky strategy, trying to get a religious man to do good by convincing him that God was within him. No, I wasn't going to try to play a religious trick on him, for I truly believed there is a God within us all.

The Justice Department Letter

Feeling much better now that I had determined what was wrong with me, I had enough energy to do some reading. I reached for my briefcase, took out the letter from the Justice Department and started reading. In the first paragraph, the Justice Department opposed the draft report or letter prepared by JAG, which the Department of the Army had submitted on behalf of the Secretary of Defense. After briefly summarizing what the attorney general called the most significant facts, and stating that the Army's report misconceived the purpose of the bill, the attorney general took what I felt was a most remarkable and intriguing position. He recommended that the Defense Department take action under existing law to set aside the dishonorable discharges

[discharges without honor] of 1906. He went on to say, "If that is done, enactment of H.R. 6866 would be unnecessary."

My pulse quickened. I had found the potential solution in the Justice Department's letter. Do it within the Department of the Army. Don't wait for the enactment of Hawkins' bill. That was the missing link in my own analysis—and I chastised myself for not arriving at that potential solution on my own.

Morning had come. Even though I hadn't gotten much sleep, I felt invigorated. It was going to be a beautiful day. I just knew it! With the sunrise came rays of light through our small kitchen window, which spread across the papers on the kitchen table. With those rays of sunlight came a new spark of hope.

My thoughts were filled with possibilities that the Justice Department's letter invoked in me—the possibility of reversing President Roosevelt's decision by revoking Special Orders Number 266, and doing it in-house. That would in effect exonerate the soldiers, activate the search for old soldier survivors, allow the actual granting of honorable discharge certificates, and finally grant compensation. That letter was powerful even though it did not mention all of those possibilities. What impressed me most was that Richard G. Kleindienst, the Acting Attorney General, signed it—not an assistant attorney general or a low-level staff lawyer. The strategy was cunningly political for obvious reasons, but clever in that it sought to achieve administratively what probably could not be attained by law through the Congress.

I suspected JAG had not mentioned the Department of Justice's position in its reply to George Shultz, so I re-read JAG's letter to find out. Nowhere in that letter did JAG mention the 'do-it-within' strategy. They simply ignored the central means to the end, which was stated in the caption of the bill, "to direct the Secretary of Defense to rectify certain official action taken as the result of the 'Brownsville Raid,' 1906." Now why hadn't JAG mentioned the Department of Justice's position? Could it be that it was hiding that most powerful position from the rest of the Army General Staff? If the rest of the staff knew of the Justice Department's position, they might not only non concur, they might agree with Justice, and ask, "Why not do it within?"

Armed with this new information, I was ready to see Williamson again. When we met in his office on Saturday morning, he looked bedraggled. His face was unnaturally pale, as if a vampire had sucked the blood out of it. He didn't show much verve. The old gusto had disappeared overnight. And he did something unusual after I sat down at his conference table—he reached across the table to shake my hand. His hand was limp. It was the congratulatory feeble shake of a coach whose team had just lost the game to the winning coach. His voice was that of a dispirited man. "Well, major, it's your nickel. You go first. Did you think about your career last night?"

I wanted to tell him, "No, sir, but I did think about your career," but I controlled the urge to use sarcasm. A flip response was inappropriate in light of the gravity of the subject. I waited a few seconds before speaking. I speculated that he was now ready for the cooperative strategy that I tried to talk him into the day before. I began speaking again about the expected benefits of cooperation with both sides winning and nobody losing.

"To be honest, sir, I was miserable last night, didn't sleep much at all, but when the morning dawned, and after reading the letter from Justice, I felt better. I became firmly convinced in my belief that the only honorable and God-sanctioned thing for us to do is to cooperate, and I am ready. I believe there is goodness buried in you that needs to be freed—and only you can do that. The God within you demands it! I believe that you believe that God is ubiquitous. He is everywhere, and if He is everywhere, then logically, rationally, He must be in you. He demands the truth as you and I both know it. We must speak together, and as officers we have a duty to speak, and to speak the truth. Our honor expects it, demands it, and will never let us rest without speaking it."

Each time I mentioned the word 'God' he trembled, and the word honor seemed to lift him up. When I finished he said, "All right, all right, let's make a deal. You drop the non-concurrence and I will see that JAG drops the opposition to the bill. You are never to mention the fact that there was no evidence of a 'conspiracy of silence,' either orally or written, in this building, as long as you and I are on active duty. Is it a deal?"

"Not yet, sir. Will JAG write a legal brief for the Secretary of the Army to exonerate the soldiers, as that letter from Justice recommended?"

"Baker, I don't have the authority to promise that, and I would be kidding you if I did. You must be aware that there are powerful forces in this building—and not all of them are in JAG—who will oppose reversing Roosevelt's decision without proving some of the men didn't shoot up that town. Some of the top brass have read the confession of Private Boyd Conyers. How would any lawyers writing a brief get around that? Well, I can tell you, JAG won't tackle it. The proof is too conclusive that some of the soldiers did it. We just don't know which ones. Of necessity, the brief would have to be conclusive before the Secretary of the Army would even consider reversing Roosevelt.

"Yes, Justice's letter recommended that we do it from within, but they didn't volunteer to prepare the brief. Justice skirted around it. They made that recommendation for political reasons. They didn't want the Nixon administration to be on record opposing it, and they wanted to avoid a nasty fight in Congress. I haven't changed my mind about Hawkins' bill. It's worthless without additional facts—and it has provided none. When the heated debate comes in the House and the Senate, I guarantee you it will never get through. That's it, Baker."

"If JAG refuses to write the brief, then who will?" I asked. "Only JAG is staffed with lawyers."

"That's not exactly true. There are civilian lawyers in the Secretary of the Army's office, and the Secretary of Defense, but they passed the buck down to the Army. Now how about that? Your only possible solution, as I see it, is to talk General Kerwin into hiring outside lawyers to do it, and I can tell you right now, General Prugh would oppose that."

From that day to this, I don't know how I managed to say it, but I blurted out, "Then dammit, I will do it. I need reassurance from you, Colonel Williamson, that the JAG will not oppose me. I need that before I can agree to a deal. You are asking a lot of me to keep silent about what I have already found out."

"I can promise you that, and more. If you're lucky enough to find the proof that none of the soldiers shot up that town, you bring it to me first and prove it to me. I will take it from there. Don't worry about the other lawyers in JAG. You just satisfy me, and I'll do the rest. For starters, you will meet with me early Monday morning. I will establish the legal scenarios and will be your point of contact in JAG," Williamson said.

Having said that, he did a surprising thing. He took the opposition memorandum prepared by Captain James W. Murdoch and with affected pomposity proclaimed, "With this pen I officially drop JAG's opposition to H.R.6866." He drew a diagonally blue line through the original copy, and handed it to me with these words, "This is yours for keeps. By God, you earned it!"

"It's a deal," I said. And from that day until now, I have kept that original memorandum.

TWENTY EIGHT

JAG SETS THE LEGAL

$$\approx$$

Parameters

The Meeting with JAG

IT WAS VERY EARLY Monday morning, June 5, 1972, when I met with Colonel Wade Williamson, Lieutenant Colonel Davis, and Captain Murdoch, who were sitting in Williamson's office around his conference table. Their faces were stark, grim, cold, and distrustful.

Williamson opened the meeting by saying that he understood that I was taking over the Army's response to the proposed enactment of H.R. 6866, and that our office would be responsible for preparing a case for the Secretary of the Army to ameliorate the action taken by President Roosevelt. He reiterated emphatically Wade Williamson's position that JAG would not prepare the case, but would have final review of any case we prepared. He got up, strode to a standing flip-top chart, turned over the first page, which was blank—and uncovered the next. On that page, he had written several premises on which, he said, any decision to reverse Special Orders Number 266 had to be based. The letters were bold and black.

PREMISES

*# 1. THE DECISION WAS ERRONEOUS AS A MAT-
TER OF LAW.*

*#2. THE DECISION WAS ERRONEOUS AS IT WAS
BASED ON THE CONCEPT OF MASS PUNISHMENT
RATHER THAN INDIVIDUAL GUILT.*

*#3. THE DECISION CONSTITUTED AN INJUSTICE
AS IT WAS PREDICATED UPON RACIAL DISCRIMI-
NATORY GROUNDS.*

After pausing briefly, Williamson turned from the chart
and asked me if I had any questions concerning the premises
as far as the law was concerned. He wanted to know if I understood what was going to be required of me from a legal
point of view to support any one of the premises. From the
tone of his voice and with his emphasis upon the words law
and legal, I suspected he intended to wrap me up in a tidy
legalized trap, where everything would appear neat and legitimate. But the devil would be in the details—details that
I would have to work out, even if the action taken by Roosevelt was considered legal, according to legal standards at
that time in history. But I was certain it was morally unjust
then, and was morally wrong now.

Never having had much faith in the law for correcting
injustices, I preferred relying upon what was "morally right"
rather than what was legal. I knew there was a fundamental
and profound difference. What is morally right is not always
legal, and what is legal is not always morally right.

But I gave Williamson credit for having asked me
whether I understood what was required of me in terms of
providing proof. What I needed him to tell me, in simple,
non-legalese language, was what JAG would accept as proof
and would not accept in support of the assumptions that he

had described as premises. So I told him, "No, Sir, I don't know what you want in legal terms. Just tell me in simple terms what you want."

To get the concepts straight in my head and to keep them that way, I asked him if he would simplify the premises. I also wanted to know why we couldn't just call the premises 'assumptions?'

"You can call them whatever you want to call them," he said, "but I will try to simplify them as much as I can."

Shaking his head, he turned back to the chart, pointed to assumption No.1 and simplified by flatly rejecting it. He said that Roosevelt's decision was, in fact, legal. It was based on ample precedents, and that at that time in history, both the President and the JAG found ample precedents for doing what they did. Then, closing the door to me to use that assumption, he said that over the years JAG had reaffirmed the legality of the decision, and even today, they had no basis for reaching a contrary result. I interpreted his comments to mean that, if I went out and tried to prove that the decision was illegal and brought it back to them, JAG would turn me down.

Maybe they had ample precedents, and maybe they didn't, but what if they didn't? Does an unjust precedent in the past doom one to suffer an injustice in the future? And if so, is that right? Moreover, it was characteristic of Roosevelt to assert something was right, simply because he, the President, said it. Instead of falling for that argument, which was specious at best, even considering the need for consistency in the administration of the law over the long term, I jotted down on my note pad, "Check precedents."

Then he moved to #2. The action taken constituted an injustice, as it was based upon the concept of mass punishment rather than individual guilt. He paused, looked at it quizzically, started to say something, then stopped, as if he changed his mind about what he was going to say. Then after a moment of hesitation, Williamson stated that JAG was not going to express a definitive opinion on the concept of mass punishment versus individual guilt. Or put another away (at least the way I perceived it), he was not going to express an opinion on the barbaric procedure practiced in medieval times (maybe even today) that if the authorities couldn't find the hand that stole the bread, they would just chop off the hands of 100 people in the marketplace, hoping to get the hand that stole the bread or worse, chop off 100 heads. He was not going to say anything about that. He was not going to repudiate mass punishment!

Disappointed that he was not going to express an opinion on the concept of mass punishment, I wondered how he could avoid discussing two of the most sacred pillars of our law—the presumption of innocence until proven guilty and the concept of due process—which were intertwined with the topic he was discussing. Saying JAG was not going to express an opinion on the relevancy of those concepts was the same as ignoring the facts that the soldiers did not receive a trial, that there was a lack of due process, and that the soldiers were punished en masse.

After moving along in his presentation, Colonel Williamson must have realized the implication of what he had just said about JAG's refusal to issue a definitive opinion on mass punishment, for he quickly qualified that statement. "Of course, we all know that it is unlikely that a similar action of mass punishment would be taken today."

Whew! I was relieved to hear him disavow the concept of mass punishment in present day, even though he was not going to say anything about the past. But he went on to warn me to be careful if I chose to use that assumption. "Great caution should be applied in giving retroactive effect to every change in the concept of due process."

I didn't have to read his mind to conclude what he meant, for he told me. "President Roosevelt cited a series of cases in his message to Congress, dated December 19, 1906 in which similar, if not identical, action was taken."

Presumably, he was talking about white military units who allegedly received similar treatment. He was suggesting that if we set a precedent by changing the discharges of the black soldiers in the same circumstances, what was I going to do about the white soldiers as a matter of equity?

Since that assumption was intertwined with the ample-precedents assumption and now the discredited conspiracy of silence theory, I underlined the words 'check ample precedents' in my notes. Then I made a mental note to myself to determine if there was, or was not, evidence of a conspiracy of silence in the other cases Roosevelt cited.

Taking his pointer, Williamson jabbed the third assumption several times, almost punching a hole in the paper chart. Obviously, he was about to say something extraordinarily important about it. "If you chose to make a case that the action taken by President Roosevelt constituted an injustice as it was predicated upon racially discriminatory grounds, you better be prepared to support such a conclusion by specific findings of fact. And I warn you, the basic problem with racially discriminatory findings by you, by their very nature, impugns the integrity of President Roosevelt and his specific disclaimer of racial prejudice made in his message to Congress."

For a moment, I thought about Williamson's warning. I took it to heart, for I knew exactly what he meant. Racial discrimination was the last thing the U.S. Army ever wanted to be accused of, even in the past. Certainly, the Army didn't want to be accused of continuing to support that past discrimination, and perhaps White America felt the same way.

Abruptly, he paused. After what seemed to me an endless silence, he looked hard at me, as if to give his message time to sink into my head. "Now," he went on to say, "I raised these issues for the sole purpose of indicating the difficulties which you may encounter in developing a persuasive case to support your position."

Four Courses of Action

Williamson furrowed his brow. "As I see it, you have four courses of action, and all of them are difficult." He turned to the second page on his briefing chart, on which he had previously written:

COURSES OF ACTION

A. Action by the Adjutant General Independent of the Secretary of the Army

B. Action by the Army Discharge Review Board

C. Action by the Army Board for Correction of Military Records

D. Action of the Secretary of the Army, Independent of the Army Board for Correction of Military Records

I scrambled to write the courses of action down on my yellow notepad. Of the four options, I was leaning towards action D–preparing a case strictly for the Secretary of the Army.

The strategy would be for us to:

1. Summarize the existing facts,

2. Search for hard evidence to prove that the soldiers didn't do it,

3. Rely heavily on the fact that no indictments were returned by the Cameron County Grand Jury, which was the only true forum of the judicial system faced by some of the soldiers, and

4. Petition the Secretary of the Army to rectify the injustice, independent of the Army Board for Correction of Military Records, based upon manifest error of the past.

I wanted to hurry things along, as I didn't have much time. Before he could continue, I broke into his presentation. "Colonel Williamson, would you kindly simplify those alternatives that you are calling courses of action? Tell me which ones you consider feasible under your rules."

"I will not. It's important that you hear and understand the full implication of these courses of action. You should know what you're getting yourself into."

Then he picked up four 3x5 cards lying on the table in front of him, on which the four alternative and detailed explanations had been typed. He started to read and talk from the cards. "You might think it would be easy for the Adjutant General, independent of any findings by the Secretary of the Army, to just issue an order rescinding Special Orders 266. That's Course of Action A. It's not that simple, and doesn't work that way, although JAG has previously expressed the opinion that the Adjutant General has the authority to change records administratively to reflect the true facts." He read the opinion numbers and the dates, "JAGA/1963/4143, 27 May 1963; JAGA 1960/3508, 12 Feb 1960."

"Sir, may I have copies of those opinions?"

"You may not," he said and continued to go through the advantages and the disadvantages of each course of action.

As he droned on and on, explaining everything in the minutest detail—disadvantage this, disadvantage that, you can't do this, you can't do that—I struggled to stay awake. Several times I caught myself nodding off. The words on his chart began to blur. My head must have been bobbing because I heard him say, "Stay awake, Major!"

"I'm sorry, sir."

I sat up straight, wished I had a cup of black coffee, and scrawled Xs over the first three alternatives. They were completely out of the realm of possibility of achieving in my lifetime.

His voice mellowed, erasing the edge which characterized the beginning of his presentation. He eyed the fourth option on my pad and said, "Well, I see you didn't scratch that one out. I'm glad you didn't because that one may be your only hope. You probably thought that the other courses of action were out of reach, but the last one is perhaps the most risky, because it involves going directly to the Secretary of the Army without any intermediary. That places a political burden squarely upon his shoulders, without allowing him any wiggle room, if anything goes politically wrong. I can tell you now that he may not like that, and he may wonder why you are coming directly to him. If he gives you a quick denial, the action is finished, dead. No appeal above him. He will simply write 'Denied' and that'll be it."

There was another reason I wanted to go directly to the Secretary of the Army to present the soldiers' case. I wanted to stand before one person—and one person only—someone who had the power to make a decision and to whom I could passionately present an objective argument. A board of officers might be afraid to set a precedent. I believed that a complex case such as this one didn't stand much chance of success by being presented dispassionately in the present. Dry, dead facts about dead people—entombed in the bones of history—were not the stuff of inspiration.

"This ball is now in your court," he said. The meeting was over.

I went back to my office, facing a difficult task that required building a case upon facts so powerful, so clear, and so compelling that the Secretary of the Army would be convinced that justice demanded rectification of the effects of Roosevelt's decision. I had to do it quickly, and I had to make sure it was politically acceptable to a conservative administration.

I have always followed the "Rule of Parsimony," or as the philosopher William of Ockham put it, that everything else being equal, the simplest way to do something is almost always the best and rational way. This is a scientific principle called "Occam's Razor."

But I realized with a heavy heart that the inherent problem in trying to disprove a negative—that the soldiers did nothing—was not a simple thing to do. I had to face that fact squarely and deal with it first.

Twenty Nine

DISPROVING

A Negative

Back to Square One

I LEFT WILLIAMSON'S OFFICE, went directly to the Law Library and started my research all over again. Disproving a negative was going to be extremely difficult, if not impossible, especially in such large-scale circumstances. I needed a new game plan and had to steel my resolve for the fight ahead. The first step was to establish a conceptual framework based upon logic, existing philosophy, or law. Hopes and dreams for success had no place here.

When I got to the library, it was virtually empty, except for the librarian, and cold. I sat at the reference table, but didn't take a single book from the shelf. I needed to think.

I began weighing the elements of proof and the historical context of the logic of the difficulty in disproving a negative. At the very heart of the theory is the claim of the existence or non-existence of something, and the fallacy of inferring general rules from limited, specific, empirical observations. This was shown to be unsound by David Hume, the 18th century Scottish philosopher. It was misleading, and inherently circular. I learned in school that this specious reasoning was a misuse of inductive reasoning.

Thus, knowing the inherent difficulty in disproving a negative, I could understand the problems faced by the black soldiers, which I also would face unless I changed the philosophical paradigm associated with the historical presumption of innocence. JAG and Roosevelt ignored that proposition in criminal allegation—that a person is to be presumed innocent until proven otherwise in a court of law. Connected thereto is where the burden of proof lies logically and legally upon anyone claiming the existence or non-existence of anything.

First, I solidified in my mind my assumption that if I claim the existence of something, or if I make a claim about anything, then I must prove it. And the only logical way for me to prove it is to produce it, or produce evidence of it, and present it to the person to whom I am making the claim.

Now the person I am making the claim to has no responsibility to prove that my claim is false. The burden of proof is on me—not on the other person to prove the negative. And if the other person says, "I don't know, I have no knowledge of it, and you have not proven it to me," then there is no requirement for that person to disprove my claim.

Following that logic, I considered the fact that each soldier was put in a position of disproving that he participated in shooting up the town. Each one denied any knowledge of it, and as Senator Foraker pointed out on the Senate floor, how else could he prove it except by denying it? Also, I considered the fact that each soldier was required to disprove that he knew who participated in the raid, even if he didn't participate himself. The soldiers were punished for being unable to disprove that they didn't know, or put another way, they were punished for not knowing.

I imagined putting an argument to philosopher David Hume. I imagined that Major Blocksom had claimed that all the catfish in the Rio Grande River were brown, and that Blocksom claimed he knew it, because so many of the towns-people in Brownsville had told him that fact. Thus, he knew it to be the truth. I envisioned further that Blocksom took Hume to the river, where he pointed out several brown cat-fish swimming in the Rio Grande. "See," says Blocksom, "I told you."

Based on Hume's theory about fallible generalizations, he would probably say, "Not on your life can you infer that all the catfish are brown in the Rio Grande from those limited observations. You would have to drain the whole river to prove that, and look for catfish everywhere in the river to prove it."

Now, I imagined that Major Blocksom demanded that the soldiers prove that there were no black catfish in the Rio Grande River, that is, disprove a negative. To put it another way, he demanded that the black soldiers prove that they didn't shoot up Brownsville. In the case of the catfish, the soldiers would encounter a similar degree of difficulty, but inherently more so, requiring them to drain the entire river, search everywhere for black catfish, and produce all the cat-fish in the river to show that there weren't any black ones. A virtually impossible task.

Suppose they tried to do just that by draining the river, but returned and told Major Blocksom that they were unable to find any black catfish, and Blocksom said that's not good enough. He might further assert that because they didn't find any didn't mean none existed in the river. Perhaps they had not searched everywhere in the river. Some may have been embedded deep in the mud. He would accuse them of getting together and intending not to find any black catfish, engaging in a conspiracy, a situation not unlike the actual one they faced. I concluded that those charges would be impossible to refute by disproving the negatives.

One would have to conclude, as I did, that the burden of proof would be illogically and illegally shifted away from Major Blocksom. After all, in his argument, he made the claim of the existence of something, that all catfish in the river were brown. He should have to prove it—not the soldiers. The burden of proof was unfairly placed upon the backs of the soldiers—the persons not stating the claim. It seemed to me that the soldiers' burden of proof would be so great that no amount of evidence would be enough to prove anything, and, in fact, would suggest that the outcome was rigged.

Under the adverse requirement of proving non-existence (a negative), the reasonable thing to do was to assume non-existence, and keep searching, which is the position of the great philosophers, the great jurists and the law of civilized people. In this position, the burden shifts from requiring those accused of crimes to prove a negative over to requiring a presumption of innocence until proven guilty. The successful shifting of that burden must be my predominant strategy for success.

THIRTY

THE LECKIE AND WIEGENSTEIN

Experiments

A Walk Back in Time

DAYS PASSED. I WENT in and out of the Law library, in and out of my office—and back again to the Library of Congress. I sandwiched my research on Brownsville between my regular office work, other projects, and my project with the White House Staff.

By the time I got to the Court of Inquiry Investigation volumes at the Law Library, my brain was becoming addled. These heavy red tomes featured more than 13,000 pages of testimony and exhibits. However, I wasn't so addled that I couldn't detect that the report was biased against the soldiers. That's when I determined that I had to go to the National Archives and study the primary documents, the old depositions, affidavits, telegrams, speeches, and court-martial records of the white officers.

As I walked up the steps of the National Archives, I had the strange feeling that I was walking back through time and into history. If the truth were ever to be found, I must search for it passionately. I would certainly find it in this neoclassical, Greco-Roman style temple with its colossal Corinthian columns, where the nation stores and maintains its most precious historic records. Once in the building and at the reference desk, I requested the Brownsville file. After a two-hour wait, an attendant rolled in a cart carrying several small, dusty green file boxes.

Now I had the actual documents in my hands. These files were the ones that President Roosevelt and all the prior investigators touched and worked with. These were the texts upon which they made their decisions.

While skimming through the documents, I found a letterhead that said "The White House." It was addressed to the War Department and signed by the President. Roosevelt wanted the adjutant general to go over the testimony of Lieutenant Harry G. Leckie. He claimed that Leckie testified falsely before the Senate committee. First, Leckie was sent to Brownsville to investigate on behalf of the defense at the court-martial of Major Penrose. And second, Leckie gave several hundred rounds of government ammunition to an outsider. Roosevelt ended the letter, "Please report to me on all of his evidence."

Why did Roosevelt ask the personnel staff officer, the AG, rather than the legal staff officer, the JAG, to do this? Was Roosevelt's vindictive side beginning to show? Let's take another look at Roosevelt's animus toward Sanders, Leckie, and Penrose.

Roosevelt's letter to the War Department said:

Sergeant Mingo Sanders, in spite of his reputation for personal courage, was as thoroly [thoroughly] dangerous, unprincipled, and unworthy a soldier as ever wore the United States uniform and that, under no conceivable circumstances, should he ever is allowed in the army.

On the last day, when the three companies of the 25th Infantry were drummed out, Penrose watched in uncontrollable grief, saying, "There goes the best battalion in the army." Roosevelt read about the statement in the Evening Star newspaper and was livid. He demanded an explanation for Penrose giving such an interview. Furthermore, Roosevelt required a full and immediate explanation for Penrose's reasons for making such a statement. Ultimately, Penrose ate his own words and denied both his laudatory comments about the black troops and his interview with the newspaper.

Roosevelt's letter led me to Lieutenant Leckie's testimony before the Senate Military Affairs Committee and the file on the court-martial of Major Penrose.

I came to the part of the Senate hearings that I imagined must have made Roosevelt's blood boil. Leckie debunked Major Blocksom's theory that the bullets were fired from Company B's barracks or from any other location within Fort Brown. In fact, Leckie showed that the bullets couldn't possibly have been fired from B Company's barracks.

The question Senator Foraker put to Leckie was, "Could the bullets that entered Yturria's house have been fired from B Company?"

Leckie was sure they couldn't:

The reason that I say that they were not fired from B barracks is that they would have to turn an angle of 90 degrees in the air, without having anything to deflect them in any way. And I do not know of any laws of motion for a bullet doing that.

Next, I turned to the court-martial record of Major Penrose. To my delight, there I found the rest of the story that caused Roosevelt angst and precipitated that War Department letter about Leckie. It, too, was based on Leckie's test results. According to the record, General McCaskey sent Leckie to Brownsville to trace the shots that hit the various houses and to see what parts of the barracks could be seen

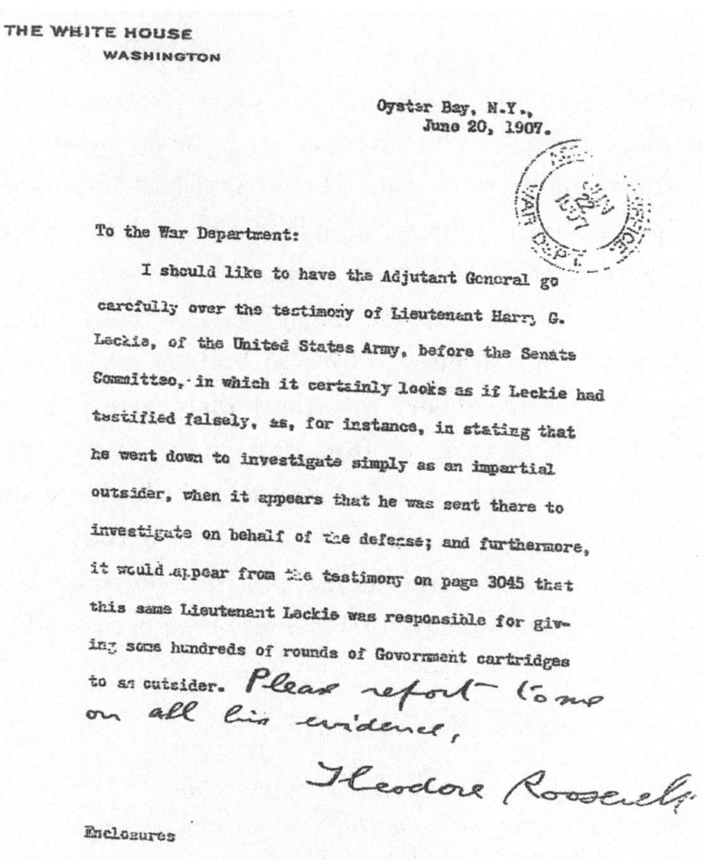

THE WHITE HOUSE
WASHINGTON

Oyster Bay, N.Y.,
June 20, 1907.

To the War Department:

I should like to have the Adjutant General go carefully over the testimony of Lieutenant Harry G. Leckie, of the United States Army, before the Senate Committee, in which it certainly looks as if Leckie had testified falsely, as, for instance, in stating that he went down to investigate simply as an impartial outsider, when it appears that he was sent there to investigate on behalf of the defense; and furthermore, it would appear from the testimony on page 3045 that this same Lieutenant Leckie was responsible for giving some hundreds of rounds of Government cartridges to an outsider. *Please report to me on all his evidence,*

Theodore Roosevelt

Enclosures

Figure 20. Letter from President Roosevelt to the War Department,
6/20/1907.
President Roosevelt directs the Adjutant General to go over the testimony of Lieutenant Leckie and report the evidence to him.
It is clear that Roosevelt is not happy with Leckie.
U.S. Archives, AG file 1135832

from the Leahy Hotel second-story windows. Leckie was also to inspect the Ruby Saloon, and see if Allison was still in jail, and why. What he found was revealing.

Starting with Cowen's house, his investigation proved that, based on where the bullets struck the house, that all of the shots had to have been fired from the rear. There were no bullet holes in the front of Cowen's house.

In the test of the upper rooms of the Leahy Hotel, the results highlighted several physical impossibilities. One could not observe C Company's barracks from the first window upstairs (the window toward the alley) in Herbert Elkins' room. Elkins told the Senate Committee that he saw flashes of gunfire from C Company's barracks. That view was obstructed by houses. No barracks except for 10 feet of the upper end of B Company's barracks could be seen.

Katie Leahy swore to the Senate Committee that from her position in the upper window she saw men shooting from both the lower and upper porches (galleries). Leckie found the view of the lower porch completely blocked by an orange tree. And only half of the upper porch could be seen from that window.

The Flash of a Rifle

Next, I turned to the Wiegenstein experiments. Lieutenant Henry Wiegenstein was admitted as an expert witness for the defense at Major Penrose's court-martial in March 1907.

On a bright, moonlit night on February 19, 1907, between nine and ten 'o'clock, Wiegenstein set up experiments to determine the accuracy of vision at night. One of his experiments simulated the conditions of an alley in a flat dry-bed gully, commonly known as an arroyo. He wanted to determine, according to his testimony, what could be seen by looking into the flash of a rifle from above, behind or in front. He set up lanterns at two locations, and posted military officers at the two locations to act as observers. As he moved a firing party, consisting of three civilians and eight soldiers, into positions, an observer shouted, "Lieutenant Wiegenstein, which way are the men facing?"

"I don't care to tell you, that's part of the test," Wiegenstein shouted back. Nor did Wiegenstein tell the observers their race or color. The men fired two volleys, then fired at will. Wiegenstein moved them up and down the simulated alley, firing at two different locations—point A and point B. The horizontal distance from the firing party to the nearest observer was about nine feet. The vertical distance was uniform at about 21 feet. When the firing was completed and the observers questioned, they said that they couldn't recognize any complexion by the light of the flash, that they couldn't see anything, not even the rifles.

Not satisfied, Wiegenstein took special pains to see if he himself could discern features or complexion. He stationed himself directly in the center of the firing party. He fixed his attention on the faces of the men immediately in front of him, not more than one-step distance. He wanted to see if at the instant of discharge, whether the flash of the guns would enable him to distinguish features or complexion. He couldn't, no matter how hard he fixed his attention on the faces as they stood before him, nor could he see the guns. The flash was instantaneous and his eyes involuntarily followed the flash.

After the firing was completed, he marched the firing party along a path out of the gully to the road where the observers stationed themselves. Then he marched the firing party single file nine feet from the observers. Wiegenstein said that the officers peered into the faces of the men separately as they went by. One of the observers remarked, "I would like to see white men marched by. I want to see if I can detect their features or complexion."

Wiegenstein testified he informed all of observers that there were white men in the firing party as well as black men and "also a Mexican."

After midnight, Wiegenstein conducted a second test. This time, unknown to the observers, he switched the firing party and used only black soldiers. The main idea, as he testified, was to note if the effect of darkness, without moonlight, would cause the flash to be more pronounced, and would enable the observers to distinguish the firing party complexion, which they had failed to do earlier on that same night while the moon was still shining. He repeated the same tests after the moon went down, on a starlit night with no clouds. The results were the same. The observers couldn't tell whether members of the firing squad were black, Mexican or white.

On March 11, Wiegenstein conducted still another test, under starlit conditions. He selected seven soldiers. This time he included a sergeant and himself among the group. Again, he didn't tell the observers the color or race of the firing party, nor did he tell them that he himself would be a member of the group. He dressed himself identically to the men. But Wiegenstein put a white collar around the sergeant's neck, gave him his (Wiegenstein's) blouse and cap, switched the sergeant to his position—and had the sergeant give the commands for firing.

From that point, the firing party repeated the same tests as those done in February and got the same results. But before the firing was terminated and when the shotgun was fired, which created more light than before, Wiegenstein heard an observer say, "There's Wiegenstein, but you wouldn't know him if he didn't have on a cap." However, the man wearing the cap was the black sergeant.

When the firing was finished, the sergeant marched the firing party out of the gully onto the road, where the observers posted themselves to determine if they could identify individuals by peering into their faces. They could not, as before.

But Wiegenstein added a new dimension to the test this time. Part of the experiment was conducted from a second-story window overlooking the street, and part was from the edge of a porch on the ground floor. He arranged for the observers to place themselves in the second story of a building and to look out a window into a side yard. Then he instructed one of the soldiers in the firing party to go into the side yard and act as if he were bent on making trouble. Then he was to run around to the front and join the firing party as they went into the street parallel to the front of the building and marched between the building and the street lamp. At about the same time, the observers came to a front window and looked into the street as the firing party went by. Wiegenstein had previously measured the distance from the upper story to the street. It was between 44 or 45 feet.

Turning around, the firing party marched back down the street between the same street lamp and the building. This time the observers sat on the front porch while the soldiers marched onto the sidewalk within 10 to 12 feet from the observers. Again the observers reported that they were unable to detect whether the firing party was black, White, or Mexican—or the color of their clothing.

I now had something to take back to Wade Williamson that would contradict the testimony of the "eyewitnesses" and Major Blocksom's theory of where the shots were fired from.

THIRTY ONE

THE EYEWITNESSES

What the Eyewitness Saw

SINCE ROOSEVELT CITED WHAT he termed "scores of eyewitnesses to the shooting," it was natural for me to re-examine the testimony of those witnesses. To get control of the testimony, I set up a credibility chart to help me move quickly through the numerous statements. I wanted to determine:

- if what the witnesses said made any sense,

- if they were under oath or not,

- if what they saw was actually possible under the circumstances of where they were,

- what they said they saw,

- the darkness of the night and so on.

I also wanted to know what evidence, if any, existed in the records to support, contradict, or refute their testimonies.

First of all, Roosevelt's count was incorrect. There weren't scores of eyewitnesses who were in any position to see what they claimed to have seen. By my count, there were only eight out of a total of 21 witnesses who, by their own statements, said they saw black soldiers. My examination of their statements revealed that they weren't statements of facts at all. They were opinions, inferences, and guesses. They were not creditable—not worthy of belief by anybody—and certainly not able to meet the standard of probable cause in a legal case. But I couldn't just take my opinion back to Wade Williamson. I had to find something substantial to contradict the eyewitness accounts.

That it was a dark night was indisputable. All prior investigators agreed. Even witnesses who said they saw the soldiers shooting up the town admitted that it was a dark night. It had been raining, and it was heavily overcast.

First, applying the Wiegenstein test standards to the powers of observation of the 14 eyewitnesses cited by President Roosevelt in his second message to the Senate discredited all of their accounts. Their statements to the various investigators could be dismissed out of hand as unbelievable.

But, because Roosevelt believed them and insisted "... that there is no possibility of their having been mistaken," I went back and re-read the key eyewitnesses' testimony given in a court of law—the court-martial of Major Penrose. Mr. George Rendall was a star witness cited by the President, so I started with his testimony.

While reading the transcript of his testimony, I imagined myself sitting in the court room, listening, making notes, as a member of the jury, as I had done many times during my career as a military officer. The décor in the reference room in the Archives—the elevated wooden reference desk, old mahogany straight-back chairs, old wooden study desks, dim lamps, heavy draperies, quiet decorum and the musty smell of the room—made a remarkable backdrop for my visualization of a courtroom.

Rendall, a witness for the prosecution, was first to take the stand. Having already given his testimony to the Citizens' Committee, Major Blocksom, and Mr. Purdy, the Assistant Attorney General, the prosecutor now considered Rendall one of his best witnesses. He was a mechanical engineer who lived with his wife on the second floor of the Western Union Telegraph building at the corner of Elizabeth and 15th Streets. The building was next door to Fort Brown and about 60 feet from the wall separating the town from the fort.

He testified that he was awakened by two pistol shots, grabbed his glasses from the nightstand, went to the window, and looked out. He swore he saw "colored soldiers" mount and jump over the wall into the street. He said he heard a voice saying, "Here we go." Furthermore, he claimed that he had heard that same voice before—it was the black soldier who came to his house seeking a room to rent for his wife and son who were to join him in a week or so in Brownsville.

Under cross-examination, the defense counsel for Major Penrose asked, "How old are you, Mr. Rendall?"

"I'm 72 years of age."

"How long have you been wearing glasses?"

"I've been wearing glasses since 1866."

"You have lost vision in one eye, I believe, have you not? When did you lose that, Mr. Rendall?"

"I lost that in 1866."

The defense counsel asked Rendall a series of questions about whom he had discussed the case with, how many times, and if he remembered anybody he had discussed it with. He said he had talked about it many times, over a hundred— but could not remember any specific person. Rendall said he gave testimony to all of the previous investigators.

Defense continued with the cross-examination.

"Could you see uniforms?

"No, sir. I could not."

"Will you tell the court how you knew those were soldiers."

"By their uniforms," Rendall said.

"And yet you say you couldn't see uniforms?"

"Those that I saw pass here." He pointed to the map. "I saw the uniforms and saw they were negro [Negro] soldiers."

"Did you see them jump over the wall at all?"

"I just saw the shapes and saw the men."

"Will you tell us how you knew those men were soldiers?"

"How do I know?" Rendall asked.

"That they were soldiers?"

"I can tell a soldier by the uniform," Rendall said.

"As a matter of fact, did you at any time during that night see any of those men that jumped over the wall close enough to see their uniforms or their guns?"

"No, sir, I didn't."

"Now, then, you got out of the bed and grabbed your glasses. Where did you go?"

"To the front window."

"And you saw some men. Which way did they go, and how many?"

"Up this way," Rendall said, pointing to the map, "Five or six."

"Did they have guns?"

"Yes, sir."

"Sure about that?" Defense asked.

Rendall hesitated, then said, "I wouldn't swear they had their guns."

"Do you know whether they were shooting a pistol or a gun?"

"No, sir. I wouldn't hesitate to say they were shooting pistols. I saw the flashes were near their faces, and the two I saw were colored men."

"How could you tell that?"

"Why, certainly because the flash of it showed their faces just the fraction of a second. It might have been white men blacked, I don't know about that, but they were not white men I saw shooting those shots."

"How far were those shots from you?"

"Sixty to seventy-five feet."

"Did you tell the Citizens Committee about that shot that went through your house?"

"I suppose so."

"Did you or did you not?"

"I don't know what I told them. I told them what I thought at the time. I don't suppose my three evidences put together would correspond at all, simply because I was mis-led in the first place of the cause of it—and the result was much different from what I anticipated and what I thought. I have been in a quandary about the whole thing. I know as far as I am concerned, all of the troops that have been there have offered nothing but friendship—and no one had any cause for anything else, particularly the soldiers."

"We want your best recollection, so this court can make up its own mind about the facts. We don't want a confused recollection," the defense counsel said.

"Well, the facts, as far as I am individually concerned, is hardly facts. What I saw and what I heard I know pretty well, but a man with all his faculties, a young man in the prime of his life, might form a little different opinion than an old man who is hard of hearing and whose eyesight is bad," Rendall said.

Seeing, but Not Seeing

As I read, or better put, listened to the testimony and the grilling of the old man, I couldn't help but have compassion for him. He said he had been misled in the first place about the whole thing, but by whom, and for what reason? The cross-examination continued.

The defense counsel read back the testimony of Rendall where he stated he recognized the voice of the man who gave the command, "Here we go," when the soldiers jumped over the wall. "Did you hear that evidence just read?"

"Yes, sir."

"Do you want this court to understand that you heard that same identical voice giving commands that night that you heard two or three days before?"

"No, sir. I don't know there is a man in that garrison that ever went over the wall, as far as I am positively sure. What I saw at that distance is very indistinct."

"You don't mean to swear before this court that the same man who gave a command that night 60 or 70 feet away from you had been talking to you about a room the day before?"

"No, sir. I don't swear he was or he wasn't. It was my impression he was."

"Stand up and look at the gentlemen in the back of the house—there are four men back there. How many men do you see back there by the stove?"

"I see one man—two men."

"Is that all you can see back there?"

At this point the judge advocate [prosecutor] objected to one of the four men standing by the stove in the back of the court room. To that, the defense counsel said, "This is not a trick. I simply want to test this man's sight to see if he can see. I want to know, and I want the court to know."

The objection was sustained, and the man was asked to leave because he was a defense witness. That left three men standing in the back.

"Will you tell the court how many people you see back there by the stove?"

"I see five," Rendall said.

The defense counsel asked Rendall if he could see color, to which he said he could. Now he was tested on the color of the clothes the three men in the back near the stove were wearing—but he wasn't able to discern much about the color of their clothing or shoes.

Defense then asked Rendall if the man on the left was a white man or a black man.

"I judge he is a white man. He may have colored blood in him. I don't know."

"What color is the man on the extreme right—your right?"

"He is a fair looking white man."

"You are sure about that."

"No, I'm not sure of that."

"How many men are there? Look carefully and tell us. Look carefully."

"I can see five. There may be one hiding behind the stove."

Finally, Defense asked Rendall what was the condition of the weather that night.

"The condition was rather dark, starlight night," Rendall said.

Mrs. Rendall, George Rendall's wife, followed him to the stand. I noted from her testimony that she looked out the same window at the same time her husband did. She was some 10 or 12 years younger than George and both of her eyes were good, yet she swore she couldn't tell the color or complexion of any of the men—in contrast to George, who claimed he could see color. However, he couldn't pick out colors in the courtroom even at shorter distances.

I dismissed the testimony of Teofilo Martinez, the caretaker in the Yturria house because, upon hearing the first shots, he quickly flattened himself on his "belly" on the floor and by his own words, stayed there all night. It was impossible for him to see anything.

Katie Leahy, the prized witness of the investigators, was the next witness to take the stand. No one could have been more anxious to see how Katie Leahy's testimony would stand up in a court of law than I was.

Her testimony first came to my attention in Blocksom's report. Then an article in the *Washington Post* (June 7, 1907) drew my scrutiny to her again when I was at the Library of Congress. The Post reported that Katie Leahy testified before the Senate Committee on Military Affairs. She recognized one of the soldiers as a "Yellow Nigger with spots," and she wished she had fought it out with them. That statement sounded preposterous. It sent me looking for her testimony before the Senate Committee on Military Affairs, then to the Purdy report and before this court.

I found her testimony consistent throughout. She was positive about what she saw and specific. She noted everything. She was in her nightgown when she heard the first shot, fired precisely at 11:55 P.M. because she looked at her clock. She counted the flashes of the guns and could see the color of the raiders' clothes and the color of their faces by light from the flashes of the guns they were shooting. They wore khaki uniforms and some wore blue shirts. Their faces were black. They were Negroes. She could see the blue steel of the rifles by the flash of the guns.

How could the prior investigators believe she could recognize a freckle-faced person, the blue steel of the rifles and all the rest that she claimed she saw from a distance of 50 feet to 280 feet, on a dark night? Especially, how she could see soldiers walking around and shooting from the lower porch of B Company, where the view was totally obstructed by an orange tree? President Roosevelt believed her testimony and relied on it. So did the prior investigators except for Senator Foraker. He certainly didn't believe her, especially when she told him: "I saw through the leaves." On a dark night?

Once she was in a court of law, however, she was subject to cross examination. As I read the defense counsel's examination, I wished I could have been there to hear it. I didn't believe Katie Leahy's story. Neither did the court or the defense counsel. Defense characterized Katie Leahy as an "overcharged bottle of seltzer." All you had to do was to push the right lever and she did the rest. Her testimony gushed forth like seltzer—and that testimony discredited her before the court.

Only Herbert Elkins' testimony was more absurd than that given by Katie Leahy. Elkins was Leahy's hotel clerk and lived on the second floor of her hotel. Under direct examination, he testified that he was in his room about five minutes to 12 when he heard some shooting—about 15 shots just inside the wall or outside the wall. He went to the window and saw "two nigger soldiers" coming up the alley. He assumed they were the leaders. About 75 to 100 feet behind them, he saw eight to 15 other raiders.

When asked who these men were, he said they were nigger soldiers. How did he recognize them as such? He answered, "By the way they were dressed." He "knew they were niggers by looking at them. They had on khaki pants, leggings, belts, and some had on those light summer shirts. And some had on coats and some of them had on caps, and some hats." But Elkins said that he didn't notice what the two men in the lead—the first two he saw about 75 to 100 feet ahead of the other raiders—were wearing.

Elkins claimed he saw the raiders turn up the alley. As they turned, they fired three or four shots into the front of Cowen's house and went on uptown. He saw the type of clothes they were wearing and the color, but didn't know whether they wore hats. He was sure they wore belts because he saw the khaki belts.1

After that group of raiders ran uptown, somewhere toward the saloons, he supposed, Elkins went on to testify that he saw soldiers shooting from C Company's barracks, some 80 feet away. He saw this firing as well from his bedroom window on the second floor. At about the same time he stepped into Judge Parks' room next door, and from Judge Parks' window he saw shots fired from the upper balcony of B Company.

Making sure Elkins had plenty of opportunity to think about what he was saying, Defense repeated its question four or five times. Elkins said definitely, that from his window he saw firing from C Company's barracks.

The defense counsel was just waiting to see if he would say that, and that's what he said. Now that was another impossibility. Elkins' view, or anybody's view, of C Company's barracks from the window of his bedroom on the second floor would be obstructed by the houses along the west side of the alley between 14th and 15th Streets, as the Leckie tests demonstrated.

---

1   Remember that Lieutenant Leckie testified that there were absolutely no bullet holes in the front of Cowen's house and the other investigators didn't find any either.

Having caught Elkins in a trap, the defense counsel moved closer to Elkins' face and pressed him. "Did you testify to Major Blocksom that you couldn't see the post from your window?"

"That I could not see the ground?" Elkins asked.

"You answer the question! Could you see the post from your window?" Caught in the trap that the defense counsel had set for him, Elkins conceded. "No, sir."

"Could you see any portion of it?"

"I could see roofs, and a little of the barracks."

Elkins surely had become rattled, for he gave even more preposterous answers to questions. He recognized the knob on the gun and the Springfield 03 rifle by the light that flashed from the guns as they were being fired. He recognized color by the flash of the gun and saw a soldier get bogged down in a mud hole.

Only part of Joe Dominguez's testimony for the prosecution required my special attention. The rest could be ignored. Dominguez stated on his own that he got confused. After testifying that he saw black soldiers shooting into Cowen's house, he admitted that another policeman had told him that. He knew nothing of his own knowledge. He said he was mistaken and, "I would like to state to this court that I get so confused I don't know whether I am stating right or not."

So, was he stating right when he earlier testified that he heard shots fired toward the fort? He said it twice. In this instance, I don't think he was confused at all. Mayor Combe admitted that the citizens fired toward the fort, while the black soldiers swore they heard bullets whizzing by over their heads.

I finished reading the testimony of all the eyewitnesses before the court. Not one claimed to have seen the raiders closer than 25 feet, except Herbert Elkins, Katie Leahy, and the policeman Dominguez. But their credibility was undermined by their own words. I found that what they claimed they saw under the conditions of darkness and distance was nothing more than a string of impossibilities and contradictions.

Most troublesome to me, however, was the testimony of Paulino S. Preciado. He was the last person to see the bartender alive. He swore to Assistant Attorney General Purdy that he saw the murder of the bartender in the courtyard of the Ruby Saloon. He said he saw the murderers under the light of the lamps and recognized them as Negro soldiers.

Again, I returned to Preciado's original sworn statement, given to the Grand Jury on September 10, 1906. Nowhere in his statement did he say anything about black soldiers doing the shooting. To the contrary, he said, "I couldn't see anybody in the alley, as it was dark out there and I was in the light. I heard no word spoken."

Maybe he did see the murderers. Maybe the bartender saw the murderers and recognized them, but not as black soldiers. Maybe he saw local hired thugs. Perhaps that's why the bartender was murdered, and why Preciado told the Grand Jury he didn't see anything—he was afraid.

Next I examined all of the original depositions and affidavits of the black soldiers and their white officers. The soldiers' testimony was consistent, credible, and compelling with respect to their innocence.

I revisited the testimony of Tamayo, the post scavenger, who was in the best position to see the soldiers jumping over the wall—if, in fact, they did. He swore on several occasions that the attack began on the town side of the garrison wall.

Another witness story supports the soldier's position. Wilbur Voshelle, a white man and the corral boss at the fort, swore he didn't see a single soldier on the streets. He saw only two policeman and four armed citizens talking about soldiers.

THIRTY TWO

THE PROOF

An Abstract Notion

KNOCKING DOWN THE EYEWITNESS' testimony was necessary, certainly. It was unreliable and flimsy, but I realized that it didn't prove the soldiers were not guilty. In fact, it didn't prove anything except that eye-witnesses did not actually see what they reported they saw. Some of them were deliberately lying. Others repeated the lies they had heard so often that they began to believe them.

The presumption of innocence was going to be my fall back strategy, if I couldn't find the proof. But I wanted more than the legal presumption, because deep down I feared that people didn't really believe in it, or at least some of them didn't. For those people, the concept of presumed innocence was an abstract notion. For example, in trials of alleged crimes, if the prosecutor didn't prove his case and the criminal went free, I have heard people say, "Well, he did it. They just couldn't prove it. He had a smart lawyer." I didn't want this to be the case.

So as I started looking for hard evidence that the soldiers didn't do it, I was ever mindful of Wade Williamson's admonition that I must find facts to refute all of Roosevelt's allegations.

To find reliable facts, I followed the written trail of Leckie and dug deeper into his testimony. There Leckie told an intriguing story that provided evidence that I could take

back to Williamson. While in Brownsville, Leckie found
more disturbing evidence that had annoyed Roosevelt. Leckie testified before the Senate that while he was in Brownsville
having a drink at Crixell's saloon, one of the Crixell brothers, Teofilo, invited him to go outside of the saloon. Once
outside, Teofilo showed Leckie how close he came to getting
killed. Teofilo pointed to a bullet hole in an upright post
supporting the awning near the door of the saloon. "That's
one of the shots fired that night."

Leckie shook his head, "You're mistaken about that."
Leckie rubbed his finger over the bullet hole. "That's about
a .44 or .45."

"No," Crixell said.

A crowd of loafers, half-drunks, and drunks came out of
the barn and gathered around the two men—the bet was on.
Leckie bet a round of drinks that the hole had not been made
by a steel-jacketed Springfield 03-rifle bullet. Leckie bored
the bullet out with a brace and bit.

Leckie was correct. It was not a Springfield 03-rifle bullet which the black troops used. Instead it was an all-lead
bullet. The bullet was later tested by Dr. Hildebrand and
"found to be a bullet of a different composition [lead, tin,
and antimony] from any of the bullets used by the black soldiers, a bullet such as the soldiers could not have fired from
their rifles."

Again I searched for hard evidence in the record of the
Court-martial of Major Penrose. There I found yet another
impossibility. The record showed that seven empty cartridges
and six clips Captain Macklin found in the early morning
after the shooting spree at the mouth of Cowen Alley were
found in a little circle whose diameter was not more than 10
inches. Macklin swore to this. However, if those bullets had

been fired on the night of the raid, the mechanical action of the Springfield rifle ejector would have scattered the empty shells randomly over a 10-foot area. I knew this from my military experience with the Springfield 03 rifle, which I had fired many times.

The defense counsel pointed out this discrepancy to the court, "Those shell casings had been put there for a purpose."

After reading that, it became apparent to me that there had indeed been a conspiracy at Brownsville, but not the one of silence so often mentioned. It was a conspiracy by other parties yet undiscovered. Who put those empty shell casings there and for what purpose? Why would the black soldiers place those shell casings in that little circle? What soldier would be so dumb as to leave that kind of incriminating evidence behind in the path of his shooting spree? I was unable to offer an explanation for such irrational behavior on the part of the soldiers, if, indeed, they did the shooting.

At Last, a Literal Smoking Gun Is Found

In his summation argument in the court-martial of Penrose, the defense counsel alluded to a certain microscopic test carried out by experts on the empty shell casings found on the streets of Brownsville. But he had been unable to get the results from the Senate. That excited me. Maybe that was the critical piece of evidence I needed.

Digging farther into the little green boxes in the National Archives, I pulled out several documents that were rolled in a neat little bundle and tied with a red cord that looked like it hadn't been untied in years. To my surprise, among those papers were the ballistic tests report (Microscopic Investigation Report) of the ordnance experts at the Springfield, MA, Armory.

Those experts had subjected the 33 exploded shells picked up in the streets of Brownsville to microscopic examinations. When analyzed together with other evidence, I was able to state conclusively that the 33 shells had not been fired in Brownsville at all. They had been fired on the rifle range at Fort Niobrara, Nebraska.

So, how did those shells get to Brownsville? For the answer, I went back to the Senate hearing report which I had quickly skimmed over earlier in my research. Now I studied and focused on the testimony of several black soldiers, white officers, and Major Penrose, in particular.

In March 1907, after Major Penrose was acquitted of the charge of "neglect of duty to the prejudice of good order and military discipline" for his men's alleged culpability in the Brownsville raid, he was called before the Senate Committee to testify about his troops' own participation. Penrose had now changed his position. He no longer believed his men were guilty.

Penrose's testimony was telling—he supported the ballistic tests report. "Those shells were brought down from Fort Niobrara to Brownsville," declared Penrose. "They were in open [boxes] on the back porch of B Company. They were open there several days, I don't remember how long. I think they were taken out there and put there."

Now, the details of the ballistic test were fascinating. I understood the Microscopic Investigation Report because of my experience at the Ballistic Research Laboratories. I hoped that I would be able to explain it to Williamson without undue complexity and tedium.

To perform the test, all 167 of the rifles assigned to the black soldiers at Fort Brown were shipped to the Springfield Armory. Each rifle was fired twice and those exploded shell casings were put under microscopic examinations. Those shell casings were then compared to the 33 Brownsville shell casings which were also put under microscopic examination.

The results were stunning—there were four guns which provided an identical match between the microscopic indentations found on the heads of all 33 exploded Brownsville shell casings and the microscopic indentations found on the heads of the shell casings belonging to Company B. The experts said it was beyond a reasonable doubt.

How did the experts identify these four guns out of the 167 they tested? That was easy. Three of the four guns from which the bullets must have been fired were identified by their serial numbers, and the Brownsville troops assigned to those rifles could be identified. So it seemed that the soldiers failed the tests. But wait! Lieutenant Lawarson testified that those men were present and accounted for and their rifles were locked in the racks and clean. Had the guns been fired at some other time and place? Had the spent shells been planted?

The fourth gun provided the inconvertible, absolute, and conclusive proof. That rifle, the fourth gun with serial number 45683 was originally assigned to Sergeant William Blaney at Fort Niobrara. On that fateful night, August 13, 1906, Blaney was not in Brownsville, but on a four-month furlough. Before he left his post in Nebraska for vacation, he turned in his rifle to Quartermaster-Sergeant Walker Mc-Curdy, who placed Blaney's name on a small piece of paper, placed that paper in the bore of the gun and locked it in the arms chest. In other words, that rifle had been placed in the arms chest at Fort Niobrara, then it had been transported to Fort Brown.

On the same night of the midnight attack on Browns-ville, Lieutenant Lawarson, the white company commander, had verified the count of all the rifles. Lawarson and Mc-Curdy, carrying an oil lantern, went to the locked storeroom, unlocked it, unscrewed the top of the arms chest and found Blaney's rifle. It was still locked in the arms chest—with the piece of paper still in the bore of the gun—with baggage, ex-tra bunk beds, and odds and ends stacked on top of it. Both Lawarson and McCurdy swore to this at the Senate Hearings.

Thus, it was impossible for that fourth gun to have been fired in Brownsville. An actual smoking gun had been found. And as the saying goes, "eliminate the impossibilities, and what remains must be the truth." The experts had conclu-sively demonstrated that Blaney's rifle had to have been fired on the rifle range at Fort Niobrara, Nebraska (or any place other than Brownsville), and the empty shells casings found on the streets of Brownsville were planted.

Two other test findings—double indentations and dou-ble insertions—corroborated the impossibility that those empty shell casings picked up in Brownsville were fired from the four guns on the night of the attack.

Double indentations meant that the experts found two dents on the head of some of the empty shell casings, which indicated that the firing pen had struck the head of the bul-let twice before it finally fired. Each time the rifle failed to fire, the ejector would have thrown the bullet 10 feet away on the ground, requiring the shooter to retrieve it and insert it again. It was highly improbable that a raider would be so foolish as to take the time to scramble around in the dark searching for an ejected cartridge, and highly unlikely he would ever find it in the dark. But it could happen on the rifle range in daylight during target practice. (I have seen it happen many times.) Several of the soldiers and officers testified that it happened on the rifle range at Fort Niobrara.

The same thing would be true for double insertions. If a soldier tried to insert a cartridge into a rifle two or more times, he would have to pull the bolt backward and the ejector would throw the cartridge out of the chamber three to 10 feet away. The testers found nine empty shell casings which had been put in the gun two or more times before the rifle finally fired. Again, what kind of night raider would chase a cartridge under such circumstances? The officers and men swore that the need for double insertions had happened several times at Fort Niobrara during target practice.

Finally! After running into many dead ends, I had found in the National Archives the pieces of technical evidence that I believed would prove conclusively that the soldiers were not involved in the shooting, and in fact, were innocent.

THIRTY THREE

PARDON

Or Exoneration

"You got it half-right."

IT WAS LATE, ALMOST nine 'o clock at night, near closing time at the National Archives. There were only two or three of us left, and the attendants were turning off the lights at the research desks. After stuffing my briefcase with copies of my research, I left the Archives by the back door on the Pennsylvania Avenue side.

The next morning I met with Wade Williamson. I was decidedly upbeat. Putting aside all sense of protocol, I spread my documents out on the Colonel's desk, not waiting for him to go to his conference table. When I started to explain the key elements in the documents that I had underlined, Williamson said, "Wait, Baker, I can read."

Williamson went through the documents, nodded his head from time to time, jotted down notes on a yellow pad as he turned page after page, and asked me pointed questions. Then after about three hours, several cups of coffee and as many trips to the bathroom, he put the papers down.

I was anxious.

He pushed his chair back from his desk, folded his arms, and said, "Boy, I think you got something here."

Then he looked embarrassed and quickly added, "Baker, you know I didn't mean anything by calling you 'boy,' it was just a figure of speech."

Even though I had been dealing with Wade Williamson only for a short time, one thing I knew for sure. He wasn't a racist and he wasn't calling me "Boy" in a pejorative sense. "Now don't you be over-sensitive," I said, "because I see your neck is getting red."

He laughed. Then he commended me for finding what he called all "this stuff" in the Archives, but added a 'but.' "How're you going to explain it to the Army staff in a one-page summary sheet?"

"I'll brief them first."

"You'll never get enough time. Look, we've been here almost three hours. Half of it I understand, half of it I don't. This stuff's technical."

"I know I can explain it," I said.

"Yes, but that's not good enough. You got it half-right. Facts alone never win anything, Baker. You've got to have a compelling legal argument! What you got here doesn't do anything to satisfy the legal argument raised by President Roosevelt that, as commander-in-chief, he had the legal power backed by precedents to discharge those soldiers 'without honor' by executive summary action."

What is he doing, moving the goal posts, changing the rules in the middle of the game? I needed more? I remembered him telling me to get the facts. Well, I had better get moving.

Beat down almost below the bricks, my head down, once again I trudged off to the National Archives to search for evidence to discredit the legal precedents—the central core in Roosevelt's argument. After crossing the street on the

Pennsylvania Avenue side, I noticed for the first time the inscription near the back-door entrance. I was inspired by what I read, "What's past is prologue."

What I found was also quite revealing. A letter from the White House dated December 7, 1906, stated that the President wished Taft to "give him some instances, of which he knows there must be many," where commanders have discharged men without honor and without court-martial. Taft replied on December 10, 1906, that no precedents in the Regular Army had been found prior to the discharge of the black soldiers of the 25th Infantry. However, Taft sent him some cases that were clearly not analogous to the Brownsville case. In fact, they weren't precedents at all.

I went back to Williamson's office and showed him what I had found. He agreed. JAG's opposition collapsed.

The Legal Argument

After all the research, consultation with JAG and other staff directorates, hits, and misses, it was now time to sit down and write the legal argument. Hiding out in one of the conference rooms with all of my files and reference books stacked on the tables, desks, and on the floor, I wrote the first draft. When I finished, I had written 40 pages.

I showed it to Wade Williamson and he promptly rejected it. "This will never fly. You need help. Cut this thing back. The lawyers in the Secretary of Defense's Office will never let this out."

I distilled the information into a two-page summary sheet and a five-page legal argument with 10 appendices.

There were five key elements:

First, the soldiers satisfied the criteria for Honorable Discharges. I proved this declaration by referencing their records that stated their service was honest and faithful.

Second, the action taken by President Roosevelt constituted an injustice as it was based upon the concept of mass punishment rather than individual guilt.

Third, the action taken constituted an injustice, enacting an extreme form of disgrace and punishment. It took away valuable property rights, retirement income, and other benefits.

Fourth, the action taken constituted an injustice as it was partly predicated upon racial discrimination.

Fifth, the action taken was erroneous as a matter of law. There were no precedents for the action in the Regular Army.

I wrapped the whole argument into a case of manifest error. It was bad on its face, a gross injustice had been done. Overlaying the whole argument was the presumption of innocence.

On August 7, 1972, based upon the case I developed, the Secretary of the Army decided to exonerate the soldiers. I was ecstatic. Then I learned that there was a hitch. The exoneration was put on hold. Some of the top lawyers in the Defense Department advocated a pardon by President Nixon as more appropriate than exoneration. I objected to the idea of a pardon, because that would indicate that the soldiers were guilty after all.

Back at Williamson's office, he cautioned me. "Baker, you got to be careful. There's a document floating around among the top people that purports to be a confession by one of the black soldiers."

I burst out laughing.

Williamson got up and closed his office door. "Baker, what in the hell's wrong with you?"

Wanting to answer him, I tried, but I couldn't. Putting my hand over my mouth, I tried to stop laughing. I felt tears streaming down my cheeks. It felt good, and a relief. Words wouldn't come. I kept laughing.

"What's so damn funny? Are you cracking up?"

Finally, I managed to get control of myself and got a few words out. "I can assure that I'm not."

This time I didn't have to go back to the Archives. I knew that the so-called Boyd Conyers confession was a fraud, and explained it to Wade Williamson.

"Do you have something to prove this?" Williamson asked.

"Yes, sir, in my files."

"Get it and give to me."

I retrieved Sheriff Arnold's sworn statement from my files. Sheriff Arnold swore that the so-called Conyer's confession was false. Williamson read it and said, "This is good enough. Leave it to me."

But I promised myself that I was going to track down the source of that document containing that old false confession. I would find its sleeping place, drive a stake through its heart, and "kill it thoroughly dead." I found it in an information folder that had been prepared by the public relations staff for the top-level people.

The Defense Department lawyers dropped the pardon idea.

On Monday morning, September 21, 1972, Mr. Belnap, legal advisor to the adjutant general, brought the draft order to my office and asked me to review it for the last time. I had reviewed a draft list before, but I still went over it again, making sure, name by name, that no soldier was left off the order.

Finally, Exoneration

The order amended War Department Special Order 266 of 1906, re-characterized the discharges of the Brownsville black soldiers, and changed their status from discharged without honor to honorably discharged, thereby exonerating all of them. Then I noticed an old clause that I had objected to before. It had been reinserted in the final draft. That clause stated, "No back pay, allowances, benefits or privileges shall accrue by reason of the issuance of this order to any heirs or descendants."

I was irritated, and greatly disappointed that that old clause had crept back into the order. I had fought it twice, won and lost, and now lost again.

With a distressed expression on his face, Belnap said, "Colonel Baker, please take what you've got. Don't overreach. The Adjutant General will never change that clause."

So I took what I had. The amended order was completed on Tuesday, September 22, 1972, and delivered to me by Belnap. It was packaged with the legal case upon which the Secretary of the Army acted to reverse President Roosevelt. I rushed into General Brook's office and gave it to him. After Brooks reviewed it, he gave it back to me, and told me to lock it in our safe until the Chief of Public Information could put out a news release. After it appeared in the newspapers, I was to take the order to the National Archives.

About mid-afternoon, General Brooks' secretary stuck her head in my office door and told me that General Brooks wanted to see me right away in the secure conference room.

I got up, and walked to the room wondering, "What's this all about?"

After I entered the conference room, General Brooks made sure the door was locked. Then he introduced me to Mr. Don Miller, the Deputy Secretary of Defense for Equal Opportunity. Brooks came straight to the point. "Bill, Don plans to announce the decision that the Army has exonerated the Brownsville soldiers at the reunion of his old regiment. What do you think about it?"

General Brooks was putting me on the spot, and I knew it. Perhaps he thought I would speak truth to power.

I hesitated. Both men looked at me intently while I struggled for a politically correct answer. When I waited too long to say anything, Miller spoke up. "I'd announce it at the 369th Infantry Regiment celebration in New York City."

"When?" I asked.

"That would be ..." Miller pulled out his calendar and glanced through it. "Sunday, October 8."

Miller's proposal would delay the exoneration, because the order had to be posted to the records in the National Archives to legally correct the records. He gave me the perfect opening to oppose it. "That'll take too long, don't you think? It might leak out."

"No, it won't. Lock it in a safe!" Miller said.

"It's already locked up," Brooks said.

I pointed out that we would be taking a big risk. JAG and several staff officers knew about it. Suppose somebody leaked it to, say, John Connolly, the former Democratic governor of Texas, now turned Republican or any other politician. He could go to President Nixon and kill it on the spot.

DEPARTMENT OF THE ARMY
OFFICE OF THE ADJUTANT GENERAL
WASHINGTON, D. C. 20315

LCC/hcw

DAAG-ASO-O (7 Aug 72)   22 September 1972

SUBJECT: AMENDMENT OF ORDERS

Action: Amendment

So much of: Paragraph 1, Special Orders 266, War Department,
9 November 1906

As reads: "discharged without honor from the Army by their
respective commanding officers and forever debarred from
reenlisting in the Army or Navy of the United States, as well
as from employment in any civil capacity under the Government."

How changed: Is amended to read: "honorably discharged from
the Army by their respective commanding officers."

Is amended to add: No back pay, allowances,
benefits or privileges shall accrue by reason of the issuance
of this order to any heirs or descendants.

Is amended to delete: The discharge certificate
in each case will show that the discharge without honor is in
consequence of paragraph 1, Special Orders, No. 266, War Department, November 9, 1906.

Pertaining to member(s) of: Company B, 25th Infantry
First Sergeant Mingo Sanders
Quartermaster Sergeant Walker McCurdy
Sergeant James R. Reid
Sergeant George Jackson
Sergeant Luther T. Thornton
Corporal Jones A. Coltrane
Corporal Edward L. Daniels
Corporal Ray Burdett
Corporal Wade H. Watlington
Corporal Anthony Franklin
Cook Leroy Horn
Cook Solomon Johnson
Musician Henry Odom
Private James Allen
Private John B. Anderson
Private William Anderson
Private Battier Bailey
Private James Bailey

Figure 21. Department of the Army Amendment of Orders, dated
September 22, 1972. Names of the soldiers whose discharges were
amended from "without honor" to "honorable" distributed to all identified locations.
Pages 344 through 346.

DAAG-ASO-O (7 Aug 72)   22 September 1972
SUBJECT: Amendment of Orders

Private Elmer Brown
Private John Brown
Private William Brown
Private William J. Carlton
Private Harry Carmichael
Private George Conn
Private John Cook
Private Charles E. Cooper
Private Boyd Conyers
Private Lawrence Daniel
Private Carolina DeSaussure
Private Ernest English
Private Shepherd Glenn
Private Isaac Goolsby
Private William Harden
Private Charley Hairston
Private John Holomon
Private James Johnson
Private Frank Jones
Private Henry Jones
Private William J. Kernan
Private George Lawson
Private Willie Lemons
Private Samuel McGhee
Private George W. Mitchell
Private Isaiah Raynor
Private Stansberry Roberts
Private William Smith
Private Thomas Taylor
Private William Thomas
Private Alexander Walker
Private Edward Warfield
Private Julius Wilkins
Private Alfred N. Williams
Private Brister Williams
Private Joseph L. Wilson

                    Company C, 25th Infantry
Quartermaster Sergeant George W. McMurray
Sergeant Samuel W. Harley
Sergeant Newton Carlisle
Sergeant Darby W. O. Brawner
Sergeant George Thomas
Corporal Charles H. Madison
Corporal Solomon P. O'Neil
Corporal Preston Washington

                    2

DAAG-ASO-O (7 Aug 72)   22 September 1972
SUBJECT: Amendment of Orders

Corporal Willie H. Miller
Corporal John H. Hill
Cook George Grier
Cook Lewis J. Baker
Musician James E. Armstrong
Musician Walter Banks
Artificer Charles H. Rudy
Private Clifford I. Adair
Private Henry W. Arvin
Private Charles W. Askew
Private Frank Bounsler
Private Robert L. Collier
Private Erasmus T. Dabbs
Private Mark Garmon
Private George W. Gray
Private Joseph H. Gray
Private James T. Harden
Private George W. Harris
Private John T. Hawkins
Private Alphonso Holland
Private Thomas Jefferson
Private Edward Johnson
Private George Johnson
Private John Kirkpatrick
Private Edward Lee
Private Frank J. Lipscomb
Private West Logan
Private William Mapp
Private William McGuire, Jr
Private Thomas L. Mosley
Private Andrew Mitchell
Private James W. Newton
Private George W. Perkins
Private James Perry
Private Oscar W. Reid
Private Joseph Rogers
Private James Sinkler
Private Calvin Smith
Private George Smith
Private John Smith
Private John Streater
Private Robert Turner
Private Leartis Webb
Private Lewis Williams
Private James Woodson

                    3

DAAG-ASO-O (7 Aug 72)
SUBJECT: Amendment of Orders   22 September 1972

Company D, 25th Infantry
First Sergeant Israel Harris
Quartermaster Sergeant Thomas J. Green
Sergeant Jerry E. Reeves
Sergeant Jacob Frazier
Corporal Temple Thornton
Corporal David Powell
Corporal Winter Washington
Corporal Albert Roland
Corporal James H. Ballard
Musician Hoytt Robinson
Musician Joseph Jones
Cook Charles Dade
Cook Robert Williams
Artificer George W. Newton
Private Samuel Wheeler
Private Charles Hawkins
Private Henry Barclay
Private Sam M. Battle
Private Henry T. W. Brown
Private John Butler
Private Richard Crooks
Private Strowder Darnell
Private Elias Gant
Private James C. Gill
Private John Green
Private Alonzo Haley
Private George W. Hall
Private Barney Harris
Private Joseph H. Howard
Private John A. Jackson
Private Benjamin F. Johnson
Private Walter Johnson
Private Charles Jones
Private John R. Jones
Private William E. Jones
Private William R. Jones
Private Edward Jordan
Private Wesley Mapp
Private William A. Matthews
Private James Newton
Private Elmer Peters
Private Len Reeves
Private Edward Robinson
Private Henry Robinson

DAAG-ASO-O (7 Aug 72)
SUBJECT: Amendment of Orders   22 September 1972

Private Robert L. Rogan
Private Samuel E. Scott
Private Joseph Shanks
Private John Slow
Private Zachariah Sparks
Private William Van Hook
Private Edward Wickersham
Private Dorsie Willis

Company A, 25th Infantry
Private James A. Simmons
Private August Williams

Company G, 25th Infantry
Private James Duncan

Unassigned, 25th Infantry
Private Perry Cisco

Troop C, 9th Cavalry
Private Alexander Ash
Private Taylor Stroudemire
Private Robert James

Troop H, 10th Cavalry
Private John W. Lewis

BY ORDER OF THE SECRETARY OF THE ARMY:

Major General, USA
The Adjutant General

DISTR:
25 - Old Military History Branch, Military Archives Division,
     Office of the National Archives NARS, GSA, 7th and Pa. Ave,
     NW, Washington, DC 20408 (thru DAPE-MPE)
5 - DAPE-MPE
1 - DAIO
1 - DAAG-PSS
1 - DAAG-ZC Rm BF712 A Pentagon

5

383

Miller discounted my concerns as unlikely and said he thought it should be announced to a black audience. His old regiment would make the perfect venue.

When I heard him say that, he convinced me that I was wasting my time. Believing he had already made up his mind, and nothing I could say would matter, I politely excused myself and left.

Togo West was a brilliant, young black officer working as the Civil Rights Staff Attorney for the Secretary of the Army. After I left the secure conference room, I went over to his office and told him about Don Miller's plan for public announcement of the exoneration.

"Why, he's trying to upstage the Secretary of the Army. I won't let him do that," West said. He put on his suit jacket and went directly over to the Secretary of the Army's office.

Not hearing anything for a day, I feared something had gone wrong. What if the exoneration had hit a political snag? Suppose there was a last ditch effort to stop it? After all, the November election was coming up. What could I do?

I devised a simple strategy, but a risky one. I would take the order to the National Archives early in the morning on Friday, September 22, 1972, and deposit it there. That would, in effect, complete the exoneration. I wouldn't wait on any press release from the Pentagon or Don Miller. Publicity was not my business anyway.

Then I was summoned to the office of the Assistant Secretary of Defense for public affairs, and was told that Melvin Laird, Secretary of Defense, might make the public announcement on Sunday, September 24, 1972, on the nation-wide television news program, Meet the Press. The public relations experts had prepared notes for him, and they wanted me to check the accuracy of those notes.

A Beautiful Day in My Heart

That Thursday night, the eve of the day I was to deliver the order to the Archives, was a bad night. I didn't sleep well. I had dreams one gets on the night before exams in a difficult course, say, nuclear physics. Dreams of bizarre impossibilities occurred all during the night. I woke up in a cold sweat each time.

One dream was unusually strange and frightening. With the documents secured in my briefcase, I dreamed I went to the Archives. The inscription at the back entrance had changed from Shakespeare's "What's past is prologue," to Dante's inscription over the gates of hell, "Abandon hope who enter here."

A man met me at the door, and said, "Welcome, Colonel Roosevelt, we've been expecting you for a long time. I see you have something for us."

"You're mistaken. My name is Baker," I said.

Turning his head slightly to the side while smiling the man said, "No, it's not. Come in, Colonel Roosevelt."

When I stepped through the door, to my amazement the Archives had turned into a beautiful green forest.

I tried to ask a question, but the man cut me off. "Give me the papers!"

When I tried to unlock my briefcase, my key wouldn't fit. The man handed me a key and said, "Try this one. It fits."

I took the papers from my briefcase and handed them to him. He read the papers, and handed them back to me. "We can't accept them."

"Why?"

"They are ashes of the past."

Frightened, I turned to leave.

"Wait, Colonel Roosevelt, you can't get out that way. You must go this way." He pointed toward the green forest.

When I started to walk toward into forest, it turned to ashes before my eyes.

"Where's the door?" I asked.

"Colonel Roosevelt, you must walk on the ashes of the forest."

The next morning I got out of bed feeling pretty groggy, as if I had spent the entire night drinking. I made my way to the bathroom. After taking a cold shower, I put on my finest military uniform, my dress blues. I didn't own a set of whites, but if I had, I would have worn them. It was a day of celebration.

Friday morning, September 22, 1972, was a day when autumn had barely arrived. No leaves had started to turn color. Summer was still hanging on. It was gray, heavily overcast, warm and humid—but it was a beautiful day in my heart. I walked out of the front door of the Pentagon. There was no Army sedan waiting for me, only my old, black, un-air-conditioned Pontiac. I got into it and drove across the 14th Street Bridge, turned right onto Constitution Avenue and on to the front entrance of the National Archives. I went through the front entrance—not the back door this time—and delivered the order.

The World Is Told the Truth

My family, a group of friends, and I sat in front of the television on Sunday, September 24, 1972 waiting for Mr. Laird to announce the good news about Brownsville. Members of the press grilled him seemingly about everything, the war in Viet Nam, the volunteer army and so on. He never said anything about Brownsville, even though there were opportunities to squeeze it in.

Would the public release be made on Monday? Surely it would be. Monday went by—nothing on the evening news. Tuesday came and went—nothing in the newspapers, TV, or radio. By Wednesday, when there still was no announcement, I began to think that maybe Melvin Laird killed the public release for political reasons and might soon ask if the order had been delivered to the Archives. Finding out that it had been, he would no doubt conclude he had been handed *fait accompli,* which is abhorrent to the military chain-of-command. Might he still try to stop the whole thing? I began to worry. Now I'm in trouble. The order is in the Archives. Suppose some researcher stumbled upon it in the records and notified the press?

I was about to go out of my mind. Then it occurred to me, call the Archives. What a relief when I found out that the order had not been filed in the records. I asked Dr. Elaine Everly, the archivist in the Old Military Branch, to wait for the official announcement by the Department of Defense before giving any publicity to the order. She agreed. Why didn't I think of that before?

On Thursday morning, September 28, 1972, the Department of Defense made the announcement. And on Friday, September 29, 1972, it seemed that newspapers all over the country carried the story. The *New York Times* carried it in a front page article, "Army Clears 167 Black Soldiers Disciplined in a shooting in1906." *The Washington Post* had a different title on page A3, "Army Clears Black Soldiers in 1906 Brownsville Incident."

It was official. The whole world knew the truth—the Brownsville soldiers were innocent.

THIRTY FOUR

THE OLD MAN'S

Claim

Dorsie Willis Is Still Alive

EVEN THOUGH THE MAIN reason propounded by the Adjutant General for the no-back-pay, no-benefits clause in the order was to avoid setting a precedent by making payments to surviving soldiers, no one in the Pentagon that I dealt with believed that any of the soldiers were still alive. Even the Justice Department had said that in writing. So it follows that the real reason for the no-back-pay, no-benefits clause was to prevent payments to living descendants. Living descendants were a more likely probability.

Even I doubted that any of soldiers were still alive, but I hadn't given up hope. Anxious to find some of the soldiers, I requested authority and funds to search for survivors. My superiors were against it. They told me there were no funds in the budget for such a project, and moreover, they said I needed to get back to work developing the Army's Affirmative Action Plan and developing plans to improve race relations in the Army.

One day Bob Dews came to my desk to give me a message. His face was sad, and he had an air of formality about him, "General Brooks is leaving. He's being replaced by Colonel Ernie Frazier."

388

I was puzzled. Then Dews added quickly, "Don't worry about Harry. It's a step up the career ladder for him. It'll probably guarantee a second star for him."

Then he got down to the real reason he came to see me. "Bill, I have been asked to tell you that there are people in this building that don't want Brownsville embellished anymore. You've done your job. You're being pulled off the case. Turn your files over to the adjutant general's staff."

I felt numb, and for some strange reason, unworthy. Only once before had I felt that way—when I returned from the war in Vietnam. I looked up at Bob. "Vietnam, all over again, no appreciation, huh?"

"I'm just the messenger. Don't shoot me," Bob said, and left. Fortunately, that was not the end of it.

One morning in early October, the secretary told me that a General Mark W. Clark was on the phone and wanted to speak to me. I picked up the phone. A gruff, commanding, man's voice came through loud and clear. "Mark Clark here. Are you the lad who knows something about back pay for the Brownsville boys?"

Sure enough, it was Mark W. Clark, the famous World War II four-star general. He told me that he knew a remarkable old Negro who had shined his shoes for the last 30 years—and wanted to know what the Army was doing to grant him back pay.

I almost leaped through the telephone. Could it be? Could it be? Words rushed out of my mouth, "General Clark. General Clark. Who's alive? Who are you talking about?"

"Don't you know?" The old general said.

"No, sir. I don't."

"You don't know? Nixon's aides told me to talk to you."

I was embarrassed for myself and the Army. I mumbled something like, "Let me get back to you."

"Well, you answered my question. You don't know anything. You're not doing anything for Dorsie Willis."

Sensing that he was about to hang up on me, I said, "General Clark, how can I reach you? I'll get back to you."

"All right. You can reach me at the Francis Marion Hotel in Charleston, South Carolina. Call 803 577 5959. Don't call me back till you have the answer to my question."

That call from Mark Clark filled me with hopeful anticipation that the Army would change its position on back pay and benefits, and provide funds for me to organize a search for survivors. I rushed into General Brooks' office and told him that we might have a survivor. Brooks wanted to know his name and how I had found out about him. In my excitement, I had neglected to first tell him about my conversation with Mark Clark. When I told Brooks that I had spoken to Mark Clark, a living World War II legend in his own right, I got Brooks' full attention.

Newspapers around the country had also discovered Dorsie Willis, and his picture appeared in stories across the country. On October 5, 1972, the *Minneapolis Star*, in a front-page banner headline heralded the story of Dorsie Willis. "Army justice was 66 years late to a man in Brownsville Affray."

A huge public outcry ensued almost simultaneously with the publicity surrounding Dorsie Willis, charging the Army with discrimination in the no-back-pay, no-benefits clause. Letters flowed into the Secretary of the Army's office praising him for exoneration of the soldiers, but asking what the Army was going to do about helping Dorsie Willis? Copies of those letters were forwarded quickly down through the chain of command to me by intermediate staff officers. Obviously, no one had told them I was no longer on the case. Dorsie Willis became a political hot potato.

Weeks passed, but the Dorsie Willis problem wouldn't go away. On Friday, October 27, 1972, Mr. Plant, Special Assistant to the Under Secretary of the Army, by-passed the chain-of-command and called me directly. "Colonel Baker, I understand that you're handling the actions pertaining to survivors of the Brownsville Incident. What's the status of benefits for Dorsie Willis?"

After hesitating for a moment, and not knowing how to respond, I said, "Mr. Plant, our office isn't handling survivors' benefits. You should talk to the adjutant general."

On November 3, 1972, Secretary of the Army, Robert F. Froehlke, received a letter from Congressman Augustus F. Hawkins criticizing the no-back-pay, no-benefits clause. Among other things, Hawkins stated, "Frankly, I consider this language discriminatory [language in the order], and I wonder if you could give me the reasoning behind it."

A day or so later, our secretary told me that I was wanted immediately upstairs at a meeting in the Assistant Secretary of the Army's office. I quickly grabbed some of my Brownsville files and hurried upstairs. I walked into a spacious office. There I found several high-level staff officers sitting at a long mahogany table. Some I knew, some I didn't. All of them had quizzical looks on their faces.

A well-dressed man sat at the head of the conference table. I didn't remember having ever seen him before. He seemed to be in charge and acted as if he knew me. "Colonel Baker, what was your rationale for including that dumb no-back-pay, no-benefits clause in your case?"

"I didn't have a rationale then, and I don't have one now. I put it in the case because General Bowers insisted on it. That's the only way I could get it by him."

"Got any proof of that?" the man said.

"Yes, sir."

"Where is it?

I fumbled through the file I had brought along. Luck was with me. I found the memorandum prepared by Mr. Fraker and signed by Colonel J.C. Pennington for the Adjutant General on June 30, 1972, a long time prior to the development of my case. I got up from the table, walked over to where the man was sitting, laid the memorandum down in front of him and put my finger on the paragraph of the memo that was the origin of the no-back-pay, no-benefits provision.

"That's all, Colonel Baker," the man said.

Even though I had been taken off the project, the staff at the higher levels kept forwarding me letters about Dorsie Willis. On November 17, 1972 the Secretary of the Army received a poignant letter from Mr. J.C. Cornelius, a wealthy banker from Minneapolis, Minnesota. He wrote that "my greatly admired friend, General Mark W. Clark," at his request, was doing all he could to find out whether or not his good friend Dorsie Willis was entitled to any benefits.

After reading that letter, not only did I feel helpless, I also felt guilty that I hadn't gotten back to General Mark W. Clark about benefits for Dorsie Willis. Why did I feel that way? I simply had nothing to tell him. Moreover, I had been taken off the project.

The Search for Dorsie Willis

Congressman Donald M. Fraser, in a letter on November 22, 1972, asked the Army to issue Mr. Willis an Honorable Discharge certificate. That letter increased the pressure against the Army for doing nothing and saying nothing about the plight of Dorsie Willis. The Secretary of the Army was being put on the spot personally for the Army's inaction. He was feeling the heat and he wanted some answers.

Having many projects to work on, I kept busy. But my main interest was still on Brownsville. Time went by fast after the long Thanksgiving weekend, and it was now mid-December. I kept my ear to the ground, listening for any information about Dorsie Willis.

Colonel Frazier, the soon-to-be director of our department, and General Brooks were summoned into a hastily called meeting with General Bernie Rogers, our new boss. Rogers had just replaced General Kerwin, the three-star general in charge of all personnel in the Army. I wasn't asked to attend.

But about 15 minutes later, I was called into the meeting. Colonel Frazier was talking when I entered the room. "General Rogers, we don't have the staff to search for survivors. Back pay and benefits are not our responsibilities. Bill Baker is overloaded."

General Rogers turned to me. "Colonel Baker, what do you have to say about this? What can we do to help Dorsie Willis?"

Before I could think clearly, words came pouring out. "We could do a lot more than nothing." Then I realized that I had been too blunt. "Sir, I mean the Army...not anybody personally."

I knew that I had better show General Rogers that I wasn't just a bag of emotions, so I said, "Let me put it this way, sir. The first thing we must do is identify this man who calls himself Dorsie Willis. Yes, there was a Dorsie Willis at Fort Brown. I know that. But is this the same man? Is he a legitimate survivor? We don't know that yet. If he is, we must issue him an Honorable Discharge certificate. The discharge certificate would enable him to apply for veterans' benefits. Also, we should determine if he is due any back pay or some sort of reparations.

"We should not allow the case of this man to be made into a cause célèbre by the news media or any other outside organizations. That's what's happening now. We must move rapidly to seize the initiative."

"That's a mouthful. Now, you tell me who's going to do the work?" Ernie Frazier glared at me.

"I'll do it," I said.

"You don't have enough time. You have too much on your plate now," Frazier said.

"I can do both, like I've been doing. I'll work at night. I'll give up my Christmas vacation, and work during the holidays."

General Rogers spoke up. "Let's give Bill a shot at it."

I went back to my office thinking that I had settled it, I was back on Brownsville. Later that day, I prepared a position paper for General Rogers recommending identification of Mr. Willis and issuance of an Honorable Discharge certificate, if appropriate.

When I made that recommendation, I knew that one of the most powerful generals in the Army with respect to military personnel policy, Major General Verne Bowers, the Adjutant General, had opposed the issuance of the

Honorable Discharge certificate to any possible survivor just a few weeks ago, even though he knew that the issuance of such a certificate would have "no legal effect on statutory entitlements to which these individuals [Brownsville survivors] would otherwise be entitled." That is what JAG told him back on November 9, 1972.

When my position paper was staffed recommending the issuance of an Honorable Discharge certificate to Mr. Willis, if his identity could be established, the Adjutant General opposed it. It took outside pressure from letters to the Secretary of the Army to get him to change his position.

The Criminal Investigation Department Steps In

On the day before General Brooks' departure, I was called into Colonel Frazier office for a special meeting on Brownsville. For all practical purposes, Colonel Frazier was now the new director of our office, and he had moved into General Brooks' office. He had a pleased look on his face when he introduced me to three men wearing cheap-looking, bell-bottom polyester civilian suits. As if on cue, all three of them immediately took out their badges and showed them to me. They were military policemen (MPs) from the Criminal Investigation Department (CID).

Colonel Frazier said, "Bill, I have asked the CID to identify Dorsie Willis. Take them to the conference room and brief them on Brownsville. They'll go to Minnesota and get this over quickly."

"Gentlemen, would you excuse us?" I said, "I want to speak to Colonel Frazier privately."

"What do you want to talk with me about? I just got you some help." Frazier said.

Colonel Frazier and I had a long and sometimes heated debate about the wisdom of sending criminal investigators out to Mr. Willis' home in Minneapolis. I was against it and told him so. I also told him my belief that the CID was the most distasteful department of the military police. Some of their methods were questionable and secretive. To seriously consider sending them out to investigate an old, arthritic man who had committed no crime was a despicable thing to do. And I told him so.

My words hit a nerve. Maybe I should've been more tactful. He stood up. His face was red and the veins in his neck bulged. As he talked and pounded his fist on his desk, he got louder and louder. He was becoming a wild man. I knew he hadn't been drinking, he was a teetotaler. Every time I tried to say something, he drowned me out saying, "Shut up! Shut up! Shut up!"

Finally, desperate to stop him, I yelled, "Colonel Frazier you're making a colossal mistake!"

"I told you to shut up! Don't interrupt me when I am talking. Now go do what I told you."

The three CID agents were waiting for me in the conference room. How can I get rid of these guys? That was the first thought that crossed my mind. Ernie Frazier had told me that they didn't know anything about Brownsville. I was betting on their ignorance. To be sure, I had better confirm it. So I began, "I know you fellows are smarter than Brown & Baldwin detectives, the Secret Service, the Grand Jury, and five prior military investigators. But you should know that they failed."

"Failed at what?" One of the agents asked.

"I'll get to that in a minute. First, I need to know who's in charge, and what authority you have to investigate an American civilian."

One of the agents spoke up. "I'm in charge. Did I understand you to say that Dorsie Willis is a civilian?"

"That's right Colonel," I said. "How does that square with the Posse Comitatus Act?

"It doesn't. Ernie didn't tell us that Dorsie Willis was a civilian. He must be slipping. He must have forgotten everything he ever learned as a CID agent. I know him from way back. I'll talk him out of this."

The Real Dorsie Willis

It was the 26th of December. The corridors of the Pentagon were quiet and people were still out on Christmas vacation. But I wasn't. I was working. By now Colonel Frazier and I had patched things up. With the telephone not ringing as much and hardly any meetings to attend, I was able to catch up on my projects and put in some serious time searching for evidence that would confirm that the real Dorsie W. Willis, who was a young soldier in 1906, was still alive.

I viewed his records in the National Archives, read interviews he gave to various newspapers, and reviewed the testimony and affidavits he made to prior investigators. I knew a lot about him. I was confident that I would be able to say whether or not he was the Dorsie W. Willis within a week or so. Thus, I felt it was time to answer some of the mail about Willis, buy some time, and work to neutralize the negative publicity the Army had recently endured. I so advised Ernie Frazier.

On December 26, 1972, on behalf of the Secretary of the Army, Ernie Frazier notified Congressman Donald Frazier

THE BROWNSVILLE TEXAS INCIDENT OF 1906

that the Army would assist Dorsie Willis in establishing his identity as a legitimate survivor. The effort would require research in the National Archives to find documentation and a personal interview of Willis by a "knowledgeable person." Based on the findings, the Army would be in a position to determine his identity as the lone survivor of the Brownsville night of terror. Upon proper identification, Willis would be issued an Honorable Discharge certificate.

The next day, December 27, at his home in Minneapolis, Minnesota, Dorsie Willis gave an extensive interview to Andrew H. Malcolm. His report, 'How Brownsville Raid Changed Life of Black G.I.,' was filed as "Special to the *New York Times*" and appeared on New Year's Eve. Willis told Malcolm his sad story, while providing me with valuable information that would have to be verified by direct contact with him.

Now that the Army had officially gone on record offering Dorsie Willis assistance, and he was talking freely to reporters, I felt that it was the right time for me to make contact with him. I called him on the telephone and introduced myself. I tried to reassure him that my job was to assist him in convincing the Army that he really was Dorsie W. Willis. I was going to help him, not interrogate him.

The first thing he said to me was, "It's a trick! You're playing a trick on me." Then he hung up the phone.

Well, that was a mistake. It was a mistake making a cold call to an old man who had no good reason to trust me, or anybody else in the Army. I needed an introduction. So I turned to Mr. J. C. Cornelius, the President of the Northwestern Bank in Minneapolis, who readily agreed to call Dorsie Willis and persuade him to talk with me. The next time I called him, he was most gracious. I didn't have to ask him a single question. He talked on and on about Brownsville and his life after being discharged. His story was essentially the same things he had told several reporters.

More Detective Work

On January 8, 1973, I developed a detailed, four-step procedure for a board of officers to follow that would assist Willis in establishing his identify.

One of the first things I did was develop a systematic approach to solving the identification problem. From the outset, I ran into problems. Fingerprint technology was not available until 1918, so that was out. I was about to fly off to Jackson, Mississippi, to get a copy of Willis' birth certificate, when I learned that Mississippi did not record births or deaths until 1912. I couldn't find any record of his dental work. What surprised me most, however, was not only could I not find any historical photos of Dorsie Willis, but in addition, he had no photos of himself as a young man. All witnesses who knew him and could identify him as a member of the 25th Infantry were probably dead. He had outlived all of them. Recordings of his voice in a historical context were not available. So voice prints were out. I was getting nowhere fast.

When everything seemed to have failed, I found historical signatures of Dorsie W. Willis in the National Archives. I also saw more recent signatures (1954) in JAG's records where Willis had appealed to the Army for an honorable discharge. I hired a graphologist, or hand-writing expert, to confirm their authenticity. I arranged for Mr. John H. Orr, an examiner of questionable documents, to meet me at the National Archives on January 5, 1973. With approval of the archivist, I had the expert examine original historic signatures signed by Willis on January 5, 1905, and three original signatures he had executed on affidavits in 1954. On the basis of his examination, the graphologist concluded that the same person executed those signatures.

The experts' determination on the signatures heartened me, but I knew that evidence alone wouldn't be enough. What I needed were his medical records. I kept digging farther into the box of records, examining paper after paper. Then on January 5, 1973, I found Willis' medical records. As I began reading the descriptive data on the physical induction card, my hands began to shake with excitement. Like a miner who had been digging for years to find that perfect golden nugget, I had found my undeniable proof. My hands shook so rapidly that it made the data difficult to read. I grabbed my right wrist with my left hand and held it tightly so I could read the document.

Here was what I needed—a full description of Dorsie W. Willis. Color of eyes, color of hair, complexion, height and weight. And scars—a quarter inch on his left cheek, a 1-inch scar on his left wrist, one one-and-a-quarter inches on his left forearm and one eighth of an inch on his right forearm. Three other scars were described in the induction physical—one on Willis' back, right thigh, and left foot.

From that information, public statements Willis had made, depositions and affidavits, I was able to develop a complete profile of a young man who was 18 years old and a private in the U.S. Army stationed at Fort Brown, Texas. I knew what he looked like then, but I didn't know what he would look like as an old man in his eighties. Now armed with these distinguishing characteristics, we could positively identify him and confirm the existence of the last living legacy of the Brownsville affair.

Meet Dorsie Willis

On January 11, 1973, I flew on Northwest Orient Airlines to Minneapolis, Minnesota, with Colonel Robert J. Kirk, a personnel expert, and Doctor L. Thomas Wolff, a medical doctor. There we interviewed Reverend Curtis Herron, Pastor of Zion Baptist Church. The substance of the interview was that he knew Dorsie Willis and the old man was a faithful member of the church.

The next morning at nine o'clock we went to the seat of financial and economic power in Minneapolis, Northwestern Bank. Jack Cornelius ushered us into his large and elaborate mahogany-paneled office. Cornelius told us he had known Dorsie Willis for 40 years, and during those years, as far back as the 1930s, Willis had told him of the unjust treatment he had received as a result of the Brownsville Incident. He had come to know Willis as a friend and described him as a hard worker who shined shoes in his bank building for many years. He said he admired his intelligence, integrity, and civic responsibility, and told us a short story of how Willis saved enough quarters from his shoeshine business to send an inner city child to summer camp every year. "In spite of how the Army had treated him," Cornelius said, "Dorsie loves our country."

We were scheduled to interview Willis at his home at two o'clock that afternoon. Becoming anxious, I called Mr. Willis and asked him if we could come a little earlier. He said, "Yes." I could hardly wait to get there.

We arrived at his home about 30 minutes early. He lived in a little white stucco bungalow on Minnehaha Street. It was a cold, sunny afternoon. The house was covered with snow and his yard glistened with ice from melted snow.

A well-dressed, distinguished-looking old man, with a face as if cast in bronze, stood at the open door leaning on a walking cane. His cheeks were fully fleshed, and he had a square chin, stocky build, and gray silver hair. He greeted us warmly and welcomed us into his home.

Figure 22. Dorsie W. Willis, 1972
Last Survivor Brownsville, Texas, Incident, 1906
Courtesy of U.S. Army Signal Corps

Sitting down in his old-fashioned leather chair seemed difficult for him. He eased slowly and carefully into it. It must have been painful. The chair and the man seemed too big for the tiny living room.

When I looked into his eyes, sadness looked back at me. Now knowing his history, I knew it was a sadness of many years—and a mourning for all his friends and fellow soldiers who passed on before him, leaving him the last man standing. His approaching mortality was reflected deep in the hollow of his eyes. He would be celebrating his 87th birthday next month in February, and we both knew there wouldn't be many more. His expression told us that he had been waiting for us, the U.S. Army, for a long, long time. His eyes seemed to ask us the question, "Why did you have to wait until now?"

Nothing had adequately prepared me to meet this man. I didn't know where to start, even though I had written out several questions on a yellow pad that was still in my briefcase. I was supposed to lead the interview. I fidgeted awkwardly with the latch on my briefcase. Failing to get it open, I gave up trying.

Willis's attention was drawn to my briefcase. He looked at it, then at Colonel Kirk's briefcase sitting on the floor, then at Dr. Wolff's black medical bag. After the four of us had sat in silence for what seemed like a long time, the old man finally spoke up softly. "You gentlemen look educated, but are you civilized?"

Then he smiled, and we all smiled. Even under these circumstances, I realized Dorsie Willis had a sense of humor. When he smiled, I noticed a scar on his left cheek. After I saw that scar, I dropped my plan for direct questioning and conducted an open-ended interview.

The story the old man told us was at once extraordinary, revealing, and compelling. His narrative coincided remarkably with my research. When he appeared to tire, I thought it time to end the interview. I wanted to get back to Washington, report our results—and get this man his Honorable Discharge certificate. I had seen and heard enough.

But we needed to do a physical examination. I asked him if he was willing to submit to a medical exam. He agreed. Dr. Wolff and Willis went into a back room for privacy where the doctor conducted the exam. The doctor found the identical scars that were on Willis' medical record at the age of 18.

We took a vote. It was unanimous—this man was, in fact, the Dorsie W. Willis we were looking for. He was a legitimate and confirmed survivor of the Brownsville Incident, and he should be recognized as such by the Department of the Army.

After 69 Years of Injustice, Justice

On Friday, February 2, 1973, Secretary of the Army, Robert F. Froehlke approved the report. Almost immediately, controversy arose over who would present Dorsie Willis with his Honorable Discharge certificate. There were a number of wild suggestions. Ernie Frazier made it known that he would clear his calendar and make the presentation himself. Of course, I wasn't consulted. I didn't care much about it, except that I was concerned that the Army would select the wrong official. I didn't want someone who was ignorant of the historical significance of the affair and what the awarding of the Honorable Discharge would mean to the 87-year-old man humbly standing before him.

Secretary of the Army, Robert F. Froehlke eventually selected Major General Dewitt C. Smith, Jr., the second-ranking public affairs official and press expert in the Pentagon, to represent him and make the presentation. Froehlke selected me to assist General Smith. Togo West explained the rationale, "Major General Smith should be accompanied by the staff officer (Lt. Col. Baker) most familiar with the case. Since Lt. Col. Baker happens to be black, the team would be racially balanced."

At that time I didn't know anything about General Smith. I checked around the Pentagon, and found out that DeWitt

Smith, in addition to his outstanding public relations reputation, was a soldier's soldier, a fair man, and a big supporter
of equal opportunity. I went to his office to see him and
asked if I could write his presentation speech, which was
customary for staff officers to do for generals and high-level
civilian officials. He thanked me, but declined. He said he
preferred to write it himself, but promised to let me read it
before he delivered it.

I made all the arrangements for the presentation. I got
approval from Reverend Herron and Dorsie Willis to conduct the ceremony on Sunday, February 11, 1973, at the
Zion Baptist Church in Minneapolis. I sent notification to
interested members of Congress, requested press coverage,
and so on. Then I went back to the Pentagon and asked
General Smith's secretary if the general had finished writing
his speech. She said, "No, Colonel Baker. He's really tense
about this speech. I've never seen him like this before. I'll let
you know when he completes it."

On Friday evening, the day before we were to leave for
Minneapolis, General Smith still hadn't prepared his speech.
I was worried.

The next morning, February 10, 1973, General Smith
and I caught a plane for Minneapolis. On that flight I noted
he was writing furiously. He sat in a seat in front of me, and
in about 20 minutes into the flight, he turned around and
handed me a pencil-written speech, "Bill, read this and tell
me what you think."

I read the speech in awe. How could this man write such
beautiful, powerful words that conveyed so much in such a
short period of time? I gave it back to him and simply said,
"Marvelous!"

On Sunday afternoon, February 11, 1973, following the regular church service, the ceremony was held in a packed church with standing room only. People filled the back and down both sides of the aisles. Willis and his family sat in the first rows with General Smith and me standing in the pulpit, wearing our Dress Blue uniforms.

General Smith, addressing the congregation in general, and Dorsie Willis in particular, said in part... "We are trying to substitute justice for injustice, to make amends, to say how much we of this generation—white men as well as black—regret the errors and injustices of an earlier generation. Colonel Baker and I signify the Army's disapproval of mass punishment. Mr. Willis, you honor us by the quality of the life you have led, by your outstanding citizenship, and by the faithful service you rendered the United States Army..." (*New York Times* quote of the day [in part], 2/12/73).

When General Smith had finished his speech, Dorsie Willis knew the moment he had waited for so long had come. He stood up and hobbled alone to the edge of the pulpit, stood as erect as he could, and leaned on his cane. He was followed by his wife, Olive Willis, and family members. Photographers, TV camera technicians, and men and women scrambled on their knees and hands along the floor in front of the pulpit, jockeying for a good view of the scene. With TV cameras rolling and flash bulbs popping, General Smith presented Dorsie Willis his Honorable Discharge certificate.

Dorsie Willis took the certificate, looked down at it momentarily, raised his head, and looked up past us. I could only imagine that he was looking back into time, to the days of his youth. To a time of broken promises and crushed dreams that could never be repaired or restored. The certificate reclaimed his honor, but not the life he had imagined.

It was not until the congregation gave him a standing ovation that he smiled.

The choir began singing the *Battle Hymn of the Republic*. The words flowed into the hearts of many people with yet a deeper meaning, for I saw them crying while singing, "Mine eyes have seen the glory of the coming of the Lord...."

Later at the cake and coffee reception in the basement of the church, I presented Dorsie Willis with an American flag. He said to me, "I'm going to use this flag to put on my coffin."

Figure 23. The Washington AFRO-AMERICAN, February 17, 1973
The American Flag was presented to 80-year-old Dorsie Willis (R) during ceremonies at the Zion Baptist Church in Minneapolis, Sunday, while his son Reginald (3rd from L) watched proudly. Willis, believed to be the sole survivor of an all-black unit dishonorably discharged from the Army in 1906 for an unsolved murder in Brownsville, Tex., was exonerated after being forced to shine shoes for 40 years.
Making the presentation is Lt.Col. William Baker. (UPI Telephoto.)

After the ceremony, and after General Smith flew back to Washington, I was inundated with requests for interviews by reporters. They assumed that I was a public relations spokesman for the Army, which I wasn't, but nevertheless, I was uncomfortably pressed into that role.

The Army's plan was that I would remain in Minneapolis to assist Willis in filling out forms for his Veteran benefits and not to talk to reporters. However, I was grilled about back pay, reparations and benefits for Dorsie Willis. What was the Army going to do? I ducked, dodged, and danced away from the questions as best I could.

One of the interviews I gave was to Andrew H. Malcolm. His report, 'Army Returns Honor to Discharged Black,' was filed as "Special to the *New York Times*" and appeared on Monday, February 12, 1973.

Sometime later another Brownsville survivor surfaced—Edwin Warfield. He was also confirmed as legitimate and presented with his Honorable Discharge certificate. That made it two, out of the 167 disgraced and dishonored soldiers, who would go to their graves knowing full well that they had been innocent of any crime.

Figure 24.
"I'm going to use this flag to put on my coffin."
Dorsie Willis, February 2, 1973.
Courtesy, U.S. Army Signal Corps

BOOK III

AFTERMATH

THIRTY FIVE

COMPENSATION

Or Reparations?

A Bid to Compensate

NEGATIVE PUBLICITY CONTINUED TO build against the Army for its failure to rescind the no benefits clause in the order. Congressman Hawkins fired off a follow-up letter to Secretary of the Army, Robert F. Froehlke, which was blunt in every detail. "I do not consider [Army] replies responsive to my inquiries...." He pressed Froehlke for answers to his previous questions. He wanted the answers in detail and in simple terms. Why didn't Froehlke consider the language in the order discriminatory? Why did Dorsie Willis and the other survivor have difficulties receiving benefits? Hawkins threatened Congressional hearings and legislation, if the Army failed to act soon.

When the Army didn't heed his warning, Congressman Hawkins introduced on February 20, 1973, H.R. 4382, a bill to "confer pensionable status on veterans involved in the Brownsville Texas Incident..." His bill would require the administrator of the Veterans Administration to make compensatory payments of $40,000 to veterans involved in the Brownsville Incident and $20,000 to their heirs.

The Chairman of the House Veterans' Affairs Committee requested Melvin Laird, Secretary of the Defense, and

Donald Johnson, head of the Veterans Administration, to submit their views on the proposed legislation. As customary, the Nixon Administration required such reports to be submitted through its Office of Management and Budget so that a consistent policy position could be presented to the Congress.

Donald Johnson of the VA opposed the bill in his written reply on May 16, 1973. On June 10, 1973, Major General Verne Bowers, the Adjutant General of the Army, in his proposed reply for the Secretary of the Army, simply deferred comments to the Veterans Administration on the merits of the bill. Richard Belnap, legal adviser to General Bowers, brought copies of Johnson's reply and General Bowers' proposed reply to my office for my review and agreement.

I disagreed with both Johnson and General Bowers on their replies, and wrote a memorandum analyzing their positions and stating my objections. My analysis of the VA's position was easy. I concluded that all of the VA's opposition points said essentially the same thing and all of them were wrong. They contended that:

Retroactive benefits for the Brownsville soldiers would be discriminatory to other veterans who had not been granted benefits for commission of similar offenses.

But there were no other similar cases of mass punishments or precedents in the Regular Army. All legal authorities agreed on that.

In deferring to the VA, General Bowers, in effect, recommended that the Army submit a negative report to the Congress. Such a report would, like Pontius Pilate, attempt to wipe the Army's hands clean of the whole sorry Brownsville affair. This effort would be a complete dodge of the unjust consequences of that affair, which was solely perpetrated by the War Department (now Defense Department), and not the modern Veterans Administration. Moreover, for the Army to defer any comments to the VA, based upon the contention that Hawkins' bill fell outside its purview, was to accept a narrow interpretation of its responsibility.

My view was that the Army should make restitution for the damage it had done in the form of direct reparations to the survivors or their heirs. I recommended that the Army support Hawkins' bill with respect to the monetary aspects, that payments should be made by the Army in individual lump sums to survivors or their heirs, and that the funds should come from the Army, not the VA.

In my opinion, though, Hawkins' bill was flawed in a major way. Unlike the notorious Willie Sutton, who reportedly once said, when asked why he robbed banks, "That's where the money is," the Hawkins bill was trying to get funding where there was little or no money. Everyone knew that the VA was almost always broke. The Defense Department was where the money was—and that's where I wanted to get it from.

General Bowers flatly and roundly denounced my plan. His opposition didn't totally surprise me. He took unsympathetic positions towards the soldiers all along. But now that his office were responsible for carrying out the remaining tasks on Brownsville, he was in a strategic position to block benefits—and that's just what he was trying to do.

Why did he choose to step out from behind the curtain of simply deferring to the VA to out-right opposition now? It occurred to me that I used the wrong word in my argument for benefits. It was my fault. By using 'reparations,' I plunged the benefits argument into controversy. Bowers thought he could gain allies now, for it was common knowledge that the mere notion of paying reparations was anathema.

When the Adjutant General still wouldn't agree to support the Hawkins bill, I recommended that our office nonconcur. Since we were at loggerheads, Colonel Loma Allen, the new deputy director of our office, took the matter up the chain of command to General Bobby Gard for resolution, but General Gard was not in his office. He was in California, testifying against Daniel Ellsberg for leaking the Pentagon Papers to the *Washington Post*. A conference telephone call was made to him.

After the conference call, Colonel Allen came to my office and stood over my desk. I looked up at him, waiting for the decision. He told me that General Gard asked three questions. Who agreed with the Adjutant General, who disagreed and what was the VA's position?

"We told him that everyone agreed except you, Bill."

"You mean everybody?" I asked.

"That's right," Allen said.

Then he told me that General Gard said that we would go along with the VA and oppose the legislation, and that I should write a paragraph ending the controversy and support the adjutant general's position.

At that point it mattered little to me what Bobby Gard said. I knew what I had to do. With Colonel Allen still standing over my desk, I turned to my typewriter and typed out a paragraph taking the opposite position of the VA:

Whereas this office does not support that part of the bill which would award benefits to second generation children, the concept of benefits to actual veteran survivors or their widows is a fair objective through congressional legislation.

Eliminating benefits to second generation children, as much as I hated to do it, was my way of ending the controversy over reparations. From then on, I substituted the word "compensation" for "reparations" when referring to back pay and benefits. I had to compromise, if I were to get benefits for Dorsie Willis and the widows of the soldiers, all of whom were old and not far removed from institutional care. They were poor people and medical bills were already falling heavily upon them. They needed the money now.

Colonel Allen was still looking over my shoulder and he didn't like what he saw. "Bill," he said, "this isn't what General Gard said. You have defied him."

It was true, I had defied General Gard's instructions, but certainly not lightly. A charge of insubordination could be serious. But moral cowardice was worse.

I took the paper out of the typewriter. My hand shook so badly that it was difficult to sign my name. I handed it to the colonel. "Colonel Allen, please take this to General DeWitt Smith."

Smith was the next general in our chain of command. He had recently been moved from public relations to the position of Assistant Chief of Staff for Personnel, reporting directly to Lieutenant General Bernie Rogers. In that position, Smith slightly outranked the Adjutant General who also worked for Bernie Rogers. Fortunately for me, Smith overruled Bobby Gard and the Adjutant General. General Smith persuaded General Bowers to include in the Army's reply to Congress part of my paragraph:

> *...some compensation to surviving members of the Brownsville incident or their widows is a fair objective through legislation...*

I barely managed to keep the Army on the side of supporting "compensation," for without the Army's support, any bill was doomed. But I hadn't in any way won a victory.

On June 5, 1973, I read a story hot off the wires of UPI:

THE NIXON ADMINISTRATION IS OPPOSING A BILL TO GRANT COMPENSATION TO Families of 167 Black Soldiers Dismissed From The Army In 1906… Rep Hawkins… Said. The Measure Is Being Opposed By Both The Veterans' Administration And The Office Of Management And Budget. Administrator Donald Johnson Said Hawkins' Bill Would Set An Undesirable Precedent And Discriminate Against Other Veterans. UPI 06-05 02:42.

Now that Hawkins had gone public against the Nixon Administration, I feared positions would harden. Something extraordinary needed to be done. Not knowing exactly what to do, almost by reflex I picked up the telephone and called Donald Johnson at VA headquarters. I was surprised when he took my call—and mildly shocked when he listened to my views on the phone and agreed to meet with me. It was risky business for me to step outside of the Pentagon's realm of control, and meet with another government official. But the risk was worth taking. I took a cab to his office, but when I got there, he was gone. Instead, he left word for me to brief his staff.

In an emotional, yet fact-filled presentation, I told them the story of Brownsville and I ended by warning them that the tide was running against them and that Hawkins' bill would pass. My friends in the White House could turn this thing around, convince President Nixon to sign the legislation, and as a consequence, the budgetary cost and burdensome staff work would be unhappily forced upon them.

Then I struck a deal with them. If the VA would drop its opposition to the bill, I would guarantee that the funds would come out of the Defense Department Budget for retirees. I also assured them that the Army would assume the administrative responsibility for payments. The staff made no commitments to me, but agreed to pass the information along to Johnson.

After leaving the VA, I hailed a cab and went to the White House (Old Executive Office Building), and met with the staff of Roy Ash, the new Director of OMB. I told them essentially the same story about Brownsville, the main element being that the Army was historically responsible for the injustice. Therefore, the Army should pay restitution in a lump sum, and should accept the administrative burden associated with payments.

Compensation Is Due, But...

On or about June 6, 1973, Secretary of the Army, Howard H. Callaway (Bo Callaway) who had recently succeeded Froehkle, received a letter from the Executive Office of the President, OMB, which essentially rejected General Bowers reply letter with one exception, the paragraph that said some compensation would be a fair objective through legislation. The Nixon Administration wanted to know specifically what form that compensation should take, and would the Army be willing to absorb the cost. Gone was the VA's opposition to any compensation.

The Administration agreed with the VA that claims should be submitted to the Department of the Army, not the VA, since claims would not be related to regular veterans' benefits. On June 8, 1973, in response to the Nixon Administration OMB letter, Belnap prepared another letter for the

Adjutant General and brought it to me for concurrence. I couldn't agree with it, and I told him why. After first praising him, telling him what a good and honest man I believed he was, I then I told him he hadn't taxed his imagination or ingenuity. He simply copied the same old letter using different words to say the same thing, and more to the point, he hadn't addressed the new offer by the Nixon Administration. My major objection was that Belnap had not included in his draft letter an unambiguous, unqualified commitment by the Army to pay for the compensation out of the Army's or Defense Department's funds.

"Well, what do you want me to do?" Belnap said.

"I want you to introduce me to General Bowers, and see if he will talk to me directly."

"I don't know about that. He's a busy man. What changes do you want us to make?"

"They want us to pay for this out of our budget. The VA wants us to do the work! Mr. Belnap, can't you see that!"

I typed the changes that I wanted to include.

> *The Department believes some compensation to surviving members of the Brownsville Incident or their widows is a fair objective through legislation. A lump sum payment should be considered through legislative enactment to those men...or to their unremarried widows. Such legislation should provide for payment currently available to the Department of Defense for military retired pay.*

In other words, I wanted the Defense Department to cough up the money because the VA was probably broke.

Handing him the proposed changes, I said, "Take me to General Bowers. I want to explain it to him directly. We can work it out."

Belnap said I should come with him to Colonel J.C. Pennington's office. He was the Executive Officer to General Bowers, the gate keeper, and the defacto second man in charge. We went around to his office on the E-ring corridor. Belknap told me to wait outside in the lobby while he consulted with Pennington.

This was the first time I had been in the suite of the adjutant general's office. The sumptuous lobby was richly appointed with thick oriental carpets, red and brown leather chairs. A great big overstuffed brown leather couch sat in front and against a long rectangular mahogany table with beautiful colorful lamps on top. Lining the mahogany-paneled walls were portraits of serious, stern-looking men, all previous adjutant generals.

Standing outside the open door to Pennington's office, I could hear they were arguing.

Belnap's voice was low, but distinctive. "We must convince General Bowers to accept Baker's changes."

Pennington's voice was loud and argumentative. "General Bowers will not take orders from a junior officer. Baker is not our boss."

"But he's right on this issue. Let's go see General Bowers."

When I heard them getting up, I moved away from the door over toward one of the portraits.

The two men went into General Bowers' office and closed the door. They weren't in there very long. Pennington came out first and walked right past me without saying a word. A few seconds later, Belnap came out, walked up to me, shook his head and said, "Colonel Baker, for your own sake, please back off." Having said that, he gave me a little written green memo slip, which I still have today. Then he turned on his heels, and went to his office. I read the note.

The Adjutant General had refused to speak to me. It was evident to me that he wouldn't be persuaded by words, and certainly not from me. He had taken a hard line. In writing, he had said that he would not change his position unless directed to do so by his immediate superior officer, Bernie Rogers, a three-star general. When any soldier says he will not act unless given an order, that's pretty strong stuff.

Bypassing Colonel Frazier and Colonel Allen, I went to see General Smith and told Joyce, his secretary, that I needed to speak to the general. I showed him the note and Smith told me to try to find out what JAG's position was on the changed language. At about five o'clock that evening I learned informally that General Prugh, the Judge Advocate General, said he would also oppose our changes. With that, Smith said for me to let him handle it.

Since Bernie Rogers was not available to resolve the dispute, I later learned that Smith took the issue to General Creighton W. Abrams, the Chief of Staff of the Army, for resolution. Abrams, a former tank commander during World War II in General George Patton's Third Army, was known for making quick decisions. He overruled the adjutant general and the judge advocate general, putting the Army squarely in support for compensation and just as important, willing to foot the bill.

On June 13, 1973, the new Secretary of the Army, Howard H. [Bo] Callaway, signed the letter to the Chairman of the House Committee on Veterans Affairs, ending the controversy in the Army, and the Nixon Administration raised no more objections to Hawkins' bill.

During the whole time I struggled to put the Army on record to support Hawkins' bill, I openly worked with Senator Hubert H. Humphrey's staff. I had been assisting them, at their request since February 13, 1973, to formulate a bill to make compensatory payments to veterans involved in the Brownsville Incident. Senator Humphrey's administrative assistant had enough political clout to get authorization from the Secretary of the Army's Office of Congressional Legislative Liaison for me to work with them without going through the time-consuming bureaucratic chain-of-command process.

Working with Senator Humphrey's staff was reassuring. The people I worked with were advocates for the Brownsville soldiers, and I felt confident that Senator Humphrey would succeed in getting some sort of bill through the Senate. On June 14, 1973, he introduced S. 1999, a bill similar to Hawkins' bill, for himself and Senator Walter Mondale. For processing, the bill went to Senator Vance Hartke, Chairman of the Senate Committee on Veterans' Affairs.

About three weeks after Senator Humphrey introduced his bill, Belnap rushed into my office and showed me a letter dated July 10, 1973, from Senator Vance Hartke. It was addressed to Secretary of the Army Bo Callaway. The Senator requested the Army's position on Humphrey's bill.

I assumed that the Army's response to Humphrey's bill would be identical to the response on Hawkins' bill, thus avoiding any more controversy. Or so I thought.

But Senator Hartke asked Callaway to provide additional information: To develop in the next two weeks a compensatory schedule (mathematical model) to calculate the amounts of payments for the Brownsville survivors. He also requested a "comprehensive historical outline of past compensation awards, especially as to amounts, dates, and factors considered, including items of legitimate damages." Finally, Hartke suggested Callaway consider, among other alternatives, paying $25,000 to surviving Brownsville veterans, $10,000 to widows—and $5,000 to children, if no widow.

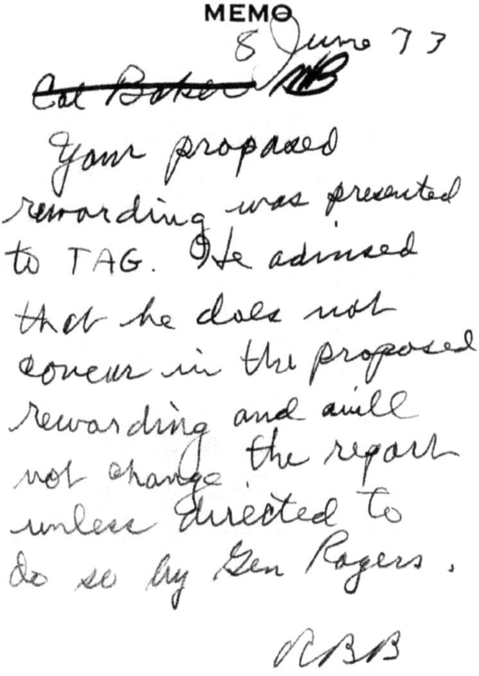

MEMO

[handwritten note]

**Figure 25. OFFICE OF THE ADJUTANT GENERAL
MEMO
8 June 73.**
Col. Baker, Your proposed rewording was presented to
TAG [The Adjutant General]. He advised that he does not
concur in the proposed rewording and will not change
the report unless directed to do so by Gen. Rogers.
RBB [Richard B. Belnap]

To satisfy Hartke's request, the adjutant general made inquiries to the Comptroller of the Army, the Board for Correction of Military Records, and JAG, seeking information about past compensatory awards in situations analogous to the Brownsville Incident. Since those agencies didn't find any records, Belnap asked me if I would develop a reasonable formula for determining a fair lump-sum payment schedule for each soldier-survivor involved in the Brownsville Incident, and each surviving unremarried widow.

Belnap said the payment schedule must be done in a day or two because of the tight Senate deadline and the requirement to get concurrence by the Army General staff. Also, the Nixon Administration had to approve any payment schedule.

"Look," I told him, "that's not my job. It's the adjutant general's responsibility. Go back and tell General Bowers to have his staff make the calculations." Belnap started for the door.

"Wait!" I called to him. "Richard, you know I'm just joking." I had never called him by his first name before, and he never called me "Bill." I couldn't hide my enthusiasm. I was so happy that he asked me to make the calculations.

He handed me the letter from Senator Hartke and said, "Thanks, Bill."

I went to work. I developed a payment schedule. My calculations showed that Dorsie Willis would receive $126,598. When I finished, I trotted over to Belnap's office and gave him the compensatory pay schedule. Later, when Belnap told me that Colonel Pennington, chief of staff for the adjutant general, and JAG agreed with the compensatory pay schedule, I felt good. I was riding high.

Two weeks went by. The deadline came and went. It was the end of July, and I hadn't heard anything about a reply back to Senator Vance Hartke. I was about to call Richard Belnap when my telephone rang. Belnap was on the other end of the line. "Bill, could you come over to my office right away?" His voice sounded tentative.

"The Japanese Problem"

What disaster has happened now? I hurried over to Belnap's office. He told me that the civilian politicians in the Secretariat rejected the compensatory pay schedule of $126,598. They were supporting the $25,000 for Dorsie Willis and $10,000 for unremarried widows—and nothing for heirs.

What could I do now? I needed time, but time I didn't have. So I called my contact on John Erlichman's domestic staff in the White House. I was told that the Nixon Administration would support no more than the $25,000 and $10,000 payments. When I asked why, I was told it's the "Japanese problem."

Questioning my contact further, he explained that the current thinking of the Administration and some other politicians was that America soon would have to free its conscience and absolve its guilt for the Japanese internments during World War II. At that time the federal government imprisoned 72,000 Japanese American citizens and aliens—men, women and children—for dubious reasons. Compensation for thousands of them was expected to be costly. Because of that likelihood, Brownsville couldn't become a costly precedent.

On or about August 3, 1973, the new secretary of the army reported to Senator Vance Hartke that research provided no record of past compensatory awards analogous to the Brownsville Incident. Therefore, no basis for compensation was available. However, the Army would have no objections to $25,000 for soldier survivors and $10,000 for unremarried widows. The Army still objected to any payments to heirs or descendants. The compensatory payment schedule that I devised, and, was agreed to by the Army staff, was not mentioned.

General Smith was unhappy about this proposal. He wrote me a note:

> *Why did the Assistant Secretary of the Army take this position? Originally, when Togo West was there, I thought they were sympathetic to Mr. Willis, et. al. Did Mr. Bennett think this was right and the wise thing to do? Ask informally and quietly.*

I knew the answer already. The decision came from on high, from the Nixon Administration—and not from my old friends in the Assistant Secretary of the Army's office. It pained me that I couldn't divulge my source to General Smith.

The Chief of Legislative Liaison, Major General Thomas H. Tackaberry, who worked for the Secretary of the Army, was carrying out political orders when he rejected my compensatory payment schedule. He wrote that my formula was based on highly-speculative assumptions and that such a formula could establish "an undesirable precedent."

Where could I go and what could I do to reverse this defeat? Nowhere to go above the political structure of the Army, I was sure. Nowhere to go in the Nixon Administration. I had been told the reason. Nowhere to go in the Congress, except to Senator Humphrey's staff. I could give them the compensatory payment formula, but that would be disloyal to the Army and I couldn't do that. We had our internal fights, but in the end, the uniform Army on the General Staff supported me. Even if the Congress endorsed my payment formula and passed Humphrey's bill, Nixon would probably veto it. I must do nothing to hurt the chances of the "some compensation position" I had managed to get the Pentagon to support. Those old people needed money now—not a political fight that would surely last beyond their lives.

Humphrey Makes a Move

In order to be successful, I have always believed that everyone had to struggle up to the top of his mountain. However, one must not misjudge it by continuing the climb and falling off the other side where disaster waited. With only lukewarm support from the Pentagon, I knew both Congressman Hawkins' bill, H.R. 4382, and Senator Humphrey's bill, S.1999, were doomed to failure in their present forms. The only thing I could do now was to wait and hope that the "some compensation clause" would stick and at least the $25,000 and $10,000 amounts would survive.

It was now the middle of November. I couldn't wait any longer for some news—good or bad. I called Senator Humphrey's staff and learned that Humphrey, the "old happy warrior," had attached his bill as an amendment to H.R. 9474, the Veterans' Pension bill, and on November 16 both houses had agreed on one bill. The $25,000 and $10,000 survived the conference process. All it needed to become law was the signature of President Nixon.

Thanksgiving passed. I had no word from the White House that Nixon would sign the bill. I knew there were problems over there with the Watergate break-in, and rumors starting to surface that Nixon would resign. After all, it was the height of the Watergate scandal. It might seem ironic, but I hoped he would hold on at least until he could sign that legislation.

66 Years Later, Compensation

Then, on December 5th at three o'clock in the afternoon, I received a call from Roger Currier, Special Assistant to Secretary of the Army, Bo Callaway. He told me that Callaway received a call from the White House staff. President Nixon invited me to the White House to witness the signing of H. R. 9474. I asked Currier if anyone else from the Pentagon were invited. He said, "Nobody else, just you."

On December 6, 1973, at twelve noon, wearing my Dress Blue uniform, I stood in the White House Oval Office and watched President Richard M. Nixon fumble with a fountain pen, struggling to hold it between his fingers. The pen kept slipping out of his sweaty hand as he nervously signed the Veterans' Pension Act, granting $25,000 compensation to the last soldier-survivor of the Brownsville incident, and $10,000 to each surviving widow. Public Law 93-177, 93rd Congress was enacted to take effect on January 1, 1974. After receiving one of the Nixon's souvenir fountain pens, I left the White House, feeling that my job was done.

Well, I was wrong about that. Even before the Act took effect, the day after Nixon signed H.R. 9474 into law, I began receiving telephone calls saying President Nixon had "an interest" in presenting the $25,000 check to Dorsie Willis at the White House. One of the calls was from Donald Johnson, Veterans Affairs Administrator—a man I had belatedly come to respect. He told me that President Nixon "desires Mr. Willis to be brought to the White House for an appropriate ceremony." He asked me to check on the availability of military aircraft to transport Mr. Willis.

Other queries came from the General Counsel of the Veterans' Affairs Committee, Senator Humphrey's office and other congressional leaders. One suggestion was to have the Army bring Willis to Washington, D.C. Bo Callaway would present him with the check in the Pentagon. Congressional leadership responsible for the legislation would be invited to the presentation ceremony as well. Others wanted the Willis family brought into the Capitol Building for the event.

Figure 26. President Richard M. Nixon signs Public Law # 93-177, the Veterans Pension Act December 6, 1973, granting $25,000 to surviving Brownsville Incident Veterans and $10,000 to any unremarried widows. Lt. Col. William Baker, Congressional Leaders, American Legion President and past Presidents, and White House Staff look on. Courtesy White House Communications Agency

Before trying to satisfy all those competing interests, I called the aging Willis on December 7 to determine his wishes in the matter. He said it didn't matter to him. "I will do anything you want me to do." But two days later, Willis told me Congressman Hawkins had asked him to have the ceremony in his office in California.

Before I went any further, I called Willis' doctor, Donald Brown, in Minneapolis and asked him what he thought about it. He said, "Colonel Baker, we're barely keeping Mr.

Willis alive. I don't recommend he take a trip to Washington or California."

Now how was I going to convince these politicians that it was too risky to bring Dorsie Willis to either Washington or California? I had to scare them off. In telephone calls to the various staff people, I simply relayed what Dr. Brown told me, planting seeds of what would be a public relations disaster in their minds. "What if the old man fell dead in the White House Oval Office, on the Pentagon steps or steps at the Capitol Building?" That did it. My telephone stopped ringing.

Secretary of the Army Callaway settled the presentation question. He decided that since almost all of the work, historical and current, which resulted in the exoneration of the Brownsville soldiers, as well as the legislation granting compensation was largely the results of Army initiatives and persistence, it followed that the Army should present the payment check to Mr. Willis. Accordingly, he decided that the ceremony would be conducted at an appropriate place in Willis' hometown. General Smith would represent him—assisted by Major Vincent Gomez and me. Interested congressional leaders would be invited.

The Army published orders making me a Class A agent responsible for drawing the checks on the U.S. Treasury and paying $25,000 to Dorsie Willis and $10,000 to eleven un-remarried Brownsville widows.

On January 10, 1974, General Smith, Vince Gomez, and I traveled to Minneapolis and hosted a presentation ceremony in honor of Dorsie Willis at the Marquette Inn. Near the end of the luncheon ceremony, and after remarks by General Smith and several testimonial speeches by Dorsie Willis'

Figure 27. Dorsie W. Willis, Lone Survivor—1973
With Lt. Col. William Baker and armed escort to deposit compensation
check in the bank.
Courtesy U.S. Army Signal Corps

friends, I presented Mr. Willis with a $25,000 check, and thanks to a ruling from the IRS, it was tax free.

"I'm very grateful for [the check]," Dorsie said. "It's a great birthday present. But it comes too many years too late. I'd hoped for $70,000, figuring $1,000 for each year of the sixty-six years I waited, plus $4,000 for medical costs I've had over the years. But this is all right."

Four years later on August 24, 1977, at the age of 91, Dorsie Willis passed away. Five days later, on a bright sunny day, the now exonerated former soldier was buried with full military honors in the National Cemetery at Fort Snelling, Minnesota. I was there. The Military Honor Guard folded the flag and handed it to me. It was the same flag I had given him at the presentation of his Honorable Discharge certificate. I said a few words at the request of his widow, Olive Willis, and then I presented her with the flag. A lone bugler played taps. The honor guard fired the gun salute and Dorsie Willis, honorably discharged U.S. Army veteran, formerly Company D, Brownsville station, was finally at rest.

Thirty Six

WHO ACTUALLY DID

The Shooting?

Unanswered Questions

MY QUEST FOR ANSWERS to unanswered questions about Brownsville didn't end with the exoneration of the soldiers or with the death of the last survivor. It led me to seek out the white descendants in Brownsville and to go to the old Fort Brown, now partly commercially developed as a resort. The University of Texas at Brownsville and Texas Southmost College occupy part of the old fort, coexisting with some of the old buildings that were standing on the night of the raid.

I located many of the white descendants, but only two of them would talk to me. The others refused. Perhaps they wouldn't want to say anything that might lead to the discovery that one of their grandfathers might have been a murderer.

Ralph Cowen, a prominent citizen and business man, talked with me freely, saying that his mother and some of his older relatives and he believed the black soldiers were dealt a dirty deal by Roosevelt. Cowen said he spent some time in Louis Cowen's old house and saw the bullet holes in it. He drew me a sketch showing where the old house once stood. I talked to Cowen several times over the years and asked him many questions, but he didn't remember hearing anything from his older kinfolks that would give me a clue as to the identity of the raiders. Without my asking, he proudly confirmed his and Louis Cowen's Jewish ancestry.

At the Brownsville Historical Society, I was introduced to Henry Krause, a dignified, well-spoken man who retired as a former State Department diplomat. I was told that he knew a lot about the history of the incident and he did. Starting from old Fort Brown, Krause took me on a walking tour of Brownsville and we retraced the route of the raiders. He pointed out some of the extant buildings and explained where some of the old buildings once stood. We turned the corner from what used to be Cowen Alley, came down 13th Street, turned that corner onto Elizabeth, then walked down a short distance. He paused and pointed to a shabby brick structure. "Over there in that building is where my great-grandfather ran a saloon."

"Who was he?" I asked.

"Joe Crixell."

I didn't tell him that I remembered Joe Crixell all too well from my research. While playing cards in his saloon, he yelled, "Nigger!" when the first shots rang out. "Close up boys, here come the niggers," He said it, without any evidence as to the identity of the raiders. Crixell was gunned down in the middle of Elizabeth Street just a few years after he swore to many lies about the soldiers. Like Ralph Cowen, Henry Krause didn't remember hearing anything from his relatives connected to the identity the raiders.

The Brownsville trail led me further across the Rio Grande River into Matamoros, Mexico, where I followed up on what turned out to be blind leads. Some of the Brownsville residents told me that the answer to who raided the town could be found across the river. I found nothing there.

Who murdered Judge Parks, the creditable witness who saw the raiders but didn't recognize them as black soldiers? That question troubled me. To my disappointment I couldn't find anything that connected Parks' death to the identity of the raiders.

I did find out who killed Judge Welch. He was murdered by Alberto Cabrera from Starr County, Texas, but I was unable to connect Cabrera in any way to the Brownsville Incident.

While unanswered questions and imponderables still dogged me, there were answers to questions about the soldiers that became absolutely clear to me. Did Dorsie Willis and the other 166 men carry secrets to the grave, concealing the identity of the raiders? Hardly. Did the soldiers have a motive for raiding the town? Not likely, and certainly not to protest segregated bars and trivial incidents. This position became especially clear when placed in a larger context of the gravity of the crime.

None of the preceding investigations found one scintilla of evidence that would lead to the conviction of any of the soldiers in a court of law. But somebody did shoot up that town and terrorize its citizens. Who was it? This mystery led me to re-examine the motives of some of the citizens and the key evidence implicating them, which hadn't been done by any of the prior investigators.

The Evidence Re-examined

The evidence was clear that the citizens didn't want black soldiers stationed in their town. Some of them threatened to drive them out in a week or so. The white saloon owners lost money when the white soldiers were replaced by black soldiers. The alleged rape of a white woman whipped up hysteria among the citizens, some of whom openly threatened to attack the fort. All of these facts suggested that some of the town's citizens had a motive to frame the soldiers to provide a pretext to force them from Brownsville.

Given my suspicion that the plot was hatched in Tillman's Ruby Saloon, I found the behavior of John Tillman and his friend, Paulino S. Preciado, the publisher of a local Mexican newspaper, strange.

When the raiders came up Cowen Alley, shooting wildly at every light they saw, Preciado said he heard several shots near the back gate of the Ruby Saloon. He followed the young bartender out the back door of the Ruby Saloon. He claimed he saw the killers come through the open gate from the alley, "advance two or three paces" into the courtyard, and shoot down Frank Natus. Light shining from the saloon's open back door allowed Preciado to recognize the raiders as black soldiers. This is what he told Assistant Attorney General Milton Purdy under oath in December 1907.

But earlier in September, Preciado told a different story to the Grand Jury. He swore he hadn't seen anything. Moreover, on the night of the shooting, he swore to the justice of the peace, who conducted the inquest over the dead body, that unknown parties fired about seven shots inside the courtyard of the Ruby saloon and killed Frank Natus. He said as much in his sworn statement which he wrote out in long hand.

One can pick his or her choice of the contradictory statements to believe. For me, I believe Preciado did see the murderers in the light flowing into the alley from the open back door of the saloon—and he knew who they were.

I believe Frank Natus, the bartender, also saw the killers and recognized them. And that's the key. The raiders realized Natus knew who they were—and killed him for it. And that's also why Preciado swore he didn't recognize the killers in his testimony at the inquest, and he told the Grand Jury the same thing.

Months later in December, when Preciado thought it was safe, he added to the growing body of lies blaming the soldiers. He also thought he could shake down the U.S. government for $10,000 in a lawsuit for an alleged wound where he claimed a bullet grazed his arm.

Not satisfied with Preciado's veracity, I went back to the National Archives and re-examined Frank Natus' original death certificate . It stated:

> There were two bullet holes inflicted by the same projectile. The orifice of entrance was the right side between the 8th and 9th ribs, and the bullet went directly through the body. The orifice of exit was in the left side about two inches lower than the orifice of entrance.

According to Dr. Fred Combe, who examined the body, the wound was caused by a [single] high-power bullet.

I found it remarkable that, if Preciado is to be believed, seven shots were fired at what had to be short range. Only one bullet hit Natus, and that lone bullet was never found. (Or, perhaps never turned in to the authorities.) Maybe somebody found the bullet, disposed of it, or put it in the coffin, and buried it with him.

After re-examining the bartender's death certificate in the National Archives, I traveled to Brownsville and searched for his grave in the old Brownsville City Cemetery, tombstone by tombstone. I found nothing. Finally, and by happenstance, I saw a large, upright, above-ground crypt almost

Figure 28. Frank Natus' Crypt, Old Brownsville City Cemetery
Lt. Col. William Baker's Private Papers
Photo: Joe Hermosa, Brownsville, Texas

hidden by weeds and overgrown brush. There I found the name Frank Natus inscribed among other names of people buried in a marble crypt. A poor man, a boy orphan, buried in that crypt. Why?

After that I turned to Bruce Aiken, historian, author, and member of the Texas Historical Commission. Like many historians, Bruce firmly believed that the soldiers were the raiders, but when I pressed upon him my distrust of Preciado's story and his possible involvement in the plot, he said, "We ought to open the crypt." The crypt was never opened.

John Tillman's behavior in the face of danger that fatal night was extraordinary. His bartender had been shot dead. He knew danger was nearby for anyone foolish or brave enough to go out into streets. Yet Tillman did. Why did he feel safe in walking down the middle of Elizabeth Street during the height of the shooting? If the raiders were black soldiers, why didn't they shoot him? I suspect that Tillman knew the raiders and the raiders knew him.

The jammed rifle story was an oddity, too. Much of what Katie Leahy said she saw was an impossibility, including her tale about seeing a raider's rifle jam. But where did she get that story? Herbert Elkins said he saw the same thing. If they didn't see it, someone must have told them about a raider having trouble with his gun. No black soldier would have known or told her that.

However, there was, in fact, a jammed rifle that night. Jose Garza carried it. He was one of Mayor Combe's part-time policemen who wasn't on duty that night. When Mayor Combe saw him with the rifle, he took it away from him, but noticed that the rifle was jammed. There was an exploded cartridge shell casing in the bore of the gun and the ejector failed to eject it when the gun was fired. Mayor Combe swore to this. Another oddity was Joe Crixell's explanation. The saloon keeper offered a quick, incredulous explanation for the jammed gun. "It doesn't work. It's probably been like that for a long time." Mayor Combe accepted the explanation, but should he have?

That the raiders knew Police Lieutenant Joe Dominguez is beyond a doubt. Four witnesses remembered hearing the raiders call out different versions of the same words, but saying essentially the same thing. "There goes the son of a bitch! Get him! Give it to him. There he goes, shoot him!"

There was no evidence that any of the soldiers even knew Joe Dominguez—and more to the point of motive, Dominguez spoke well of the soldiers and hadn't had any negative contact with them. As far as I could determine, the soldiers didn't have any accounts to settle with the policeman. But the raiders surely did and they tried to kill him.

With the exception of the shooting of Joe Dominguez, which appeared to be the settling of a score, and the killing of Frank Natus, I concluded that the raiders weren't trying to kill anyone, let alone women and children. With the firing of an estimated 300 to 500 rounds of ammunition, it would be a near-miracle that more people weren't killed or wounded, or that more bullet holes weren't found in buildings. Unless the raiders were simply poor marksmen, maybe they weren't really trying to shoot anybody. This latter explanation appeared to me to be more plausible when placed in context with the other facts that I unearthed.

Experience taught me to look for patterns—or the lack of them—in about everything I observe, study, or do. To me it was evident, and it should have been obvious to prior investigators, that because the raiders fired consistently at houses and buildings wherever they saw lights, they created a pattern of their behavior. This was compelling evidence that they were trying to conceal their identity by shooting out the lights. It also suggested to me that the raiders were civilian rather than soldiers.

I say that because I walked and ran the historic route, some 350 yards that the raiders took, to better visualize what happened in 1906. I concluded that the route of the raid into town and back to the fort wasn't favorable to the soldiers. But it was favorable to civilians who could seamlessly melt back into the rush of people running about the town.

No soldiers in their right minds would plan an attack like the Brownsville Affray and seriously believe that it would work. It started with firing from the porches of their barracks (as alleged by the citizens), which would alarm the whole town and wake up the white officers at the fort. Some of their compatriots were then expected to jump the wall, while other soldiers continued to cover the attack by randomly shooting into town, endangering the lives of their fellow soldiers from friendly fire.

To carry out such a plan, they would first have to break into the gun racks or steal the keys from the pockets of the charge of quarters. Then they would have to steal 300 to 500 rounds of ammunition, shoot up the town, sneak back to camp undetected, fall in line, and answer their names at roll call. Later that night they would have to clean their rifles in the dark in order to pass rigid inspections by the white officers and complete all of this activity without being discovered. Yet this fanciful scenario is precisely what some of the citizens claimed happened. It is also what six investigations said occurred, forming the basis for the drastic action taken by President Roosevelt.

The chance that this occurred in the manner alleged was an impossibility that I eliminated. What remained must be the truth. It didn't happen.

Now just for the sake of argument, and maybe a little enlightenment, if some of the soldiers shot up the town, would it be impossible, under the circumstances alleged by the citizens, for dozens of the other soldiers not to know their identities? This line was Roosevelt's argument. If that supposition were true, then the men who knew had kept that secret for years while enduring several investigations, the rigors of cross examinations, and relentless pursuit by detectives and Secret Service agents. They resisted bribes of money, whiskey and employment, and suffered threats of imprisonment and death by hanging in Texas. Was it possible that they could have withstood such an ordeal for years without being discovered or without at least one of them cracking, and pointing the finger at the raiders, if he knew? It was not possible.

The Heart of a Conspiracy

I found creditable evidence that a black citizen of Brownsville named Mack Hamilton knew who the raiders were. Hamilton worked for John Tillman at the Ruby Saloon, primarily serving the few black soldiers who came into his segregated back room. According to Napoleon B. Marshal, a black lawyer, and Brigadier General Aaron S. Daggett, the soldiers' defense counsels during the military court of inquiry hearings, Hamilton said he overheard white civilians in Tillman's Ruby Saloon conspiring to attack the fort. They even asked Hamilton, a former soldier who most likely knew Fort Brown, to be their guide.

On the night of the raid, Sheriff Garza locked up Hamilton and kept him in jail for a week. The detention was for his own protection, since there was a rumor circulating in the Mexican community that Hamilton knew as many as 16 people who made up the shooting party, and that the ringleader was a photographer.

After I examined the sworn testimony of ex-corporal Willie H. Miller, I was convinced that Hamilton had crucial evidence to tell the Senate Committee, the Military Court of Inquiry, and the jury at the court-martial of Major Penrose, but they wouldn't let him testify.

Corporal Miller was Hamilton's cousin. On the night of the raid, Miller was trapped in an uptown Mexican saloon, drinking beer during the shooting. He had been on a 24-hour pass in Mexico and did not know about the curfew. Miller went to Hamilton's house, presumably after the shooting stopped, but before the sheriff threw Hamilton in jail. Miller swore before the court of inquiry that Hamilton told him that the citizens wanted him to join them and to go to the post that night and take somebody out. But he refused. Miller testified that his cousin wouldn't give him the names of the conspirators because he was afraid they might find out that he talked and "people might do something to him down there."

The Senate Committee did, in fact, bring Hamilton to Washington, but found a flimsy excuse for not calling him to testify. "He seemed to be in a terror-stricken frame of mind," Marshal said, further explaining that Hamilton was afraid of retribution against his family and wanted transportation for them to be moved out of Brownsville. It appeared that even the U.S. Senate was afraid to put him on the stand for what was termed as a case of "extreme humanity...." Or were the senators afraid that his testimony would break the case wide open and embarrass a sitting President?

Later that year, Captain Howland, the recorder "prosecutor" for the Court of Inquiry, also wouldn't allow Hamilton to testify. Howland opposed the subpoena for Hamilton, offering a thin excuse, "There is no money to bring Hamilton here."

Even at Penrose's court-martial, the defense counsel for Penrose was unable to get Hamilton to testify before the court. He was too frightened to take the stand.

The absence of any bullet holes in any of the buildings at Fort Brown gave rise to the question, "If the Brownsville people did the shooting, isn't it remarkable that not a single building at Fort Brown was struck?" In my opinion, that kind of reasoning ignores testimony that the soldiers heard bullets whistling high over the garrison, and Mayor Combe's testimony that some of the citizens fired at the Fort. The easy conclusion is that the raiders didn't hit anything simply because they aimed high.

But Hamilton had a better answer:

> It was their purpose to shoot over the buildings and not to shoot into them...the object being to draw the men out and draw their fire, so it would appear that the men did the shooting there in the city of Brownsville.

I believe that baiting the soldiers to shoot back into the town was at the heart of the plot of the Brownsville, Texas, conspiracy.

At the end of my search for evidence, I reflected on the incident, its aftermath, relevancy, and ramifications. What was it all about? I knew it was not just about a 10-minute shooting spree in Brownsville, Texas. It was about much more, and to me, it was not simply about racism, although there was plenty of that. Numerous threads came to my mind—honor versus dishonor, mass punishment versus individual guilt, manifest error, an error so egregious that it was deemed bad on its face, injustice versus justice, due process of law, the presumption of innocence, and other constitutional guarantees vs. the summary action of President Roosevelt to punish by executive order. It was about all of those themes intertwined with the principle that might makes right—a throwback beyond the Enlightenment to medieval times and the ancient Greeks. Of course, President Roosevelt was a modern man. But with the Brownsville Incident, he still believed that might made right. Therefore, he, the President, the stronger, the most powerful, decided what was right and imposed his will on the weaker.

Knowing that might makes right won in Brownsville and Washington for 66 years caused me to distrust certain judicial expressions that often give the illusion of justice—the sort of stereotyped bromides that politicians and judges are given to, such as, "All men are equal before the law," and the inscription over the U.S. Supreme Court building, "Equal justice under law." President Roosevelt made similar statements as he rationalized his action against the Brownsville soldiers. His statements were barren then, and such lofty pronouncements are barren now, and will always be barren, for they assume the law is just.

I am convinced that justice is not always inspired or achieved by the law, and certainly not by well-meaning platitudes, and not even by just having constitutional rights. Those rights must be activated. It was goodness, the God within, and struggle that achieved a measure of justice for the soldiers. What they got was delayed, imperfect, but redemptive. Truth prevailed. And in this case, "truth crushed to the earth" did rise again.

Too many innocent people live out their lives in prison waiting for justice.

Noted historian and winner of the Pulitzer Prize, Doris Kearns Goodwin, in her book *The Bully Pulpit*, wrote, "Roosevelt's handling of the Brownsville affair is a permanent scar on his legacy."

Morris, Edmund. Historian Theodore Rex (Modern Library Paperback Edition 2002) left no doubt that the evidence showed that the "black soldiers were innocent, and Roosevelt knew it."

It is my position as well—that the black soldiers were innocent and President Roosevelt knew it. All of the facts and evidence that I excavated so many years after the incident pointed to the truth. But what more could the black soldiers have done to prove their innocence? Nothing.

Thirty Seven

THE OFFICER'S FATES

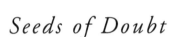

Seeds of Doubt

A Change of Mind?

PRESIDENT ROOSEVELT WROTE A letter to the Secretary of War, William Howard Taft requesting whether the white officers "are or not blamable." He ordered a "thorough investigation."

Major Penrose was acquitted of the charge of "neglect of duty, to the prejudice of good order and military discipline" for his men's alleged culpability in the Brownsville raid. Penrose recanted his earlier report that the black soldiers under his command raided the town.

Captain Edgar A. Macklin was tried by court-martial in April 1907 for neglect of duty on one count, having been the officer of the day on August 13, 1906. He was acquitted.

Captain Samuel P. Lyon was tried by court-martial and acquitted.

These white officers were acquitted using the same evidence that Roosevelt denied to the black soldiers.

Sometime later, after the President drummed out the black soldiers, he was walking along the Potomac River with Owen Wister. They were old friends.

Apparently, President Roosevelt had a change in mind about the disparity in his treatment of the black soldiers and their white officer's commanders, especially after talking to Owen Wister.

"When you turned those niggers out of the army at Brownsville," Owen Wister asked Roosevelt, "Why didn't you order a court of inquiry for the commissioned officers?"

"Because I listened to the War Department, and I shouldn't [have]," Roosevelt replied. He paused. "Of course, I can't know all about everything."

Defensively, he launched into a long disquisition on the fickleness of financial advisors. Wister heard him out.

Roosevelt continued, "And so, the best you can do is to stop, look and listen—and then jump... Yes. And then jump. And hope I've jumped right."

Extraordinary, I thought. Roosevelt entertained the thought that he could have made a mistake in dishonorably discharging all 167 black soldiers. He was not sure if he did the right thing. He just didn't know. He hoped he did. Too late, too late.

The defense counsel for Major Penrose in his court-martial said:

> *...but we become a world power, and while I recognize and appreciate that, certainly during this generation, and whether there is going to be prejudice against the negro,...I certainly hope for the good of this country — and that the time is not very far distant — when the uniform of the United States will protect the black man or the brown man, just as it does the white man. That prejudice is of that general nature that we all recognize against*

the negro race... but particularly against the African; but I certainly hope that we, and each of us, will make it our effort to cultivate sentiment in this country that will protect these colored men...

Unfortunately for the black troops of the 25th Infantry stationed in Brownsville on August 13, Texas, 1906, Roosevelt's later doubts notwithstanding, that sentiment did not arrive in time to save them.

Author's Bio

Lieutenant Colonel (RET) William Baker was born November 26, 1931 and grew up in Amsterdam, Georgia. When he was 11 months old, he was adopted by Angeline and Ned Keaton after the death of his mother, Julianne Lee Baker, and the remarriage of his father, Roosevelt Baker. Angeline, and Ned Keaton, a freed slave, raised him as their grandson.

Baker graduated valedictorian of his class from the college preparatory program of Attapulgus (Georgia) Vocational High School in 1949. He was a Georgia State Quiz Contest winner, earning a full scholarship to Howard University, where he graduated *cum laude*. The top-ranked cadet in the ROTC program there, he received the Distinguished Military Graduate Award.

The author received his MBA in Controllership from Syracuse University, distinguishing himself at the Ballistic Research Laboratories, Aberdeen Proving Ground, Maryland. While at Aberdeen, he published *The Role of Cost Discounting in Weapons Systems Evaluations* in 1969. It was co-authored with his assistant Robert Williams and published by the U.S. Department of Commerce which sold it around the world for more than 40 years. This work is now archived by the National Science Foundation.

He was assigned to the Office of Equal Opportunity at the Pentagon in 1972 where, in addition to other duties, he developed Operation Aware in conjunction with the White House staff, which permitted black soldiers to air their concerns directly to influential black businessmen and the Department of the Army.

Bill Baker's crowning life's achievement was the reinvestigation of the Brownsville Texas Incident of 1906. After extensive research, he prepared a case for the Secretary of the Army that resulted in the reversal of President Theodore Roosevelt's decision to dishonorably discharge the soldiers of the First Battalion, Twenty-fifth Infantry. Based on Baker's research, the Secretary of the Army made the decision to correct the injustice and change the soldiers' discharge to 'Honorable.'

The resolution was signed by President Richard M. Nixon, bringing national acclaim to Baker and the United States Army. Baker received the coveted Pace Award from the Secretary of the Army and the Legion of Merit in 1973 as a result of his painstaking work.

Secretary of the Army Robert F. Froehlke described Baker's contributions best when he said, "Baker's achievement has brought favorable acclaim to the Army in the field of Civil Rights and has had a positive commitment to elimination of racial injustice."

Baker is also the recipient of two Bronze Stars, two commendation medals with oak leaf clusters, and other medals for service in Korea, NATO, and Vietnam. In his post-military retirement, he was employed as a financial manager for Rohm and Haas Chemical Company, Philadelphia, PA, (now Dow Chemical), and retired in 1993.

He was a member of Alpha Phi Alpha Fraternity and a charter member of the Delta Epsilon Boule, Sigma Pi Phi Fraternity. Though Lieutenant Colonel Baker died on September 24, 2018 just weeks after the ink on the final page of his manuscript had dried, his wife, Dr. Bettye Foster Baker, has brought his important work to light through the publication of this book.

Source Notes

The reconstruction is based primarily on official government reports and on original source documents in the US National Archives. The original source documents are located in boxes 4499 through 4504, the adjutant general document file number 1135832. I have referenced many of these materials in the narrative of the book. By far the most important materials I have relied on were—the sworn affidavits, depositions, testimony of the soldiers, townspeople and officials; court-martial records and technical reports by ballistic experts and others.

The government reports constituted the official records of the Brownsville Affray as the incident was called at that time in history. These records included three presidential messages, War Department reports, the hearings of the Senate Military Affairs Committee, the courts-martial reports of Major Charles W. Penrose and Captain Edward Macklin, and the military court of inquiry proceedings, all published by the US Government Printing Office in Washington. D.C. These published reports included many volumes, some of which constituted thousands of pages. They purported to tell the story of what really happened at Brownsville. Although these published government documents offered valuable information, as I reviewed and analyzed them, I grew to distrust much of their information and I rejected many of their conclusions.

Other sources included telegrams, cablegrams, memoirs, contemporary newspaper accounts, letters, and autobiographical materials of some of the major characters.

The second part of the book, My Quest for Justice, is based largely upon the evidence culled from the same government records and the same original source documents in the National Archives I relied upon for the reconstruction, plus official government letters and memoranda from 1971 to 1974, my interviews with the last surviving soldier, Dorsie Willis, my private papers and memory.

Selected Bibliography

National Archives
700 Pennsylvania Avenue, NW
Washington, DC 20408

Library of Congress
101 Independence Avenue, SE
Washington, DC 20540

The Law Library in the Pentagon
1400 Defense Pentagon
Arlington, VA 22202

U.S. Army War College
Army Heritage and Education Center
950 Soldiers Drive. Carlisle Barracks, PA 17013-5021

The Brownsville Historical Association (Society)
641 E Washington St.
Brownsville, TX 78520

The University of Texas at Brownsville
1 W University Blvd
Brownsville, TX 78520

Books

Dostoyevsky, Fyodor, 2001. *Crime and Punishment* Translated by Constance Garnett. Dover Publication, Mineola, New York.

"His profound understanding of the tragic side of life and the workings of the psyche make him one of the greats of Russian literature. His fascination with the theme of crime and the problem of conscience arose from his own firsthand experience." Dostoyevsky's protagonist...experiences a profound sense of alienation from humanity after his crime, and his isolation from society accentuates his moral dilemma. Embodied in this inward struggle is the notion of good and evil vying for supremacy of the soul, and a recurring of Dostoyevsky."

Voltaire, 1884. *Candide*, Edited by Francois-Marie Arouet, 112 pages. (0-486-6689-3).

Doctor Pangloss in Voltaire's Candide, a Satire, proclaimed that "This is the best of all possible world," notwithstanding all kinds of disasters he encountered.

Goodwin, Doris Kearns, 2013. *The Bully Pulpit*. Simon and Schuster, p 515

"Roosevelt's handling of the Brownsville affair is a permanent scar on his legacy."

Morris, Edmund. Historian, 2002 *Theodore Rex* (Modern Library Paperback Edition).

Morris said that Roosevelt had a failure when he agreed with the white citizens of Brownsville and had succumbed to white racist pressure.

Alighieri, Dante. *The Divine Comedy, 1935*. A long poem in book style. Sources of the select passages are: The Divine Comedy of Dante Alighieri 1265-1321. Inferno, Purgatory, Paradise, New York: The Union Library Association, Print.

Inscription over the gates of hell. "Abandon hope all ye who enter here." [37749].

BDH	*Brownsville Daily Herald*
CI	Senate Document, 701, 61st Congress, 3rd Session. (1910).

Report of the Proceedings of the Court of Inquiry Relative to the Shooting at Brownsville, TX. Twelve Volumes. (US Government Printing Office 1911).

DA	Department of the Army
CMA Com- mittee	On Military Affairs, U.S. Senate. Senate Document, 402, 60th Congress, 1st Session (1907).

Affray At Brownsville, Tex. Hearing Before the Committee on Military Affairs, US Senate. (US Government Printing Office 1907).

DAML	Department of the Army Memoranda, Letters and Notes, 1971-1974.

These documents are listed by their subjects and file symbols. They should be available at Department of the Army or its record storage facilities.

NAUS	National Archives—boxes 4499 through 4504, the adjutant general document file number 1135832.
NYT	*New York Times*
PG- CM-M	*Affray at Brownsville, Texas, August 13 and 14,* 1906. Proceeding of a General Court Martial...in the Case of Edgar A. Macklin, (Government Printing Office 1907).
PG- CM-M	*Affray at Brownsville, Texas, August 13 and 14,* 1906. Proceeding of a General Court Martial...in the Case of Edgar A. Macklin, (Government Printing Office 1907).
PGCM-P	*Affray at Brownsville, Texas, August 13 and 14,* 1906. Proceeding of a General court Martial...in the Case of Major Charles W. Penrose, (Government Printing Office 1907).
SD-155 Part 1	Senate Document, 155, 59h Congress, 2d Session, 1906. Summary Discharge or Mustering Out of Regiments or Companies. Message From The President of the United States (US Government Printing Office 1906).
SD-155 Part 2	Senate Document, 155, 59th Congress, 2d Session, 1907. Summary Discharge or Mustering Out of Regiments or Companies. Message From The President of the United States (US Government Printing Office 1907).
SD-389	Senate Document, 389, 60th Congress, 1st Session (1908). The Brownsville Affray.
SD-430	Senate Document, 430, 60th Congress, 1st Session (1908). Names of Enlisted Men Discharged on Account of Brownsville Affray with Applications for Reenlistment.

SD-587   Senate Document, 587, 60th Congress, 2nd Session
            (1908). Special Message of the President of the United
            States. Contains the Report of Investigation of Mr. Her-
            bert J. Brown. (US Government Printing Office 1908).

SR-355   Senate Report No.355, Parts 1 and 2, 60th Congress, 1st
            Session (1908). The Brownsville Affray. (US Government
            Printing Office 1908).

WBPP   William Baker Private Papers.

Newspapers

BDH   *The Brownsville Daily Herald.* Aug. 14,1906.

            "The Brownsville Raid. EVIDENCE POWERFUL AND
            COMPELLING." Retired Lt. Colonel William Baker led
            the government's investigation into the 1906 Brownsville
            Raid. This is his account of that time. SPECIAL TO THE
            HERALD:

            Their contents proved surprising. It was found that no ev-
            idence had been gathered to prove a conspiracy of silence
            on the part of the members of the battalion. The whole pro-
            ceeding in fact was based on the assumption of the officers
            who made the inquiry that those who did not take part in the
            riot at Brownsville 'must know' who did.

SPPE   *St. Paul Pioneer Press*, St. Paul., MN, Monday, February
            12, 1973

TBHC   *The Brownsville Heritage Complex*

WP   *Washington Post*

Periodicals

JBB   Bishop, Joseph Bucklin. *Theodore Roosevelt and his Time.*
            (Scribner's, 1920.)

JMC   Carroll, John M. *Twenty Fifth Infantry,* (The Old Army
            Press, 1972).

CC   Clark, Champ. *My Quarter Century of American Politics,*
            (Harper's, 1920).

DB   Du Bois, W.E.B. *The Souls of Black Folks.*

AWD   Dunn, Arthur Wallace

JBF   Foraker, Joseph Benson, 1916, *Notes of a Busy Life* (2 vols.),
            (Stewart and Kidd Co., Cincinnati,1916.)

JBF   Foraker, Joseph Benson, April,1908, *A Review of the Tes-*
            timony in the Brownsville Investigation, (North American
            Review, April 1908.)

JF   Foraker, Julia Bundy. I would Live It Again (Harper's, 1932).

JH   Franklin, John Hope. From Slavery to Freedom (Knopf, 1967).

CF   Fuller, Charles. The Brownsville Raid. (A Play by Charles Fuller produced by the Negro Ensemble Company, 133 Second Avenue, New York City, 1975)

EM   Morris, Edmund. Theodore Rex (Modern Library Paperback Edition 2002).

ABP   Paine, Albert Bigelow. Captain Bill McDonald: Texas Ranger (J.J. Little & Ives Co., New York, 1909).

HFP   Pringle, Henry F. Theodore Roosevelt (Harcourt, Brace, 1931).

MCT   Terrell, March Church. A Colored Woman in a White World (Ransdell Inc Publishers, Washington, D.C., Arno Press, New York, 1980).

NYT   Speaking less charitably of Garlington's report, the New York Times characterized it as:

            Extraordinary...Not a particle of evidence is given in the 112 pages of the document to prove that any enlisted man had certain knowledge of the identity of any participants in the riot. (November 22, 1906).

JAT   Tinsley, James A. The Brownsville Affray. (Master of Arts Thesis, University of North Carolina, Chapel Hill, 1948).

            —"Roosevelt, Foraker, and the Brownsville Affray" (Journal of Negro History, January 1956).

JEW   Watson, James E. As I knew Them. (Bobbs-Merrill, 1935).

JDW-1   Weaver, John D. The Brownsville Raid. Paperback. (W.W. Norton & Co., Inc, New York, 1973).

JDW-2   —The Senator and the Sharecropper's Son: Exoneration of the Brownsville Solders (College Station, 1997)

Backstory

4 Brownsville Awaits the Final Decision

The fact that a certain amount of race prejudice: SD-155 Part 1, p.301.

He's been fornicating with a Mexican woman: "3rd Indorsement. Fort Reno, Okla, Jan.16, 1906 [1907]" to letter from Sam P. Wreford to President Theodore Roosevelt 1-3-07. NA.

...he's not a resident, and hasn't paid his taxes in several years: Ibid. he was, in fact, a resident of Mexico! Ibid.

These are the brave soldiers who captured El Caney: BDH, 7/31/06, pp. 1,3. "Talks About a Fight." he began to read from the paper: Ibid, p.1.

...he even practices nepotism with his sister: I first heard about this type of demagoguery used in the old South by George Smathers against the late Senator Claude Pepper in a race for the U. S. Senate in Florida during the 1950s.

5 Buffalo Soldiers Are Coming To Brownsville

The people in Texas are gonna give you hell! Don't go down there: This account was drawn from the deposition of John Amos Holomon, January 8, 1908, p.24. NA.

...the five white officers dreaded taking these black troops to Texas: SD-701, p. 1625.

He had been schooled at West-Point: SR-355, Part 2. p. 2. Officials at West Point deny that Penrose was a graduate. Letter to Lt. Col Baker, 12/13/2002 from US Military Academy. WBPP. From the standpoint of health and physique: The description of Major Penrose was based on his medical records as recorded by doctors at Walter Reed Army General Hospital. NA. "these damn niggers trading down here." CI, p. 724.

6 The Troops Go To Town

It seems kinda funny, I can't buy salve in a drugstore: PGCM-P, p. 1090. ...you black son-of-a bitch, don't you know this is a white man's town: Deposition, Private McGuire taken by Lt. Col. L. A. Lovering. NA. Also see SD 155-PART 1, p. 160.

It was rumored that back in 1904 Bugs headed a secret society of thugs: This account of Bugs' character was drawn from a sworn statement dated January, 1907 by Samuel P. Holman. It was attached to a letter from Holman to Roosevelt, December 30, 1908. Holman was a deserter from the Army when he made the statement to Detective Browne. NA.

Private John Amos Holomon...had a talent for making money: The description of Holomon's money making ventures was taken from his deposition. NA.

Then he began pistol-whipping him about the head and shoulders: There are several versions of Tate's pistol-whipping of Private Newton's version is in his affidavit, Penrose reporting, SD 155-PART 1, p. 69. Tate's version, SD 155-PART 2, pp. 454-455. Deposition, Private Frank J. Lipscomb, taken by Lt. Col. L. A. Lovering: NA. Also see SD 155-PART 1, p. 133. Ibid, pp. 209-210.

"You damned niggers are too smart around here, anyway.": SD 155-PART 2, p. 479.

7 THE YELLOW ROSE OF TEXAS

"That's a colored soldier's song.": The best historic evidence I could find shows that the song "The Yellow Rose of Texas" was probably written by a black person. Private Reid was correct. The song had been sung by black soldiers for years, long before Texas became a state. There was a fair skin African American woman named Emily West Morgan who was "The Yellow Rose of Texas." See In Search of the 'Yellow Rose of Texas' by Mark Whitelaw. http://www.markw.com/yelrose.htm.

Mrs. Evans, a white woman, alleged that she had been accosted by a big black soldier: PGCM-P, pp. 1146-1148."...report this outrage on my wife.": CMA, p. 2381."...with the number of Mexican prostitutes in this town, I hardly think rape would be necessary.": PGCM-P, p. 1147. Also see "...as prostitutes are too common in town.": SD 155-PART 1, p. 69.

8 MIDNIGHT ATTACK ON BROWNSVILLE, AUGUST 13, 1906

...a big black dog had cornered several children who were huddled in a group: PGCM-M, p.181....then Trooper began racing up and down along the wall, barking loudly: PGCM-M, p. 61....sixteen to twenty men emerged from the darkness near the garrison wall: The location of the beginning of the attack was reconstructed from the testimony of the two most credible witnesses in a position to know. Testimony of Private Joseph H. Howard, Sentinel on Post No. 2.: PGCM-M, p .60. Also see: PGCM-P, pp. 1057-1058. See deposition of Matias G. Tamayo, post scavenger [garbage collector] 12/29/06, p. 2. NA.

...a single frame house...stood alone, its lights still burning: The description of Cowen's House, how it was shot up, and how the family was terrorized was drawn from the testimony of Anna A. Cowen. CMA, p. 2790-2803. A student lamp...was shot out. The lantern in the kitchen...shattered with a single shot, as was a large Rochester lamp. Ibid., pp. 2794, 2795. The raiders were bent on shooting out the lights for obvious reason.

"Madame, Madame! 'Tis the day of judgment!": Ibid., p. 2794. "The soldiers are going to kill us.": Ibid.

Louis Cowen's house was being shot up: Anna Cowen and her husband Louis Cowen testified that the soldiers did not have a "grudge" against their family. Ibid., pp. 2796, 2809-2810.

...they fired sporadically at the Western Union Telegraph building, Yturria's house, and Martinez's Cottage from their position in Cowen's Alley: I reconstructed the route of the attack from the trail of damages and by sorting out the conflicting testimony of many witnesses. Also see map of Brownsville: JAT, p. xvi.

"Git the light.": The single shot missed the oil lamp in Hale Odin's room in the Miller Hotel. Deposition of Hale Odin before Assistant Attorney General Purdy, 1/4/07, pp. 7-9. NA.

"Close up your doors. Here come the niggers.": Joe Crixell's testimony, CMA, pp. 2483-2518.

Mr. S. C. More testified he heard a raider say, "There go the son of a bitch. Let's git 'im.": Deposition of S.C. Moore, January 1, 1907, p. 1. NA. "The colored soldiers are firing into houses and killing the people!": PGCM-P, p. 118. Policeman Dominguez testified he heard the raiders say, "Give him hell.": Ibid., p. 118. ...fired a volley in the direction of the policeman, shooting him in the arm and shooting his horse: Ibid.

...one of the men was having trouble with his gun: CMA, pp. 2893-2923. "Don't go out! I heard noises in the alley.": See Nicholas S. Alanis' testimony. PGCM-P, pp. 422-427. Also see his testimony before Assistant Attorney General Purdy, pp. 100-102. "A group of five or six armed men appeared in the alley and fired.": Preciado's testimony before Assistant Attorney General Purdy. NA. Frank exclaimed, Ay Dios and fell down.": See contradiction in Paulino Preciado's testimony before the grand jury, p. 1. NA.

A lantern was burning in Fred Starck's house. A hail of bullets hit the two-story house, knocking out the lantern: CMA, p. 154. "Fred, hug the wall. They are shooting down the street.": CMA, p. 2383. "Don't go any farther, mayor. You will be shot.": Ibid., p. 2384. "What are you doing with that rifle, Garza?: Ibid. ...there was an empty cartridge inside the magazine, which the ejector had failed to eject: See Joe Crixill's testimony. Ibid., p. 2515.

9 DID THE SOLDIERS SHOOT UP THE TOWN OF BROWNSVILLE?

"I saw Colored soldiers." "...the soldiers have shot up the town.": That was the "universal expression." CMA, p. 2385. "I don't know what the word fear means.": PGCM-P, p. 86. "Yellow Nigger with Spots.": WP, (June 7, 1907). Also see PGCM-P, p. 86. "I served with those troops, ...know them to be...efficient...splendidly armed... valuable lives will be lost.": CMA, p. 2386. Your men have gone into town... killed one man...": Ibid., p. 2387. "... I can hardly believe that...": Ibid. ...no evidence that any weapons had been fired: Ibid., pp. 1933-1934. "Well, Macklin, it looks as if our men...": Ibid., pp. 1933. "...what do you think of this evidence? Your men did this.": Ibid., p. 2392. "...this is almost conclusive evidence,...": Ibid.

11 INVESTIGATIONS BY THE CITIZENS' COMMITTEE AND PENROSE

"... your men did this shooting.": CMA, pp. 2394-2395. "No one else has those arms or ammunition.": Ibid., p. 2395. "I would give my right arm...": Ibid. "Regret to report serious shooting...": SD 155-PART 2, pp. 430-431. "We know that this outrage...": SD 155-PART 2, p. 449. 'God damn him!': Ibid. "I don't know if they were Negroes...,": Ibid. "...we ask you to have the troops... removed... and replaced by white soldiers."...": Telegram to Roosevelt from Citizens Committee, 8/15/06. SD 155-PART 1, pp. 20-21.

'Come out, you black sons of bitches.': Affidavit of Private Map, 9/25/06. SD 155-PART 2, p. 516. '... we will kill all of you.': Affidavit of Private Rudy, 9/12/06. SD 155-PART 2, pp. 512-513. "I saw some civilians running ...": Affidavit of Corporal John H. Hill, 9/24/06, p. 69. NA. "After further investigation...": Telegram, Penrose to Military Secretary, Dept. of Texas, 8/14/06. NA.

12 THE BLOCKSOM INVESTIGATION

"SAVE US FROM NIGGER HUSBANDS.": JDW-1, p.115. "The cause of the disturbance...": SD 155-PART 1, p. 38. ...recommended the removable: Ibid. "Our position is misunderstood.": SD 155-PART 1, p. 26. Roosevelt approved ...recommendation... ordered the removal: SD 155-PART 1, pp. 34-35.

13 A TEXAS RANGER COMES TO TOWN

...don't have the authority to enter the fort: I based this account on, ABP, p. 324. "...that Brownsville business." Ibid. "Why, them hellions...": Ibid. McDonald faced down: I based this account on Paine's book. Ibid., p. 198. "...you'd like to take it up.": Ibid. "...done took it up.": Ibid. "I'm Captain McDonald...here to investigate...show you niggers something...Put up them guns!": Ibid., p. 328. Quotations are from McDonald' autobiography as told to Paine. "You, as their officers, ...": Ibid., p. 337. "Judge, nobody gonna move...": Based in part from Paine. Ibid., p. 345. "Military authorities are trying to take our prisoners...": Ibid., p. 346.

15 FORT RENO

Author's note. I have named the hills the troops ran up and down after two hills at Fort Knox, Kentucky that I used to drill my troops on during basic training.

17 A CONSPIRACY OF SILENCE

He imbibed too much and fell out the window: Senator Foraker questioned whether Judge Parks was pushed or fell out the window. CMA, p. 2423. He didn't see a single soldier on the streets: Deposition of Wilbert Voshelle, 10/24/06, p.1. NA. "That the raiders were soldiers… cannot be doubted.": SD 155-PART 2, p. 427. "All enlisted men of the three companies present…discharged … without [honor]…": Ibid., p. 429. "It must be confessed that the colored soldier is much more aggressive…": Ibid., p. 430.

18 THE GRAND JURY INVESTIGATES

"[the] unprovoked, murderous midnight assault…": CMA, pp. 3297-3298. …the soldiers now being held in jail were entitled to go free: SD 155-PART 1, pp. 107-108. "…evidence did not point with sufficient certainty to any individual…": CMA, p.3242. "The reasons for the selecting of these men…": SD 155-PART 1, p.66.

19 THE ULTIMATUM

"…to secure information that will lead to the apprehension and punishment…": SD 155-PART 2, p. 527. "…every black soldier stationed at Fort Brown would be discharged 'without honor…": Ibid. "I lived with them,…": CMA, p. 2733. "The action of President Roosevelt in entertaining that nigger, …": Quote is from the Y

"You have until nine o'clock…": SD 155-PART 2, p. 530. "Unless you men with guilty knowledge come forward….": Ibid., p. 527. "All of you have entered into a general understanding …": Ibid., p. 529. All of them must be punished: Ibid., p. 531. "Theodore Roosevelt came to me, …shared our supply of hardtack with his command.": Affidavit of Sergeant Mingo Sanders, 9/24/06, p.1. NA. Sergeant Mingo Sanders knew Colonel Roosevelt in Cuba and thought he would not let him down.

20 PRESIDENT ROOSEVELT MAKES HIS DECISION

"…blacker than black….": Roosevelt said, "A blacker never…" SD-389, p. 14. …calling them murderers, midnight assassins, criminals: See Roosevelt messages to the senate. Ibid., pp. 14-20. …accused all of them of engaging in a conspiracy of silence: Ibid., p. 14. Roosevelt made his decision. Ibid., p. 8. War Department issued Special Order 266: NA. Also see SD-389, pp .8-10.

21 A PUBLIC OUTCRY

"…I've come on behalf of the colored soldiers.": The major source I have used on Taft's suspension of Roosevelt's order is the account given by Mary Church Terrell in her memoir. MCT, pp.268-271. …suspend the order dismissing the soldiers…": Ibid. "Is that all you want me to do, Mary?": Ibid. "…suspend an order issued by the President of the United States…" Ibid. He suspended the order of the President: SD 155-Part 1, p.187. Also see NYT, 9/20/1906,

p. 1. "Discharge is not to be suspended ...": JAT, pp. 51-52. Taft revokes suspension. SD 155-Part 1, p. 189.

22 WITHOUT HONOR

"There go the best men, the best soldiers...": The source of this quote is an interview with Major Penrose in the Washington, DC. Evening Star,9/27/06. Roosevelt complained about the article. See letter from the White House to Taft, 9/27/06. NA

23 THE GRIDIRON CLUB DINNER DEBATE

Roosevelt and Foraker were destined to collide: The major sources I used for reconstruction of the debate are cited here in their short form abbreviations. CC, pp. 443-449; JEW, pp. 70-73; AWD, pp. 178-189; JBB, pp. 31-32; JBF, pp. 249-257; WP, 1/28/07. "I wants to see de President. I'se an old nigger...": JDW-2, p. 125. "All coons look alike to me.": AWD, p. 180. Also see JEW, p.71. The Mob! The Mob! The Mob!: JBF, p. 255. "The government ought not to conduct the business.": Quote is from a speech TR gave in Harrisburg, Pennsylvania on 10/4/06. JBB, p.32. He shook his fist: CC, p. 445. "No man in this country is so high: JBF, p. 251. ...When legal and human rights are involved.": Ibid. "...academic discussion.": Ibid., p. 255. "Mr. President, there was a time.": Ibid., p. 252. "Some of those men were bloody butchers...ought to be hung.": CC, P.447.

24 THE LAST INVESTIGATIONS

Louis Cowen was the head devil...Cowen was really ...": AJL, p.64. Brown & Baldwin detectives spread out: See letter from Browne to Taft, 5/9/1908. NA. Browne reported...that Boyd Conyers...had confessed: Letter from H. J. Browne to G.B. Davis, JAG, 6/15/08. NA. "I have...sufficient evidence...to convict, and hang...": Letter from H. J. Browne to G.B. Davis, JAG, 7/30/08. NA. "This report enables us...": SD-587, p. 3. "It's the most absolutely false...": JBF, p. 306.

It was signed into law...creating a military court of inquiry: JAT, p. 124. It concluded that the soldiers shot up the town: CI, p. 1635. ...allowed fourteen men to re-enlist: Ibid.

25 THE PENTAGON 1972

"....supplemented it in the shape of a successful conspiracy of silence...,: SD 389, p. 14.

26 SEARCH FOR EVIDENCE OF A CONSPIRACY OF SILENCE

"Almost no evidence against men arrested...,": SD 155-PART 2, p. 437. Testimony as to the expression heard...–'Black sons of bitches...,: Ibid., p. 458. "The following men...prove an alibi.": Ibid., p. 457. "The President directs that you proceed ...": Ibid., p. 527. "The uniform denial indicated a possible general understanding

...but I could find no evidence of such understanding.": Ibid., p. 529. "I could get no information ...assumed a wooden, stolid look...": Ibid., p. 528. "The secretive nature of the race...,": Ibid. "...plenty of precedents for the action taken.": SD 389, p. 15. "[I] lay before the Senate the following facts...": Ibid., p. 11. "...the evidence proves conclusively that a number of soldiers...": Ibid., p. 14. "There contents proved surprising.": NYT, 11/22/1906. "Extraordinary...Not a particle of evidence...": Ibid.

28 JAG Sets the Legal Parameters

...he had written several premises: DAML, file symbol: DAJA-AL 1972/4430 (20 Jun 72). Memo Col. Williamson to Maj. Baker, 30 Jun 1972. Affirmative Action by DA to Re-characterize Discharges as a Result of the Brownsville Incident.

30 The Leckie and Wiegenstein Experiments

Roosevelt ended the letter..., "Please report to me on all of his evidence.": NA.

"The reason that I say that they were not fired from B barracks...": CMA, p. 3222. ...they had to be fired from the rear: PGCM-P, pp. 1126-1127.

Wiegenstein set up experiments: Ibid., pp. 989-1028. ...which way are the men facing?: Ibid., p.1012. "I don't care to tell you...": Ibid. "I would like to see white men...want to see if I can detect ....": Ibid, p. 991. "I informed all of observers...": Ibid. "There's Wiegenstein...": Ibid., p.997. But the man who had on the cap was the black sergeant: Ibid.

31 The Eyewitnesses

Since Roosevelt cited what he termed "scores of eyewitnesses": SD 389, p. 11. "... that there is no possibility of their having been mistaken": SD 389, p. 20.

Rendall, ... was the first witness to take the stand: See Rendall's testimony. PGCM-P, pp. 6-25, 43-45. Mrs. Rendall, George Rendall's wife, followed him to the stand: PGCM-P, pp. 25-43.

Katie Leahy, the prized witness of the investigators: Ibid., pp. 73-93. The defense counsel characterized Katie Leahy...": Ibid., p. 1230. "I saw through the leaves.": CMA, p. 2902.

Only Herbert Elkins' testimony was more absurd: PGCM-P, pp. 442-479. ...he said they were nigger soldiers: Ibid., p. 443. By the way they were dressed, he knew "they were niggers by looking at them.": Ibid. "They had on khaki pants...": Ibid. "You answer the question!: Ibid., p.473.

...in Dominguez's own words he stated that he got confused: Ibid., p. 131. ...he admitted that another policeman...he knew nothing of his own knowledge: Ibid., pp. 130-131. "I would like to state to this court that I get so confused…": Ibid, p. 131. See Dominguez's testimony. Ibid., pp. 116-153.

Most troublesome to me was the testimony of Paulino S. Preciado. See his testimony to Assistant Attorney General Purdy. NA. …the last person to see the bartender alive: Ibid. I returned to the original sworn statement, given to the Grand Jury. **"I couldn't see anybody in the alley, as it was dark out there and I was in the light. I heard no word spoken.":** Ibid.

32 THE PROOF

"That's one of the shots fired that night.": CMA, pp. 1892-1894. "That's about a .44 or .45.": Ibid. It was an all-lead bullet: Ibid. …tested by Doctor Hildebrand, "Found to be a bullet of a different composition …from any of the bullets used by the black soldiers…, a bullet such as the soldiers could not have fired from their rifles.": SR 355 Part 2, pp. 42-43.

…seven empty cartridges…were in a little circle whose diameter was not more than 10 inches: CMA, p. 3024. Macklin swore to this: SD-389, p. 92. Also see PGCM-P, p. 1237. "Those shells were brought down from Fort Niobrara…": CMA, p. 3025. "I think they were taken out there and put there." Ibid., p. 3025. That rifle, this fourth gun, serial number 45683: CMA, p. 1748. See all of Sergeant Blaney's testimony. Ibid., pp. 1748-1752. …it was still locked in the arms chest: SD-389, pp. 96-97; 98-99. …there was, among those papers, the ballistic tests report (Microscopic Investigation Report): NA. Also see CMA Vol.2, pp. 1309-1326.

33 PARDON OR EXONERATION

"…give him some instances…where commanders have discharged men without honor and without court-martial.": Letter from the White House, 12/ 7/ 1906, signed by Roosevelt. NA. …no precedents in the Regular Army had been found: SD 155-Part 1, p. 311. Huge amounts of information were distilled into a two-page Summary Sheet: DAML, file symbol: DAPE-MPE (18 JUL 72). Summary Sheet. Affirmative Action by DA to Re-characterize Discharges as a Result of the Brownsville Incident. Contact Officer Baker.

36 MY QUEST

Judge Welch was found murdered in his bed: Alberto Cabrera was convicted for the murder of Judge Welch in 1908. It appears that it was a political murder. "The Handbook of Texas Online, Welch, Stanley. The Texas State Historical Association. **…thought he could shake down the U.S. government for $10,000 in a lawsuit:** SR 355, Part 2, p. 42. My examination of the death certificate revealed…": See Certified Copy of Inquest Proceeding dated 8/14/06, Verbal by Victoriano S. Fernandez. NA. "It doesn't work. CMA, p. 2515. It's probably been like that for a long time.": Ibid. Also see, p. 2386.

Op.cit. It started with firing from the porches of their barracks (alleged by the citizens): Katie Leahy said the shooting started from the balconies, PGCM-P, pp. 73-74. Herbert Elkins testified he saw the soldiers shooting from the barracks. Ibid., p. 452.

Mack Hamilton...overheard [white] civilian conspirators...cooking up plot to attack the fort: CI, p. 980. ...examined the sworn testimony of ex-corporal Willie H. Miller: CMA, pp. 855-867, also see CI, pp. 333-343. "He seemed to be in a terror-stricken frame of mind...,": Ibid., p. 980. There is no money to bring Hamilton here.": CI, p. 981. "It was their purpose to shoot over the buildings...": Ibid., p. 981. ...as a case of "extreme humanity: CI, p. 982.

37 COURT MARTIAL OF THE OFFICERS, THE LAST CHAPTER

Owen Wister: "Two old friends were out walking together, along the shore of the Potomac."

pp. 474-475. *Theodore Rex*, Edmund Morris. "'When you turned those niggers out of the army at Brownsville," Owen Wister asked Roosevelt, "Why didn't you order a court of enquiry for the commissioned officers?'"

"'Because I listened to the War Department, and I shouldn't," Roosevelt replied. He paused. "'Of course, I can't know all about everything.'"

"'Defensively, he [Roosevelt] launched into a long disquisition on the fickleness of financial advisors, Wister heard him out.'"

Roosevelt continued, "'And so, the best you can do is to stop, look, and listen -- and then jump.'" "Yes. And then jump. And hope I've jumped right."

DEPARTMENT OF THE ARMY
THE PACE AWARD: 1973
FOR EXCEPTIONAL SERVICE
AWARDED TO

𝕷𝖎𝖊𝖚𝖙𝖊𝖓𝖆𝖓𝖙 𝕮𝖔𝖑𝖔𝖓𝖊𝖑 𝖂𝖎𝖑𝖑𝖎𝖆𝖒 𝕭𝖆𝖐𝖊𝖗

Lieutenant Colonel William Baker, Office of Equal Opportunity Programs, Office of the Deputy Chief of Staff for Personnel, distinguished himself by exceptional performance of duty during a reinvestigation of the Brownsville Incident of 1906. This event resulted in every soldier assigned to the all black unit of the 1st Battalion, 25th Infantry being discharged without honor and barred forever from re-enlisting in the Army or Navy and from civilian employment with the Government. After extensive research, Lieutenant Colonel Baker prepared a case upon which the Secretary of the Army made the decision to correct the injustice by changing the discharges of these soldiers to honorable. In addition, he developed the process for identification of survivors; assisted in the location of a bona fide survivor; and formulated the Army position favoring legislative approval of a bill which was signed by the President and provided compensation to survivors and unremarried widows of soldiers involved in the Brownsville Incident. Lieutenant Colonel Baker's accomplishments reflect great credit upon himself and have brought national acclaim to the United States Army.

WASHINGTON, D. C.

Howard H. Callaway
Secretary of the Army

Department of the Army PACE Award: 1973 for Exceptional Service
Awarded to Lt. Col. William Baker based on his investigation of the
Brownsville, Texas Incident of 1906

List of Illustrations

Index

S

T

X

Y

Z

2 1982 02942 2445

CPSIA information can be obtained
at www.ICGtesting.com
Printed in the USA
LVHW052037300820
664592LV00015B/1597